PRIVATE CLIENT: WILLS, TRUSTS AND ESTATE PLANNING

The University of Law
133 Great Hampton Street
Birmingham B18 6AQ
Telephone: 01483 216041
Email: library-birmingham@law.ac.uk

PRIVATE CLIENT: WILLS, TRUSTS AND ESTATE PLANNING

Lesley King LLB, Dip Crim (Cantab), Solicitor

Published by

College of Law Publishing,
Braboeuf Manor, Portsmouth Road, St Catherines, Guildford GU3 1HA

British Library Cataloguing-in-Publication Data
A catalogue record for this book is available from the British Library.

ISBN 978 1 915469 27 4

Typeset by Style Photosetting Ltd, Mayfield, East Sussex
Tables and index by Moira Greenhalgh, Arnside, Cumbria

Preface

The aim of this book is to provide a comprehensive introduction to the legal and taxation implications arising from estate planning work for clients within the private client department of a solicitor's practice. At the beginning of **Chapter 1**, there is reference to the problem of definition of private client. In view of this it has been necessary, but difficult, to define the scope of the text, although the subtitle to this book has helped to a considerable extent.

We have had the benefit of helpful, and often long, discussions with many practitioners, from whose suggestions we hope to have arrived at a consensus. However, we remain aware that the private client department of a London firm is often very different from a provincial practice. We should like to express our appreciation to the many busy private client partners who have so willingly provided their advice and suggestions, and their time, in relation to the content of this book.

This book is written primarily to complement the elective, Private Client, but it is hoped it will provide a useful introduction to others interested in this type of work.

Until 2016/17, this book was co-authored with Helen Cousal, who put in an enormous amount of work. Much of the text remains hers and we owe her an enormous debt.

For brevity, we have used the masculine pronoun to include the feminine. The law is stated as at 30 September 2022.

Throughout, we have endeavoured to provide the principal statutory references to enable further research to be made into a topic where this is required. In a subject as broad-based as Private Client (even as interpreted within this book), there are many relevant textbooks and precedent books to which a student or practitioner may wish to refer; these include:

Lasting and Enduring Powers of Attorney

Cretney & Lush on Lasting and Enduring Powers of Attorney, 9th edn (LexisNexis Butterworths, 2022)

Trust Law

Parker and Mellows, *The Modern Law of Trusts*, 9th edn (Sweet & Maxwell, 2015)
Hanbury and Martin, *Modern Equity*, 22nd edn (Sweet & Maxwell, 2021)

Precedents

Practical Will Precedents (Sweet & Maxwell)
Practical Trust Precedents (Sweet & Maxwell)
Encyclopaedia of Forms and Precedents (LexisNexis Butterworths), Trusts and Settlements

Estate and Tax Planning

Estate Planning (Tolley)
Tax Planning (Tolley)
Taxation of UK Trusts (Tolley)

Wills and Probate

Barlow, King and King, *Wills, Administration and Taxation Law and Practice*, 13th edn (Sweet & Maxwell, 2020)
Williams on Wills, 11th edn (LexisNexis Butterworths, 2021)

Revenue Law

Revenue Law: Principles and Practice, 37th edn (Bloomsbury Professional, 2019)

LESLEY KING
The University of Law

Contents

Table of Cases

Table of Statutes

Table of Statutory Instruments and Practice Rules

Table of Abbreviations

The following abbreviations are used throughout this book.

A & M	accumulation and maintenance
AEA 1925	Administration of Estates Act 1925
AEA 1971	Administration of Estates Act 1971
AIM	Alternative Investment Market
AVCs	additional voluntary contributions
BMT	trust for bereaved minors
CGT	capital gains tax
COB Rules	SRA Financial Services (Conduct of Business) Rules
CPA 2004	Civil Partnership Act 2004
EPA	enduring power of attorney
EPAA 1985	Enduring Powers of Attorney Act 1985
FA	Finance Act
FCA	Financial Conduct Authority
FSAVCs	free-standing additional voluntary contributions
FSMA 2000	Financial Services and Markets Act 2000
ICTA 1988	Income and Corporation Taxes Act 1988
IHT	inheritance tax
IHTA 1984	Inheritance Tax Act 1984
IPDI	immediate post-death interest
ISAs	Individual Savings Accounts
ITA 2007	Income Tax Act 2007
ITEPA 2003	Income Tax (Earnings and Pensions) Act 2003
ITPA 2014	Inheritance and Trustees' Powers Act 2014
ITTOIA 2005	Income Tax (Trading and Other Income) Act 2005
LCT	lifetime chargeable transfer
LPA	lasting power of attorney
LPA 1925	Law of Property Act 1925
MCA 2005	Mental Capacity Act 2005
OEIC	open-ended investment company
PAA	Perpetuities and Accumulations Act
PEP	personal equity plan
PET	potentially exempt transfer
PHI	permanent health insurance
PR	personal representative
RAO 2001	Financial Services and Markets Act 2000 (Regulated Activities) Order 2001
RDR	Retail Distribution Review
SERPS	State Earnings-Related Pension Scheme
SLA 1925	Settled Land Act 1925
SRA	Solicitors Regulation Authority
TA 1925	Trustee Act 1925
TA 2000	Trustee Act 2000
TCGA 1992	Taxation of Chargeable Gains Act 1992
TESSAs	Tax Exempt Special Savings Accounts

TIA   Trustee Investments Act 1961
TLATA 1996   Trusts of Land and Appointment of Trustees Act 1996
VTA 1958   Variation of Trusts Act 1958

CHAPTER 1

PRIVATE CLIENT – AN INTRODUCTION

1.1 WHAT IS PRIVATE CLIENT WORK?

Lord Denning, in *Griffiths v JP Harrison (Watford) Ltd* [1962] 1 All ER 909, HL, said, 'We can recognise a "trade" when we see it. ... But we are hard pressed to define it'. In that case, he was considering whether an activity was a trading activity. He might have said much the same thing had he been considering 'private client work'.

At its broadest, private client work may be said to include all work except commercial work, although even commercial work has a private client dimension. At its narrowest, it will generally be taken to exclude such topics as conveyancing, family law, litigation and employment law, leaving a residual category of personal taxation, wills, probate and trust work. An increasingly large elderly population has seen an increase in work directed at the needs of the elderly, for example, lasting powers of attorney, deputyships and provision for the cost of care.

Some firms have separate departments with partners and assistant solicitors who concentrate exclusively on serving the needs of their private clients. In recent years, many large practices have developed a policy of concentrating on commercial work and referring any private client work to other firms specialising in that area.

The subtitle to this book, 'Wills, Trusts and Estate Planning', describes, and places a limit on, the scope of the book. Therefore, it covers private client work in the narrow sense. Other aspects of private client work as more broadly defined are the subject of other books in this series.

Extensive discussion with City of London firms, provincial city firms and many other firms with private client departments has confirmed that the main emphasis of their work within the private client department is 'estate planning'. This emphasis has led to an equivalent main theme for this LPC Guide.

1.2 PRIVATE CLIENT WORK AND THE COMPULSORY SUBJECTS OF THE LEGAL PRACTICE COURSE

1.2.1 Probate and estate administration

The study of private client work follows naturally from a study of probate, estate administration and related succession issues. Many of the topics introduced in the LPC Guide, **Legal Foundations**, for example lifetime gifts and the use of annual tax exemptions, are developed further. Many new topics and ideas for estate planning are also introduced. In some cases, reference is made to particular aspects of other LPC Guides. It will be necessary to re-read some of the material contained in those books.

1.2.2 Revenue law

The three principal taxes applicable to private individuals are relevant to this area of work. The principles of these taxes are set out in the LPC Guides, **Legal Foundations** and **Business Law and Practice**.

1.2.3 Financial services

Estate planning for clients will inevitably involve a consideration of financial planning, particularly in relation to investments. For example, clients may want advice in relation to their existing shares, or as to what investments they should make in the immediate future.

In some cases, a solicitor may become involved in other investment activity for a client. After giving advice, the solicitor may follow this up by making arrangements for the client to acquire (or sell) investments. In some cases, the solicitor may even be prepared to manage a client's investment portfolio. However, this is relatively uncommon since the Financial Services and Markets Act 2000 (FSMA 2000) increased the regulatory burden on firms involved in such work.

Not all solicitors' firms will wish to carry out investment business for clients, even though they undertake a substantial amount of private client work. Many practitioners prefer to 'hive off' the financial aspects of a client's business to specialist independent financial advisers leaving the solicitor to concentrate on the purely legal aspects of the work. However, some of the larger firms, as well as many medium-sized or smaller firms, take the opposite approach. They see financial services work as potentially lucrative for the practice. Thus, using their existing client database as their prime source of investment business, firms which decide to become involved in financial services work may often set up a separate financial services department. This may be 'headed up' by a solicitor with the necessary expertise or by an individual brought into the firm for the purpose. Such a person would normally have qualifications and experience gained from working in the financial services industry. Departments of this type will work closely with the private client department but will also provide a support role for other areas of the practice. Firms have to decide whether they are prepared to comply with the requirements of FSMA 2000 and be regulated by the Financial Conduct Authority (FCA), or whether they wish to limit themselves to activities that can be carried out under the regulation of the Solicitors Regulation Authority (SRA).

This book presupposes that the solicitor's firm has opted for regulation by the SRA. However, we will consider the nature of the various investment products available on the market, their similarities and differences and their suitability or otherwise for any particular client. Such a client, within the context of this book, may either be an individual or a trustee.

1.3 OWNERSHIP AND DISPOSITION OF ASSETS

Private client work for any client will involve the solicitor in two separate, though closely related, matters.

1.3.1 Ownership of assets

The decision to acquire assets, for example the family home or investments, is for the client to make, although the solicitor may be asked to offer advice. Even where clients do not require advice as to the selection of particular assets, they may need advice on how family assets should be owned. In particular, the solicitor can advise on the tax and practical advantages and disadvantages of sole ownership, joint ownership (as joint tenants or as tenants in common) and holding assets through a trust. Another important aspect of asset ownership is providing for the owner's possible loss of mental capacity, and so the solicitor will also frequently advise on lasting and enduring powers of attorney. Hence, this book deals with (inter alia):

(a)   financial planning; and

(b)   estate planning.

1.3.2 Disposition of assets

Clients who have substantial assets will want to consider how to pass them on to family members in the most tax-effective way. The options available are:

(a)   lifetime gifts: these may be outright gifts to individuals or into trusts; or

(b)   gifts by will: these may also be outright gifts to individuals or into trusts.

SUMMARY

Private client work can cover a very broad range of legal work. This book focuses on the law and practice most relevant to advising clients how best to hold and pass on their wealth within their family unit.

FINANCIAL PLANNING

LEARNING OUTCOMES

After reading this chapter you will be able to:

- explain the role of a lawyer in financial planning for clients
- identify the regulatory constraints within which lawyers work
- explain the matters which a specialist financial adviser will consider.

2.1 A LAWYER'S ROLE IN FINANCIAL PLANNING

As a private client lawyer, you will often act for clients who want more than a will or a lifetime settlement. While such clients may want to make sure that they can pass on their property to their family in a tax-efficient manner, they will also want to make sure that they maximise the benefit they get from their property during their lifetime. This requires successful financial planning.

Regulatory constraints mean that you will not usually provide advice on financial planning yourself. However, you will need to understand what the client and the other professionals involved are trying to achieve.

This chapter provides a brief introduction to financial planning. It looks at the regulatory constraints applying to lawyers and at the basic principles of financial planning.

The object of financial planning is to maximise the wealth (capital and income) of an individual.

Financial planning is a continuing process. It requires the development of a strategy based on short- and long-term forward planning. Ideally, a plan, an investment strategy, should be developed for the client. Any immediate needs identified by the plan can be implemented at once. Longer-term planning can be given effect as the opportunities develop.

The range of financial planning and investment opportunities available to private clients is very wide. In view of this, the key to successful advice to clients lies in:

(a) knowing all the circumstances of the particular client; and

(b) devising a financial and investment plan which is appropriate to meet those circumstances.

2.1.1   Financial planning

Financial planning covers savings, for example in a bank or building society, investments, life assurance and pension arrangements, mortgages, school fee schemes (see **Appendix 2**) and tax planning generally (see **Chapter 4**).

2.1.2   Investment planning

Investment planning is one aspect of financial planning. In everyday use the phrase is understood as covering a wide range of investments from unit trusts, investment trusts, and other stocks and shares (see **Appendix 2**) to specialist items such as works of art, stamp collections and investment in woodlands. It is not confined to 'investments' as defined in the FSMA 2000 (see **2.2**).

2.1.3   The Retail Distribution Review

The Financial Services Authority, now the Financial Conduct Authority (FCA), identified various problems existing in relation to advice to consumers on investment products and the basis of charging for it.

Traditionally, those advising consumers on investment products could be paid either by the consumer in the form of up-front charges or by commission from the product provider. There was obvious scope for abuse in the commission arrangement as the product carrying the highest commission may not be the one best suited to the particular consumer. Further difficulties for consumers existed because it was not always apparent whether those advising where 'tied' to particular products, or were independent and able to advise on all investment products. Moreover, not all advisers were particularly well qualified.

On 1 January 2013, new rules came into effect changing the way advisers can operate. Known as the Retail Distribution Review (RDR), the objective was to raise professional standards in the industry by requiring mandatory qualifications and ongoing professional development, introducing greater clarity between the different types of advisory service available, and making the cost of advice clear to those buying it.

Types of adviser

Under the RDR there are only two types of financial adviser – 'independent' or 'restricted' – and all advisory companies have to decide which they become. Some firms have opted to offer both services to different types of customer.

An independent adviser is required to research the whole market for products which might be suitable for their client's needs and every asset class that could potentially be suitable. This includes more 'exotic' products, such as investment trusts, exchange traded funds, enterprise investment schemes or venture capital trusts, where these are deemed potentially suitable products.

A restricted adviser may consider a select range of investment products and product providers that might be suitable. The number of products and providers considered before selection may vary significantly. For example, one restricted adviser could opt to select from just 20, while another could choose from several hundred.

Although the term 'restricted' might carry certain negative connotations, many commentators believe that restricted advice is likely to be appropriate for the majority of people. A restricted adviser may specialise in certain areas, but can still research a very broad range of products and providers (even the whole market, if they wish), in order to offer tailored recommendations suited to a client's financial objectives.

Charging

The other big change introduced by the RDR is the charging system. Previously, there were a number of ways that investors could pay for advice, including up-front hourly fees, or initial and ongoing commission paid by the company selling the investment product. Now, all financial advisory companies are required to set out clearly the charges the client will pay and agree them prior to providing any advice – to ensure clients are fully aware of the costs involved. Providers of investment products are no longer able to pay commission to advisers.

2.1.4 The RDR and regulatory requirements for solicitors

Originally, solicitors could only refer clients to independent advisers. However, as a result of the changes introduced by the RDR, the SRA, following consultation, formed the view that there might be situations in which a restricted adviser would be more suitable for a particular client's needs than an independent one, and changes were made to Chapter 6 of the SRA Code of Conduct 2011 to allow recommendations to restricted advisers provided that:

(a)   the recommendation was in the client's best interests;

(b)   the client was fully informed of any financial or other interest the firm had in the referral;

(c)   the client was in a position to make an informed decision; and

(d)   the firm was not paid a prohibited referral fee.

The Law Society was concerned that this change was not necessarily in the best interests of clients, and on 29 November 2012 the then Law Society Chief Executive, Desmond Hudson, issued a statement warning solicitors that they might become more open to negligence claims as a result of recommending restricted advisers and risked becoming 'embroiled in the type of mis-selling scandal that has plagued the financial services industry in recent times'.

The SRA's position was that the change to the Code of Conduct was necessary to allow solicitors to refer to the financial adviser who offers the best outcome for the client. Only allowing solicitors to refer to those advisers deemed 'independent' might be contrary to that object.

Agnieszka Scott, SRA Director of Strategy and Policy, said:

> The amendment has been brought in to remove any barriers solicitors may face when trying to achieve the best outcome for their client. Doing away with the prescriptive rule about what kind of financial adviser should be referred to achieves this aim. It needs to be reiterated that we are not making a judgement on who provides the best financial advice – independent advisers or otherwise – which is what a lot of people who responded to the consultation did. We have simply removed an administrative blockage, allowing the solicitor to make a considered judgement on what's best for their client.

The 2019 Code is less prescriptive, but Principles 4, 5 and 7 require those regulated by the SRA to act with honesty and integrity and in the best interests of each client.

Paragraph 3.4 of the Code for Solicitors, RELs and RFLs requires those regulated by the SRA to consider and take account of the client's attributes, needs and circumstances. Paragraph 5.1 includes the following:

> In respect of any referral of a client by you to another person, or of any third party who introduces business to you or with whom you share your fees, you ensure that:
>
> (a)   clients are informed of any financial or other interest which you or your business or employer has in referring the client to another person or which an introducer has in referring the client to you;
>
> (b)   clients are informed of any fee sharing arrangement that is relevant to their matter;
>
> (c)   the fee sharing agreement is in writing;
>
> (d)   you do not receive payments relating to a referral or make payments to an introducer in respect of clients who are the subject of criminal proceedings; and
>
> (e)   any client referred by an introducer has not been acquired in a way which would breach the SRA's regulatory arrangements if the person acquiring the client were regulated by the SRA.

Obviously, a solicitor referring a client to any type of adviser must be satisfied of the competence of that adviser and of their suitability for the client's needs. The client must be fully informed of any restrictions on product range and on the basis of charging.

2.2   THE FINANCIAL SERVICES AND MARKETS ACT 2000

The FSMA 2000, is discussed in the LPC Guide, **Legal Foundations**. Any firm which is involved in developing and implementing an investment strategy for a client must comply with the relevant provisions of FSMA 2000 and the Financial Services and Markets Act 2000 (Regulated Activities) Order 2001 (RAO 2001), SI 2001/544. Remember that carrying on a regulated activity without the necessary authorisation is a criminal offence under FSMA 2000, s 19.

Under FSMA 2000, firms carrying on regulated activities as defined by the RAO 2001 have to be regulated by the FCA.

However, Pt XX of FSMA 2000 makes special provision for professional firms which do not carry on mainstream investment business but which may carry on regulated activities in the course of other work such as probate and trusts. This enables firms regulated by the SRA to be treated as 'exempt professional firms' and to carry on 'exempt regulated activities' under the supervision of the SRA, which is a Designated Professional Body for this purpose.

In this book we deal with exempt professional firms but not with regulation by the FCA. Readers interested in obtaining authorisation from the FCA should consult a specialist text.

2.2.1   Regulation by the SRA

Designated Professional Bodies are required to make rules to ensure that their members only carry on regulated activities arising out of or complementary to the provision of professional services to the client. The SRA Financial Services (Scope) Rules 2018 set out the scope of activities that can be undertaken within the Pt XX exemption. It is most important not to stray outside the Scope Rules, as this is likely to amount to a criminal offence under FSMA 2000, s 19.

In the course of probate and trust work, firms will frequently perform services which fall within the definition of regulated activities in the RAO 2001. They need to ask the following questions:

(a)   Does the activity involve a specified investment?

(b)   Is the activity capable of being a specified activity under the RAO 2001?

(c)   If so, does it fall within any of the exclusions in the RAO 2001?

(d)   If not, does it fall within the Scope Rules?

There is a further issue. The FSMA 2000 provides that any communication which amounts to an invitation or inducement to engage in an investment activity must be made (or in some cases approved) by an FCA-authorised person.

Those regulated by the SRA must be careful not to breach this requirement. Communication may be oral or written. Almost anything said or written in connection with many legal transactions could be construed as a financial promotion. For example, advising executors to sell the deceased's shares could be inviting them to deal in investments.

Fortunately there is an exemption for 'one-off' communications, which will normally apply unless the communications are part of an organised marketing campaign.

2.2.1.1   Does the activity involve a specified investment?

Investments are specified in RAO 2001, arts 74–89. They include:

(a)   shares or stock;

(b)   debentures;

(c)   government securities;

(d)   unit trusts and open-ended investment companies (OEICS);

(e)   insurance contracts;

(f)   mortgages;

(g)   deposit bank accounts;

(h)   rights under a funeral plan contract;

(i)   rights under a regulated home reversion plan;

(j)   rights under a regulated home purchase plan;

(k)   certain greenhouse gas emission allowances and emission allowances consisting of any units recognised for compliance with the requirements of the emission allowance trading directive.

The following are not investments:

(a)   National Savings products such as National Savings Certificates, Premium Bonds, SAYE contracts;

(b)   current bank accounts;

(c)   cash ISAs.

2.2.1.2   Is the activity capable of being a specified activity under the RAO 2001?

The activities are listed in Pt II of the RAO 2001, and usually the activity is expressed in relation to a particular type of investment, so it is the combination of activity plus particular investment which produces the specified activity.

Some of the activities have particular exclusions associated with them which are dealt with below.

Specified activities include:

(a)   dealing in shares as principal or agent;

(b)   advising on or arranging the acquisition or disposal of shares;

(c)   advising on or arranging the assignment of life policies;

(d)   arranging deals in investments;

(e)   safeguarding and administering investments on behalf of clients;

(f)   managing investments;

(g)   custody of investments (which involves safeguarding and administering investments);

(h)   taking deposits.

Note: Advising means giving specific advice about a specific investment. It is possible to give generic advice to a client without carrying on a specified activity, for example advising on the relative merits of buying shares as opposed to land.

2.2.1.3   Does the activity fall within any of the exclusions in the RAO 2001?

If the activity falls within one of the exclusions then the activity is not regulated and the firm will not be subject to the Scope Rules at all in connection with the activity. There are a number of exclusions. The most relevant to private client work are discussed below.

Articles 22, 29 and 33 – using an authorised person or introducing a client to an authorised person

Those regulated by the SRA can:

(a)   Introduce a client to an authorised person with a view to the provision of independent advice (art 33).

It is important to do no more than introduce the client to the adviser. If any sort of ongoing role is retained (for example, acting as a channel of communication, discussing the matter with the client or explaining the meaning of certain terms) this will amount to more than mere 'introducing'.

(b)   Arrange deals for a client who enters into them with or through an authorised person:

   (i)   on the advice of an authorised person, or

   (ii)   where it is clear that the client, in his capacity as investor, borrower, reversion seller, plan provider, home purchaser, agreement provider or (as the case may be) agreement seller, is not seeking the advice of the legal adviser (or if the client did seek it, the legal adviser declined to give it and recommended that the client obtained advice from an authorised person) (art 29).

(c)   Enter into deals as agent for a client with or through an authorised person:

   (i)   on the advice of an authorised person, or

   (ii)   where it is clear that the client, in his capacity as investor, is not seeking the advice of the legal adviser (or if the client did seek it, the legal adviser declined to give it and recommended that the client obtained advice from an authorised person) (art 22).

In order to come within arts 29 or 22 the legal adviser must not receive any pecuniary reward or other advantage from anyone other than the client which is not accounted for to the client. In each case the legal adviser must be careful not to comment on the advice of the authorised person in such a way that it amounts to separate advice.

These exclusions will not apply if the transaction involved is an insurance contract, so solicitors who advise on or make arrangements for a PR client to obtain, for example, a missing beneficiary insurance policy will not be able to benefit from any of these exclusions.

Article 66 – trustees

This exclusion relates to various functions which trustees or personal representatives (PRs) might perform in relation to investments. The exclusion does not apply if the trustee/PR receives any additional remuneration on top of remuneration received for acting as trustee or PR. The trustee/PR is not regarded as receiving additional remuneration if they simply receive remuneration calculated on a time basis for time spent dealing with the investments (art 66(7)). The functions include:

(a)   *Arranging.* Arrangements made by a legal adviser acting as trustee or PR will be excluded if for, or with a view to, a transaction which is made by:

   (i)   the legal adviser and any fellow trustees or PRs, acting in their capacity as PRs or trustees;

   (ii)   a beneficiary under the trust, will or intestacy.

   It is only available where the legal adviser acts *as* trustee or PR and not where the legal adviser acts *for* them. However, it is available where a member of the firm carries out the activity on behalf of the trustees.

(b)   *Managing.* Managing investments as a trustee or PR is excluded. Again there must be no additional remuneration. This exclusion is not available if the legal adviser holds themselves out as providing a discretionary management service over and above that which a lay trustee would provide.

(c)   *Safeguarding.* There is an exclusion for safeguarding investments, but it is not available if the legal adviser holds themselves out as providing a discretionary management service over and above that which a lay trustee would provide. Again there must be no additional remuneration.

(d)   *Advising.* There is an exclusion for a person acting as trustee or personal representative who gives advice on investments, regulated home reversion or purchase plans, sale or rent back agreements to:

   (i)   a fellow trustee or PR for the purposes of the trust or estate; or

(ii) a beneficiary under the trust, will or intestacy concerning his interest in the trust fund or estate.

This exclusion does not apply to contracts of insurance.

Article 67 – necessary part of other professional services

There is an exclusion if the activity may reasonably be regarded as a necessary part of other services provided in the course of that profession or business. The exclusion does not apply if the service is remunerated separately from the other services. This simply means that the legal adviser must not make a separate charge on the bill.

An example of reasonable necessity in connection with probate work would be arranging the sale of *all* assets to provide funds for payment of debts and inheritance tax. A decision as to *which* asset to sell to provide funds is unlikely to be 'necessary' as the trustees can always go elsewhere for the advice.

This exclusion is unlikely to apply to insurance contracts.

2.2.1.4 Does it fall within the exemption for professional firms?

The exemption is contained in s 327 of the FSMA 2000. There are three main conditions.

Section 327(4) – the manner of providing the service must be 'incidental to the provision' by the firm of professional services

To satisfy this condition the exempt regulated activities must not be a major part of the firm's practice. The FCA will consider whether the scale of regulated activity was in proportion to other professional services provided; whether the regulated activities were held out as separate services and the impression given through the firm's advertising of the way in which the firm provides the regulated activities.

In addition the regulated activity must be incidental to the particular client. A firm cannot carry out a regulated activity in isolation for a particular client. The professional service must be the primary service and any regulated activity should be subordinate to that professional service. Thus, in a probate matter where the client is the executor, advice given to a beneficiary will not satisfy the test.

Section 327(3) – the firm must account to the client for any pecuniary reward or other advantage which the firm receives

If a firm receives any pecuniary reward or other advantage from a third party because of acting for or giving advice to a client, the firm must account for the reward to the client. Accounting to the client does not mean simply telling the client that the firm will receive a reward. It means that the reward must be held to the order of the client (see FCA Handbook, PROF 2.1.12). Firms will still account to the client if they have the client's informed consent to keep the reward.

If the firm is charging the client on a fee basis, the firm can offset the reward against the firm's fees. The firm must send the client a bill or some other written notification of costs to make the position clear.

The requirement for informed consent will not be satisfied by the firm seeking a blanket consent in its terms of business to the keeping of unspecified rewards.

The firm must be able to demonstrate that the client has given informed consent to any retention of the reward, having had full disclosure of the amount.

Section 327(6) – the activity must not be on the list of activities prohibited from coming within Pt XX

Rule 3 of the SRA Financial Services (Scope) Rules lists the prohibited activities as follows:

(a)   an activity that is specified in an order made under section 327(6) of FSMA;

(b)   an activity that relates to an investment that is specified in an order made under section 327(6) of FSMA;

(c)   entering into a regulated credit agreement as lender except where the regulated credit agreement relates exclusively to the payment of disbursements or professional fees due to you;

(d)   exercising, or having the right to exercise, the lender's rights and duties under a regulated credit agreement except where the regulated credit agreement relates exclusively to the payment of disbursements or professional fees due to you;

(e)   entering into a regulated consumer hire agreement as owner;

(f)   exercising, or having the right to exercise, the owner's rights and duties under a regulated consumer hire agreement;

(g)   operating an electronic system in relation to lending within the meaning of article 36H of the Regulated Activities Order;

(h)   providing credit references within the meaning of article 89B of the Regulated Activities Order;

(i)   insurance distribution activities in relation to insurance-based investment products; or

(j)   creating, developing, designing or underwriting a contract of insurance.

2.2.1.5   Insurance mediation

Clients may be interested in obtaining life assurance either as a personal investment or to provide funds for family members or to pay IHT. Private client practitioners must remember that the Government extended the financial services legislation to comply with the Insurance Mediation Directive (2002/92/EC).

As a result of the amendments, any assistance given to a client to obtain insurance, even the introduction of a client to an insurance broker, will be a specified activity. The main exclusions do not apply to insurance contracts, so a firm which offers any assistance to a client in relation to insurance will commit a criminal offence unless covered by the exemption under s 327 of the FSMA 2000 for professional firms.

Assistance with the provision of insurance may be incidental, as described at **2.2.1.4**, and unremunerated, but there are additional requirements that must be complied with. The firm must appoint a compliance officer and be registered in the FCA Register.

2.2.2   The Conduct of Business Rules

If the firm carries out an exempt regulated activity it must comply with the SRA Financial Services (Conduct of Business) Rules (COB Rules), the current version of which came into effect from 31 December 2020, as well as with the Scope requirements.

The COB Rules apply only when firms are carrying out an exempt regulated activity and not when the firm is doing something which does not amount to a regulated activity at all, say, using an authorised third party. However, it is safest to make sure that the firm always follows the COB Rules, as this will avoid any risk of accidental non-compliance. In any event, the Rules merely set out good practice.

Of particular relevance to private client departments are the following:

(a)   Rule 5 – The firm must keep records of all commissions received in respect of regulated activities and how that commission was dealt with.

(b)   Rule 6 – Where a firm safeguards and administers another's assets it must operate 'appropriate systems' for safeguarding those assets, including the keeping of appropriate records, which provide for the safekeeping of assets entrusted to the firm by clients and others. Where such assets are passed to a third party, the firm should obtain an acknowledgement of receipt of the property; and if they have been passed to a third party on the client's instructions, the firm should obtain such instructions in writing.

2.3 DEVELOPING THE INVESTMENT STRATEGY FOR CLIENTS

Although you will not be developing such a strategy unless you have special expertise, it is important to appreciate what professional investment advisers should be doing.

2.3.1 'Know your client'

When taking instructions in relation to any financial planning for clients, it is essential to 'know the client'.

There are two main aspects to this:

(a) investigating, ie, ascertaining from the client all relevant personal and financial details, including appetite for risk; and

(b) determining the suitability of investments, ie, only recommending investments suitable to the particular client.

2.3.2 The client's personal details

The information which should be obtained will include the following four major categories:

(a) Personal details:
    (i) name, address and occupation;
    (ii) dates of birth and retirement;
    (iii) whether single, married or in a civil partnership, divorced, or widow(ed);
    (iv) whether employed, or self-employed.

(b) Family details:
    (i) spouse or civil partner (name and age);
    (ii) children, grandchildren (names and ages).

(c) Gifts previously made (including the amounts and whether outright or in trust).

(d) Provision by any will (including the date of will).

The Money Laundering, Terrorist Financing and Transfer of Funds (Information on the Payer) Regulations 2017 (which came into force on 26 June 2017 and were amended by the Money Laundering and Terrorist Financing (Amendment) Regulations 2019 and the Money Laundering and Terrorist Financing (Amendment) (EU Exit) Regulations 2020) require solicitors to take measures to identify not merely clients but also 'beneficial owners' who are not clients. In the case of trusts, a beneficial owner for this purpose is defined in reg 6(1) as each of the following:

(a) the settlor;

(b) the trustees;

(c) the beneficiaries;

(d) where the individuals (or some of the individuals) benefiting from the trust have not been determined, the class of persons in whose main interest the trust is set up, or operates;

(e) any individual who has control over the trust.

In relation to an estate of a deceased person in the course of administration, 'beneficial owner' is defined in reg 6(6) as the executor, original or by representation, or administrator for the time being of a deceased person.

These Regulations also impose significant identification obligations on trustees of express trusts who must place details of beneficial owners on the Trusts Register (unless the trusts are within the small class excluded from the need to register set out in Sch 3A to the 2017 Regulations).

2.3.3   The client's financial details

The financial details obtained from the client will generally concentrate on two broad areas:

(a)   the client's current assets and liabilities; and

(b)   the client's current income and expenditure.

Generally, there will be some 'signpost' or 'indicator' in the client's existing financial affairs which leads to the opportunity to provide financial planning advice. Some of these indicators are set out at **2.3.3.1–2.3.3.5**.

A recent problem for many clients has been maintaining a reasonable income stream at a time when interest rates and yields on shares and bonds have been falling. This is a particular problem for trustees where there may be different classes of beneficiaries, some interested in income return and some in capital growth.

2.3.3.1   Savings predominantly on deposit in a bank or building society account

Savings in a bank or building society are relatively 'safe' and convenient in that the money can be withdrawn quickly (although some accounts do require up to 90 days' notice to be given unless interest is to be lost, see further **Appendix 2**). Interest payable is subject to income tax. The main danger in holding a lot of money in such an account is the loss of purchasing power because of inflation. Inflation is the investor's number one enemy. At 5% inflation, £100 today will be worth £95 next year. Money in excess of the state guarantee (normally £85,000) is at risk if the institution collapses.

Although it is prudent to hold some money in savings accounts as a ready source of money in case of emergency, it is rarely sensible to hold large amounts. Clients should consider withdrawing some of it for investment elsewhere.

2.3.3.2   Investments all yielding high income returns

High income yields will be superficially attractive to the client, but there are features of such a return which indicate a review of the investment strategy, for example because:

(a)   high yields may be earned at the expense of high risk, ie, there may be a higher risk of losing the invested capital because of the nature of the investment. If so, it may be prudent to diversify the investment portfolio to an appropriate extent; and

(b)   high income indicates the probability of income tax rates of 45% and loss of personal allowances. This may be alleviated by the transfer of some investments into the name of the client's spouse if he or she pays income tax at a lower rate, or by rearranging the investment portfolio into assets where the concentration is on capital growth rather than income yield.

2.3.3.3   No life assurance

For a consideration of the available types of life policy, see **Appendix 2**. Although premiums do not generally attract income tax relief, it is always prudent to use life policies as a method of saving to produce substantial sums of money on the occurrence of anticipated future events. Traditionally, these are the repayment of a mortgage, the retirement of the client and the death of a client. They can also be used to cover school fees.

2.3.3.4   No occupational pension scheme or personal pension

Ideally, anyone who is in work should be able to look forward to retirement in the knowledge that he will then benefit from a pension which provides an acceptable level of income. Payment of National Insurance contributions during working life will ensure receipt of the State retirement pension. This is payable at State pension age. In some cases, a 'top up' pension will be payable as well, ie, the State earnings related pension. However, further 'top up' through an occupational pension scheme and/or a private pension is also desirable.

Occupational pension schemes

The absence of contributions by an employee to an occupational pension scheme should not necessarily be taken as meaning that the employee will not benefit from an occupational pension on retirement. These schemes may be offered by employers on a 'non-contributory' basis, ie, only the employer pays contributions. If approved by the Revenue, occupational pension schemes attract considerable tax advantages for employer and employee contributions and for the pension fund itself. The increasing cost to employers means that many non-contributory schemes are closing.

Occupational pension schemes used to offer a defined amount based on final salary and length of service. The cost of providing such schemes has risen inexorably given falling interest rates and increased longevity. They are now extremely rare and have effectively been replaced by defined contribution schemes where the amount that is paid out depends on investment returns.

The government has required all employers to introduce 'auto-enrolment'. Automatic enrolment means that most UK employers must put in place a qualifying workplace pension scheme and automatically enrol their qualifying workers. The scheme was phased in and was fully in place by April 2019. A minimum 8% contribution is shared: 3% from the employer and 5% from the employee. Employees have the right to opt out of the scheme.

Personal pension schemes

Personal pension schemes are available to all, and are of particular importance to the self-employed and to employees who are either not offered an occupational pension scheme by their employers or who prefer not to join that pension scheme. If approved by the Revenue, these schemes also attract considerable tax advantages for contributions to the scheme as well as for the fund itself.

Stakeholder pension schemes

These became available on 6 April 2001 and are really a type of personal pension scheme. They are low cost and available to everyone, even those who are not in paid employment. They are much more flexible than traditional personal pension schemes, as contributors can contribute varying amounts and stop and restart contributions. Employed people can take the pension with them when they change jobs. They have substantial tax advantages, as the Revenue will contribute even where the contributor is not a taxpayer.

Passing on pension 'pots'

Originally people who saved into a pension scheme had to use the funds available at retirement to buy an annuity. This requirement became increasingly unpopular because:

(a)   the capital saved could not be accessed;

(b)   annuity rates fell progressively as life expectancy increased; and

(c)   those who died shortly after buying an annuity failed to benefit fully from the funds saved and could not normally pass on the investment fund to family members.

The rules requiring annuity purchase were progressively relaxed.

The current rules (which take effect for pension fund death benefits payable on or after 6 April 2015) are contained in the Taxation of Pensions Act (TPA) 2014. Not only do they allow much more flexibility in the way taxpayers can access their pension funds during their lifetime, but, crucially, they allow undrawn pension funds:

•   to be passed on;

•   more than once; and

•   sometimes, completely tax free.

See **Appendix 2** for a more detailed discussion of pensions. Note that pensions are an increasingly important part of estate planning and should always be considered alongside provision by will and lifetime transfer.

2.3.3.5 Assets held in the name of one spouse alone

The home, investments and other assets may, with advantage, be transferred into the joint ownership of spouses through the use of a joint tenancy or a tenancy in common. The various estate planning opportunities available to spouses are discussed in **Chapter 4**. It is frequently preferable to own as beneficial tenants in common rather than as beneficial joint tenants as this gives greater flexibility.

2.3.4 Suitability of investments for a particular client

The investment strategy for the client will reflect the information obtained from the client. Three particular factors will be the age of the client, the client's existing investments and earnings and the client's attitude to risk.

2.3.4.1 The client's age

Younger clients, especially if married with children, may have little spare money beyond what is needed for everyday life, including mortgage payments. Because of the risk of a sudden need for cash, it is important to try to build up a cushion in the form of assets which can be quickly realised. This really means a deposit account. Rates of interest have been at a historic low for some years. However, 2022 has seen the return of inflation carrying with it significant rate rises. In any event, even when returns are low, it is necessary to have funds available which are relatively free from risk and can easily be recovered if needed. Should further money be available, a more complex strategy will be needed.

Middle-aged clients, with growing families, should begin planning for retirement and old age by improving their income and capital position as far as possible. They may, however, be burdened by the costs of school and university fees. So far as possible, they should try to fund pensions. Spare earnings and investment income should be invested to produce maximum capital growth.

Retirement-age clients, who no longer have mortgage and school fee commitments, may need to change the emphasis of their investment strategy from capital growth to income yield. Loss of earnings will need to be balanced as far as possible by investment yields and pension income. If a tax-free capital lump sum is withdrawn from the pension fund at retirement, this should be invested to improve the income position.

Elderly clients, often with low incomes, need to ensure that maximum advantage is taken of the increased levels of personal tax allowances – the age related allowances (see **Appendix 1**) – by holding high income yielding investments where possible. Interest payable to depositors in banks and building societies used to be paid net of basic rate tax (20%) under s 851 of the Income Tax Act 2007 (ITA 2007). Non-taxpayers could recover this tax by submitting an appropriate claim to the Revenue. However, for tax year 2016/17 onwards all financial institutions pay interest without deducting income tax. This makes life simpler for non-taxpayers but more complicated for taxpayers who now have to include interest on their tax returns.

Planning the financial and other affairs of clients will become difficult where they are unable to take part in decision-making through loss of mental capacity. In order to overcome problems caused by loss of mental capacity, from 1985 individuals were able to make enduring powers of attorney (EPAs) to appoint someone to deal with their property and affairs. Since 1 October 2007, when the relevant provisions of the Mental Capacity Act 2005 came into force, it has no longer been possible to make new EPAs. However, it is possible to make lasting powers of attorney (LPAs). It is appropriate for advisers to recommend to clients that they make an LPA. The client may choose to appoint a member of the family, or a professional, as their attorney.

Note that LPAs should not be regarded as something reserved for elderly clients. People of any age can lose capacity as a result of accident or illness. They will then need someone to deal with their affairs for them. It is often convenient to raise the question of making an LPA at the same time as the client is making a new will or codicil. This is considered in detail in **Chapter 3**.

2.4 PORTFOLIO PLANNING

Every client is different, and each client will have different requirements. Excluding the buying of a house, a general plan for investments will probably be:

(a)   'ready cash' saved in a bank or building society;

(b)   protection through life assurance for the client and dependants;

(c)   pension; and

(d)   longer-term investments purchased with any spare cash.

2.4.1 High risk/low risk

Investments can be categorised as low, medium or high risk. Often the higher the return, the higher the risk. Each category might include the following.

Low risk

(a)   savings accounts in the bank or building society;

(b)   government stock ('gilts');

(c)   National Savings, for example National Savings premium bonds.

Medium risk

(a)   unit trusts;

(b)   investment trusts;

(c)   shares in public companies, ie, in blue chip 'equities';

(d)   loans to companies, financial institutions and local authorities.

High risk

(a)   shares in small public companies and in private companies;

(b)   'collectibles' such as works of art and stamp collections;

(c)   woodlands.

2.4.2 Short-term/longer-term

Short-term investments often mean 'savings', ie, short-term cash investments made for the purchase of a particular item such as a new car. Probably the bank or building society offers the best opportunity but interest rates may be low (and no capital growth).

Longer-term 'investment' depends on the client's available resources, personal likes and dislikes etc, and may include many of the investments in **Appendix 2**.

2.4.3 Capital growth/income yield

If the client has adequate income, he may prefer to invest for capital growth rather than for dividends or interest. Company shares are the most likely type of investment if capital growth is required, although companies showing good capital growth usually pay good dividends as well. In the last few years, it has proved unusually difficult to obtain capital growth.

If income yield is required, savings in higher rate bank and building society accounts may be sensible. So too may be investment in certain companies where the dividend record is good, or even government stocks ('gilts').

2.4.4   Income tax and capital gains tax

'Savings' producing an income and 'investments' producing both an income and capital growth will mean that both income tax and capital gains tax will affect the client. Some savings and investments are tax free and should always feature in the portfolio planning for clients who are, or who become because of the investment, taxpayers. Examples include ISAs (see further **Appendix 2**).

2.5   INTRODUCTION TO TYPES OF INVESTMENT PRODUCTS

There are very many different types of investment product on the market. The term 'investment product' covers savings, ie, money deposited in a bank or building society, as well as stocks, shares, unit and investment trusts, ISAs, life policies, etc. All these products have different characteristics, uses and tax positions associated with them. They must be selected with care to suit the particular type of client.

The main categories of savings and investments producing tax-free income are detailed in **Appendix 2**. Some of these investments are free of capital gains tax as well as income tax.

SUMMARY

(1)   A lawyer must understand what clients and their financial advisers are trying to achieve in relation to financial planning.

(2)   Regulatory constraints mean that lawyers will not normally provide financial advice except in the limited circumstances covered by an exclusion or the exemption for professional firms.

(3)   Lawyers must understand the principles of portfolio planning so that they can understand why the client wishes to take certain steps.

REVIEW ACTIVITY

You are acting for the PRs of an estate who need to sell some of the quoted shares owned by the deceased to raise money to pay debts and legacies. They have asked you to help them decide which shares to sell.

Your firm is not regulated by the FCA. You do not wish to carry out a regulated activity without authorisation.

Which ONE of the following statements is CORRECT?

A   You will not be carrying out a regulated activity if you advise the PRs which shares to sell.

B   You will be carrying out a regulated activity but will be protected by the art 66 exclusion.

C   You will be carrying out a regulated activity but will be protected by the art 67 exclusion.

D   You will be carrying out a regulated activity but are likely to be protected by the exemption for professional bodies.

Answer: D

Advising on the sale of shares is a regulated activity. Neither exclusion applies. Article 66 applies only to those who *are* PRs or trustees, not to those who advise PRs or trustees. The sale involves an element of choice and selection and so is not 'necessary'. The exemption is likely to apply as the service is incidental but you must account for any pecuniary or other rewards received.

CHAPTER 3

ENDURING POWERS OF ATTORNEY, LASTING POWERS OF ATTORNEY AND LIVING WILLS

LEARNING OUTCOMES

After reading this chapter you will be able to:

- understand the importance of enabling someone, in advance, to deal with the affairs of a person who lacks capacity
- understand the rules on the creation, format and registration of an enduring power of attorney (EPA) and a lasting power of attorney (LPA)
- understand the scope of EPAs and LPAs in relation to giving away the donor's assets
- appreciate the purpose and operation of living wills and advance decisions.

3.1 INTRODUCTION

It is sensible for clients to consider what will happen if at any time they are unable to manage their own affairs, whether temporarily or permanently. It is usually better if they have previously chosen and authorised other persons to act on their behalf. This can be done by creating a power of attorney. There are various types of power, and they can be used to authorise an attorney to act generally for the donor of the power or just in relation to specific matters. For example, a client who needs to sign a document at a time when he will be unavailable to do so may authorise someone just to sign this document on his behalf.

An ordinary power of attorney, whether granted under the Trustee Act 1925 (TA 1925) or as a short form power under the Powers of Attorney Act 1971, ceases to have effect when the donor of the power loses his mental capacity. This means that the attorney appointed by the power is no longer able to act just at the moment when the power is most needed.

This chapter considers the special types of power of attorney that can be used where a person lacks mental capacity, looking at how they are created and how they operate. The focus is on enabling persons to act in relation to financial matters, but it also gives an outline of matters concerned with the health and welfare of an individual.

3.1.1   Background to enduring and lasting powers of attorney

Enduring powers of attorney (EPAs) and lasting powers of attorney (LPAs) allow an attorney to act for a donor who has lost mental capacity.

The EPA was introduced by the Enduring Powers of Attorney Act 1985 (EPAA 1985). When the relevant provisions of the Mental Capacity Act 2005 (MCA 2005) came into force on 1 October 2007, the EPAA 1985 was repealed, and so it is no longer possible to create a new EPA. Instead a person can create an LPA. However, EPAs created before 1 October 2007 (whether registered or not) will continue to be valid and operate in accordance with Sch 4 to the MCA 2005, which largely repeats the relevant provisions of the EPAA 1985.

It is necessary, therefore, to understand the rules applying to both LPAs and EPAs.

The Law Society has produced a practice note to assist solicitors advising on having an LPA, solicitors who act as attorneys under an LPA and solicitors dealing with EPAs. It has also issued a practice note on meeting the needs of vulnerable clients.

3.1.2   Who should have an EPA or LPA?

It is appropriate for anyone to have an EPA or LPA. Loss of mental capacity may occur at any age as a result of accident or illness. However, although older clients might consider asking a solicitor about this, it is less likely that younger clients will do so. It is usual, therefore, for solicitors taking instructions for a will to suggest that the client also consider an LPA. Persons with an EPA may wish to create a personal welfare LPA (see **3.4** below), as decisions as to welfare and medical treatment cannot be taken under an EPA.

3.1.3   What happens if no attorney is appointed?

An application can be made to the Court of Protection to appoint a deputy to deal with the property and affairs of the person who has lost capacity ('P') and, if necessary, to deal with health and personal welfare issues.

The Court is usually unwilling to appoint a health and personal welfare deputy, taking the view that such decisions are usually best made consensually by those involved with P's day-to-day care.

In *Re Lawson, Mottram and Hopton (appointment of personal welfare deputies)* [2019] EWCOP 22, a preliminary issue was listed in three applications for permission to apply for the appointment of a personal welfare deputy, namely 'what is the correct approach to determining whether a welfare deputy should be appointed?'. In particular, the question was whether such appointments should only be made – as the Code of Practice suggests (at 8.38) in 'the most difficult cases'. The applications were made by parents of young adults with impaired decision-making capacity. Hayden J said that all decisions made on behalf of incapacitous persons ('P') had to be made in their best interests and there were no presumptions or rules. However, in practice, personal welfare deputies will not often be appointed, in particular because the appointment should not be seen, in and of itself, as less restrictive of P's rights and freedoms than collaborative decision making.

Both attorneys and deputies are in much the same position. They are in a fiduciary position and must act in P's best interests. However, there is clearly a possibility of abuse where one person manages the financial affairs of another. In August 2017 retired Court of Protection senior judge Denzil Lush made some controversial comments on the *Today* programme on BBC Radio 4, expressing his personal concerns about the risks posed by the creation of a lasting power of attorney (LPA), claiming that they were fraught with opportunities for abuse and that he personally would prefer the (albeit more time-consuming and costly) alternative of a deputyship.

Where the court has appointed a deputy on behalf of an individual ('P'), it requires certain safeguards to protect against the misuse of P's funds. These include:

- a security bond that will pay out in the event that funds are misused (the court can decide that a bond is unnecessary, for example if the person's estate has a low value);
- a regular support meeting between the deputy and a court-appointed visitor;
- an annual report regarding P's finances that is reviewed by the court.

Deputies win on security (although it is possible to require attorneys to have accounts audited annually by a professional) but lose on cost.

The initial court fee on creation is normally £371 (plus an additional £494 if the court decides the case needs a hearing), with an annual fee which is normally £320 (although in cases where the amount managed is less that £21,000 this fee is reduced to £35) plus an annual fee for the security bond. The amount payable for the security bond depends on the value of the estate and how much of the estate the deputy controls. The fees are payable from the estate of the person who has lost capacity. There are also ongoing costs in having to make an application to the court for interim orders (for example when wanting to sell a house).

Financial abuse can and does happen under both deputyships and LPAs, but clearly the security bond is an added layer of protection in the case of deputyships. For an example of a bond being called in, see *Re Meek* [2014] EWCOP 1. The decision as to whether to go for an attorney will largely depend on the level of trust within the family.

Where financial abuse has occurred, it is worth noting that there is a specific criminal offence under s 4 of the Fraud Act 2000 where a person occupies a position in which he is expected to safeguard, or not to act against, the financial interests of another person, and he:

(a) dishonestly abuses that position; and

(b) intends, by means of the abuse of that position:

   (i) to make a gain for himself or another, or

   (ii) to cause loss to another or to expose another to a risk of loss.

3.2 ENDURING POWERS OF ATTORNEY

3.2.1 What is an EPA?

An EPA is a power of attorney created (though not necessarily registered) before 1 October 2007, in accordance with the EPAA 1985. The donor must have been an adult with the appropriate mental capacity to make the EPA. This means that the donor must have understood the nature and effect of the power, ie that the attorney may assume authority over his affairs and that the power may continue if he becomes mentally incapable.

Once created, the EPA may continue despite the loss of mental capacity of the donor, but special duties then arise for the attorney (see **3.2.5** below). In particular, the attorney must apply to the Public Guardian to register the EPA. The Public Guardian is appointed by the Government to deal with various matters concerning people who lack mental capacity.

Any authority given by the EPA is limited to acts relating to the donor's property and financial affairs. The EPA may give the attorney general or specific authority to act on the donor's behalf. If general authority is given, this confers authority 'to do on behalf of the donor anything which the donor can lawfully do' in relation to their property and financial affairs (although there are statutory limitations on the ability to make gifts under an EPA). If specific authority is given for a particular activity, the authority is limited to that activity, for example, to contract to sell and execute a transfer of the donor's freehold property.

3.2.2 Who can be an attorney under an EPA?

Any non-bankrupt adult or a trust corporation may be an attorney, and more than one person may be appointed. Where two or more are appointed, the donor must specify whether they are joint attorneys or joint and several attorneys. Failure to do so means that the EPA is invalid.

Joint attorneys must all act together; if one should die, become bankrupt or lose mental capacity, the power ceases to be effective. Joint powers provide protection for the donor but are inconvenient. Joint and several attorneys can act independently of the other or others. This may be convenient but could lead to lack of protection for the donor's property. A joint and several attorney can continue to act when a co-attorney has died or lost capacity.

3.2.3   Creation of an EPA

3.2.3.1   The Enduring Power of Attorney (Prescribed Form) Regulations 1990

Although these Regulations lapsed on the repeal of the enabling authority, the provisions are re-enacted in Sch 4 of the Mental Capacity Act 2005. An EPA is validly created only if the instrument complies with the following requirements:

(a)   The EPA is in the form prescribed in the 1990 Regulations. The Act provided that 'immaterial differences in form' could be ignored.

(b)   The EPA form incorporates the prescribed explanatory information together with all the relevant marginal notes. Part A of the form, entitled 'About using this form', must be included together with Parts B and C. The entire form must have been explained to the donor of the power before it is signed.

(c)   The EPA must have been executed in the prescribed manner by both the donor and the attorney, in each case in the presence of an independent witness. If the donor (or the attorney) was physically disabled then the EPA could be executed on his behalf, but in this case the signature must have been made in the presence of two independent witnesses.

3.2.3.2   Postponing the attorney's authority to act

Once the EPA has been correctly executed, the attorney may act under its authority immediately and without further formality. The execution of the EPA does not deprive the donor of the ability to take decisions on his own behalf should he so wish; indeed, he can revoke the power at any time. However, if he is to act on his own behalf or revoke the power, he must retain sufficient mental capacity.

Some donors did not want the attorney to act until the donor had lost or was losing his capacity. In such cases the EPA was drafted to include an appropriate restriction on the attorney's authority. For example, the authority may be delayed until such time as the attorney believes that 'the donor either is, or is becoming, mentally incapable', ie the authority will arise at the same time as Sch 4 to the MCA 2005 places a duty on the attorney to register the EPA with the Public Guardian (see **3.2.5** below).

3.2.4   Authority under an EPA

3.2.4.1   Generally

Any authority given by the EPA is limited to acts relating to the donor's property and financial affairs. Thus, it can cover such transactions as buying and selling shares or a house on behalf of the donor. But even an EPA giving general authority is significantly limited. It does not cover such matters as where the donor should live, whether or not medical treatment should be given or withheld, or the execution of a will for the donor. This limitation on the authority of the attorney will not necessarily matter until such time as the donor of the power loses mental capacity. Until then, decisions relating to matters not covered by the EPA will be taken by the donor of the power and not by the attorney. If the donor of the EPA does not have sufficient mental capacity to make a will, the Court of Protection may be asked to make a 'statutory will' on behalf of the donor. The MCA 2005 contains provisions for dealing with a person who lacks capacity to make decisions about other matters not covered by the EPA (see **3.3**).

3.2.4.2 Authority to give away donor's property

Clearly the attorney may use the donor's property to provide for the donor but, unless expressly excluded in the power of attorney, there is also limited authority to use the donor's property to provide for others under paras 3(2) and (3) of Sch 4 to the MCA 2005 (previously s 3(4) and (5) of the EPAA 1985).

Providing for the needs of others

Paragraph 3(2) provides as follows:

> Subject to any conditions or restrictions contained in the instrument, an attorney under an enduring power, whether general or limited, may (without obtaining any consent) act under the power so as to benefit himself or other persons than the donor to the following extent but no further —
>
> (a)   he may so act in relation to himself or in relation to any other person if the donor might be expected to provide for his or that person's needs respectively, and
>
> (b)   he may do whatever the donor might be expected to do to meet those needs.

Thus, assuming there is no express restriction in the power, the attorney must consider:

(i)   Is the provision required to meet a need?

(ii)   Might the donor be expected to provide for this person's needs?

(iii)   What would this particular donor have done to meet these needs?

'Seasonal' and charitable gifts

Paragraph 3(3) provides as follows:

> Without prejudice to sub-paragraph (2) but subject to any conditions or restrictions contained in the instrument, an attorney under an enduring power, whether general or limited, may (without obtaining any consent) dispose of the property of the donor by way of gift to the following extent but no further—
>
> (a)   he may make gifts of a seasonal nature or at a time, or on an anniversary, of a birth or marriage or the formation of a civil partnership, to persons (including himself) who are related to or connected with the donor, and
>
> (b)   he may make gifts to any charity to whom the donor made or might be expected to make gifts,
>
> provided that the value of each gift is not unreasonable having regard to all the circumstances and in particular the size of the donor's estate.

Again, assuming there is no express restriction in the power, the attorney should consider:

In relation to 3(3)(a)

(i)   Is the recipient related to or connected with the donor?

(ii)   Is the gift taking place at an appropriate time?

(iii)   Is the value of the gift not unreasonable in all the circumstances?

And in relation to 3(3)(b)

(i)   Is the recipient a charity?

(ii)   Did the donor previously make gifts to this charity, and if not might the donor be expected to make such gifts?

(iii)   Is the value of the gift not unreasonable in all the circumstances?

The attorney can make gifts to charity at any time. Gifts to non-charities can be made only if they are seasonal (eg, at Christmas), or for a birthday or marriage. It is doubtful whether 'seasonal' extends to the end of one tax year and the beginning of another. Presents given for particular events such as christenings, engagements, graduations, barmitzvahs or confirmations are effectively excluded.

3.2.5 Registration of the EPA with the Public Guardian

3.2.5.1 Donor's mental incapacity

Unlike an ordinary power of attorney, an EPA is not revoked by the donor's subsequent loss of mental capacity. However, once the donor has become incapacitated the attorney is unable to act under the authority of the EPA until it has been registered with the Public Guardian (MCA 2005, Sch 4). The registration fee is £82. Schedule 4 imposes special duties on the attorney which arise once the attorney 'has reason to believe that the donor is or is becoming mentally incapable'.

3.2.5.2 Special duties

The attorney must notify the donor of the EPA and certain specified relatives of his intention to apply to the Public Guardian for registration of the EPA.

The specified relatives who must receive notification of intention to apply for registration of the EPA include:

(a)   the donor's spouse or civil partner;

(b)   the donor's children (including illegitimate children);

(c)   the donor's parents;

(d)   the donor's brothers and sisters, whether of the whole or half blood;

(e)   the widow, widower or surviving civil partner of a child of the donor;

(f)   the donor's grandchildren.

The list continues with further remoter categories of relatives.

Three individuals must be ascertained by working from the top of the list. All members of a particular category must be notified once any member of the category is counted to establish the minimum number of three. However, there is no requirement for the attorney to notify, inter alia:

(a)   a person who has not attained 18; or

(b)   himself, even if he is a specified relative, but he should be included when counting the number of relatives to notify.

EXAMPLE

Adam is married with five adult children and a number of other surviving relatives. He has appointed his solicitor, Brian, to be his attorney. When Adam becomes incapable of managing his affairs, Brian must notify Adam's wife and all five children (plus Adam himself unless the court dispenses with this).

The Public Guardian has a general power of dispensation from the duty of notification. It can order dispensation if satisfied that it would be undesirable or impractical for the attorney to give notice, or if no useful purpose is likely to be achieved by it. However, clear medical evidence of detriment to health is required before the court will dispense with notification to the donor.

3.2.5.3 Effect of registration

The registration of the EPA with the Public Guardian effectively revalidates the EPA and restores to the attorney the powers granted by the EPA. Once registered, the donor can no longer revoke, extend or restrict the extent of the EPA.

3.2.6 Effect of the Trustee Delegation Act 1999

Prior to the Trustee Delegation Act 1999 (TDA 1999) it was possible for trustees to delegate their powers by using an EPA (EPAA 1985, s 3(3)). Section 3(3) had been drafted in haste in response to the decision in *Walia and Others v Michael Naughten Ltd* [1985] 1 WLR 1115. There was a feeling that the section had gone too far. There were three main problems with it:

(a)   The delegation remained effective indefinitely, unlike a delegation under s 25 of the TA 1925 which could last for only 12 months.

(b)   Various safeguards present in s 25 of the TA 1925 were not present in the EPAA 1985. The trustee did not have to give notice to the person entitled to appoint new trustees and was not liable for the acts of the delegate.

(c)   The delegation remained effective after the trustee lost capacity.

Section 5 of the TDA 1999 therefore provides (subject to one important exception) that any delegation of trustee functions must comply with s 25 of the TA 1925, as substituted by s 5. The delegation cannot exceed 12 months; the trustee must give notice to any co-trustees and to any person able to appoint new trustees; and the trustee will remain liable for the acts of the attorney.

The exception is contained in s 1 of the TDA 1999, which allows a person who is beneficially interested in land (or the proceeds of sale of land) to delegate trustee functions without complying with s 25 of the TA 1925. The appointment can, therefore, continue for more than 12 months. The exception is useful for co-owners as it allows one co-owner to delegate authority to another co-owner (or third party) for longer than 12 months.

However, the usefulness of the s 1 exception is to some extent eroded by s 7 of the TDA 1999, which provides that where two trustees are required (for example, to give a good receipt for capital money), the requirement is not fulfilled by one person acting in two capacities, as a trustee and as an attorney of another trustee.

> **EXAMPLE**
>
> H and W are co-owners of a house. H appoints W as his attorney under an EPA. He becomes mentally incapable and W registers the power. W wants to sell the house but she will not satisfy the requirement for two trustees. She can, however, appoint a further trustee as permitted under s 8 of the TDA 1999.

3.3   EFFECT OF THE MENTAL CAPACITY ACT 2005

The MCA 2005 contains a number of provisions of general application in relation to mental capacity.

Section 2 introduced a single test for capacity. It provides that:

(a)   a person lacks capacity *in relation to a matter* if at the material time he is unable to make a decision for himself in relation to the matter because of an impairment of or a disturbance in the functioning of the mind or brain;

(b)   it does not matter whether the disturbance is permanent or temporary.

Section 3 provides that a person is unable to make a decision for himself if he is unable to:

(a)   understand the information relevant to the decision; or

(b)   retain the information relevant to the decision; or

(c)   use the information relevant to the decision as part of the process of making the decision; or

(d)   communicate the decision (whether by talking, using sign language or any other means).

A person is not to be treated as unable to make a decision simply because he makes an unwise one. A person is not to be treated as unable to make a decision unless all practicable steps to help him to do so have been taken without success. The fact that a person is able to retain information relevant to the decision only for a short time does not prevent him being regarded as able to make the decision. The information relevant to making a decision includes information about the reasonably foreseeable consequences of:

(a)   deciding one way or another; or

(b)   failing to make the decision.

Section 1 provides, for the purposes of the Act, that a person is to be assumed to have capacity until the contrary is established on the balance of probabilities. It also states that anyone making a decision on behalf of a person who lacks capacity must act in the best interests of that person. When deciding what is in the best interests of a person who lacks capacity ('P'), the matters set out in s 4 of the Act must be considered. These include the past and present wishes and feelings of P (and, in particular, any relevant written statement made by him when he had capacity).

Part 2 of the MCA 2005 deals with the powers of the Court of Protection to make decisions on behalf of persons who lack capacity. The Act provides that if a person wishes to make decisions on behalf of P, he may do so informally in relation to many matters, particularly those involving personal welfare. However, for some decisions, including most decisions concerning property and financial affairs, it will be necessary to make an application to the Court of Protection (unless there is an effective EPA or LPA). The Court may empower a person to make a specific decision or may appoint a deputy or deputies to make decisions on an ongoing basis.

Section 42 of the MCA 2005 provides for the Lord Chancellor to issue a code or codes of practice giving guidance to persons with various duties and functions under the Act. The Mental Capacity Act Code of Practice ('the Code') was issued in April 2007 and is regularly updated. Various persons, including attorneys acting under an LPA, must have regard to the Code when making decisions on behalf of others.

The Act also provides for the creation of LPAs and the creation of advance decisions to refuse treatment.

3.4   LASTING POWERS OF ATTORNEY

From 1 October 2007, when the relevant provisions of the MCA 2005 came into force, it is no longer possible to create an EPA (see **3.1**). Instead a person may create an LPA.

3.4.1   What is an LPA?

According to s 9 of the MCA 2005, under an LPA a person (the donor) is able to confer on the attorney(s) authority to make decisions about the donor's health and care and/or financial affairs for the donor, including authority to make such decisions in circumstances where the donor no longer has capacity (as defined in ss 2 and 3). There are two separate types of LPA: one allowing the appointment of attorneys to deal with decisions on financial affairs, and the other allowing the appointment of attorneys to deal with decisions on health and care. A person can choose to create both types of power or just one, and can appoint the same person or different people to act as an attorney under each power.

3.4.2   Who can be appointed as attorney?

Section 10 of the MCA 2005 provides that the attorney must be an individual over the age of 18, or, if the authority is only in relation to the donor's property and affairs, a trust corporation.

The donor may appoint more than one attorney, and may specify whether the appointment is joint, or joint and several. It is possible to provide that for some functions the attorneys must act jointly, and for other functions they may act jointly and severally. Although this provides flexibility, it may cause difficulty for the attorney in using the power. An institution such as a bank, when dealing with one of several attorneys, may refuse to comply with that attorney's instructions because it cannot assess if the circumstances are such that the attorney may act severally rather than jointly. If the donor does not specify, the appointment will be regarded as joint.

Attorneys appointed with joint authority cease to be able to act if one dies, loses capacity or (in the case of a property and financial affairs power) is declared bankrupt. However, if there are joint and several attorneys, the bankruptcy of one of the attorneys will not affect the validity of the appointment of the other non-bankrupt attorneys. A bankrupt can act as an attorney of a health and care LPA.

The donor may provide for a successor or substitute attorney to replace an attorney in specified circumstances, for example the death, loss of capacity or bankruptcy of the attorney. It is, therefore, particularly important to appoint a replacement in the case of joint appointments. It is possible to appoint the surviving attorney(s) as replacement(s). See *Miles v Public Guardian* [2015] EWHC 2960 (Ch).

3.4.3   Creation of an LPA

3.4.3.1   Prescribed form

Only an adult with capacity can create an LPA. It must be made in the form prescribed from time to time in regulations, and contain prescribed information, including:

(a)   that the donor has read and understood the prescribed information and intends to confer authority to make decisions in circumstances where he has no capacity;

(b)   who the donor wishes to be notified of any application for the registration of the LPA (up to a maximum of five), or that he wishes no one to be notified;

(c)   that the attorney has read and understood the prescribed information and understands his duty to act in the best interests of the donor;

(d)   a certificate, signed by a person of a 'prescribed description', as to the capacity of the donor. (Before 1 July 2015 it was necessary to supply two certificate providers where the donor did not indicate that anyone was to be notified of the application for registration.)

The Lasting Powers of Attorney, Enduring Powers of Attorney and Public Guardian Regulations 2007 (SI 2007/1253) ('the Regulations') set out the format of each type of LPA. As a result of various extra features, the LPA is much longer than the EPA. The forms contain a considerable number of sections, and it is vital to complete the forms fully and correctly. An LPA may be refused registration if it contains any defect. In some cases the defect may be corrected simply on supplying further information, but if a new LPA is needed this will only be possible if the donor still has capacity to make one. The Office of the Public Guardian has issued a detailed guide to making and registering an LPA (Form LP12).

The forms have been redesigned more than once since 1 October 2007, and the most recent versions (known as LP1F for financial decisions and LP1H for health and care decisions) came into effect on 3 March 2017.

There are sections on each type of LPA in which the donor can set out 'instructions' and 'preferences'. It is for the donor to decide what, if anything, to include here. It used to be essential for anyone who wanted their attorney to be able to use discretionary fund management to include a clause authorising the attorney to do so. Some risk-averse financial institutions took the view that an attorney is a delegate and therefore cannot delegate the exercise of discretions to another without authorisation (the principle of *delegatus non potest delegare*). The Office of the Public Guardian agreed that this was necessary.

The following wording was commonly used:

> My attorney(s) may transfer my investments into a discretionary management scheme. Or, if I already had investments in a discretionary management scheme before I lost capacity to make financial decisions, I want the scheme to continue. I understand in both cases that managers of the scheme will make investment decisions and my investments will be held in their names or the names of their nominees.

However, on 14 March 2022 the Law Society announced that the Office of the Public Guardian had agreed to change its guidance on the need to have express provision for the management of investments via a discretionary fund manager.

Given that financial institutions can make their own decisions as to whether or not to accept instructions, cautious advisers may continue to suggest including express authorisation.

3.4.3.2   Certificate of capacity

Paragraph 8 of the Regulations provides that the persons who may provide a certificate of capacity are:

(a)   a person chosen by the donor who has known the donor personally for at least two years immediately prior to the signing of the certificate;

(b)   a person chosen by the donor who, on account of his professional skills and expertise, reasonably considers that he is competent to make the judgments necessary to certify that the donor has sufficient capacity to make the LPA.

The Regulations give examples of the persons who might fall into the second category, and these include registered health care professionals, social workers, and barristers and solicitors. Note that persons in this category do not need to have known the donor for at least two years.

There are a number of persons listed in the Regulations who are not permitted to provide a certificate under either category. These include the intended attorney, or a person who is attorney under any other lasting or enduring power created by the donor, a business partner of an attorney, a family member of the donor or the donee, and those involved in running a care home in which the donor resides. 'Family member' is not defined in the Regulations or the MCA 2005. In *Re Kittle* [2010] WTLR 651 the Court of Protection ruled that a cousin was not a family member for this purpose.

The Office of the Public Guardian's guide to making and registering an LPA includes examples of relationships which would make a person ineligible to provide a certificate. These include persons related by marriage to the donor or donee and unmarried partners, whether or not living with the donor or donee (see also *Re Phillips* (Court of Protection, Judgment, May 2012)).

The certificate provider must certify that in his opinion, at the time the donor makes the LPA:

(a)   the donor understands the purpose of this LPA and the scope of the authority conferred under it;

(b)   no fraud or undue pressure is being used to induce the donor to create the LPA; and

(c)   there is nothing else which would prevent an LPA from being created.

3.4.3.3   Execution

Paragraph 9 of the Regulations sets out detailed rules for the execution of the power, and states that a power must be executed in accordance with these.

The rules require that the donor must first read all the prescribed information, then 'as soon as reasonably practicable' after this the donor must complete section 9 of the power and sign it in the presence of a witness (who must not be an attorney or replacement attorney).

As soon as reasonably practicable after this the certificate provider must complete and sign section 10 of the power. Lastly, as soon as reasonably practicable after this, the attorney(s) must read the prescribed information and then complete and sign section 11 of the power, in the presence of a witness (who must not be the donor).

As a result of the Covid-19 pandemic, the government announced that it would introduce a temporary relaxation of the rules on execution of wills to allow 'virtual' witnessing using platforms such as Zoom. However, no relaxation was announced in relation to LPAs which continue to require witnesses to be actually present.

3.4.3.4 Registration

Unlike EPAs, which could come into operation as a power of attorney from the moment of execution, the LPA will not have any effect at all until it is registered with the Public Guardian.

There is no obligation to register the LPA once it has been executed. However, the donor or attorneys (or, where there are joint and several attorneys, any of them) may choose to do so at any time after the power has been executed, and it is common to do so as soon as the LPA is made. This will involve using a prescribed form and paying a fee of £82. Whoever applies for registration must have first notified anyone named by the donor as a person to be notified in such circumstances. To encourage early registration, the latest version of the LPA form also contains sections dealing with the application to register the LPA.

Unlike EPAs, there is no obligation on the attorneys to register the power if the donor loses capacity, although if this does happen it is very likely that the attorney or attorneys would seek to register the power.

On receipt of an application for registration, the Public Guardian must notify:

(a)   the attorneys if the donor applied; or

(b)   the donor if the attorneys applied (and any attorneys who did not join in the application to register).

The donor, attorneys or the other persons notified can object to the registration on various grounds, but otherwise the Public Guardian will register the power and notify the donor and attorneys of this. The Public Guardian keeps a register of LPAs.

Once registered, the LPA is valid and may be used by the attorney(s), subject to any express restrictions in the LPA.

3.4.4 Authority under an LPA

An attorney making a decision under an LPA for a person who lacks capacity must act in the best interests of the donor, which means complying with MCA 2005, s 4, which sets out various matters to which the attorney must have regard, including the past and present wishes of the person who has lost capacity. The attorney must also have regard to the Code.

3.4.4.1 LPA for financial decisions

An attorney who has authority to make financial decisions may act even though the donor has capacity (unless the power contains express restrictions preventing this).

The attorney cannot dispose of the donor's property by making gifts, unless in accordance with s 12 of the MCA 2005. Section 12(2) provides that the attorney may make gifts:

(a)   on customary occasions to persons (including the attorney) who are related to or connected with the donor; or

(b)   to any charity to which the donor made or might have been expected to make gifts.

In either case the value of the gift must not be unreasonable in all the circumstances. Cases such as *Re Buckley* [2013] EWHC 2965 (COP) (involving attorneys) and *Re GM* [2013] EWHC 2966 (COP) (involving deputies under similar restraints to attorneys when making gifts) indicate that on this point each case will turn on its own facts, taking many factors into consideration.

'Customary occasions' is defined in s 12(3) to mean:

(a)   the occasion or anniversary of a birth, a marriage or the formation of a civil partnership; or

(b)   any other occasion when presents are customarily given within families, or among friends or associates.

Unlike EPAs, therefore (see **3.2**), gifts to non-charities can be made other than at 'seasonal' times. *Re Treadwell* [2013] EWHC 2409 (COP) was a Court of Protection case involving deputies appointed to administer the affairs of a person lacking capacity. The deputies were under very similar restraints to those in s 12 of the MCA 2005 when making gifts. In this case gifts made as housewarming and graduation presents were accepted as being made on 'customary occasions' (although on the facts the value of the gifts was not reasonable). However, gifts made to set up child trust funds, to take advantage of a government tax-free savings vehicle, were not made on 'customary occasions'.

The donor cannot include express provisions in the LPA widening the scope of s 12 powers to make gifts, but can include express restrictions. Individuals commonly attempt to widen the powers of attorneys to make gifts beyond what is permitted under s 12. A power will not be registered with an offending clause. Instead the Public Guardian (OPG) will sever the clause so that the rest of the power can be registered. MCA 2005, Sch 1, para 11(2) requires the OPG, unless the court directs otherwise, to refuse to register an LPA containing a provision which would:

(a)   be ineffective as part of an LPA;

(b)   prevent the instrument from operating as a valid LPA.

The OPG had been quick to require clauses which it regarded as asking attorneys to make unauthorised gifts to be severed if the LPA was to be registered. However, the decision in *Re JG and Others* [2017] EWCOP 10 is important as it has substantially changed the approach of the OPG. In *Re JG*, Eldergill J had to consider a number of cases in which the OPG wanted to sever provisions which it regarded as objectionable. He made the point that the Act is an enabling Act and obstacles should not be put in the way of carrying out P's intentions, if at all possible.

In one of the applications, the person creating the power (P) had written in the 'Preferences' section of the LPA: 'I would like my attorneys to consider Thomas G (my son) as my main priority when making decisions.'

The view of the OPG was that the words had to be severed. They would have prevented the instrument acting as an LPA because the attorneys were not required to act in 'the best interests' of P. Eldergill J disagreed. P had not imposed any conditions or restrictions on the authority of the attorneys which would prevent the instrument from operating as a valid LPA or which were ineffective as part of an LPA. She had merely specified that she would 'like' her attorneys to consider her son as her main priority. The Act entitled her to make a written statement concerning her wishes and feelings (s 4(6)(a)) which the attorneys, and the court, were required to consider when deciding what decision was in her best interests. She had done no more than exercise that right. Moreover, in the judge's opinion, it was a misunderstanding of the Act to take the view that acting in an incapacitated person's best interests in some way precludes giving any weight to the interests of other persons dear to them.

Unlike EPAs, there is no provision authorising an attorney to make gifts to meet the reasonable needs of persons the donor of the power might be expected to provide for. Until Eldergill J's decision in *Re JG and Others*, it was assumed that attorneys had no power to meet 'reasonable needs' of family members or dependants unless P was under a legal obligation to maintain such persons – there is an obligation for a spouse or civil partner to maintain the other and for a parent to maintain a minor child. However, Eldergill J said that this was not the case. An LPA attorney is able to make all financial decisions on behalf of P in his or her best interests subject only to specific limitations on the power to make gifts. He considered that meeting a need was not the same as making a gift.

If the payment is not a gift for the purposes of s 12 but the meeting of a need, and there is no condition or restriction in the instrument which prevents such payments, then the attorney must apply the principles in MCA 2005, s 1 and the best interests considerations in s 4. The attorney must consider matters such as the donor's past and present wishes and feelings, their beliefs and values, any written statements made by them, including statements in the LPA itself, and all other relevant considerations such as the donor's own needs and the nature of their relationship with the potential recipient, and decide whether such a payment is in the donor's best interests.

He said that it was not possible to define precisely the boundary between a gift and a payment to meet a person's needs because each person's situation, circumstances and resources are unique. However, in very general terms, gifts lack the regularity of weekly, monthly and other periodic payments to meet the needs of family members and dependants, and often are not supported by a history of frequent similar periodic payments predating the onset of incapacity.

Payments on customary occasions such as birthdays will generally be gifts, not payments to satisfy a need. Likewise, the making of one-off payments in the absence of good evidence of a sudden present need which historically the donor would have met or be likely to meet from his or her own funds may be construed by the court as a gift. Where an attorney is uncertain as to whether a proposed payment is a gift or meeting a need and the gift would not come within s 12 of the MCA 2005, the prudent course will be to apply for the court to authorise the payment.

It will also be helpful for the donor to leave an indication of his or her wishes in the preferences section of the LPA.

Current OPG guidance on making gifts is contained in 'Gifts: Deputies and EPA/LPA Attorneys', updated in February 2018 to reflect the comments of Eldergill J in *Re JG*.

More recently, Hilder J considered the boundary between making a gift and meeting a need in *In the Matter of Various Lasting Powers of Attorney* [2019] EWCOP 40. She concluded that a gift is something which is entirely voluntary and given without obligation. She also confirmed that:

(a) provisions within an LPA requesting attorneys to use the donor's funds to benefit persons other than the donor may be valid as a written statement of the donor's wishes as long as they are expressed in precatory terms, but will be ineffective if expressed in mandatory terms;

(b) provisions within an LPA that provide for attorneys to use the donor's funds to benefit themselves do not infringe the rule against self-dealing and are valid because any conflict has been authorised by the donor and, in any event, the attorney must act in the donor's best interests.

Under s 23(4), the court may authorise gifts not covered by s 12(2), eg a gift made for tax planning purposes. Because P's past and present wishes and feelings must be taken into account when deciding what is in P's best interests, evidence of previous gifts made when P had capacity will make it more likely that the court will authorise future gifts (provided there are sufficient surplus funds).

Evidence of P's past wishes and feelings is particularly important in relation to gifts for tax planning purposes. In *PBC v JMA* [2018] EWCOP 19, Hilder J said:

Mitigation of tax, ... even by completely lawful 'vanilla' means, is a matter on which there may be a range of views. The Mental Capacity Act does not permit the Court to rely on default positions, assumptions or generalisations in making a decision about whether gifts to effect tax mitigation are in the best interests of a particular protected person. The Court must decide the application on nothing more and nothing less than a case-specific application of section 4.

This was endorsed by District Judge Ellington in *Re MJL, FL v MJL* [2019] EWCOP 31 where she expressly rejected any 'default position in favour of or against tax planning'. In both these cases the court decided that the gifts were in P's best interests and that there was sufficient evidence of a wish to save tax.

3.4.4.2   LPA for health and care decisions

An attorney acting under such an LPA may make decisions about the social and health care of the donor. Unlike an attorney making financial decisions, the attorney of a health and welfare LPA can act only if the donor does not have capacity to make a particular decision. The MCA 2005 contains various restrictions on the attorney, eg the attorney cannot vote on behalf of the donor. The donor may also include express limitations in the power, eg permitting the attorney to make decisions as to the social care of the donor but not health care. If the attorney is not expressly restricted then he may give or refuse consent to health care treatment; although if the decision involves the refusal of life-sustaining treatment, the attorney must have express authority in the LPA to make such a decision.

A person who makes both types of LPA can choose the same person(s) as attorneys but it is possible, and not uncommon, to choose different persons. Although the attorney making financial decisions holds the purse strings, they will be expected to work with those dealing with P's health and care – see *Mrs P v Rochdale District Council* [2016] EWCOP B1. That case involved a deputy, but the principle is the same. A solicitor was removed as a property and financial affairs deputy because he had refused to respond to requests from those dealing with Mrs P's care. He had made no funds available for new clothes to fit her after her illness or for hairdressing and manicures and, most importantly, had refused to facilitate visits from her beloved dog after he had been rehomed.

3.4.4.3   Comparison with EPAs

Both LPAs and EPAs are intended to deal with similar circumstances, but there are a number of differences between them. A selection of the main differences is set out below.

LPAs	EPAs
Created on or after 1 October 2007	Created before 1 October 2007
Two types – one for financial decisions and one for health and care decisions	One type – only for property and financial affairs
Prescribed format for powers, requiring execution by donor, certificate provider and attorneys	Prescribed format for powers, requiring execution by donor and attorneys
Failure to specify if attorneys are joint or joint and several does not invalidate the power – attorneys treated as joint	Failure to specify if attorneys are joint or joint and several invalidates the power
Only effective on registration	Can operate from execution
No obligation for attorneys to register if donor loses capacity	Obligation for attorneys to register if donor loses capacity
Registration procedure includes notifying persons nominated by donor (if any)	Registration procedure includes notifying persons prescribed by statute

LPAs	EPAs
Attorneys authorised to make financial decisions may make gifts under a property and affairs LPA in limited circumstances: MCA 2005, s 12	Attorneys may make gifts in limited circumstances: MCA 2005, Sch 4, para 3(2) and (3)

3.5 LIVING WILLS AND ADVANCE DECISIONS TO REFUSE TREATMENT

3.5.1 Living wills

Living wills (also known as advance directives) are intended to allow individuals to specify the extent and nature of the medical treatment they would or would not find acceptable should they lose capacity in the future. The term 'living will' can be confusing since such documents have no connection with ordinary wills, but this term is probably too well established to change.

A mentally capable adult has no right to demand a particular treatment, but has the right to refuse any medical treatment (*Sidaway v Board of Governors of the Bethlem Royal Hospital and Maudsley Hospital and Others* [1985] AC 871).

The right to refuse treatment extends to a refusal made in advance. There are various cases which support advance directives.

After the Tony Bland case (arising from the Hillsborough stadium disaster), a *Practice Note (Persistent Vegetative State: Withdrawal of Treatment)* (26 July 1996) [1996] 4 All ER 766 was issued dealing with the procedure to be followed when an application is made to withdraw treatment from a person in a persistent vegetative state. It included the following statement:

> Previously expressed advance directions of the patient, in writing or otherwise, will be an important factor, and the High Court may determine the effect of advance directives as to future medical treatment.

In *Re T (Adult: Refusal of Treatment)* [1992] 2 FLR 458, the Court of Appeal said that an advance refusal is legally binding, provided:

(a)   the person making it had capacity at the time of making it;

(b)   a situation has arisen which was envisaged when the directive was made;

(c)   the person making it was not under any undue influence at the time the directive was made.

3.5.2 Advance decisions to refuse treatment

The MCA 2005 provides for an adult with capacity to make an advance decision to refuse specified medical treatment in future specified circumstances. Advance decisions made before the MCA 2005 came into effect continue to be valid provided they comply with the formalities set out in the MCA 2005, s 25(6).

If the provisions contained in the advance decision apply to the particular circumstances encountered by the persons supplying treatment, it will be as if the person had capacity to refuse the treatment, and those persons will not be liable for complying with the advance decision to refuse treatment. Such persons will also not be liable if they reasonably believe the advance decision to apply. If, as is usually the case, the advance decision concerns the refusal of life-sustaining treatment in specified circumstances, s 25(6) provides that the decision is not valid unless:

(a)   it is in writing;

(b)   signed by P or by another person in P's presence and by P's direction;

(c)   the signature is made or acknowledged by P in the presence of a witness; and

(d)   the witness signs it, or acknowledges his signature, in P's presence.

The advance decision can be revoked or modified by the person who made it at any time when he has capacity to do so. If a person who has made an advance decision later makes an LPA giving express authority to an attorney to make decisions on such matters, this LPA will supersede the advance decision.

The advance decision will not take effect if P has done anything clearly inconsistent with the advance decision remaining his fixed decision. For a recent example of an advance decision which was held to be ineffective because of P's inconsistent behaviour, see *Re PW (Jehovah's Witness: validity of advance decision), Re; University Hospitals Birmingham NHS Foundation Trust v PW (by her litigation friend, the Official Solicitor)* [2021] EWCOP 52. P had given her children, whom she knew were hostile to the Jehovah's Witnesses denomination, authority to make decisions about all medical treatment, other than life-sustaining treatment, on her behalf, without mentioning to them or including in the written LPA any preference or requirement not to receive a blood transfusion or blood products. She had requested the removal of a 'do not resuscitate' notice, without qualification and without telling her children or her clinicians about her advance decision to refuse a blood transfusion or blood products. The judge found that these actions were inconsistent with the advance decision remaining her fixed decision. He also considered it to be significant that the advance decision had been made 20 years earlier and had not been reviewed or updated. Practical points arising from this case for those making advance decisions are the importance of regular reviews and the need to make family members aware that they exist.

It is not easy to draft effective advance decisions. It is difficult to anticipate the circumstances that may arise and make the direction sufficiently specific. In *Re B (Consent to Treatment: Capacity)* [2002] EWHC 429 (Fam), [2002] 1 FLR 1090, Ms B had made a living will but it was not appropriate to deal with the circumstances that arose. Doctors therefore ignored it.

The charity, Compassion in Dying, works to inform and empower individuals to exercise their rights and choices around end-of-life care. It offers an Advance Decision (Living Will) pack containing an Advance Decision form and comprehensive guidance notes, and it has on its website a series of questions and scenarios which, when completed, will generate an advance decision ready for signature and witnessing online.

Even if a person has written a perfectly effective advance decision, there is the further problem that an emergency doctor may give treatment before becoming aware of the existence of the advance decision.

An alternative approach is to give a health and care attorney power to accept or refuse life-sustaining treatment.

SUMMARY

(1) Enduring and lasting powers or attorney do not cease to be effective if the donor loses mental capacity.

(2) Enduring powers of attorney (EPAs):

    (a) cannot be created after 1 October 2007 but any correctly created before then will continue to operate;

    (b) are effective upon execution, unless restricted;

    (c) must be registered by the attorney (who must comply with the notification procedures) if he has reason to believe that the donor is or is becoming mentally incapable, so that the power can continue to be used;

    (d) allow the attorney only to deal with the donor's property and affairs and, unless restricted, make limited gifts of the donor's property.

> (3) Lasting powers of attorney (LPAs):
>
>   (a) can only be created on or after 1 October 2007 and must be made in a specific format, including a certificate by a prescribed person confirming that the donor understands the purpose of the LPA and that there is no fraud or undue pressure;
>
>   (b) are not valid until registered with the Public Guardian, which can be done at any time after the power has been executed.
>
> (4) LPAs for financial decisions allow attorneys to deal with decisions on property and financial affairs, including making some limited gifts of the donor's property and meeting reasonable needs of family members and dependants provided this is in P's best interests.
>
> (5) LPAs for health and care decisions allow attorneys to deal with decisions on personal welfare on behalf of a person who lacks capacity.
>
> (6) A person may create one or both types of LPA and may appoint the same or different person(s) to act as attorney under each.
>
> (7) It is possible to attempt to provide for refusal of specified medical treatment in the future using an advance decision, but there are difficulties with these.

REVIEW ACTIVITY

Question 1

Andrew created an EPA on 1 June 2005. He appointed his wife, Bella, and sister, Clare, as his joint attorneys, and put no special provisions or restrictions in the power. In May 2021 Andrew begins to lose mental capacity. His only relatives are Bella, Clare, and his adult children, David, Ewan, Fiona and Gina, and he has assets of £2 million.

Which ONE OR MORE of the following is/are CORRECT?

A   The EPA was usable from 1 June 2005.

B   The EPA should have been registered in June 2005.

C   Registration of the EPA requires notification of David and Ewan only.

D   If the power is registered, Bella and Clare can pay £5,000 of Andrew's money to Gina who is getting married.

E   Bella and Clare can use the power to authorise medical treatment for Andrew.

F   If Clare becomes bankrupt in 2022, Bella can carry on acting alone as attorney.

Answer: A and D

The obligation to register the power arises only when the donor starts to lose mental capacity. Before this the power is usable, unless it contains restrictions.

On registration, three relatives must be notified, in accordance with the statutory list. Bella is one of the three (though need not actually notify herself) and then the next category is the adult children. All persons in this category need to be notified, even though this means more than three people in total.

There is power under para 3(3) of Sch 4 to the MCA 2005 to make gifts from the donor's estate to persons related to the donor on certain occasions, which include marriage. The amount must not be unreasonable having regard to all the circumstances.

The power allows the attorneys to deal only with the donor's property and financial affairs. A bankrupt person cannot act as attorney. As the power is joint rather than joint and several, Bella cannot continue to act alone and the power becomes ineffective.

Question 2

Laura created a financial decisions LPA on 1 August 2016. She appointed her husband, Mark, and daughter, Nina, as her joint attorneys, and put no special provisions or restrictions in the power. The power states that her brother, Simon, is to be notified of registration. In January 2021 Laura begins to lose mental capacity. Her only relatives are Mark, Nina, and her brothers, Peter, Simon and Tony. She has assets of £2 million.

Which ONE OR MORE of the following is/are CORRECT?

A   The LPA was usable from 1 August 2016.

B   The LPA should have been registered in August 2016.

C   Registration of the LPA requires notification of Mark, Nina, Peter, Simon and Tony.

D   If the power is registered, Mark and Nina can pay £5,000 of Laura's money to Nina who is getting married.

E   Mark and Nina cannot use the power to authorise medical treatment for Laura.

F   If Nina becomes bankrupt in 2022, Mark can carry on acting alone as attorney.

Answer: D and E

There is no obligation to register the power but it is unusable until it is. On registration, it is the person(s) indicated in the LPA who must be notified.

There is power under s 12(2) of the MCA 2005 to make gifts from the donor's estate to persons related to the donor on certain occasions, which include marriage. The amount must not be unreasonable having regard to all the circumstances.

The power allows the attorneys to deal only with the donor's property and financial affairs (although if Laura had also made a health and care LPA, this would have allowed such decisions to be made).

As the power is joint rather than joint and several, Mark cannot continue to act alone and the power becomes ineffective, unless Laura had provided for a substitute attorney to take over on the happening of this event.

CHAPTER 4

ESTATE PLANNING

LEARNING OUTCOMES

After reading this chapter you will have an understanding of the numerous factors relevant to advising a client on making lifetime outright gifts, including:

- making use of tax exemptions and reliefs
- avoiding tax pitfalls
- practical matters.

4.1 INTRODUCTION

Estate planning very broadly involves maximising wealth and then passing it on efficiently in a way that achieves the client's aims. Solicitors will deal with a range of clients with different circumstances and objectives, but the clients offering the greatest scope for estate planning are wealthy, married (or in a civil partnership), with children (and possibly grandchildren).

We have already considered financial planning in **Chapter 2**. This is an important element of estate planning as it should help clients maximise their wealth by the appropriate choice of investments. Estate planning also involves arranging for this wealth to be passed on. This may simply mean giving advice on making a will (see **Chapters 11** and **12**), but some clients will also be in a position to pass on some of their wealth before they die. They may do this by making outright gifts or by setting up trusts. Using a trust allows the client to shed his assets for tax purposes, whilst imposing a certain amount of control over assets given away. You will consider lifetime creation of trusts in detail in **Chapter 5**.

In this chapter we consider only the making of outright lifetime gifts, with particular focus on making these within the family unit to a spouse or civil partner and/or to children.

Much of estate planning work relies on using tax exemptions and reliefs appropriately. As a preliminary, therefore, this chapter contains a reminder of the key elements of inheritance tax (IHT) and capital gains tax (CGT), including the exemptions and reliefs commonly used in estate planning. It then considers making gifts of particular types of asset, indicating the tax advantages as well as possible disadvantages.

Marriage (Same Sex Couples) Act 2013

This Act permits same sex couples to marry under the law of England and Wales. Its main provisions came into effect on 13 March 2014, enabling the first same sex marriages to take place on 29 March 2014. Same sex married couples are treated in the same way as couples in opposite sex marriages, subject to any contrary provision in the Act or future legislation. For tax purposes there is no difference between same and opposite sex marriages. References in this chapter to 'husband', 'wife' and 'spouse' mean parties of both opposite and same sex marriages, for all tax purposes.

Civil partners

Since 5 December 2005 when the Civil Partnership Act 2004 came into force, persons who have entered into a civil partnership are treated for tax purposes in the same way as married persons.

For the sake of brevity this book will generally refer only to spouses and marriage, but exactly the same principles apply to the parties to a civil partnership.

Originally, civil partnership was available only to same sex couples. When the Marriage (Same Sex Couples) Act 2013 came into force, same sex couples had two options for obtaining legal recognition of their relationship, whereas opposite sex couples had only one. Section 15 of the 2013 Act required the Secretary of State to arrange for a review of the operation and future of the Civil Partnership Act 2004 to begin as soon as possible and to include a full public consultation. Following two public consultations and a debate in Parliament, the Government decided to wait to see how extending marriages to same sex couples impacted on civil partnerships before making a final decision as to how to deal with the situation.

In R (Steinfeld and another) v Secretary of State for International Development [2018] UKSC 32, the claimants sought judicial review of the Secretary of State's failure to bring forward changes to the 2004 Act on the basis that it had become incompatible with Article 14 of the Convention for the Protection of Human Rights and Fundamental Freedoms read with Article 8 – it was discriminatory on grounds of sexual orientation because it enabled same sex couples, but not opposite sex couples, to form a civil partnership. The Supreme Court held that the delay was unjustified. The Government had been obliged by the Convention to eliminate immediately the inequality of treatment resulting from the coming into force of the 2013 Act, either by abolishing civil partnerships or by extending them to different sex couples.

The Civil Partnerships, Marriages and Deaths (Registration etc) Act 2019 came into force on 26 May 2019. Section 2(1) authorised the Secretary of State to make regulations to amend the Civil Partnership Act 2004, so that opposite sex couples would become eligible to form civil partnerships in England and Wales (provided that they would be eligible to do so apart from the question of sex).

The Civil Partnership (Opposite-sex Couples) Regulations 2019 came into force on 2 December 2019. The formation of new opposite sex civil partnerships became possible from 31 December 2019 onwards (existing overseas opposite sex civil partnerships were recognised from 2 December 2019).

Part 8 of the 2019 Regulations limits the Marriage (Same Sex Couples) Act 2013 to maintain the current position on conversion rights, so that only same sex civil partners will be able to convert their civil partnerships to marriage for now. Paragraph 91 of Implementing Opposite-Sex Civil Partnerships: Next Steps (the government guidance published with the Regulations in July 2019) states:

> This approach avoids making short-term changes ahead of the outcome of the public consultation on the future of conversion rights conducted earlier this year ... Further regulations on conversion rights may follow next year, depending on the outcome of the consultation.

The impact of the legislation in relation to drafting private documents such as trusts and wills is considered in **Chapters 6** and **11**.

4.1.1 Aims of estate planning

The aims of a client are usually to:

(a)   provide financial security for self and family; and

(b)   reduce tax liabilities.

It is not always possible to achieve both objectives, and tax savings should not be attempted at the expense of financial security.

Whereas the intention when tax planning through wills is to limit the amount of IHT payable on a death, the intention of lifetime estate planning is often as much concerned with avoiding CGT or minimising an income tax bill as it is with IHT. Because of the interaction of the taxes, clients may have to accept a small CGT bill as part of the cost of avoiding a large IHT bill, or a potential IHT charge for a considerable saving of CGT.

EXAMPLE

James, who is divorced, has been told that to give away assets which are likely to increase in value is sound IHT planning. Accordingly, in 2022/23 he plans to give his daughter his 10,000 shares in a quoted company which have considerable growth potential. He hopes to reduce the IHT payable at death on his already large estate. Stockbrokers have advised that he will realise a gain of £20,300 if he gives the shares away now. There are no relevant reliefs which James can claim. He has made no other disposals in this tax year. James is a higher rate taxpayer.

Compare the following:

Lifetime gift

(a)   CGT: chargeable gain of £8,000 (£20,300–£12,300 annual exemption) taxed at 20% = £1,600.

(b)   IHT, potentially exempt transfer (PET): even if death occurs within seven years, IHT will be calculated on the value of the shares at the date of the gift. The increase in value will occur in James's daughter's estate, not in his estate.

No lifetime gift: tax on death

(a)   CGT: none (tax-free uplift to value of shares at the date of death).

(b)   IHT: on value of the shares at death as part of James's estate attracting tax of up to 40%.

4.1.2 Some ground rules

When advising clients, solicitors should consider the following.

4.1.2.1 How much to give away?

The obvious answer is not too much, as once property is given away it cannot be claimed back if the donor later falls on hard times. It is important to consider the effect of factors such as possible future ill health, care home fees, separation, divorce, retirement and death of any of the parties involved in the gift. In addition, the likely effects of inflation on the purchasing power of income and on the value of retained capital, and the possibility of loss of wealth through investment losses, all may suggest that it is prudent to retain more rather than less.

4.1.2.2 What to give away?

Where possible, assets likely to appreciate in value should be considered for lifetime giving. Shares in a private company will often rise substantially in value if the company is floated on the Stock Exchange. So too may the value of a painting following the death of the artist. Making the gift *before* the value increases ensures the growth occurs in the estate of the donee. It 'freezes the value' of the property (ie, a PET) at the value at the time of the gift, which will be relevant should death occur within seven years. Yet if the value of the asset falls, the taxpayer is allowed to substitute the reduced value when the calculation of IHT due on death is made (IHTA 1984, s 131) – an unusual example of a win–win for the taxpayer.

A 'disposal' for CGT will occur, but the disposal consideration will be the market value at the date of the gift. Assets that qualify for tax exemptions or reliefs should also be considered, although there may be non-tax reasons for not giving those away.

The introduction of the additional residence nil rate band available for deaths on or after 6 April 2017 where a residence or interest in a residence is inherited by lineal descendants may have a distorting effect. The additional nil rate band is only available where the residential interest passes on death, not where it passes by lifetime transfer. A parent with a holiday cottage may decide to keep the cottage until death and give away other assets by lifetime transfer.

4.1.2.3 How to give away?

Outright gifts are straightforward but are inflexible; if circumstances change, the property given away cannot be recovered. If the proposed donee is a minor, such a gift (if substantial) would not be sensible. The donor may come to regret making an outright gift; for example, the donee may become addicted to drugs or prove financially irresponsible. In either case, the money might be better held by trustees for the benefit of the donee.

4.1.2.4 Gifts into trust provide flexibility

Because unexpected events do occur, flexibility is an important part of planning, and therefore trusts are attractive. However, trusts require proper administration. Dealing with income and investment of trust funds, preparing trust accounts, dealing with registration and updating of personal details as required by the Money Laundering, Terrorist Financing and Transfer of Funds (Information on the Payer) Regulations 2017, and making tax returns for the trust all cost time and money. These disadvantages must be weighed against the advantages of flexibility obtained by using a discretionary trust. So too must possible adverse change in tax law affecting trusts. Over recent years, such changes have made lifetime trusts less attractive to estate planners and their clients.

A Family Limited Partnership provides an alternative to a trust as a means of giving away assets to family members whilst retaining some element of control, and there has been more interest in this structure since changes were made to the way trusts are taxed in 2006. However, although the Family Limited Partnership may offer some tax advantages, it has disadvantages in terms of lack of flexibility and operational expense and is not considered further here.

4.1.2.5 Don't let the tax tail wag the dog

The objective is to plan affairs so that the client's property is enjoyed by the beneficiaries (often the family) to the best advantage. In achieving this, tax efficiency is only one aspect.

The solicitor must balance the cost of the legal work involved against the tax saving to ensure that the costs of the scheme do not outweigh the advantages. Making lifetime property transfers may give rise to an immediate tax bill which may make the proposal unattractive to the client even though it will save tax in the long run. Clients may also have to accept that the payment of some tax is inevitable (whether during their lifetime or on death) in order to ensure the best practical financial arrangements for the family.

There are many non-tax concerns too, and The Law Society has issued a practice note (15 July 2022) giving advice to solicitors dealing with clients who wish to make lifetime gifts. It highlights, among other things, the need to advise fully on the benefits and risks of making such gifts.

4.1.2.6 Is the gift in the donor's best interests?

Professional advisers should be alert to the possibility of elderly people being over-persuaded by others into making lifetime gifts which are not in their best interests.

The test of capacity for making a substantial lifetime gift is the same as that for making a will. See *Re Beaney (Deceased)* [1978] 1 WLR 770 where an elderly mother gave her only significant asset (her house) to one of her children. Martin Nourse QC sitting as a deputy judge said that if the effect of a gift is to dispose of the donor's only asset of value and thus for practical purposes to pre-empt the devolution of his estate under his will or on his intestacy, then the degree of understanding required is as high as that required for a will, and a donor must understand the claims of all potential donees and the extent of the property to be disposed of.

Advisers should be alert to the possibility of undue influence. Where a gift is made to a person in whom the donor placed trust and confidence and the transaction requires an explanation, there is a presumption of undue influence which the donee must rebut if the transaction is challenged.

4.1.2.7 Interaction with will drafting

A client considering lifetime estate planning must also consider making a complementary will. If a client dies intestate, or leaves a will that does not take lifetime planning into account, unexpected claims can arise, for example from HMRC for additional tax. There may be a claim in negligence against the solicitor by a surviving spouse or children who receive less than was intended.

4.2 TAX AND ESTATE PLANNING

The following paragraphs contain reminders of some of the rules relating to the taxation of individuals; many of these rules also apply to the taxation of trustees (see **Chapters 10** and **14**). The basic rules are covered in the LPC Guides, **Legal Foundations** and **Business Law and Practice**. This chapter groups together all the points that are relevant when considering the various estate planning ideas put forward here. More complex tax law is explained in detail either in this section or in context in the rest of the chapter.

4.3 INHERITANCE TAX

Broadly, IHT is chargeable whenever a person makes a transfer of value. Assessing the tax on this transfer involves the following elements:

(1) *Identifying that there is a transfer of value.* Transfers occur when a person dies and also if he gives away property during his lifetime, whether outright or into a trust. Some lifetime transfers are chargeable to tax at the time that they are made, but others are only chargeable if the transferor does not live at least seven years from the date of making the transfer.

(2) *Identifying the value transferred.* The value transferred on death is everything which the deceased owned beneficially or is deemed to own for IHT purposes, less debts and funeral expenses. The value transferred by a lifetime transfer is the loss to the estate of the donor. This is often the value of the property given away, but may be more, for example where a transfer of shares causes the transferor to lose control of a company.

(3) *Identifying relevant exemptions and reliefs.* These may extinguish or reduce the value transferred. There are a number of exemptions available for lifetime transfers but fewer for transfers on death.

(4)   *Identifying the appropriate rate of tax.* This depends on how much nil rate band is available for the transfer in question and on whether it is a lifetime or death transfer. If it is the latter, the rate also depends on how much has been left to charity.

4.3.1   Rates of IHT chargeable on the death estate

Generally the position is:

- 0% on the first £325,000 (nil rate band) from 6 April 2009;
- 40% on the balance.

The nil rate band is frozen until 5 April 2026.

The amount of the estate that is charged at 0% depends upon the value of chargeable transfers made by the deceased in the seven years before death.

> **EXAMPLE**
>
> Jake, a bachelor, dies having made chargeable transfers of £800,000 in the seven years before he died. He has no nil rate band available and so all of his death estate will be taxed at 40%.
>
> If, instead, Jake dies having made a chargeable transfer of £225,000 four years previously, he will have £100,000 (£325,000 – £225,000) of nil rate band available for his death estate. This means that the first £100,000 of his death estate is taxed at 0% and the rest at 40%.

The position is different where a person (S) dies on or after 9 October 2007, having survived a spouse or civil partner (F) (no matter when this first death occurred). In such a case, if F had unused nil rate band on his death, then the unused proportion of F's nil rate band may be claimed by S's estate on S's death. This is done by calculating the unused percentage of the nil rate band in force at the date of F's death. S's estate is then allowed to have the nil rate band that is in force at the date of S's death increased by the same percentage.

> **EXAMPLE 1**
>
> Fred dies on 10 April 2007, when the nil rate band is £300,000. He leaves his whole estate (£500,000) to his civil partner, Stuart. There is no IHT to pay on Fred's death at this point as it is covered by the civil partner's exemption. Stuart dies on 19 September 2019, leaving his whole estate (£750,000) to his brother. As Fred used none of the nil rate band available at his death he had 100% unused, and this percentage can be claimed by Stuart's estate. When Stuart dies the nil rate band level has risen to £325,000, and so this can be increased by 100% to £650,000. The tax on Stuart's death would therefore be £650,000 @ 0% and £100,000 @ 40% = £40,000.

> **EXAMPLE 2**
>
> If in Example 1 Fred had left £150,000 to his sister, and the rest to Stuart, it would have meant that he had used 50% of the £300,000 nil rate band in force at his death, and thus had 50% unused. On Stuart's death the nil rate band of £325,000 would be increased by 50% (£162,500) to a total of £487,500.

For deaths on or after 6 April 2012, there is a possible lower rate of IHT (36%) where, broadly, at least 10% of a person's estate is left to charity. Establishing whether a person's estate meets this 10% requirement can be complex (see **4.8.1**).

The residence nil rate band

Although the nil rate band will remain at £325,000 until 5 April 2026, an additional nil rate band is available in certain circumstances. New ss 8D–8M are inserted into the IHTA 1984 which provide for an additional residence nil rate band where a person dies on or after 6 April 2017 and certain conditions are satisfied. The value was £100,000 in 2017/18, rising by £25,000 per tax year to £175,000 in 2020/21. For estates valued at £2 million or more, there will be a tapered reduction of the additional nil rate band of £1 for every £2 over the £2 million threshold. The estate of a surviving spouse or civil partner can claim any percentage of the additional nil rate band unused on the death of the first spouse or civil partner.

The additional nil rate band applies only where a residence or interest in a residence is 'closely inherited'. 'Closely' requires the residential interest to pass to one or more of the following:

- the deceased's lineal descendants;
- the current spouse or civil partner of the deceased's lineal descendants; and
- the widow, widower or surviving civil partner of a lineal descendant who has predeceased the deceased, unless such persons have remarried or formed a new civil partnership before the deceased's death.

The residence nil rate band is 'capped' at the value of the residence or interest in a residence inherited and is limited to one property. Where there is more than one residential interest which is closely inherited, the personal representatives must select which one to claim the residential nil rate band on. If one is worth less and one is worth more than the residential nil rate band available at death, it is sensible to choose the more valuable so as to get the maximum benefit for the estate. If both are worth more, it is irrelevant which is chosen.

'Inherited' is defined in s 8J(2) as a disposition on death effected by will, the intestacy rules or otherwise. Events occurring after death, such as a sale of the property or appropriation by the personal representatives, are irrelevant. However, post-death variations (dealt with in **Chapter 12**) passing a residential interest to lineal descendants will attract the residence nil rate band (other requirements being satisfied) because the variation is read back to the date of death for all inheritance tax purposes.

Property left for the benefit of lineal descendants to certain sorts of settlement will be treated as 'inherited' under s 8J(4). The settlement must be one of the following:

- an immediate post-death interest (IHTA 1984, s 49);
- a disabled person's interest (IHTA 1984, s 89 or s 89B); or
- bereaved minor's or bereaved young person's interests (IHTA 1984, s 71A or s 71D) .

Note how few settlements qualify. A discretionary settlement is not included even if all the beneficiaries are lineal descendants. A typical grandparental settlement, 'to such of my grandchildren as reach 21', will not qualify because it is a relevant property trust. For more detail on types of settlement, see **Chapter 5**.

However, IHTA 1984, s 144 provides that where trustees make an appointment from a relevant property trust within two years of death, the appointment is read back into the will for all IHT purposes. Hence, trustees of a relevant property trust *can* retrospectively secure the residence nil rate band for an estate within two years of death by appointing a residence or interest in a residence to lineal descendants absolutely or modifying the trusts on which the residence or interest in a residence is held to create immediate post-death interest trusts. Section 144 is discussed in **Chapter 13**.

A 'residence' is defined (s 8H) as a dwelling which has been the deceased's residence at some time during his period of ownership. There is no requirement that it be the deceased's main residence or a UK property (although, to qualify, a residence must be subject to UK inheritance tax). A holiday home will qualify. A property which was never a residence of the deceased, such as a buy-to-let property, will not qualify. However, the property does not have to have been the deceased's residence for the whole period of ownership or at the date of death. It is sufficient that it was the deceased's residence at some point during the period of ownership.

> **EXAMPLE**
>
> Marjorie has to leave her home to go into care. Her children rent out her home and use the income to pay her care fees. Marjorie dies leaving the house (now commercially let) to her children. The residence nil rate band is available because the house was Marjorie's residence at some time during her ownership.

There was concern that if a person has to die owning a residential property in order to get the allowance, the property market might be distorted by elderly people clinging on in unsuitable houses when they ought to be moving into residential care or sheltered accommodation. The Government therefore consulted on a 'downsizing' allowance.

The Finance (No 2) Act 2016 made further amendments to the legislation by inserting new provisions into the IHTA 1984 which allow a downsizing allowance to be claimed where a person disposes completely of a residence or moves to a less valuable residential property on or after 8 July 2015. The allowance is calculated by reference to the amount lost and is capped at the value of assets left to lineal descendants (and their spouses and civil partners). A residence is 'disposed' of for this purpose at completion rather than exchange of contracts. See IHTA 1984, s 8FE(8) and HMRC's *Inheritance Tax Manual* at IHTM 46054.

4.3.2 Rates of IHT for lifetime chargeable transfers

The rates are 0% on the first £325,000 (nil rate band), and 20% on the balance. The amount of nil rate band available for any lifetime chargeable transfer is reduced by the total value of chargeable transfers made in the seven years prior to that lifetime chargeable transfer.

Many lifetime transfers are PETs, which become chargeable only if the donor dies within seven years. These are therefore ignored while a person is alive when calculating the total value of chargeable transfers made by that person. However, since 22 March 2006 the lifetime creation of all trusts, except for trusts for the disabled (see **5.2.4.1**), will be immediately chargeable. Inheritance tax must be reassessed at death rates if the settlor (the person creating the settlement) dies within the following seven years. Credit is given in the recalculation for any tax already paid, ie, when the settlement was created.

> **EXAMPLE 1**
>
> In 2022/23 Helen, who is single, gives property with a value of £371,000 to the trustees of a discretionary trust. She has made no previous chargeable lifetime transfers and there are no available exemptions and reliefs. The trustees agree to pay the IHT.
>
> | | | £ |
> |---|---|---:|
> | IHT at lifetime rates | £325,000 @ 0% = | nil |
> | | £46,000 @ 20% = | 9,200 |
>
> Helen dies 14 months later – the IHT is reassessed.
>
> | | | £ |
> |---|---|---:|
> | IHT at death rates | £325,000 @ 0% = | nil |
> | | £46,000 @ 40% = | 18,400 |
> | | | 18,400 |
> | Less: IHT already paid at lifetime rates | | 9,200 |
> | Additional IHT as result of Helen's death | | 9,200 |
>
> If Helen, not the trustees, had agreed to pay the IHT when she created the settlement, the loss to her estate then would have included the IHT payable, ie, the legacies would be 'grossed up' when calculating the value transferred. This is considered further in **Chapter 5**.

Note that when calculating tax on lifetime transfers, at the time of the transfer, there is no increase in the nil rate band for a person who has survived a spouse with unused nil rate band. However, when the transferor dies, and there is a recalculation of the tax on the lifetime transfer, the increased nil rate band may be available.

EXAMPLE 2

Simon's wife died some years ago with 100% unused nil rate band. In May 2019 Simon, who has made no previous transfers apart from using his annual exemption each April, gives £355,000 cash to the trustees of a discretionary trust. The trustees agree to pay the IHT.

| IHT at lifetime rates | £325,000 @ 0% = | nil |
| | £30,000 @ 20% = | £6,000 |

(Simon's nil rate band does not benefit at this point from any increase resulting from his wife's unused nil rate band, as this is a lifetime transfer.)

Simon dies 10 months later – the IHT is reassessed. The nil rate band available to Simon on death is now increased by 100% (the proportion unused by his wife) to £650,000.

| IHT at death rates | £355,000 @ 0% = | nil |

There is no further tax to pay, but there is no repayment of the tax paid on the lifetime transfer.

(There is £295,000 nil rate band remaining which is available for Simon's death estate.)

4.3.2.1 Tapering relief (IHTA 1984, s 7(4))

If a transferor dies more than three years after the date of a transfer, the full death rate of tax is reduced and only the following percentages are charged:

(a) transfers within 3 to 4 years before death 80% of death charge;
(b) transfers within 4 to 5 years before death 60% of death charge;
(c) transfers within 5 to 6 years before death 40% of death charge;
(d) transfers within 6 to 7 years before death 20% of death charge.

Notice that tapering relief is of no benefit if the transfer is within the nil rate band. This is because it operates to reduce the rate of tax charged. If the rate is nil, there can be no reduction.

EXAMPLE 1

Ash dies in December 2022 with an estate of £500,000. Five-and-a-half years before this, Ash gave £125,000 to a discretionary trust. Other than always using his annual exemption for IHT on 6 April each year, Ash made no other lifetime transfers. At the time of making the chargeable transfer, no IHT was paid as the whole amount fell within the nil rate band.

On Ash's death, the tax on the chargeable transfer is recalculated at death rates. It is still within the nil rate band and so there is no tax to pay on it as a result of death. Tapering relief is therefore irrelevant. The death estate will have a nil rate band available of £325,000 – £125,000 = £200,000.

In the case of transfers which were immediately chargeable to tax, the effect of tapering relief may be that no further tax is payable. The relief never results in a refund of tax already paid.

EXAMPLE 2

Suppose in Example 1 in **4.3.2** above that Helen died 6 years and 4 months after making the transfer to the discretionary trust.

The effect of tapering relief is that only 20% of the tax at the full death rates is payable. The full death rate tax was £18,400 so only £3,680 is payable. The trustees have already paid £9,200. No further tax is payable but the trustees are not entitled to a refund.

4.3.3   Potentially exempt transfers (IHTA 1984, s 3A, as amended by FA 2006)

Potentially exempt transfers (PETs) are lifetime transfers made by an individual on or after 18 March 1986 which, apart from s 3A, would be chargeable transfers. The following are PETs:

(a)   Gifts to other individuals, provided the donee's estate is increased or the property transferred becomes comprised in his estate.

(b)   Transfers to trustees of a trust for the disabled.

(c)   Transfers made on or after 22 March 2006 to trustees of a 'bereaved minor's trust' on the ending of an 'immediate post death interest' (see **Chapter 12**).

Before 22 March 2006 some transfers made to trustees were PETs:

(d)   Transfers to the trustees of an interest in possession settlement because the estate of the beneficiary with the life interest includes the property in which that interest subsists, ie, the settled property (IHTA 1984, ss 5 and 49).

(e)   Transfers to the trustees of an accumulation and maintenance trust (IHTA 1984, s 71).

Transfers to trustees are considered further in **Chapter 5**.

No charge arises at the time the PET is made and it is treated as fully exempt unless the transferor dies within the following seven years. There is no obligation on the transferor to notify the Revenue of the PET. Should the transferor die within the seven years following the PET, it becomes chargeable and is treated as if it had always been chargeable. Tax is calculated in the usual way, and tapering relief (see **4.3.2.1**) may apply to reduce the tax payable. It must be reported to the Revenue.

EXAMPLE

Suppose in Example 1 in **4.3.2** above that Helen gave £400,000 to her nephew five years before she made the trust. This PET would not have been chargeable to tax at the time it was made and would therefore not affect the calculation of tax on the later lifetime chargeable transfer at the time it was made. When Helen dies within seven years of making the PET, however, it becomes chargeable.

Tax on the PET of £400,000

The first £325,000 of the PET is taxed at 0% and the remaining £75,000 (£400,000 – £325,000) is taxed at 40% = £30,000. Helen has died between six and seven years after making the PET, and so tapering relief is applied, resulting in only 20% of the tax (£6,000) being payable.

Tax on the immediately chargeable transfer of £371,000

The tax on this is recalculated as a result of death within seven years. Now that the PET has become chargeable, the total value of chargeable transfers made in the seven years before the immediately chargeable transfer exceeds the nil rate band. The whole value transferred is therefore taxed at 40% = £148,400. Tapering relief does not apply, but the £9,200 tax actually paid at the time of the transfer can be deducted, leaving £139,200 to pay.

A transfer which is covered by an exemption is fully, not potentially, exempt.

4.3.4 Exemptions applying to lifetime transfers (IHTA 1984, ss 18–23)

(a) Any property passing to a UK-domiciled spouse or civil partner. The position is different where the recipient spouse or civil partner is not domiciled in the UK as there is a limit on the exempt amount that may pass (IHTA 1984, s 18(2)). For transfers made before 6 April 2013 this was £55,000, but for transfers made in the tax year 2013/14 and onwards it is £325,000. Since 6 April 2013 it is possible, in some circumstances, for a non-domiciled spouse or civil partner to elect to be treated as domiciled in the UK (Finance Act 2013, s 177).

(b) Gifts to charity. Various ways of giving to charity are considered in **4.8**.

(c) Small gifts. Gifts not exceeding £250 to any one person in any one year are exempt. Because of this limitation, it is not possible to combine the small gift exemption with another exemption, for example the annual exemption. The gift must be outright, not in trust.

(d) Transfers of £3,000 per annum (any unused annual exemption can be carried forward one year).

> **EXAMPLE**
>
> In Year 1, a donor makes his first ever gift of £1,000. The unused part of the annual exemption is carried forward to Year 2. In Year 2, he may give away £5,000 in exempt transfers. If the £2,000 carried forward from Year 1 is not used in Year 2, it is lost and may not be carried further forward. For example, if the donor in Year 2 makes a gift of £4,000, this is wholly exempt (£3,000 from the annual exemption for Year 2 and £1,000 from the unused annual exemption from Year 1), but in Year 3 the donor only has a £3,000 annual exemption available.
>
> A husband and wife who each use the annual exemption over a 25-year period could between them give their children a total of £156,000. By the simple use of an exemption, considerable estate planning for the parents could be achieved.

(e) Gifts in consideration of marriage: up to £5,000 per parent of the couple (lesser amounts for other donors). The gift may be outright or into trust provided the beneficiaries do not include persons other than the couple or their issue (or spouses of their issue). It must be 'in contemplation' of a particular marriage, and should be so evidenced in writing.

(f) Normal expenditure out of income: if claimed (it is not given automatically), this exemption applies to a gift of cash that:

(i) is part of the normal expenditure of the donor;

(ii) taking one with another, is made out of income; and

(iii) after other such gifts, leaves the donor with sufficient income to maintain his usual standard of living.

It is a question of fact whether a gift qualifies for the exemption. What is 'normal expenditure' for one person is not necessarily so for another. Even though it is not one of a series of regular payments, a gift may none the less be 'normal' if there is evidence that payments of an ascertainable amount are intended to recur, for example *'any income in excess of [a stated figure]'* (see further *Bennett v Inland Revenue Commissioners* [1995] STC 54). It is important, to avoid later arguments when the client has died and cannot provide answers, to keep good records to show that the three elements are satisfied.

Those with high levels of income can transfer very significant amounts entirely tax free. The exemption allows funds to be paid into a discretionary trust without the usual charge on the initial transfer. Note, however, that the Revenue requires such transfers to be reported (unless they would fall within the nil rate band, if chargeable) so that it can investigate whether the exemption is properly available.

The exemption is commonly used to fund the payment of premiums on policies of assurance written in trust, for example:

(i)   an endowment policy written in trust by a parent in favour of a child on which the parent pays the annual premiums;

(ii)   premiums on a policy written in trust to be used to fund a potential IHT liability should the donor die within seven years of a PET.

The exemptions listed in (a) and (b) above also apply to transfers of the death estate.

4.3.5 Valuation

4.3.5.1 Market value

The IHT legislation contains provisions relating to the valuation of property given away by a donor. The normal rule is that property is valued at 'the price [it] might reasonably be expected to fetch if sold on the open market at the time; but that price shall not be reduced on the grounds that the whole property is to be placed on the market at one and the same time'. Thus, it is not possible to argue for a reduced valuation because 'the market is flooded' where a lot of a similar type of property is available at once (IHTA 1984, s 160).

The 'open market rule' applies on a death, although changes in value of an estate caused by the death can be taken into account (IHTA 1984, s 171). For example, life policies which mature on death are valued at the maturity value (whereas if they are given away during lifetime the value transferred is generally the surrender value) and personal goodwill in a business is valued at a figure (usually lower) after allowing for the loss of the proprietor of the business.

The value of assets is a snapshot at the date of death, so it is a matter of the luck of the draw. In December 2019, the stock market was at a high, and just three months later the Covid-19 pandemic caused prices to fall dramatically before bouncing back.

4.3.5.2 Joint ownership of assets

Co-owners of land can discount the value of their respective shares to take into account the fact that it may be difficult to sell a share in co-owned property on the market; the purchaser will occupy the property with the other co-owner. A discount of 10%–15% is normal.

> **EXAMPLE**
>
> Two brothers own a house equally. If the open market value of the house is £200,000, the value of a one-half share may be agreed by the Revenue to be £90,000.

The Revenue will normally agree 15% on a residential property but only 10% on a commercial property – see *St Clair-Ford v Ryder* [2006] WTLR 1647.

Valuation of other jointly-owned assets does not attract such a discount. In these cases, the open market value is divided proportionately between the joint owners.

Where spouses or civil partners are co-owners of land, a discount is not normally available. This is because of the related property rules (see **4.3.5.5**) which require each party's interest to be valued as a proportion of the whole.

4.3.5.3 Quoted shares

For IHT (as for CGT) the price is taken to be the price 'one quarter up' from the lower to the higher price for dealings on the day in question on the stock market. Thus, if a share is shown as 100p–104p for the day of dealing, the valuation would be 101p per share held by the donor.

4.3.5.4 Shares in unquoted companies

Shares in private/family companies are notoriously difficult to value; such a valuation is not an exact science. The principal reason for the difficulty is the lack of any real market. Final agreement of value may take many years of negotiation between the donor's valuers and the Revenue. Many factors will be relevant, including:

(a) The success or otherwise of the company.

(b) Other recent dealings in the shares (if any).

(c) The number of shares as a percentage of the entire issued capital of the company:
- a 75% holding   can pass special resolutions;
- over 50% holding   can pass ordinary resolutions;
- 50% or less   a minority holding, with less voting influence (especially if small holding).

(d) The existence of typical pre-emption rights in the company's articles of association requiring shares first to be offered to other shareholders. Here the lack of a market is the real problem. Nevertheless, the courts have over a long period held that shares must be valued on the assumption that the shares could be sold on the open market but that the purchaser will then himself become subject to the restrictions contained in the articles of association.

(e) The significance to the company of the deceased (companies sometimes take out key person insurance policies to cover this risk).

To reach agreement the Revenue will need from the company or its advisers a great deal of information, including:

(a) a full description of the business carried on by the company;

(b) the last three years' accounts of the company published before the date of valuation;

(c) if minority holdings are to be valued, details of any restrictions on the transfer of shares;

(d) if there are different classes of shares, a statement of the rights of each class, in particular those concerning voting, dividends and distributions on a liquidation of the company.

4.3.5.5 Related property (IHTA 1984, s 161)

Assets which make up a pair or set are worth more than the aggregate value of each item valued separately; for example, one of a pair of valuable earrings is not worth a lot on its own. The related property rules are designed to prevent taxpayers who can make exempt transfers (eg spouses) avoiding IHT by dividing ownership of valuable assets between them. Section 161(1) provides 'where the value of any property comprised in a person's estate would be less than the appropriate proportion of the value of the aggregate of that and any related property, it shall be the appropriate proportion of the value of that aggregate'.

EXAMPLE

Harriet has a 60% holding in H and T Ltd, an unquoted trading company. She transfers half of this to her husband, so that they now each have a 30% holding. (This transfer is exempt for IHT and at no gain or loss for CGT purposes.) Taken separately, each holding is valued at £25,000, but together the controlling holding of 60% is valued at £75,000. Harriet considers giving her shareholding to their child, Rick. Under the related property rule, her shareholding would be valued as the appropriate proportion of the value of their total holding, ie, £75,000 ÷ 2 = £37,500.

If Harriet makes her gift, she will make a PET. If she dies within seven years the PET will have become a chargeable transfer. Business property relief at 100% will be available if Rick owns the shares when his mother dies, and the conditions for relief are satisfied at that date.

4.3.6 Reliefs

4.3.6.1 Agricultural property relief (IHTA 1984, ss 115–124)

Agricultural property relief is given automatically for transfers of value of 'agricultural property'. 'Agricultural property' is defined as including agricultural land and pasture; and cottages, farm buildings and farmhouses together with the land occupied with them as are of a character appropriate to the property.

The Revenue is quick to argue that farmhouses are not of a 'character appropriate' in an attempt to deny the relief.

The relief is given against the 'agricultural value' of the agricultural property. Agricultural value is defined as the value which would be the value of the property if the property were subject to a perpetual covenant prohibiting its use otherwise than as agricultural property. Thus, any value attributable to possible development or to mineral deposits under the land would not be eligible.

Agricultural property relief applies to property which was either:

(a)   occupied by the transferor for agriculture throughout the two years immediately before the transfer; or

(b)   owned by the transferor throughout the seven years immediately before the transfer (provided it was occupied by someone (the transferor or another) for agriculture throughout the seven-year period).

For these purposes, periods of occupation and ownership by a deceased spouse can be included.

100% relief

Available where the transferor had the right to vacant possession immediately before the transfer, or the right to obtain it within the next 12 months or, by concession (ESC F17), within 24 months from the date of the transfer. To encourage agricultural tenancies, this relief is also available where property is let on a tenancy starting on or after 1 September 1995 (FA 1995, s 155).

50% relief

Available on any other qualifying agricultural property, for example where agricultural property is let on a long tenancy.

> **EXAMPLES**
>
> Giles, who farmed Greenacre for 28 months, has just died. Agricultural property relief is available at 100% against the vacant possession value due to the owner occupation.
>
> Javed ceased farming Blackacre 25 years ago. He let the farm to his son, who has continued to farm it. Javed retained the freehold reversion. Javed has just died. His PRs will be able to claim agricultural property relief at 50% against the tenanted value of the agricultural property.

Agricultural property in settlements

Subject to the time-limits, the relief can apply to agricultural property held by trustees. There is a distinction between trusts with and without a 'qualifying' interest in possession. A trust with a 'qualifying' interest in possession means a trust where the life tenant is deemed for IHT purposes to be entitled to the settled property, ie the agricultural property. Broadly, such trusts are those with an interest in possession created on death at any time, or by lifetime transfer before 22 March 2006 (see **Chapter 5**).

If it is a trust with a qualifying interest in possession, the life tenant is the 'transferor' and 'owner' of the agricultural property for the purposes of the relief. The life tenant must therefore satisfy the conditions of two years' occupation of the property or seven years' ownership of it. For other trusts, the trustees will instead be the 'transferors' and 'owners' of the agricultural property. The occasions of charge to IHT on discretionary trusts are discussed in **Chapter 10**.

Agricultural property relief is given in priority to any available business property relief.

4.3.6.2 Business property relief (IHTA 1984, ss 103–114)

Business property relief operates to reduce the value transferred by a transfer of value of relevant business property by a certain percentage.

Business property relief is not available on certain types of business, most importantly those which consist wholly or mainly of holding investments (IHTA 1984, s 105(3)). This may not sound a particularly important limitation but, in fact, it is huge. A number of cases have held that taking an income from land is an investment activity. See *McCall v RCC* [2009] STC 990 and *IRC v George* [2003] EWCA Civ 1763. Businesses which take an income from land include commercial and residential rentals, grazing licences, markets, car parks, DIY livery stables, marinas, caravan sites and holiday lettings. The whole area is a battleground between taxpayers and the Revenue. Taxpayers frequently argue that their business is a mixed business which consists partly of taking an income from land and partly from providing other services, but they are often notably unsuccessful. See, for example, *Trustees of David Zetland Settlement v HMRC* [2013] UKFTT 284 (TC) (an office block); *Best v HMRC* [2014] UKFTT 077 (TC) (an out-of-town business centre); *Pawson v HMRC* [2013] UKUT 50 (TCC) and *Ross v HMRC* [2017] UKFTT 507 (TC) (holiday lets). For rare victories for the taxpayer, see *PRs of Vigne v Commissioners for HMRC* [2017] UKFTT 632 (TC) (livery stables) (affirmed on appeal at [2018] UKUT 357) and *PRs of Graham v Commissioners for HMRC* [2018] UKFTT 306 (TC) (self-catering cottages).

The question of whether a business is 'wholly or mainly' an investment business is one of fact to be decided by an intelligent business owner who would consider the use to which the asset was being put and the way it was being turned to account (*Brander v Revenue and Customs Commissioners* [2009] SFTD 374, aff'd [2010] STC 2666).

The relief is for the whole business so, if available, the 'investment' element obtains relief as well as the non-investment element. Conversely, if the business is mainly investment, no relief is available on the non-investment element. Mixed businesses approaching the 'tipping' point may consider separating into two separate businesses if this can be done without triggering a capital gains tax charge.

EXAMPLE

Tariq has a property development business. He buys properties, improves them and sells them at a profit. The business is non-investment and would qualify for 100% relief. However, during a slow-down in the property market, Tariq finds it difficult to sell properties and starts renting them out. He finds this to be an easier way of making money, and by the time he dies the business is mainly a rental business. No business property relief will be available on any part of the business.

If he separated the two elements into a rental business and a property development business, relief would be available on the latter.

A reduction of 100% of the value transferred is allowed for transfers of certain assets. They are:

(a)   a business or interest in a business (eg, a partnership share);

(b)   shares which are not quoted on the Stock Exchange (companies on the Unlisted Securities Market and the Alternative Investment Market (AIM) count as unquoted for this purpose).

A reduction of 50% of the value transferred is allowed for transfers of any other assets which qualify for business property relief. They are:

(a)   shares which are quoted on the Stock Exchange and where the transferor had control; control exists broadly where the transferor's entire holding yields over 50% of the votes on all resolutions;

(b)   land, buildings, machinery or plant owned by the transferor personally but used by a partnership of which he is a member or by a company of which he has control.

The relevant business property must have been owned by the transferor for at least two years immediately prior to the transfer. An exception to this rule applies where a spouse inherits business property under the will or intestacy of the deceased spouse. In that circumstance only, the surviving spouse is deemed to have owned the property from the time it was originally acquired by the deceased spouse.

EXAMPLE 1

In 2011, James acquired 75% of the shares in X Ltd, a private company. James died in June 2021 leaving those shares to his wife Kim. In May 2022, Kim dies leaving all her estate, including the shares, to her son. The 100% relief will be available on Kim's death.

The exception does not apply where the relevant business property is transferred to the spouse by lifetime transfer.

EXAMPLE 2

In Year 1, Judy sets up her own business, Y Ltd, and holds 100% of the shares.

In Year 5, she transfers 20% of those shares to her civil partner, Kelly.

In Year 6, Kelly dies leaving the 20% shareholding to her son.

No relief is available against the value of the 20% holding as Kelly has owned the shares only for one year and acquired them from Judy by lifetime transfer so cannot benefit from Judy's period of ownership.

These inter-spouse transfer rules also apply to agricultural property relief.

Lifetime transfers – availability of relief

Where the charge to IHT arises as a result of a PET or chargeable lifetime transfer (eg, a transfer to discretionary trustees) which is followed by the death of the transferor within seven years, any IHT (or additional IHT) will be calculated with the benefit of business property relief *provided*:

(a)   the transferee still owns the assets (or replacement assets which qualify as business property) at the death of the transferor (or, if earlier, the transferee's own death); and

(b)   the asset qualified as business property immediately before the transferor's death but (for this purpose) ignoring the two-year ownership requirement.

There is, therefore, the danger that at the time of the death relief will not be available.

> **EXAMPLE**
>
> Mum gives a 20% shareholding in an unquoted trading company to her daughter and dies one year later. The transfer is, therefore, chargeable. Relief will be available provided the daughter still owns the shares at Mum's death and the shares still qualify for relief. If, for example, the company has become an investment company, the shares will not be eligible as a result of IHTA 1984, s 105(3). Similarly, if the company has floated on the stock exchange, relief will not be available as relief is only available on majority holdings in quoted companies.

Business property in settlements

As with agricultural property relief, relief can be available where business property is held by trustees.

If it is a trust with a 'qualifying' interest in possession (see **4.3.6.1** above), the availability of this relief is gauged by reference to the position of the life tenant. If the *life tenant* satisfies the two-year ownership test, 100% relief is available where the assets in the trust are either a business or unquoted shares; 50% relief is available for controlling holdings in quoted companies and for land, buildings, machinery or plant in the trust used in the life tenant's own business or a company which he controls.

For an example of an enormous amount of tax becoming payable where the trustees terminated a qualifying interest in possession which had existed for less than two years, see *Burrell v Burrell* [2005] EWHC 245 (Ch).

For other trusts, relief will be available if the *trustees* satisfy the conditions. The occasions of charge to IHT on trusts are discussed in **Chapter 10**.

4.4 CAPITAL GAINS TAX

4.4.1 Rates

Capital gains are added to a taxpayer's income for the year. Since 6 April 2016, to the extent that they are below the threshold for higher rate tax, they are taxed at 10% (except for gains on residential property and carried interest which are taxed at 18%); to the extent that the threshold for higher rate tax is exceeded, gains are taxed at 20% (or 28%). Where gains qualify for business asset disposal relief (formerly known as entrepreneurs' relief) or investors' relief, there is a 10% rate (see **4.4.5.3**). Personal representatives and trustees are charged to CGT at 20% (or 28%) irrespective of their level of income or gains.

4.4.2 Calculation

The gain is calculated as the difference between the disposal consideration (less the costs of disposal) and:

(a)   the acquisition cost (less the cost of acquiring); and

(b)   any cost of improvements/enhancing expenditure.

Capital losses are normally set against capital gains of the same year. To the extent that losses exceed gains for the year, they can be carried forward to the following year and beyond until used up.

4.4.3 Exemptions

These include the following:

(a)   The first £12,300 (£6,150 for trustees) of chargeable gains in 2022/23. (Note that spouses and civil partners are each entitled to their own annual exemption.) The annual exemption is frozen at £12,300 until 5 April 2026.

(b)   Any gain arising on the disposal by gift or sale of the taxpayer's main or only residence. Where a taxpayer owns more than one residence, he may elect for one to be treated as his main residence. Spouses and civil partners living together have only one principal private residence exemption, and they may jointly elect where they own more than one property (either in sole or joint names).

(c)   Any gain on the disposal of a property owned by trustees where the property is the residence of a beneficiary entitled to occupation under the terms of the trust or at the discretion of the trustees.

For a further discussion of the points mentioned in paragraphs (b) and (c) above and other matters relating to the main residence, see **4.7.3** and **4.7.4**.

4.4.4   Death (Taxation of Chargeable Gains Act 1992 (TCGA 1992), s 62)

Death provides an automatic CGT-free revaluation of assets. The probate value becomes the acquisition cost for subsequent disposals by PRs. This is because there is no disposal on death but there is an acquisition by the PRs. One consequence is that inbuilt gains accruing during the lifetime of the deceased person are not charged to CGT. This point needs careful consideration as part of general estate planning. Disposal of the same asset during lifetime could well result in immediate liability to tax if the gain exceeds the annual exemption and no hold-over relief is available.

If PRs sell assets during the administration period, they will incur a liability to CGT if the gain exceeds their annual exemption (equal to an individual's but only available for the tax year of death and the two following tax years). In the case of sales by UK residents of UK residential land on or after 6 April 2020 giving rise to a CGT liability, the transaction must be reported and the tax paid within 30 days of completion of the sale (Finance Act 2019, s 14 and Sch 2). Failure to do so will result in penalties and interest. Professional advisers should make the PRs aware of this requirement.

No liability arises when assets are vested in legatees by the PRs; the PRs' acquisition (on death) is taken to be the legatees' acquisition for their future CGT purposes. A 'legatee' includes any person inheriting under a will or intestacy whether beneficially or as a trustee if a trust arises following the death.

> **EXAMPLE**
>
> Shares worth £50,000 at death were acquired by the testator 10 years earlier for £5,000. The gain of £45,000 over the period of ownership does not attract CGT. Gains on all subsequent disposals by the person(s) inheriting will be based on an acquisition cost of £50,000. If instead the deceased had made a lifetime gift of the shares, the gain on the lifetime disposal would attract CGT unless relief was available.

A similar CGT-free revaluation of trust assets occurs when the life tenant of a qualifying interest in possession trust dies (TCGA 1992, s 72) (see **4.3.6.1** above for the meaning of 'qualifying').

> **EXAMPLE**
>
> A trust was created in 2000. The trustees have been holding quoted shares worth £100,000 at the date of creation of the trust 'for Saira for life, remainder to Gregor'. Saira has just died and the shares are worth £250,000.
>
> (a)   The gain of £150,000 during the trust period does not attract CGT.
>
> (b)   The trustees are 'deemed' to dispose of the investments at market value at Saira's death.

> (c) The investments transferred to Gregor are 'deemed' acquired by him for his future CGT purposes at their market value at Saira's death. Not all the investment will be transferred to Gregor because some will have been sold by the trustees to pay IHT due as a result of Saira's death.

The position of the trustees where a 'deemed disposal' occurs is considered further in **10.1.4.2**.

4.4.5 Reliefs

4.4.5.1 Inter-spouse transfers

Inter-spouse transfers are deemed to occur at no gain no loss (as are those between civil partners). Effectively, tax on any gain since the acquisition by the donor spouse is deferred until there is a disposal by the donee spouse (TCGA 1992, s 58).

EXAMPLE

In 2001, Arshad bought a painting for £10,000. He gave his painting to his civil partner, Barraq, in 2020 when its value had increased to £18,000.

	£
Arshad's deemed disposal consideration	10,000
less: Acquisition cost	10,000
	nil

Barraq's acquisition cost is Arshad's disposal consideration, ie, £10,000. If Barraq sells the painting two years later for £22,000, he will make a gain of £12,000.

4.4.5.2 Hold-over relief

How the relief operates

Hold-over relief is provided in relatively limited circumstances by TCGA 1992, ss 165 and 260. These two provisions operate in the same way, by permitting gains which accrue to the donor to be held over. Tax is effectively deferred by permitting the donee to acquire the gifted property at the donor's acquisition cost. Tax remains deferred until the donee disposes of the property when he either cannot, or chooses not to, make a further hold-over election. Business asset disposal relief (if available) is not applied if hold-over relief is claimed (see **4.4.5.3**).

To obtain hold-over relief, an election is required by both the transferor and the transferee, although where the transferee is a trustee only the election of the transferor is required. Once made, the result of the election is that:

(a) the amount of any chargeable gain which the transferor would otherwise have made on the disposal; and

(b) the value at which the transferee would otherwise be regarded as having acquired the asset,

shall be reduced by an amount equal to the held-over gain on the disposal.

EXAMPLE

John gives his shares in his personal company, which he acquired for £30,000 in 2003, to his daughter Julia. Their market value is £100,000.

Hold-over relief is available (see below) and a joint election for hold-over relief under s 165 is made.

			£
(a)	Disposal consideration (market value)		100,000
	less: Cost price		30,000
		held-over gain	70,000

1. John's gain on disposal is reduced to nil.
2. Julia's acquisition cost is reduced to £30,000 (£100,000 – £70,000).

(b) Julia later sells her shares for £150,000. Her gain is calculated as follows:

		£
Disposal consideration (sale proceeds)		150,000
less: Cost price (see above)		30,000
	gain	120,000

Julia's chargeable gain is made up of the gain during her period of ownership of £50,000 (£150,000 – £100,000) and £70,000 (the gain held over).

On which disposals is the relief available?

Disposal of business assets within s 165

Under s 165, hold-over relief applies where a person makes a gift (either outright or into a trust) of business assets.

Section 165 defines business assets as:

(a)   An asset, or an interest in an asset, used for the purposes of a trade, profession or vocation carried on by:

(i)   the donor; or

(ii)   his personal company; or

(iii)   a company which is a member of a trading group of companies of which the holding company is the donor's personal company.

(b)   Shares or securities of a trading company or of the holding company of a trading group where:

(i)   the shares or securities are not quoted on a recognised stock exchange; or

(ii)   the trading company or holding company is the transferor's personal company.

(c)   Agricultural property, or an interest in agricultural property, which is not used for the purposes of a trade carried on as mentioned in (a) above.

A 'personal' company is one in which the individual (i) owns not less than 5% of the voting rights, and (ii) in the case of a disposal made on or after 29 October 2018, the transferor must be entitled to at least 5% of the distributable profits and at least 5% of the assets, available on a winding up or disposal of the whole of the ordinary share capital of the company.

Disposal of business assets held in settlements

Section 165 relief in a modified form is extended to deemed disposals of business assets owned by trustees by TCGA 1992, Sch 7. The asset must be used in a business carried on by the trustees, ie, the trustees of a discretionary settlement, or by a beneficiary of a settlement with an interest in possession in the settled property, ie, the life tenant. In the case of disposals of shares in a trading company by trustees, the company must be unquoted, or at least 25% of the voting rights must be exercisable by the trustees.

Disposals within s 260

The assets gifted do not have to be business assets for the purposes of hold-over relief under TCGA 1992, s 260. Private client practitioners are likely to meet three types of disposal which attract hold-over relief under s 260:

(a) *Chargeable transfers within the meaning of IHTA 1984 (and transfers which would be chargeable transfers but for IHTA 1984, s 19 (the annual exemption)) and which are not potentially exempt transfers (s 260(2)(a)).*

The effect of this relief is that a gift which is immediately chargeable to IHT (even at 0%) is not also charged to CGT at the time. A double charge to tax is thus avoided. PETs do not attract IHT (at least immediately) and so CGT will normally arise on the disposal (unless s 165 relief applies).

If the donor dies within seven years of making a PET and as a result the PET becomes chargeable, relief is still not available since it was not immediately chargeable when made.

The lifetime creation of all types of trusts, except trusts for the disabled, on or after 22 March 2006 is an immediately chargeable transfer, and so relief will be available under s 260. There are other circumstances involving the termination of certain types of trust where there will be an immediate charge to IHT and also relief under s 260 (see **Chapter 10**).

EXAMPLE

Kalima transfers assets valued at £325,000 to the trustees of her newly created discretionary settlement. She has made no other transfers. Even though no IHT is actually payable, because the transfer is within her available nil rate band, there is an occasion of immediate charge (at 0%). Hold-over relief is available at Kalima's election. The trustees do not need to join in the election.

(b) *Exempt transfers within IHTA 1984, s 24 (transfers to political parties), s 26 (transfers for public benefit), s 27 (transfers to maintenance funds for historic buildings) and s 30 (transfers of designated property) (s 260(2)(b)).*

(c) *Termination of accumulation and maintenance trusts, trusts for bereaved minors and 'age 18–25 trusts', where a beneficiary becomes absolutely entitled to the settled property (s 260(2)(d), (da), (db)).* (See **Chapters 8** and **12**.)

The termination of these types of settlement is specifically within the provisions even though IHT is not chargeable (see **Chapter 10**).

The creation and termination of trusts is dealt with in **Chapters 5** and **10**.

Hold-over relief and settlor interested trusts

Since 10 December 2003, hold-over relief has not been available under s 260 or s 165 for any disposal to a trust which is 'settlor interested' immediately after the disposal.

When this anti-avoidance measure was introduced a 'settlor interested' trust meant one where any property may be payable to the settlor or the settlor's spouse in any circumstances. From 6 April 2006 it also includes a trust which may benefit the settlor's unmarried minor children (see **6.2.11**). 'Child' includes 'step-child' for this purpose. This extension severely limits the occasions on which hold-over relief can be claimed (see **Chapter 5**). The lack of hold-over relief makes transfers to such settlements unattractive unless the settlor has assets which have not increased in value since acquisition or has cash available.

If a settlement becomes a settlor interested trust within six years of the making of the gift on which hold-over relief was granted, the relief is clawed back. See TCGA 1992, s 169C.

EXAMPLE

Janice transfers some shares in various quoted companies to trustees to hold on trust for 'my children who reach 25'. Janice has two children, currently aged 18 and 19. Janice elects to claim hold-over relief under TCGA 1992, s 260 on the disposal of the shares.

> Two years later, Janice has another child who, under the definition, becomes a beneficiary of the trust. As there is now an unmarried minor child of the settlor who may benefit, this is a settlor interested trust and has become so within six years of creation. The CGT on the held-over gain must now be paid.

Hold-over relief and the foreign element

Neither s 165 nor s 260 applies where the transferee is not resident in the UK. Thus, disposals of chargeable assets to non-resident individuals or settlements are, for this reason, not particularly attractive.

A clawback of CGT can arise where the donee emigrates within six years following a hold-over election. If the donee ceases to be resident in the UK, CGT liability on the held-over gains is immediately triggered. The CGT is primarily payable by the donee (now overseas). If he fails to pay the tax within 12 months it can be recovered from the donor who has a (probably worthless) right of recovery from the donee.

Because of the risk of a clawback charge, the donor should be advised to consider insurance cover, retention of part of the gifted property for six years and indemnities from the donee (see **Chapter 15**).

Gifts attracting IHT and CGT

If chargeable gains on a disposal are held over, the transferee may add any IHT paid on the transfer to him to his CGT acquisition cost. In this way, some relief against the overlap between IHT and CGT is available.

EXAMPLE

Jason transferred assets acquired for £120,000 and currently worth £200,000 to the trustees of his recently established discretionary settlement. He elected to hold over the gain of £80,000. Assume £20,000 IHT was paid. The trustees now sell the assets for £250,000 and re-invest the proceeds. The calculation of the trustees' CGT liability is:

	£	£
Disposal consideration		250,000
less: acquisition cost		
(200,000 – 80,000)	120,000	
IHT paid	20,000	140,000
GAIN		110,000

Note: the principle illustrated in the example also applies if the lifetime gift was a PET which later becomes chargeable. Provided a CGT hold-over election was made by the donor and donee, the IHT payable on the donor's death can be added to the transferee's acquisition cost, as in the example.

Some planning considerations in relation to hold-over relief

The fact that hold-over relief is not generally available on lifetime gifts may make them less attractive for tax planning purposes.

A gift made today which attracts CGT at 10% or 20% to save IHT at 40% in the future may not be particularly appealing in cash-flow terms. The same gift made by will would avoid CGT and give the donee the benefit of an uplift in his acquisition price (to market value at the date of death) for future CGT purposes.

However, CGT is charged on gains whereas IHT is charged on full values (subject to reliefs).

Gifts of assets expected to appreciate in value may attract an immediate CGT charge on the gain to date but IHT will be limited to the value of the asset at the time of the gift, ie, 'asset freezing' applies should the PET become chargeable. If the value of the assets is within the transferor's nil rate band, there may be an advantage to transferring the assets to a discretionary settlement (a lifetime chargeable transfer, but chargeable at 0%) and then claiming hold-over relief.

Section 165 of IHTA 1984 provides that CGT paid by the donee reduces the value transferred by the chargeable transfer for IHT. Normally CGT is payable by the donor but, in circumstances where hold-over relief is not available, consideration should be given to the donee paying the tax to take advantage of the IHT reduction. For this to happen, agreement must be reached between the donor and donee.

A disposal (such as a PET) giving rise to a chargeable gain which cannot be held over, followed by the death of the donor within seven years, could cause IHT to become payable by the donee. In such a case any CGT paid by the donor will not be treated as part of the loss to the estate (IHTA 1984, s 5(4)). As discussed in the previous paragraph, if the donee pays the CGT, the value transferred is treated as reduced by the CGT paid (IHTA 1984, s 165(1)) and therefore the IHT bill for the donee will be reduced.

EXAMPLE

A donor makes a gift (PET) of quoted shares worth £500,000 which gives rise to a CGT liability of £50,000.

(a)   If the donor pays the CGT, the value transferred for IHT is £500,000. It is not £550,000, ie, the loss to the estate of the donor is not increased by the CGT paid.

(b)   If the donee pays the CGT, the value transferred for IHT is £450,000, ie, it is reduced by the CGT paid.

   Obviously the donee will need to be in a position to fund both tax liabilities. Insurance against the potential IHT may be possible but not the CGT because this is an immediately quantifiable amount.

4.4.5.3 Business asset disposal relief (formerly entrepreneurs' relief)

This relief was introduced by the FA 2008 and is contained in ss 169H–169R of the TCGA 1992. The relief applies only in relation to disposals (by sale or gift) made on or after 6 April 2008.

As the original name suggests, the relief was intended to stimulate entrepreneurial activity, but in recent years it became apparent that it was not working as intended. Changes were introduced in the Finance Act 2019, and much more far-reaching changes in the Finance Act 2020, s 23 and Sch 3. The 2020 changes have severely limited the value of the relief. The name of the relief has also been changed and is now 'business asset disposal relief'.

The relief applies where there is a 'qualifying business disposal'. This occurs where there is a disposal of certain types of business asset, which meet certain further criteria.

(1) The disposal of the whole or part of a business

This includes a business run by a sole trader or a partnership, and the disposal may be of:

(a)   the business (or part of it) as a going concern; or

(b)   the assets used in the business following the cessation of that business.

However, in either case only those assets used for the purposes of the business carried on by the sole trader or partner are eligible for relief. Shares and other assets held for investment purposes are not eligible.

Where the disposal is on or after 6 April 2019 and is of the business (or an interest in it), the transferor must have owned his interest in the business for the period of two years ending with the date of disposal. For disposals made on or after 6 April 2008 and before 6 April 2019, the period of required ownership is only one year.

Where the disposal is on or after 6 April 2019 and is of assets following the cessation of a business then the transferor must have owned the business for two years ending on the date of cessation of the business, provided that the disposal occurs within three years after the cessation of the business.

For disposals made on or after 6 April 2008 and before 6 April 2019, the period of required ownership is only one year.

(2) The disposal of company shares

To qualify for the relief:

(a)   the company must be a trading company;

(b)   the company must be the transferor's 'personal company', that is (i) the transferor must have a shareholding that gives at least 5% of the voting rights; and (ii) in the case of a disposal made on or after 29 October 2018, the transferor must be entitled to at least 5% of the distributable profits and at least 5% of the assets, available on a winding up or disposal of the whole of the ordinary share capital of the company; and

(c)   the transferor must be an officer or employee of the company,

and where the disposal is on or after 6 April 2019, the conditions set out above must be satisfied during either:

(a)   a two-year period ending with the date of disposal; or

(b)   a two-year period ending with the date when the company ceases to be a trading company, provided that the disposal occurs within three years after the company ceases to be a trading company.

Where the disposal is made on or after 6 April 2008 and before 6 April 2019, the period is only one year.

(3) The disposal of assets owned by an individual but used by a partnership or company

To qualify for the relief:

(a)   the assets disposed of must have been used for the purposes of a business run by:

   (i)   a partnership in which the transferor was a partner; or

   (ii)   a trading company which was the transferor's personal company and of which the transferor was an officer or employee; and

(b)   the disposal of the assets must be associated with a qualifying disposal of the transferor's interest in the partnership or company arising from the withdrawal of the transferor from the business. From 18 March 2015, the associated disposal must be of at least 5% of the partnership assets or 5% of the shares in the company (TCGA 1992, s 169K as amended by Finance Act 2015, s 41); and

(c)   the assets must have been in use for the purposes of the business during the period of one year ending with the earlier of:

   (i)   the date of disposal of the partnership interest or company shares with which the asset disposal is associated; and

   (ii)   the cessation of the business of the partnership or company using the asset.

(4) The disposal by external investors of shares in unlisted trading companies (investors' relief)

To encourage an investment culture and help companies access the capital they need to expand and create jobs, the Finance Act 2016 amended Part V of the TCGA 1992 to extend entrepreneurs' relief to gains accruing on the disposal of ordinary shares in an unlisted trading company held by individuals. It is referred to as 'investors' relief'.

The investor must not be a remunerated director or employee of the company in question at any time during the period of share ownership, and nor can any person connected with him be an officer or employee.

This restriction – which applies throughout the share-holding period for the shares in question – was modified to exclude only 'relevant employees'. The position is set out in s 169VB(2)(g) and s 169VW – the latter defining the term 'relevant employee'. Broadly, non-executive directors who had no pre-existing connection with the company, and people who become employees after acquiring the shares where there was no reasonable prospect that this would occur, are not relevant employees.

In order to qualify for the relief, a share must:

(a) be newly issued, having been acquired by the person making the disposal (or their spouse or civil partner) on subscription for new consideration;

(b) be in an unlisted trading company or unlisted holding company of a trading group;

(c) have been issued by the company on or after 17 March 2016 and have been held for a period of three years from 6 April 2016; and

(d) have been held continually for a period of three years before disposal.

Effect of the two reliefs

Relief is not automatic. Transferors may choose whether or not to claim relief. If they do so, the effect is that any losses arising from the qualifying disposal are first offset against the gains from that disposal. For disposals on or after 23 June 2010 the net gain is taxed at 10% (even if the taxpayer's income is such that the gain would normally be taxed at the higher rate). Taxpayers may deduct the annual exemption in the way that is most beneficial to them. Hence they can deduct the exemption from gains that do not qualify for the relief before applying it to those that do.

The use of both reliefs is subject to a lifetime cap. This cap was set at £1 million of qualifying net gains for disposals made during the period 6 April 2008 to 5 April 2010, but rose in stages, reaching £10 million for disposals made on or after 6 April 2011.

The Finance Act 2020 amended the TCGA 1992, s 169N to reduce the limit for business asset disposal relief, but not investors' relief, to £1 million for disposals on or after 11 March 2020.

The limits are separate for the two reliefs. Each time a person claims the relief, the value of the net gains for which they claim is added to their lifetime total, and once the person exceeds the limit they will not be able to claim the relief in relation to any further qualifying gains. The reduction of the business asset disposal relief limit to £1 million in 2020 means that any individual who has already claimed relief on gains of £1 million or more will no longer qualify for relief on any future disposals of business assets.

> **EXAMPLE**
>
> For five years Nicky has been a director of two companies, A Ltd and B Ltd, and has held a 10% holding in each company fulfilling the requirements for entrepreneurs' relief. In August 2018 Nicky sells his holding in A Ltd, realising a gain of £4 million.

> If Nicky elects to claim entrepreneurs' relief, his net gain of £4 million is taxed at 10%, leaving £6 million of his £10 million lifetime limit available.
>
> If he sells his shares in B Ltd in tax year 2019/20, realising a gain of £8 million, he can claim the relief only in relation to £6 million of this gain, and the remaining £2 million is taxed at Nicky's top rate.
>
> If, however, he delayed the sale of the shares in B Ltd to tax year 2020/21, no relief would be available and the whole of the gain would be taxed at his top rate.

There is an important planning point. Someone who is a director and shareholder may wish to cease active involvement with the company but retain the shares. If the individual is likely to later sell the shares, it may be worth continuing as a director until the date of the sale to retain the benefit of business asset disposal relief.

The total of qualifying disposals for any person will include not only those made by that person as an individual but also those made by a trust where the person is a 'qualifying beneficiary' (see below).

It is not possible to claim the reliefs and hold-over relief.

The Finance Act 2015 contained anti-avoidance provisions designed to stop taxpayers winding up a company, claiming entrepreneurs' relief and then recommencing the same trade. The effect is that if, within two years of the date of the distribution, the individual receiving the distribution – or someone connected with him or her – carries on any trade or other similar activity previously carried on by the company (whether as a sole trader or via a partnership, LLP or new company), the distribution will retrospectively be charged at income tax rates.

Business asset disposal relief and investors' relief and settlements

The reliefs operate in limited circumstances in relation to business assets or qualifying shares held within a settlement.

For business asset disposal relief to apply, there must be a disposal of trust business assets. This occurs where:

(a)   the trustees of a settlement make a disposal of 'settlement business assets';

(b)   there is an individual who is a 'qualifying beneficiary'; and

(c)   s 169J(4) and (5) of the TCGA 1992 is satisfied.

Settlement business assets are:

(a)   company shares; and

(b)   assets used for the purposes of a business (as indicated above, these will not include shares or other investment assets);

which are part of the settled property.

A person is a qualifying beneficiary if he has an interest in possession in the settlement in the whole of the settled property or the part of it which includes the settlement business assets being disposed of. If the interest in possession is for a fixed term, for example for a period five years, the beneficiary is not able to be a qualifying beneficiary.

The further requirements contained in s 169J(4) and (5) of the TCGA 1992 are that:

Where the disposal is of shares:

For a period of two years ending not later than three years before the disposal:

(a)   the company was:

    (i)   a trading company; and

(ii) the qualifying beneficiary's personal company; and

(b) the qualifying beneficiary was an officer or employee of the company.

Where the disposal is of assets used within a business:

(a) the assets must be used for the purposes of the business carried on by the qualifying beneficiary (including a business carried on by a partnership of which he is a partner) for the period of one year ending not earlier than three years before the disposal; and

(b) the qualifying beneficiary must have ceased to carry on the business on the date of the disposal or within the three-year period before the disposal.

Both the trustees and the qualifying beneficiary must claim the relief. Where it is claimed, the effect will be similar to the position for an individual claiming the relief. The lifetime cap also applies, and will include not only gains made by the trustees involving this qualifying beneficiary but also any qualifying gains made by the qualifying beneficiary as an individual.

Note: The conditions applying to the requirements for a personal company apply equally to settlements.

Time at which an individual must be a qualifying beneficiary

In 2017, an HMRC Capital Taxes Liaison Group meeting advised that HMRC considered that the individual who was the 'qualifying beneficiary' had to be a qualifying beneficiary throughout the stipulated time period. The conditions for relief would not be met if the individual had been 'parachuted in' as a beneficiary of the settlement shortly before the trustees' disposal. In *Skinner v RCC* [2019] UKFTT 516 (TC) the first-tier tribunal held that the ordinary and natural meaning of the words of s 169J(4) did not require a 'qualifying beneficiary' to hold their interest in the shares disposed of for the stipulated period. However, HMRC appealed successfully. In *RCC v Skinner* [2021] UKUT 0029 (TCC) the Upper Tribunal held that in order for relief to be available, a beneficiary must have been a qualifying beneficiary throughout the required period. In *Skinner v RCC* [2022] EWCA Civ 1222 the Court of Appeal overruled the Upper Tribunal. It accepted that the drafting of s 169 is confusing in parts, but considered that the drafting of s 169J 'pointed strongly' away from the idea that an individual who is a qualifying beneficiary at the date of disposal must also satisfy the requirements of that definition throughout the stipulated holding period. 'The identification of a qualifying beneficiary depends on an examination of the trusts of the settlement as at the date of the disposal. There is no requirement ... that the individual should have had the interest in possession for any minimum period, but only that the interest should exist at the time of the disposal.'

In the case of investors' relief, a new s 169VH provides that relief is available where trustees dispose of qualifying company shares and there is a beneficiary who has had an interest in possession throughout the period of three years ending with the date of the disposal, and at no time in that period has the individual been a relevant employee in respect of the company.

4.5 TRANSFERS BETWEEN SPOUSES AND CIVIL PARTNERS

4.5.1 Financial and estate planning

Although since 9 October 2007 there is the opportunity to transfer unused nil rate band from the first to die to the estate of the survivor on the latter's death, it is still advisable for the wealth of a married couple to be split between them. Whilst the division need not be equal, it is inadvisable for one spouse to own the majority of the assets. 'Equalisation' will provide greater financial security for the 'poorer' spouse, and the greatest scope for tax planning.

The introduction of the residence nil rate band as from 6 April 2017 provides another reason to avoid aggregating assets in one estate. The residence nil rate band is gradually withdrawn once an estate exceeds the taper threshold.

4.5.1.1   Life insurance

Insurance on the taxpayer's own life

Most clients who have partners or young children should consider personal life insurance (see **Appendix 2**).

If nothing further is done when the life cover is purchased, the insured sum will be paid to the PRs on the death of the insured and will form part of his estate. A grant of representation will be required before the proceeds are available, and the amount will be taxable if left to a beneficiary other than the deceased's spouse (or charity). Both problems can be avoided if the life insurance policy is written in trust.

Where a new policy is being purchased as part of financial advice, it can be written in trust from the outset. Life insurance companies have standard trust documents which the insured can complete with the names of the trustees and the chosen beneficiary or beneficiaries.

Existing policies can also be written in trust but whenever possible it is better to create the trust at the time of purchase. This is because existing policies may have a surrender value, meaning that if the insured cancels the policy before his death he will receive a lump sum based on the amount of premiums he has paid. When an existing policy is written in trust, the insured gives up this surrender value to his beneficiary and this is a transfer of value for IHT purposes. Usually the policy will be valued for IHT at the higher of the market value or cost of providing the policy, ie, the premiums already paid (IHTA 1984, s 167). In practice this is rarely a problem as the value in the first few years is relatively small compared with the maturity value and is likely to be covered by the insured's £3,000 annual IHT exemption. To the extent this is exceeded the transfer of the surrender value will be a PET. It does mean, however, that in the year the policy is put into trust, the annual IHT exemption may not be available to set against other non-exempt gifts.

Once a policy has been written in trust, the annual premiums paid by the insured to the insurance company are paid by the insured for the benefit of the beneficiary. These premiums are transfers of value for IHT but, unless disproportionately large when compared with the annual income of the insured, they should be exempt as normal expenditure out of income, or if not then covered by the £3,000 annual exemption. They are not PETs (IHTA 1984, s 3A). This is because s 3A(2) provides that a transfer of value is only a gift to another individual to the extent that the value transferred is attributable to property which becomes comprised in the estate of that other individual, or increases their estate.

Insurance on the life of another

Where a couple have young children it is quite possible that one parent does not have paid employment. The couple should calculate how much it would cost to employ a housekeeper and nanny or purchase child care if the non-earner were to die. Where the earner's income is unlikely to be sufficient to cover the cost, the couple might consider insuring the non-earner's life so that a lump sum will be available to cover the costs of care. As the insurance cover is likely to be required only whilst the children are of school age, term assurance (see **Appendix 2**) could be considered.

EXAMPLE

Adam and Betty have two children aged 6 and 4 respectively. Betty does not work and Adam's income is £32,000 per annum. He calculates the family's expenditure to be £22,000 per annum, and believes home help and child care would cost an extra £12,000 per annum if Betty died. This could not be supported by his income. If he insured Betty's life he would receive a lump sum on her death from which to pay the £12,000 per annum.

Obviously if the earning spouse or civil partner dies, the income will cease. However, many employers provide pension schemes with death in service benefits, so a lump sum will be available to the family. If the earning spouse does not have the benefit of such a scheme, the couple should take out life assurance on the earning spouse.

4.5.1.2   The matrimonial home

Sole ownership versus co-ownership

The matrimonial home is often the major asset owned by an individual, married couple or civil partners. Unless there are personal reasons for not doing so, it is normally advisable for spouses and civil partners to own the matrimonial home as co-owners rather than in the sole names of either.

Co-ownership can reflect the contributions each has made to the purchase price, or may provide a non-contributing spouse or civil partner with the security of legal ownership. The couple may make the initial purchase as co-owners, or a sole purchaser may subsequently transfer an interest in the property to the other. Most lenders insist that a property which is to be used as a family home is held in co-ownership. This may be either a joint tenancy or a tenancy in common.

Joint tenancy

Holding a property as joint tenants means that on the death of one spouse or civil partner, his or her interest in the property immediately and automatically passes to the survivor, ie accrues by survivorship. This cannot be prevented by anything said about the property in the will. All that the surviving joint owner needs to prove absolute ownership of the property is the death certificate of his or her spouse. Joint tenancy therefore avoids the costs and delays involved in obtaining a grant of representation on the death of the first joint tenant to die and, because the survivor is a spouse or civil partner, the interest in the property is IHT exempt on that first death.

EXAMPLE

Carla and David own a house worth £600,000 as joint tenants. David dies in 2022 and the house vests in Carla absolutely. There is no IHT payable as the transfer is spouse exempt. Assuming that David did not use his nil rate band by making gifts to non-exempt beneficiaries, his 100% unused nil rate band will be transferred to Carla. Carla dies six weeks later, in November 2022, leaving her estate (the house) to her daughter, Emma. Carla's nil rate band of £325,000 is increased by 100% to £650,000. Whether IHT will be payable on Carla's estate depends on the value of her other assets. If the house is Carla's residence as opposed to an investment property, residence nil rate band and transferred residence nil rate band will be available.

Tenancy in common

Property held under a tenancy in common passes by will or intestacy, not automatically to the surviving co-owner. A tenancy in common provides greater flexibility as it allows the first spouse to die to leave his or her share to someone other than the survivor, for example children. However, as the effect would be shared ownership between the survivor and the children, there is a danger that the children may want the house sold to realise their inheritance or that their interest may have to be sold because they have been declared bankrupt.

Mortgage

Where the matrimonial home, however owned, is subject to a mortgage, that mortgage debt should be covered by suitable insurance (see **Appendix 2**). This will enable the mortgage to be paid off in full on the death of the borrower without the need for the house or other assets to be sold to meet the debt. Where two people are jointly responsible for the mortgage, they can choose whether the insurance should pay out on the first or second death. It is normally more satisfactory for the payment to be on the first death.

4.5.2   Transferring assets (other than the matrimonial home) into joint ownership

4.5.2.1   Practical reasons

The reasons for making such a transfer are likely to be practical. The transfer allows each spouse or civil partner access to particular assets and means that, on the first death, the survivor automatically becomes sole owner of those assets. There is no need to obtain a grant of representation (so the administration is quicker and cheaper) and the survivor has immediate access to finances.

4.5.2.2   Effect for IHT

Joint ownership offers no IHT saving. Although on the first death the transfer is spouse exempt, the combined estates are taxed on the second death. If the second spouse dies on or after 9 October 2007, he or she will have the benefit of any nil rate band unused on the death of the first spouse. However, this is no different from the owning spouse dying and leaving the assets to his or her spouse. The same unused proportion of nil rate band can be transferred to the surviving spouse.

There may be an IHT disadvantage to joint ownership if the second spouse dies on or after 6 April 2017. There will be loss of the residence nil rate band if the second spouse's estate exceeds the taper threshold. Owning assets separately will allow the first to die to leave some assets directly to lineal descendants.

4.5.2.3   Effect for income tax

The basic rule is that any income arising from a jointly held asset will be treated as belonging equally to spouses or civil partners (ITA 2007, s 836). This is so, irrespective of how they contributed to the account or purchase of the asset or account (eg, with a bank or building society).

> **EXAMPLE**
>
> Habibah has a building society account into which she periodically pays additional savings. She transfers this account into the joint names of herself and her husband, Ibrahim. Ibrahim makes no contributions to the account. For income tax purposes he is nevertheless treated as owning one half of the annual income.

Spouses and civil partners can override this general 50:50 rule by making a declaration to HM Revenue & Customs of how they, in fact, beneficially enjoy the income. The declaration relates to both the income and to the underlying property. The income cannot be shared in proportions different from the property which produces it. The maximum split is 1:99. The declaration has effect from its date; notice must be given to the Inspector of Taxes within 60 days of a declaration which must be made on Form 17.

Where one spouse or civil partner has insufficient income from his or her own resources to be paying income tax, or is paying income tax at the basic (20%) rate whilst the other spouse is a higher (40%) or additional (45%) rate income taxpayer, it may be sensible to transfer some part of the beneficial ownership in the jointly owned property to the person with the lower tax rate, followed by a declaration that the lower earner is entitled to an equivalent proportion of the income. The transfer of the beneficial ownership will generally be by declaration of trust made by the spouses.

> **EXAMPLE**
>
> Jane and Kate are civil partners and the joint holders of a building society account. The annual interest is £100 gross. Jane pays income tax at 40%. Kate pays income tax at 20%.

(a)	Without a declaration			
	Jane will pay 40% tax on her one half	£50 × 40%	=	£20
	Kate will pay 20% tax on her one half	£50 × 20%	=	£10
	Total income tax			£30
(b)	Transfer of beneficial ownership and declaration that Kate is entitled to 90% of the interest			
	Jane will pay 40% tax on her 10% share	£10 × 40%	=	£ 4
	Kate will pay 20% tax on her 90% share	£90 × 20%	=	£18
	Total income tax			£22

The introduction in 2016/17 of the starting rate for income tax and the personal savings allowance and divided allowance makes it particularly important for spouses and civil partners to consider adjusting ownership of income-earning assets.

Since 6 April 2015 a spouse or civil partner may transfer part of his or her personal allowance (£1,260 in 2022/23) to his or her spouse or civil partner, provided that the transferor is a non-taxpayer and the transferee is a basic rate taxpayer (higher or additional rate taxpayers are not eligible for this allowance).

Both spouses must have been born on or after 6 April 1935 (if not, there is another relief available).

EXAMPLE

Andy and Liz are a married couple, both born after 6 April 1935, and their only income is their salaries. Andy receives £8,000 and Liz £20,600 income in the year 2022/23. There is no tax to pay on Andy's income which is covered by his personal allowance of £12,570, whereas Liz's income in excess of her personal allowance is taxed at basic rate.

Andy can make a claim to transfer £1,260 of his personal allowance to Liz. Andy's personal allowance is now £11,310, which is still more than his income, and thus there is no tax on this. Liz no longer has to pay tax on £1,260 of her income, which reduces her tax liability.

4.5.2.4 Effect for CGT

The transfer of an asset from a sole name into the joint names of the husband and wife is at 'no gain no loss' (see **4.4.5.1**).

On a subsequent disposal, whether a sale or by gift, each spouse will be regarded as owning a half share of the asset and charged to CGT accordingly. This allows each spouse to use his or her annual exemption and to make the best use of the lower rate of CGT.

EXAMPLE

Len transfers a shareholding which he bought for £2,000 into the joint names of himself and his wife Mary. Len is a higher rate taxpayer and Mary pays at basic rate.

The shares are sold for £28,600 in 2022/23 (assume that they make no other disposals in the tax year).

	Len will pay	Mary will pay
	£	£
Disposal consideration	14,300	14,300
less: Acquisition cost	1,000	1,000

		13,300		13,300
less: Annual exemption		12,300		12,300
		1,000		1,000
Chargeable gain		£1,000 @ 20%		£1,000 @ 10%
		= £200		= £100

If Len had sold the shares without sharing ownership with Mary, he would have realised a gain of £26,600 (£28,600 – £2,000). Setting only his own £12,300 annual exemption against this would result in a chargeable gain of £14,300 and a tax liability of £2,860 (£14,300 @ 20%).

Where a declaration as to the beneficial enjoyment of the income from a jointly owned asset has been made, it will have a corresponding effect for CGT purposes.

EXAMPLE

Rafael and Maya declare that the income from a shareholding is enjoyed 25:75. They will have a corresponding beneficial ownership of the shareholding. The shares were bought for £400 and have just been sold for £16,000. Assume that they make no other disposals in the tax year.

	Rafael's chargeable gain		*Maya's chargeable gain*	
	£	£	£	£
Disposal		4,000		12,000
less: Acquisition cost	100		300	
less: Annual exemption	12,300		12,300	
		12,400		12,600
Chargeable gain		nil		nil

4.5.2.5 Conclusion

Transferring assets into joint names of spouses or civil partners may provide beneficial effects. It allows both spouses or civil partners access to the assets. It is a means of making provision for the recipient without the donor losing control of the property. Since 9 October 2007 there is no IHT disadvantage in joint ownership in relation to the nil rate band, as any unused nil rate band from the first to die can be transferred to the survivor. From 6 April 2017 there will be a disadvantage in relation to the residence nil rate band if joint ownership results in the survivor's estate exceeding the taper threshold of £2 million.

Some clients value the independence and control of having assets in their sole name over and above any tax saving which may result from holding assets jointly. This is particularly likely in the case of second marriages.

4.5.3 Transferring assets outright from one spouse or civil partner to the other

Another way to achieve the 'equalisation' of a couple's estates is for the wealthier individual to make an outright transfer of assets to the poorer individual.

4.5.3.1 Income tax reasons

As seen in **4.5.2**, wherever possible, spouses and civil partners should ensure that they each utilise their own personal allowance as well as their own basic rate bands before either of them starts paying income tax at the higher rate. If one of them is an additional rate taxpayer it is even more worthwhile, and even if the other is a higher rate taxpayer there is still a 5% saving in the taxation of the income. Since 6 April 2015 a spouse or civil partner may transfer part of his or her personal allowance (£1,260 in 2021/22) to the other, provided that neither is a higher or additional rate taxpayer.

4.5.3.2 CGT reasons

A transfer from one spouse or civil partner to another is at 'no gain no loss'. Spouses and civil partners are each entitled to an annual exemption of £12,300 in 2022/23, but any unused annual exemption cannot be transferred to the other, nor can it be carried forward for use in future years. All clients (whether married, in a civil partnership or single) should be advised to use the exemption each year if possible.

It is also sensible to take advantage of one spouse or civil partner being able to pay CGT at only 10%, rather than 20%.

4.5.3.3 IHT reasons

Inheritance tax savings are often the main purpose in making transfers between spouses or civil partners. Whilst no tax saving is achieved from the transfer itself, because such transfers are IHT exempt, having assets in the individual ownership of each spouse does allow maximum use of exemptions and reliefs for passing on family wealth during lifetime to children and other relatives.

> **EXAMPLE**
>
> Hari has assets of £500,000, but his wife, Sahana, has assets of only £9,000. The couple would like to make some immediate gifts to their family. They decide to each give away £3,000 each year to their children, to utilise the annual exemption for IHT. Unless Hari transfers some of his wealth to Sahana she can only make gifts using the annual exemption on three occasions.

Using lifetime exemptions

There are several lifetime exemptions. For example, each parent can give £5,000 to a child on the occasion of the child's marriage; each parent can make annual gifts of £3,000; each parent can make gifts using the normal expenditure out of income exemption. Before these exemptions can be claimed, each parent must have sufficient assets to make the gifts. Unused exemptions cannot be transferred from one spouse or civil partner to the other.

Anti-avoidance rules

The anti-avoidance legislation and cases (see **4.10**) should not be a problem in the context of straightforward family estate planning, provided that at the time of the inter-spouse transfer the recipient spouse is not under a binding obligation to use the property as directed by the donor spouse.

Transfer of nil rate band on death

Before 9 October 2007 it was also important to transfer assets between spouses and civil partners to ensure that each member of the couple could make maximum use of his or her nil rate band when making gifts by will. This reason is less important since 9 October 2007 because it is now possible to transfer unused nil rate band between spouses and civil partners.

> **EXAMPLE**
>
> Assume Sahana in the Example above dies before Hari has a chance to transfer any of his wealth to her, leaving her £9,000 estate to Hari. There is no tax on Sahana's death and she has a 100% unused nil rate band. It does not matter that she could not have used more than £9,000 of her nil rate band because of the size of her estate. Hari then dies in the tax year 2022/23, leaving his £509,000 estate to his children. The nil rate band available for Hari's estate is increased by 100% to £650,000, so there is no IHT payable.

Transfer of unused residence nil rate band

A spouse or civil partner who dies without using the residence nil rate band can transfer it to the survivor. The only danger is that if the entire estate is left to the survivor, the aggregated estate will exceed £2 million and some or all of the residence nil rate band will be lost.

> **EXAMPLE**
>
> Harry and Maude own the matrimonial home worth £1 million and a seaside cottage worth £700,000 as beneficial joint tenants. They each have £1 million of other assets.
>
> If Maude dies leaving everything to Harry, he will have an aggregated estate of £3.7 million. If he dies in 2022/23 leaving everything to their children, his estate will have two ordinary nil rate bands but the two residence nil rate bands (2 x £175,000 in 2022/23) will be tapered to zero because of the size of his estate.
>
> From an IHT perspective, it would be preferable for Maude to use her residence nil rate band to leave an interest in the seaside cottage directly to the children. However, there may be CGT disadvantages and there will be the possibility of the children forcing a sale of the cottage or being declared bankrupt.

Loss of business or agricultural property relief

It may not be sensible to make a transfer of property qualifying for business or agricultural property relief because of the risk of losing the relief if the donee spouse dies within two years of the lifetime transfer.

> **EXAMPLE**
>
> Pavan and Ramani wish to minimise the amount of IHT that their daughter Saria will pay on their deaths. Pavan transfers his 40% shareholding in their private company Z Ltd worth £800,000 to Ramani as part of the 'equalisation' process. He has owned the shares for four years. Ramani dies six months later leaving everything to Saria.
>
> The shareholding is taxable on its full value as Ramani has not owned the shares for two years (see **4.3.6**).
>
> Had Pavan retained the shares and given them by lifetime gift or by will to Saria, 100% business property relief would have been available.

4.6 TRANSFERS FROM PARENTS TO CHILDREN AND REMOTER ISSUE

Most parents wish to provide for their children, and those who can actually afford to do so wish to ensure that such provision is made in the most tax-effective way.

It is not always possible to achieve the client's intentions and avoid a tax bill. The skill is to put forward ideas that will satisfy the practical objectives at the minimum tax cost.

Again, the solicitor must be aware of the interaction of the capital taxes; for example, is the CGT cost of a course of action less than the IHT bill which will arise if the action is not taken?

The choice for parents is a lifetime gift either outright or through the creation of a trust (see **4.6.4**), or by will which is either an outright gift or gift into trust. The use of will trusts is discussed in **Chapter 12** and will not be considered in detail here.

4.6.1 Outright gifts

A gift is an immediate outright transfer of property from one person to another. The donor loses control of the property.

When making gifts of small sums of money or family possessions, or wishing to benefit an adult child, an outright gift may be the most sensible and appropriate course of action. However, where the intended recipient is a minor or is irresponsible with money, the donor may feel that it is inappropriate to hand over valuable assets or large amounts of cash. In such circumstances, consideration might be given to the provision of the intended benefit via a trust (but see **4.6.4.1**). A minor is unable to hold the legal estate in land so it is impossible to make an outright gift of land to a person under 18 years of age. Where such a gift is attempted, TLATA 1996 imposes a bare trust.

4.6.2 The taxation of outright gifts

4.6.2.1 Inheritance tax

The current IHT legislation encourages lifetime giving, whether by a parent, grandparent or others, and, wherever possible, clients should take full advantage of the exceptions and reliefs offered (see **4.3.4**).

PETs (IHTA 1984, s 3A) – 'asset freezing'

All gifts between individuals are PETs when they are made, whereas the lifetime creation of any trust, except a trust for the disabled, on or after 22 March 2006, will be an immediately chargeable transfer (charged at half the death rate). The effect of a PET is that no IHT is payable at the time of the transfer. The transfer becomes exempt from IHT if the transferor lives for seven years. Should the transferor die within the seven-year period, the PET becomes chargeable. The value which is taxed is the value of the property at the date of the transfer, unless the value has fallen, in which case it is the lower value that is taxed – see below. It is therefore sensible for clients to consider giving away assets which are likely to increase in value. Rates at the date of the death are used unless they have increased since the gift. If so, the rates at the date of the gift are used instead.

EXAMPLE

Kalan owns a painting by an elderly living artist. He paid £20,000 for it and believes that its value will quadruple after the artist's death. Kalan utilises his annual exemptions on other transfers.

Year 1: Kalan gives the painting (value £20,000) to Laura (PET).

Year 4: Kalan dies and the painting is valued at £115,000. IHT rates have not increased subsequently. The gift of the painting becomes a chargeable transfer and tax is charged on £20,000, which, assuming Kalan had made no previous transfers, will be covered by his nil rate band.

Where a PET is of an amount which exceeds the transferor's nil rate band, IHT will be payable by the donee if the transferor dies within seven years. Whilst this tax cannot be avoided, the transferee or transferor can mitigate its effect by insuring the transferor's life for seven years (for an explanation of such term assurance, see **Appendix 2(16)**) for a sum equal to the potential tax bill. If the transferor insures his own life, the insurance policy should be written in trust for the transferee.

EXAMPLE

Mike, a divorced man, who has made no gifts in excess of £3,000 per annum, gives his daughter, Nina, £500,000 in 2022/23 to buy a house.

If Mike dies within seven years, Nina could face a tax bill of up to £70,000.

Unless she insures her father's life (which she may not be able to afford to do) Nina therefore has the choice of only spending £430,000 and putting the rest aside to meet the possible tax bill, or having to mortgage the house on Mike's death to raise the tax.

> Alternatively, Mike could insure his life for £70,000 for seven years and assign the benefit of the insurance policy to Nina. The annual premiums should be covered by his normal expenditure out of income exemption. If Mike dies within seven years, Nina receives cash of £70,000 with which to pay the tax and so can safely spend the full £500,000 on buying her house.

PETs – loss in value

If property other than cash is given away and the property falls in value between the date of the PET and the death, relief is provided by IHTA 1984, s 131. Inheritance tax is calculated on the reduced value instead of the original value (the relief applies similarly following a lifetime chargeable transfer). This relief reduces the value which is taxed; it does not affect the value of the original PET. This means that the original value remains in the transferor's cumulative total when calculating any IHT on later lifetime transfers and on the estate on the death. Any taper relief is based on the IHT actually payable, ie, the IHT payable on the reduced value.

Inheritance tax is charged at the rate(s) in force at death unless the rates have increased, in which case the rates in force at the date of the PET are used.

EXAMPLE

In January 2018 Harold gave his grandson his shares in Z plc, which were then worth £400,000. Harold died in May 2022 when the shares were worth £341,000. Apart from using his annual exemptions, Harold has made no other transfers.

(a)   On Harold's death within seven years, the PET becomes chargeable on the reduced value of £341,000.

(b)   IHT, at rates in force when Harold died (assuming 40%):

		£
nil rate band	£325,000	nil
balance	£16,000 @ 40%	6,400
		6,400

(c)   Taper relief – Harold died more than four but less than five years later.
£6,400 @ 60% = £3,840 (payable by Harold's grandson).

(d)   The original value of £400,000 remains in Harold's cumulative total when calculating the IHT due on his estate at death.

Note: if Harold's grandson had sold the shares for £341,000, IHT on Harold's death would be calculated in the same way as above. If he had given them away, no relief is given and IHT would, instead, be calculated on the full value in 2017, ie, £400,000 (IHTA 1984, s 131(1)).

Order of gifts – some considerations

Clients planning a number of gifts, some PETs and some lifetime chargeable transfers such as transfers into a settlement, should be advised that the possible IHT consequences may differ depending upon the order of the gifts.

Transfers made on the same day (IHTA 1984, s 266)

If a number of PETs are intended and all are made on the same day, there is, of course, no IHT payable at the date of the gifts. If the donor should die within seven years so that IHT becomes payable, it is charged on each PET on a pro rata basis. Each gift benefits from a proportion of any available nil rate band. Had the gifts been made on separate days, the earlier gifts would benefit from the donor's available nil rate band whereas the donees of later gifts would suffer IHT once the nil rate band was exceeded.

PETs and relevant property trusts (lifetime chargeable transfers – LCTs)

Discretionary settlements and all lifetime settlements created after 22 March 2006 (except trusts for the disabled) are referred to as 'relevant property trusts'. Such trusts have their own IHT rate, which is calculated partly on the value of transfers from the settlement and partly on the settlor's cumulative total immediately before he created the settlement (see **Chapters 5** and **10**). This makes the order of gifts important.

There is an advantage to the later taxation of relevant property settlements if the settlement is made before (or at the latest on the same day as) the PETs. If the PETs come first and later become chargeable, they will be taken into account when calculating IHT payable by the trustees during the life of the relevant property settlement. This liability of the trustees is considered in **Chapter 10**. If the client intends creating more than one relevant property settlement, the gifts to the trustees should be made on different days so as to avoid the settlements being treated as 'related settlements' (IHTA 1984, s 62). The effect of related settlements on the calculation of the trustees' IHT liability is considered at **10.2.4**.

Effect on PETs and relevant property settlements (LCTs) of death between three to seven years

Although it is beneficial to the subsequent taxation of relevant property settlements to make the LCT before the PET, there are circumstances where this can result in the payment of more tax on the transfers themselves. This occurs where the donor dies more than three years, but less than seven years after his gifts, as illustrated in the examples which follow. Assume that no annual exemptions are available.

EXAMPLE 1: PET PRECEDES LCT BY ONE DAY

			IHT £
(a)	PET	£330,000	nil
(b)	LCT	£466,000	
	first	£325,000 – nil	
	balance	£141,000 @ 20%	28,200
(c)	Donor dies after six years.		
	PET	£330,000 – £325,000 = £5,000	
		£5,000 @ 40% × 20% (taper relief)	400
	LCT	£466,000 @ 40% × 20% (taper relief)	37,280
		credit (tax already paid)	(28,200)
	IHT due on LCT		£9,080
	Total IHT – £37,680		

EXAMPLE 2: LCT PRECEDES PET BY ONE DAY

			IHT £
(a)	LCT	£466,000	
	first	£325,000 – nil	
	balance	£141,000 @ 20%	28,200
(b)	PET	£330,000	nil
(c)	Donor dies after six years.		
	LCT	£466,000	
	first	£325,000 – nil	

balance	£141,000 @ 40% × 20% (taper relief)	11,280
	credit (tax already paid – no refund)	(28,200)
		no IHT due
(d) PET	£330,000 @ 40% × 20% (taper relief)	£26,400
Total IHT – £54,600		

The difference arises because in Example 2 the benefit of the tapering relief on the LCT is largely lost as it reduces the tax payable below the level of the tax already paid and no refunds are available. No nil rate band is available to the PET as it has already been used by the LCT.

Lifetime transfers – transfers on death

Clients who are estate planning through a combination of lifetime giving and gifts by will should be aware of the effect of PETs on their death estates. Lifetime gifts which become chargeable on death have first call on the deceased's nil rate band and this may result in more IHT being payable on property passing under the will.

EXAMPLE

Oswald has always used his annual exemption but otherwise has made no previous lifetime transfers.

Year 1: Oswald makes a will leaving a legacy of £325,000 to his children and the residue to his wife.

Year 2: He makes a PET of £100,000 to his eldest son.

Year 3: Oswald dies.

Step 1: The PET becomes chargeable, but as Oswald had made no previous lifetime transfers the £100,000 is covered by his nil rate band.

Step 2: The £100,000 is cumulated with his death estate and means that only the remaining £225,000 of the nil rate band is available to set against the legacy to his children. The balance of the legacy (£100,000) is taxable at 40% (subject to grossing up); the residue passing to his wife is exempt but is reduced by the tax paid on the gift to the children.

Use of a 'formula clause' limiting the legacy to the amount available of the nil rate band at death (here £100,000) when drafting the will can anticipate and avoid this situation (see **11.2.5.3** and **12.5.1**).

Using reliefs

Property which attracts business property relief or agricultural property relief (especially at 100%) should, where possible, be given to non-exempt beneficiaries rather than exempt ones, as otherwise the benefit may be wasted. There is also the danger of losing the relief completely where the conditions for business property relief are not fulfilled at the date of death (see **4.3.6.2** for an example).

It may be preferable to make the gift of such property by will because there is a risk that the donee of a lifetime gift will no longer own the property on the death of the donor within seven years of the transfer, thus losing the relief.

Excluded property – inheritance tax

Section 5 of IHTA 1984 defines a person's estate as including everything 'to which he is beneficially entitled ... but does not include excluded property'. By IHTA 1984, s 48 a reversionary interest (with three anti-avoidance exceptions – see below) is excluded property. Section 47 defines any future interest under a settlement as a reversionary interest, whether the interest is vested or contingent, and includes the interest expectant on the termination of an interest in possession, ie, the interest which falls into possession on the death of a life tenant. The interest of a beneficiary under a discretionary settlement is not, therefore, within the definition.

Because a reversionary interest is not included in an individual's estate, it can be given away as part of estate planning without liability to IHT (and without CGT liability, see below).

Perhaps the most common example of excluded property is 'an interest in remainder' following a qualifying life interest.

EXAMPLE

In 2005, during his lifetime, Sam settles £200,000 on Angela for life, remainder to Bernard absolutely.

At the date of Angela's death, the trust property is valued at £400,000 and her free estate is £100,000.

Sam ⟶ Angela for life

↓

remainder to Bernard

Angela has a qualifying interest in possession in this trust because the interest was created by lifetime transfer before 22 March 2006. While Angela is alive Bernard has an 'interest in remainder'. Assume Bernard has shares and cash totalling £400,000 and lives in rented accommodation. He is divorced and intends to leave everything to his daughter Davina. He has a full nil rate band available.

(a)   If Bernard does nothing:

On Angela's death, her free estate is worth £100,000. The trust fund of £400,000 is taxable as part of her estate. (Assume that she is unmarried, her residuary estate is exempt and her cumulative total is zero.)

IHT on £500,000 with a nil rate band available of £325,000 is:

£175,00 x 40% = £70,000

This is apportioned between the free estate and the trust.

Angela's PRs are liable for:

£70,000 x 100,000/500,000 = £14,000

The trustees are liable for:

£70,000 x 400,000/500,000 = £56,000

Bernard receives £344,000.

When Bernard dies his estate is £344,000 + £400,000 and Davina will pay IHT of £167,600.

(b)   If Bernard gives his interest in remainder to Davina while Angela is still alive.

There will be no IHT (IHTA 1984, s 5) and no CGT on the gift (see below; TCGA 1992, s 76)

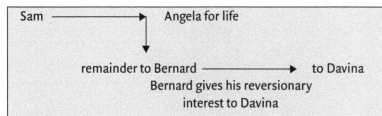

On Angela's, death, Davina will receive £344,000 (as Bernard did in (a)).

When Bernard dies his estate is £400,000 as the trust fund no longer forms part of his taxable estate. Davina will now pay IHT of £30,000 on her father's estate (£75,000 x 40%). This represents a tax saving of £137,600, ie, IHT at 40% on the £344,000 trust fund.

The three anti-avoidance exceptions within s 48 where the reversionary interest is not excluded property are:

(a)   where the interest was purchased for money or money's worth;

(b)   where the interest is one to which the settlor or his spouse is beneficially entitled;

(c)   where it is the lessor's interest expectant on the ending of a lease granted for life; where such a lease for life is granted, a settlement exists for IHT.

Excluded property – capital gains tax

No gain arises for CGT where a beneficiary disposes of his beneficial interest under a settlement, provided that it had never previously been acquired for a consideration in money or money's worth (other than consideration consisting of another interest under the settlement, for example, on a 'swap' of interests by beneficiaries). Once any consideration in money or money's worth has been given, all future disposals of the interest will attract CGT (TCGA 1992, s 76).

In the previous example, where Bernard gave his interest to Davina, neither he nor Davina would pay CGT. Whether she sold or gave away the interest subsequently, she would not pay CGT.

If, instead, Bernard sold his interest to Davina, no CGT would be payable by him (assuming no prior consideration had been given for the interest) because s 76 would apply. On Davina's later disposal of the interest (by sale or by gift) she would be liable to CGT on any gain she realises.

4.6.2.2   Capital gains tax

Although a gift may not result in an IHT charge, it may attract an immediate charge to CGT. A gift is a disposal by the donor and, if it is of a chargeable asset, CGT will be calculated in the usual way (subject to appropriate reliefs and exemptions).

> **EXAMPLE**
>
> Aadila gives quoted shares worth £60,000 to her daughter Badrai and cash of £50,000 to her son Camil.
>
> Both gifts are PETs for IHT purposes and the cash is not a chargeable asset for CGT.
>
> Aadila will pay CGT on the difference between the purchase price of the quoted shares and their open market value at the date of the gift to Badrai, after taking into account the annual exemption.

Where the gift is of a business asset hold-over relief will be available (for the definitions and conditions, see **4.4.5.2**), but if the donor's annual exemption is available or he has unused losses, it may be better not to claim the relief.

EXAMPLE

In 2022/23 Wahid gives his 10% shareholding in O Ltd to his daughter Yasmin. Wahid acquired the shares for £200 and they are currently worth £13,500. Yasmin expects to sell the shares within the next two years. In the previous year, Wahid made capital losses of £2,000. (Assume that the annual exemption and tax rate remain unchanged in future years.)

(a)   If hold-over relief claimed:

Wahid pays no CGT and retains losses of £2,000.

Yasmin acquires the shares at £200.

In two years' time she sells the shares for £14,500. Assume Yasmin makes no other disposals in the tax year.

CGT is payable on any chargeable gain.

	£
Disposal consideration	14,500
less: Acquisition cost	200
	14,300
less: Annual exemption	12,300
Chargeable gain	2,000

(b)   If hold-over relief not claimed and assuming neither makes other disposals in the relevant tax year:

Wahid's gift is a disposal of a chargeable asset.

	£	£
Disposal consideration	13,500	
less: Acquisition cost	200	
		13,300
Part of unused losses	1,000	
Annual exemption	12,300	
		13,300
Wahid's chargeable gain		nil
When Yasmin sells:		
Disposal consideration		14,500
less: Acquisition cost	13,500	
less: Annual exemption (part)	1,000	14,500
Yasmin's chargeable gain		nil

Note: Brought forward losses need only be used to reduce gains to the level of the annual exemption, unlike current year losses which must be used to reduce gains to zero before any portion of the loss can be carried forward.

Payment of CGT by instalments (TCGA 1992, ss 280, 281)

The normal date for payment of a CGT liability is 31 January following the end of the tax year of the disposal. In limited circumstances, the tax may be paid by equal yearly instalments starting on 31 January. Interest is payable on the outstanding tax.

Capital gains tax may be paid by instalments if the following apply:

(a)   Sales (s 280) – if the consideration is payable over a period exceeding 18 months and the Revenue is satisfied payment of the tax in a lump sum would cause hardship. The instalment period is eight years (or the payment period if the consideration is payable over a shorter period).

(b)   Gifts or deemed disposals by trustees (s 281 – see **10.2.7**) – where the property is land, a controlling shareholding in either a quoted or an unquoted company, or a minority holding in a company whose shares are unquoted, provided that hold-over relief was not available under either TCGA 1992, s 165 or s 260, ie, neither the asset (s 165) nor the occasion (s 260) was appropriate to enable hold-over relief to be claimed. Failure to make the appropriate election for hold-over relief, in cases where it is available, does not mean that the tax can then be paid by instalments. When available, the CGT may be paid by 10 equal annual instalments.

Accelerated reporting and payment of CGT on UK residential land

The Finance Act 2019, s 14 and Sch 2 introduced accelerated reporting and payment dates for CGT on UK land disposed of by non-residents starting in tax year 2019/20. A report is required even if there is no tax due.

The date of disposal is fixed by reference to the date of unconditional exchange of contracts. For completions on or after 27 October 2021, the return and payment must be submitted within 60 days of completion of the disposal. For completions before that date the time period was only 30 days.

The change also applies to disposals of UK residential land by UK residents on or after 6 April 2020 *but only where tax is due*. It applies to disposals made by PRs and trustees as well as to disposals by individuals.

No reports are required for disposals where no tax is due, for example because the gain is:

*   within the annual exemption;
*   covered by existing losses;
*   attracts main residence relief; or
*   to a spouse or civil partner (no gain/no loss disposal).

The reporting process is done online and is completely standalone. It does not use self-assessment returns or references. Instead, the taxpayer needs to set up an online CGT UK Property Account.

The calculation of tax is made on the basis of events so far in the tax year with an approximation of the level of income expected during the year. The payment made is on account of the tax due at the end of the year. However, it is not necessary to submit a self-assessment tax return if the tax paid was correct and there is no other need for a return.

The payment may turn out to be too little (for example where the taxpayer's combined income and gains unexpectedly exceed the higher rate limit) or too much (for example, where income is less than expected or losses are made later in the tax year). Where too little has been paid, the additional amount is simply paid with the rest of the tax. If an overpayment has occurred as a result of an amendment or due to a further UK Property Disposal return, there is a section on the UK Property Disposal online return to request a repayment.

4.6.2.3   Income tax

An outright gift of an income-producing asset to an adult child by his parent will give the child an increase in his taxable income (taxable at his own rates) and a corresponding decrease in the level of the parent's taxable income (and a saving of tax at his own rates). The potential saving of tax, possibly at 40% or 45%, by the parent makes such gifts attractive, particularly when the child's rate of tax may be at basic rate or less.

Parental gifts for minor children (ITTOIA 2005, s 629)

Despite the obvious practical advantage of an outright gift, there is a potential income tax problem if the child is unmarried and under 18 years when the gift is made. Income tax rules state that any income (of more than £100) paid to or for the benefit of the unmarried minor child from a 'settlement' created by his parent will be taxed as though it is still the income of the parent (s 629). This is deliberate policy to prevent a parent who pays income tax at 40% or 45% from benefiting the child who pays income tax at lower rates or possibly is not a taxpayer at all. If income is accumulated and not paid to or for the benefit of the minor child, it will not be taxed as income of the settlor. However, it will be taxed as income of the settlement, and the settlement rates of tax are unattractively high. See **Chapter 14**.

'Settlement' is defined in very wide terms by ITTOIA 2005, s 620, as including 'any disposition, trust, covenant, agreement, arrangement or transfer of assets'. An outright gift by a parent to a minor child is clearly within the provision, so that any income of the property given away is taxed as if it still belongs to the parent. The actual 'ownership' of the income does not belong to the parent even though it is deemed his for income tax purposes. The parent has a right of reimbursement from the child for the extra tax suffered where the income is deemed to be his for income tax purposes (s 646). Once the child attains 18 or marries, s 629 ceases to apply. The income is then taxed as the child's, not his parent's.

4.6.3 Post-death disclaimers and variations

Where a parent leaves assets by will to a wealthy adult child, that child may in turn decide to give that property to his own children. A post-death variation of the will may be the most tax-effective way of passing inherited property to the next generation. Where the requirements for post-death alterations are met, the gift is treated for the purposes of IHT and CGT as made by the deceased, not by the legatee. (See **Chapter 13**.) Note, however, that the parental settlement rules, discussed at **4.6.2.3** above, will apply to a post-death variation for income tax purposes.

4.6.4 Gifts into trust

The practical advantage of a gift into trust over an outright gift is flexibility. By using a settlement, the settlor (the person making the gift into the trust) can determine who will benefit, when and how. Conditions can be imposed, for example, 'To Ben if he attains 21 years of age', so that Ben will receive the trust fund (gift) only if he reaches his 21st birthday; or to limit the amount of the gift received, for example 'the income to Carol during her life and on her death the income and capital to Doreen'. This is not possible with an outright gift.

There are various types of trust, and each trust has its own particular uses and conditions. The most commonly used types are considered in more detail in **Chapter 5**. Trusts with trustees resident outside the UK also play a considerable role in tax and estate planning. These are considered in **Chapter 15**.

4.6.4.1 Parental settlements (ITTOIA 2005, s 629)

The income deeming provisions discussed at **4.6.2.3** apply to 'settlements' as defined by s 620. If, therefore, a parent creates a trust of any of the types just mentioned of which his minor unmarried child is a beneficiary, s 629 will apply to income paid out to the child for so long as the child remains under 18 years and unmarried.

The income produced by the property in the settlement will be taxed as though it is still the income of the parent/settlor. The income remains the income of the trustees who will use it under the terms of the trust for the benefit of the beneficiaries. The parent/settlor has a right to recover from the trustees the extra income tax he pays because of these provisions.

The provision does not apply if income is accumulated. However, the trustees will have to pay the trusts rate of tax which is unattractively high. See **Chapter 14**.

4.6.5   Gifts with a reserved benefit (Finance Act 1986, s 102 and Sch 20)

4.6.5.1   Tax implications where there is a reservation of benefit

No estate planning involving gifts can take place without at least a brief consideration of the rules governing 'reservation of benefit'. Anybody, whether parent, grandparent, uncle, etc, making a gift must ensure that the donor does not continue to have any interest (with minor exceptions) in the subject matter of the gift or the gift will be ineffective for IHT purposes. This principle applies to outright gifts and gifts into trust, and is illustrated by the following examples.

EXAMPLE 1

Gina gives her nephew, Henri, a valuable painting which hangs in her living room. Henri does not take the painting away and Gina keeps it hanging on her wall.

EXAMPLE 2

For many years, Indrajit has owned a country cottage in which he spends his holidays. He transfers the ownership of the cottage to his son Jagan but spends his holidays there as before.

In both examples there has been a valid gift for succession and CGT purposes and a PET for IHT purposes. However, the Revenue will not fully recognise the gift for IHT purposes because there has been a reservation of benefit – the continued enjoyment of the Matisse and the occupation of the cottage.

The death of the donor within seven years will attract IHT in the usual way on the PET. However, because the gift is caught by the 'reservation of benefit' provisions, the property will also be taxable as part of the donor's IHT estate at death. This prima facie double liability is, to an extent, alleviated by the Inheritance Tax Double Charges (Relief) Regulations 1987 (SI 1987/1130).

If the reservation ends before the donor's death, he is treated as making a PET at that time. Again, the 1987 Regulations provide relief should each PET (the original gift and the ending of the reservation) be within seven years of the donor's death.

4.6.5.2   When do the provisions apply?

The reservation of benefit provisions apply where an individual disposes of any property by way of gift and either:

(a)   full possession and enjoyment of the property is not bona fide assumed by the donee at or before the beginning of the relevant period (s 102(1)(a)); or

(b)   at any time in the relevant period the property is not enjoyed to the entire exclusion, or virtually to the entire exclusion, of the donor by contract or otherwise (s 102(1)(b)).

The relevant period means the period ending on the date of the donor's death and beginning seven years before that date, or if it is later, on the date of the gift.

EXAMPLE 1

David gives away (ie, transfers the legal title to) his house to his only child Ella. David moves out and Ella moves in (or rents out the property, keeping the rent):

(a)   If David dies two years later – full possession and enjoyment at the beginning of the relevant period (of two years) – no reservation.

(b)   If David dies eight years later – as before, no reservation.

> (c)   However, if after one year David resumes occupation for six months to write his autobiography, the property is no longer enjoyed to the entire exclusion of David – gift with reservation.

EXAMPLE 2

Faria settles a property on discretionary trusts naming herself as one of the discretionary beneficiaries. Even though she has no more than an expectation of benefiting as a beneficiary of a discretionary settlement, all the trust property will remain taxable as part of her estate on death.

The Revenue has provided guidance and examples in relation to the interpretation of s 102(1) in its tax manuals (IHTM 14311 onwards). As indicated above, s 102(1)(b) requires that 'the property' is 'enjoyed to the exclusion ...' etc. Identifying the property given is not normally difficult but is obviously essential before the rules can be applied appropriately. It also requires 'virtually entire exclusion' from the gifted property. Some continued enjoyment of the property is therefore possible. There is no statutory definition but the Revenue interprets the phrase as meaning (and therefore including) 'to all intents' or 'as good as' (IHTM 14333). Flexibility is applied by the Revenue when applying the interpretation so that a donor can have limited access to the property given away.

The following are some of the situations which, according to the Revenue, will not bring the rules into play:

(a)   A house which becomes the donee's residence but where the donor subsequently:

    (i)   stays, in the absence of the donee, for not more than two weeks each year, or

    (ii)   stays with the donee for less than one month each year.

(b)   Social visits, excluding overnight stays, made by a donor as a guest of the donee, to a house which he had given away. The extent of the social visits should be no greater than the visits which the donor might be expected to make to the donee's house in the absence of any gift by the donor.

(c)   A temporary stay for some short-term purpose in a house the donor had previously given away, for example:

    (i)   while the donor convalesces after medical treatment;

    (ii)   while the donor looks after a donee convalescing after medical treatment;

    (iii)   while the donor's own home is redecorated.

(d)   A house together with a library of books which the donor visits less than five times in any year to consult or borrow a book.

(e)   A motor car which the donee uses to give occasional (ie, less than three times a month) lifts to the donor.

(f)   Land which the donor uses to walk his dogs or for horse riding, provided this does not restrict the donee's use of the land.

Conversely, the following are instances (in the Revenue view) where the rules may apply:

(a)   A house in which the donor then stays most weekends, or for a month or more each year.

(b)   A second home or holiday home which the donor and the donee both then use on an occasional basis.

(c)   A house with a library in which the donor continues to keep his own books, or which the donor uses on a regular basis, for example because it is necessary for his work.

(d)   A motor car which the donee uses every day to take the donor to work.

The reservation of benefit provisions do not apply (inter alia) to transfers qualifying for the four following IHT exemptions:

(a)   the spouse exemption;

(b)   the small gift exemption;

(c)   the gift in consideration of marriage exemption; and

(d)   the gifts to charity exemption.

4.6.5.3   Full consideration exclusion in relation to land and chattels

Schedule 20, para 6(1)(a) to the FA 1986 states that if land or chattels are given away and a donor provides full consideration for his future enjoyment of the property, the reservation provisions do not apply. The Revenue has indicated that full consideration must be paid for the whole of the relevant period. In relation to what constitutes full consideration, the Revenue has indicated that it would be unlikely to object where the arrangement resulted from:

(a)   a bargain negotiated at arm's length;

(b)   by parties who were independently advised; and

(c)   which followed the normal commercial criteria in force at the time it was negotiated (IHTM 14341).

Further aspects of the reservation rules and the family home are discussed at **4.7.4**.

4.6.5.4   Income tax charge on pre-owned assets

The FA 2004 introduced income tax provisions (s 84 and Sch 15) with the aim of catching situations not covered by the IHT reservation of benefit regime. The effect is that where a person owns certain assets (land, chattels or intangible property) and disposes of them, other than by sale at arm's length, but still derives some benefit from them, that person will suffer an income tax charge on the annual value of this benefit. The charge also applies if a person has contributed towards the purchase of such property by another, and derives some benefit from the property. These provisions came into effect on 6 April 2005, but the charge affects anyone who has owned and disposed of assets since 17 March 1986, or contributed to the purchase of an asset since that date.

This charge will not apply in various situations, including:

(a)   where under the reservation of benefit rules the asset is treated as part of the IHT estate of the donor;

(b)   where the annual value of the benefit is below £5,000; or

(c)   where the asset is owned by the donor's spouse.

4.7   THE FAMILY HOME

The principal tax-saving opportunity available to the home owner is the CGT private residence exemption. As a substantial asset in its own right, home owners will frequently raise questions about gifts of the home, or at least an interest in it, as part of estate planning with a view to saving, principally, IHT on its value at death. There are many problems associated with gifts of this type, some of which are discussed later.

4.7.1   Insurance cover

It is sensible to provide insurance cover designed to repay the mortgage secured on the family home. In the case of property owned jointly by a husband and wife the policy will normally mature on the death of the first spouse to die leaving a mortgage-free property for the survivor. Various types of policy are available and are discussed in **Appendix 2(16).**

4.7.2   Joint tenancy and tenancy in common

Joint tenancy and tenancy in common have already been discussed (see **4.5.1.2**) as the two common ways property is held by spouses. For IHT purposes, there is no distinction made between joint tenancy and tenancy in common; it is the beneficial interest behind the trust of the legal estate that is important when considering the 'estate' of each spouse. The differences between joint tenancy and tenancy in common from a succession point of view have also been considered earlier.

4.7.3   Capital gains tax main residence exemption (TCGA 1992, ss 222–226)

Gains on residential property are taxed at 18% or 28%, not the normal 10% or 20%. However, many people pay no tax on such property because of the important main residence exemption.

Gains made on the disposal by sale or by gift of an individual's dwelling house used as his only or main residence, including grounds of up to 0.5 hectares (or such larger area as is reasonably required for its enjoyment), are exempt. It is a question of fact in each case as to what constitutes a dwelling house. A caravan was held to be a dwelling house in *Makins v Elson (Inspector of Taxes)* [1977] 1 All ER 572 but not in *Moore v Thompson* [1986] STC 170 (the caravan not having its own water or electricity supply).

Problems can also arise in deciding whether separate buildings can constitute the taxpayer's residence. For example, a separate bungalow occupied by a caretaker and situated in the grounds of the taxpayer's house was within the exemption when sold, ie, physical separation of the buildings did not deny the taxpayer the exemption (*Batey (Inspector of Taxes) v Wakefield* [1982] 1 All ER 61). Later cases (where CGT was payable) show that the separate building must be physically close to the main building so as to enhance the taxpayer's enjoyment of it (*Markey (Inspector of Taxes) v Sanders* [1987] 1 WLR 864 – bungalow 130 metres away), or within the 'curtilage' of the main building (*Lewis (Inspector of Taxes) v Lady Rook* [1992] 1 WLR 662 – cottage 200 yards away).

4.7.3.1   Land and residence disposed of separately

The order of disposals can be important where the taxpayer plans to sell or give away land used with the main residence and the main residence itself. Land of up to 0.5 hectares (or a permitted larger area) is within the exemption if used in connection with the residence. Thus disposal of the residence with its grounds will be exempt, but gains on the later disposal of the retained land will be chargeable (*Varty (Inspector of Taxes) v Lynes* [1976] 3 All ER 447).

4.7.3.2   Part business user

Use of part of the house exclusively for business purposes will mean that part of the gain on the disposal is chargeable. Exclusive use can easily be avoided, for example, by having a television set in a room otherwise used as an office for a business run from home.

4.7.3.3   More than one residence

A taxpayer with more than one residence can elect for one to be treated as his main residence (TCGA 1992, s 222(5)). This avoids difficult questions as to which of two or more residences is the only or main residence for the purposes of the relief. The election should be made within two years of acquiring the second residence. Failure by the taxpayer to elect will mean that the Inspector of Taxes will do so. The relative CGT liability on each property will generally influence the election of a particular property, for treatment as the taxpayer's main residence.

A married couple can have only one main residence between them, and the same is true of civil partners. When a couple marry, each owning a residence, the election for treatment as their main residence must be made within two years of the marriage or civil partnership.

4.7.3.4   What is a residence?

Simply spending time in a property on a temporary basis does not make it a residence. There must be some expectation of permanence or continuity. For examples of cases where this point was in issue, see *Goodwin v Curtis* [1988] STC 475, *Dutton-Forshaw v RCC* [2015] UKFTT 478 (TC) and *Bailey v HMRC* [2017] UKFTT 0658 (TC).

EXAMPLE

Finola, a highly paid banker, exchanges contracts on a flat in Canary Wharf. Before completion, she decides that banking is no longer what she wants to do. She puts the flat back on the market and exchanges contracts on a croft in the Highlands of Scotland. She completes the purchase of the Canary Wharf flat and moves in while she waits to complete the purchase of her Highland croft. She spends six weeks in the flat. Her occupation is on a temporary 'stop-gap' basis and the Revenue is unlikely to accept that she used the flat as a residence.

However, if she moved in, intending to make the flat her home, but after a few weeks decided that banking was no longer for her and put the flat back on the market, the exemption would be available because she had an expectation of permanence and continuity when she moved in.

4.7.3.5   Non-qualifying periods of ownership

Periods of absence

Exemption is available if a taxpayer occupies a property as his only or main residence throughout the period of ownership. Periods of absence will therefore cut back the exemption so that a proportion of the gain on disposal is chargeable.

Certain periods of absence can be ignored (so not prejudicing the exemption). These include:

(a)   the first 12 months' ownership due to delay in building or alteration (see CGTM 65003 and Extra Statutory Concession D49);

(b)   periods not exceeding three years in total, provided there was no other available residence and the property was occupied before and after the periods of absence;

(c)   for disposals on or after 6 April 2020, the last nine months of ownership, eg, where the owner moves into new property and experiences delay in selling the former.

(For disposals before 6 April 2020 and on or after 6 April 2014, the period was 18 months. For disposals before 6 April 2014, the last three years of ownership were ignored. This period will continue to apply after 6 April 2014 in some situations where the person disposing of the property is a disabled person or has gone into care.)

Periods of non-residence

For disposals on or after 6 April 2015, a further period of ownership does not qualify as occupation of the property as a main residence, and will therefore reduce the use of the exemption. This is any tax year or part tax year in which (i) neither the owner nor spouse was resident for tax purposes in the country where the property is located, and (ii) the owner spent fewer than 90 days in the property; see further **4.7.3.7**.

4.7.3.6   Main residences occupied under the terms of a trust (s 225)

If the trustees sell a dwelling house occupied by a beneficiary as the beneficiary's main residence under the terms of the trust, their capital gain is exempt. The exemption will apply where the beneficiary has an interest in possession, ie, is entitled to occupy under the terms of the settlement.

The exemption will also apply if the beneficiary occupies as a result of the exercise of a discretion, for example, where the trust is discretionary and the trustees exercise a power in the settlement to permit one (or more) members of the discretionary class to occupy (*Sansom and Another v Peay (Inspector of Taxes)* [1976] 3 All ER 375).

Chapter 5 discusses the essential differences between interest in possession and discretionary trusts.

Since 10 December 2003, the TCGA 1992, s 226A provides that where hold-over relief is claimed under TCGA 1992, s 260 on a transfer of a house to a discretionary settlement, the main residence exemption will not be available if the trustees allow a beneficiary to occupy that house and the trustees then dispose of it. If hold-over relief is not claimed when the house is transferred to the settlement, the main residence exemption will be available on a later disposal by the trustees (assuming that they have first allowed a beneficiary to occupy the house).

4.7.3.7 Main residence exemption and non-residents

The Government has been looking at ways to make the tax system fairer, which means widening the tax base so that more people pay more tax on more transactions, rather than increasing the rates generally. In particular it is concerned to obtain tax from individuals who spend only limited time in the UK.

To achieve this, new ss 222A–222C are inserted into the TCGA 1992. As from 6 April 2015, a person's residence, whether UK or non-UK, will not be eligible for the exemption unless either:

(a)   the person making the disposal was tax resident in the same territory as the property for that tax year; or

(b)   where not tax resident in the territory, the person spent at least 90 midnights in that property (or across all of their properties in that territory) in that tax year.

Helpfully, only gains arising as from 6 April 2015 will be taxed. Further, when calculating the gain, the taxpayer can normally choose whether to use:

(i)   a re-based 5 April 2015 value; or

(ii)   a time-apportionment of the whole gain; or

(iii)   the whole gain or loss for the period of ownership.

Also helpfully, the 90 days include occupation by the individual or spouse or civil partner, although each midnight can count only once.

EXAMPLE

Irena is resident in Italy and owns a flat in London, in which she stays on 80 midnights in one tax year for pleasure and on her occasional work trips to the UK as a political journalist.

Her husband Gianni accompanies her on 30 of those nights, but he also stays on alone for an extra 12 midnights. Irena passes the 90 midnights test because the property has been occupied by either her or Gianni for 92 midnights.

But if Gianni only arrives home by midnight on nine of those 12 extra nights, the test will fail because the property will have been occupied for only 89 midnights. The test is explicit: the individual must be present 'in' the property at midnight.

> A person who spends more than 90 days in the UK is likely to become resident for tax purposes under the 'sufficient ties' test (see **15.2.2**). For many non-residents, especially where single, it will in practice be difficult to obtain the exemption and not become resident. In effect, the new rules are a neat way for the Government to restrict the availability of the exemption to, in most cases, residents and the few non-residents who can juggle their affairs down to the 90th midnight with exact perfection.

4.7.4   Estate planning and the family home

The dilemma here is, on the one hand, the wish to give away part or all of the value of the home to save IHT; and on the other hand, the necessity to maintain a roof over the donor's head. Saving tax in relation to the home (bearing in mind its value in the client's estate) is an obvious consideration but the best advice is often 'don't let the tax tail wag the dog', ie, it is frequently better not to enter into arrangements just to save IHT.

The residence nil rate band that is available from tax year 2017/18 is only available where an interest in a residence is inherited, not where it is given away by lifetime transfer. This would appear to discourage lifetime gifts. However, despite the deceased's residence having been disposed of before death, the residence nil rate band is available in some cases where the gift is made with a reservation of value, or a downsizing allowance may be available where the disposal is on or after 8 July 2015.

Reservations of benefit

Where a residence is taxed as part of the death estate because of a reservation of benefit, the residence nil rate band is available *if, and only if*, the person to whom the disposal was made is a lineal descendant of the donor or spouse or civil partner of a lineal descendant (s 8J). This produces some inconsistent results.

> **EXAMPLE**
>
> Dad gave his home to his son in 2015. Dad goes travelling but spends several months each year staying with his son. Dad dies in 2020. There is a reservation of benefit. The residence nil rate band is available because the disposal was made to the son.
>
> However, if Dad settled the residence on himself for life, remainder to his son absolutely, even though there is a reservation of benefit, the residence nil rate band is not available because the disposal was not to the son.

Downsizing allowance

Where a person disposes completely of their residential property or moves to something cheaper on or after 8 July 2015, a downsizing allowance is available to their death estate provided assets are left to lineal descendants. The allowance is capped at the value of assets left to lineal descendants. The calculation of the allowance is complex, but, basically, the value of the residence disposed of is expressed as a percentage of the residence nil rate band available at the date of the disposal. That percentage is then applied to the residence nil rate band available at the date of death. The percentage is limited to 100%.

> **EXAMPLE**
>
> In September 2017 Fred, who is divorced, gives his son, Sam, the family home worth £3 million and goes into residential care. The residence nil rate band in 2017/18 is £100,000. The downsizing percentage will be limited to 100%.
>
> Fred dies in 2021/22 when the residential nil rate band is £175,000. His estate does not exceed the taper threshold.

Potentially, Fred has a downsizing allowance of £175,000 available, but it is capped at the value of the amount inherited by lineal descendants. If Fred leaves Sam less than £175,000, the allowance will be reduced.

Normally, IHT planning considerations will revolve around a gift of the house, or of an interest in it, to another individual who will usually be the donor's child.

There is a danger in giving the family home, or an interest in it, to a child (even where the family relationship is harmonious). The child may become bankrupt or be divorced. The donor's house would then be taken by the child's trustee in bankruptcy, or be at risk in the divorce settlement.

The gift with reservation of benefit provisions (FA 1986, s 102) and the pre-owned assets regime discussed at **4.6.5** present the main obstacle to estate planning where the family home is involved. There are some exceptions to the reservation rules, the more important of which are discussed below.

4.7.4.1 'Occupation virtually to the entire exclusion of the donor' (FA 1986, s 102(1)(b))

A gift of the home to a child followed by occasional visits (as interpreted in HMRC tax manuals) should have no adverse IHT consequences.

4.7.4.2 'Occupation resulting from change of circumstances of the donor' (FA 1986, Sch 20, para 6(1)(b))

A gift of land which is subsequently reoccupied by the donor following unforeseen and unintentional change in his circumstances is excluded by para 6, provided:

(a) the donor is through age or infirmity unable to maintain himself;

(b) the reoccupation is reasonable provision by the donee for the care of the donor; and

(c) the donee is a relative, spouse or civil partner of the donor.

The scope of this exemption is clearly limited as shown in the following example.

EXAMPLE

A father on his retirement gives to his daughter the family bungalow. He later returns to live there following serious ill health. No IHT consequences should follow from the reoccupation.

4.7.4.3 'Occupation of land and possession of a chattel for full consideration in money or money's worth' (FA 1986, Sch 20, para 6(1)(a))

A gift of the home and the arrangement of a right of continued occupation through a lease or licence should have no adverse IHT consequence. Full consideration is required throughout the period of occupation so that a full rent, reviewed regularly, will be essential (see **4.6.5**). A scheme using this paragraph will reduce the donor's estate for IHT but requires the donor to have sufficient income to pay the rent in full and regularly.

4.7.4.4 'Co-ownership' between the parents (donors) and the children (donees)

The Finance Act 1986 introduced some specific exceptions which apply where there is a gift of an undivided share of an interest in land.

Section 102B(4): sharing arrangements

There is no gift with reservation where:

(a) there is a gift of a share in land; and

(b) the donor and the donee both occupy the land; and

(c)   the donor does not receive any benefit, other than a negligible one, which is provided by or at the expense of the donee for some reason connected with the gift.

EXAMPLE

Joe gives 75% of his house to his son, Sid (who lives with him). If Sid then pays all the bills for the property (eg council tax, heating and lighting), Joe has reserved a benefit.

If Sid agrees to pay 75% of both the property and the household bills (so including 75% of the food bills) then again Joe has reserved a benefit.

If Sid agrees to pay 75% of the property bills but the household bills are shared equally then possibly Joe has not reserved a benefit: the property bills are being split in accordance with the ownership ratio whilst each is paying his share of the living expenses (the position might be different if Sid were merely an occasional occupier).

If Joe continues to pay all the bills, there cannot be a problem. In a sense, this is erring on the side of caution (Sid could be made responsible for some of the bills without jeopardising the IHT planning, but as the earlier examples show it is not clear just what he can safely pay), but if Joe can afford it, it is the most attractive solution. And it may be sensible IHT planning for Joe to deplete his estate in this fashion.

Note

(1)   It must be a gift of a share. If the donor gives the whole of the property, the section does not apply.

(2)   There is no ceiling on the size of the share that can be gifted and so a donor could gift 90% of his interest in the property, retaining only a 10% share. However this may not be wise:

    (a)   The gift is a PET and so the donor must survive seven years if tax is to be avoided. Remember that a gift of 20% will cause a bigger than 20% reduction in the value of the transferor's estate because there is now a co-ownership discount.

    (b)   The donee may die before the donor. The gifted share is part of the donee's estate and there may be insufficient funds to pay the IHT due. (Moreover because the sharing arrangement has come to an end, the protection of the exception is lost and the donor will become subject to the reservation of benefit rules.)

(3)   There must be joint occupation, but persons can occupy more than one property, for instance, a town flat and a country cottage, and the length of time spent at each is not determinative in terms of whether or not he occupies the property. Provided a person has the right to come and go at will, has possessions in the property and uses the property from time to time then it is possible to argue that he is in occupation. HMRC is likely to ask questions about length of time spent, registration with GP, direction of mail, electoral roll, but no one element is conclusive.

(4)   It does not matter if the donor moves out but it is fatal if the donee does. These arrangements should only be contemplated where the family arrangement is stable.

(5)   Take care in relation to expenses. The donor must not receive a benefit (other than a negligible one) if a gift with reservation is to be avoided.

(6)   A pre-owned assets tax charge could, in principle, apply to a donor who gives away an interest in land which he continues to occupy. Accordingly, there is a specific exclusion for property which would be subject to a reservation of benefit but for s 102B(4).

Section 102B(3): non-occupation

There is no reservation of benefit where there is a gift of a share in land and the donor does not occupy the land. Hence, if a donor gives away an interest in land which is let but continues to enjoy the income, there is no reservation as a result of s 102(3)(a) (but there will be CGT issues if the property has been owned for some time and has increased in value).

> **EXAMPLE**
>
> Dad buys a rental property and gives 90% of it to his daughter. She agrees that she will let him keep all the income. Dad derives a benefit from the property but is within the statutory exception from the gift with reservation rules.

A simple agreement does not protect the donors. To make the position secure, it would be necessary to settle the gifted share into a trust under which the donors retain a life interest.

> **EXAMPLE**
>
> Parents settle 90% of a let property on trusts for themselves for life then to their son. They are entitled to all the income from the property under the terms of the trust, so are secure. Section 102B(3) protects them from any reservation of benefit.
>
> Because the transfer is to a settlement, it will be immediately chargeable to IHT, so the transfer is unattractive if the value exceeds the available nil rate band.

4.8 GIFTS TO CHARITY

In addition to, or perhaps instead of, gifts to family and friends, a taxpayer may wish to make gifts to his favourite charity or charities.

Although not always considered part of estate planning, such gifts can be achieved in a number of tax-efficient ways and the method chosen will normally be determined by the timing and anticipated amount of the gift.

4.8.1 Inheritance tax

All gifts to a charity, whether made by lifetime gift or by will, and regardless of the amount, are exempt from IHT (IHTA 1984, s 23). A wealthy client may well make sizeable lifetime gifts to charity. These will be exempt and never enter his cumulative total.

Many clients will not be able to afford or wish to make such lifetime donations but will make provision for a charity in their will. This may take the form of a legacy or a gift of residue. The amount given must be deducted as an exemption in the calculation to find the deceased's total chargeable estate.

The will or intestacy of a deceased person may also be varied (see **Chapter 13**) to provide an exempt gift to charity.

Reduced IHT rate on estates

For deaths on or after 6 April 2012 the rate of tax is reduced from 40% to 36% on some or all of the estate if enough of the estate passes to charity (FA 2012, s 207 and Sch 33, which inserted a new Sch 1A into the Inheritance Tax Act 1984). Clearly, if a person leaves all of his estate (or all of the estate in excess of available nil rate band) to charity there will be no tax to pay on the estate. The provisions contained in the FA 2012 are aimed at encouraging those who might want to give some, but not all, of their estate to charity to give more than they might have done in order to get the benefit of the lower rate. The lower rates may mean there is more available for the other non-charitable beneficiaries. The method of calculation to ascertain if enough of the estate is passing to charity can be complex.

The reduced rate applies where a person leaves at least 10% of his net estate (referred to as 'the baseline amount') to charity. Where a person's estate does not contain any property passing by survivorship or any trust property that he is deemed to own then the calculation is relatively straightforward. The baseline amount is the estate less debts, funeral expenses, any exemptions and reliefs other than the charity exemption, and the available nil rate band. The gift to charity needs to be at least 10% of this value for the 36% rate to apply.

EXAMPLE

John, a single man, dies with assets worth £830,000, all in his sole name. These include £20,000 of shares that qualify for 100% business property relief. John's debts and funeral expenses total £10,000, and in his will he leaves £50,000 to a charity and the rest to his great-nephew. John made only one chargeable transfer in the seven years before he died when he gave £25,000 (after applying the annual exemption) to his great-nephew.

The baseline amount is therefore:

	£
Estate	830,000
Less	
Debts and funeral expenses	10,000
	820,000
Less exemptions (ignoring charity) and reliefs	
100% BPR on the shares	20,000
	800,000
Less available NRB	
(£325,000 – £25,000)	300,000
	500,000

As the £50,000 gift to charity is at least 10% of this baseline amount, it means that the 36% rate applies to the estate.

To calculate the tax payable:

	£
Estate	830,000
Less	
Debts and funeral expenses	10,000
	820,000
Less exemptions (charity)	50,000
	770,000
and reliefs	
(100% BPR on the shares)	20,000
Chargeable estate	750,000
Tax	
First £300,000 @ 0%	0
£450,000 @ 36%	162,000
Total tax	162,000
Amount to charity	50,000
Amount to great-nephew	608,000

If the gift to charity had not been enough to meet the 10% requirement, for example if it had been only £45,000, then the tax payable would have been £182,000 instead (£455,000 @ 40%) and the great-nephew would have received only £593,000. It is clearly in the interests of the great-nephew (and the charity) that the gift is the higher amount.

However, when drafting the will, the testator will not be able to state a precise value for a charitable gift to ensure meeting the target and may have to consider using a clause that gives a 'formula' rather than a set amount – for example, a legacy of an amount which will enable the reduced rate to be available on the rest of the estate.

Alternatively, if a will gives too little for the reduced rate to be available, the beneficiaries could choose to make a post-death variation, increasing the gift to charity and securing the reduced IHT rate (see **Chapter 13**).

Whilst the calculation of the baseline amount is relatively straightforward in the example above, the position is more complex where an estate is made up of different elements. The legislation states that, for the purposes of calculating the baseline amount, an estate is made up of the following components:

- property passing by survivorship;
- property within a trust that the deceased is deemed to own (ie where the deceased had a qualifying life interest in trust property);
- property subject to the gift with reservation rules;
- 'general property' that does not fall into the above categories.

Each component is looked at separately, and if at least 10% of that component is left to charity, tax on the rest of that component is charged at the reduced rate.

EXAMPLE

Marsha is the life tenant of a trust created in her father's will which after her death is to pass half to her children and half to charity. The value of the trust fund is £400,000 and she has £200,000 of free estate which she leaves to her children. Clearly more than 10% of the baseline value of the trust component is passing to charity, so the reduced rate is available on the half of the trust fund passing to the deceased's children.

Where an estate consists of more than one component, in order to calculate the baseline value of each component, it is necessary to apportion the nil rate band between the different components. It is possible to elect to merge the components (see below). The effect of a merger election is that the merged components are treated as one for the purposes of the 10% test. Merger elections are therefore useful where a significant portion of one component is left to charity as the reduced rate may then be available on the whole merged value (as would be the case in the previous example where half of the trust fund is passing to charity). The election is made by the 'appropriate persons' who are the surviving joint tenant(s) for the joint property component, the trustees for the settled property component, the donee in the case of property subject to a reservation and the personal representatives in the case of the general component.

There is detailed explanation and guidance on how to calculate tax in these circumstances in the IHT manual available on the GOV.UK website, but the following provides an illustration of the position where there is more than one component.

EXAMPLE

Ben has died. His nil rate band available for the death estate is £325,000. Ben owned a house with his brother as joint tenants. His share, after allowing the co-ownership discount, is worth £100,000. He owned other assets that fall into the general component totalling £435,000. Debts and funeral expenses are £10,000.

He leaves £25,000 to charity and the rest to his friend, Ken.

This time the baseline amount is calculated as follows:

General component	£
Value of general component	435,000
Less	
Debts and funeral expenses	10,000
	425,000

Less exemptions (<u>including</u> charity exemption – this is required by the legislation in order to calculate the correct nil rate band apportionment) and reliefs

Gift to charity	25,000
Net general component	400,000
Add the survivorship component	100,000
Total of net components	500,000
Apportion the nil rate band between the two components by dividing the net general component (£400,000) by the net total components (£500,000) and multiplying by £325,000	260,000
Deduct the apportioned nil rate band from the net general component	400,000 –260,000
	140,000
Add back the value of the gift to charity	25,000
The baseline amount	165,000

The gift to charity (£25,000) is at least 10% of this baseline amount so the tax on the general component of the estate will be 36%. The tax on the joint tenancy property will be 40%, unless an election is made to merge the two components, ie add them together to assess if the gift of £25,000 is at least 10% of the total merged figure. If that is the case then the 36% rate will apply to both components. In this example, the baseline value of the merged components, after deducting debts and the full nil rate band, is £200,000. The gift to charity is more than 10% of this, so the 36% rate can apply to both components.

The legislation permits personal representatives to opt out of assessing if the lower rate of tax may apply. This would be of use where the cost of valuing assets in the estate would outweigh any possible tax savings.

4.8.2 Capital gains tax (TCGA 1992, s 257)

The most common form of charitable gift is of cash and therefore CGT is not relevant.

Where, however, a taxpayer is transferring chargeable assets to a charity, the gift will be at no gain no loss (the rule works in a similar way to inter-spouse transfers, see **4.4.5.1**).

For property left to charity by will, the organisation will receive the property at probate value at the testator's death. As with lifetime gifts, when the charity disposes of the property any gains should be exempt from CGT.

4.8.3 Income tax

There are various schemes for lifetime payments to charity which are income tax effective for the donor and which should, therefore, be especially attractive to higher rate taxpayers. These include payroll giving (ITEPA 2003, s 713), gift aid (ITA 2007, ss 414–416) and charitable gift relief (ITA 2007, ss 431, 434).

4.9 STAMP DUTY AND STAMP DUTY LAND TAX

Stamp duty is a tax on documents, not transactions. Broadly, it now applies in relation to transactions involving shares and other marketable securities. Therefore where a document effects the transfer of these types of property, that document is subject to stamp duty. For documents executed on or after 13 March 2008 there is no ad valorem stamp duty if the transaction is for consideration of £1,000 or less, and if the document effects a voluntary transfer there is no fixed duty.

From 1 December 2003 stamp duty was abolished in relation to land transactions. Instead, transactions in land are subject to stamp duty land tax.

A transaction in land is subject to the charge if, according to FA 2003, it is:

(a)   a land transaction;

(b)   effected for consideration;

(c)   which is not exempt.

Voluntary transactions are thus not liable to the tax.

Stamp duty land tax rates depend on the value of the property purchased (see below). However, since 6 April 2016, a person buying a second property (or having an interest in a second property) pays an additional 3%.

There is an exception where the property purchased replaces a main residence. The question of whether or not a residence is a main residence is a question of fact. Taxpayers cannot elect for this purpose.

EXAMPLE

(1)   Fred has a main residence. He buys a holiday home. He will pay the additional rate on the holiday home.

(2)   Fred has a main residence and a holiday home. He sells his main residence and replaces it with another. He does not pay the additional rate on the replacement main residence.

Special provision is made for the (relatively common) situation arising where purchases and sales are not synchronised to avoid buyers becoming subject to the additional rate.

In the case of trusts, the additional rate is payable unless a beneficiary has either a right to occupy a dwelling owned by the trust for life or is entitled to the income from a dwelling owned by the trust, in which case the beneficiary will be treated as the purchaser. Whether or not the additional rate is payable will depend on whether the beneficiary has a second property (or interest in a second property). Note the difference for this purpose between a beneficiary with an occupation right which must be for life and the right to receive income which does not have to be for life.

EXAMPLE

Ben has a right to income from a trust for 10 years. The trust buys a dwelling which is rented out. Ben is entitled to the income, so if he does not own another dwelling, the additional 3% is not payable. However, as he is treated as the buyer of the trust property, the additional 3% would be payable if he bought his first home while still entitled to receive the income from the trust.

Rates from 1 October 2021 are as follows:

Property or lease premium or transfer value	SDLT rate
Up to £125,000	zero
The next £125,000 (the portion from £125,001 to £250,000)	2%
The next £675,000 (the portion from £250,001 to £925,000)	5%
The next £575,000 (the portion from £925,001 to £1.5m)	10%
The remaining amount (the portion above £1.5m)	12%

The additional 3% is payable if the purchase is of an additional residence (unless it is a replacement of a main residence, as explained above).

First time buyers' relief is available to buyers who have never owned a residence or interest in a residence and who buy property for no more than £625,000 (increased from £500,000 for purchases on or after 23 September 2022). Tax is at 0% on the first £425,000 and 5% on the balance.

The conditions for this valuable relief are contained in the Finance Act 2003, Sch 6ZA, and are that:

(1)   the purchased dwelling is a major interest in a single dwelling;

(2)   the consideration is no more than £625,000;

(3)   the purchaser (or each of them, if more than one) is a 'first time buyer' who intends to occupy as their only or main residence; and

(4)   the transaction is not linked to another, or is only linked in relation to a garden of the dwelling or an interest or right to land benefitting the dwelling or its garden.

'First time buyer' is defined to exclude anyone who has previously acquired any equitable interest in a dwelling, either by purchase or by gift or inheritance. It picks up any previous interests owned, whether or not as a personal home. Hence a person who inherited an interest in a dwelling is not a first time buyer even if the dwelling is subsequently sold.

> **EXAMPLE**
>
> Grandma died in 2015 leaving her four grandchildren a 10% share in her property, with 20% to each of her three children. When she died, the property was worth £100,000 and was kept for two years, and let out for income, before being sold. Each of the grandchildren is now denied first time buyers' relief (though they will not be liable for the additional 3%).

Schedule 6ZA, para 1(7) provides that first time buyers' relief is not available if the higher rates are payable on a purchase. This can catch beneficiaries of trusts who are buying their first dwelling.

> **EXAMPLE**
>
> Wanda is a widow who has never owned a dwelling. Her husband died and left the family home to her for life, remainder to their children.
>
> Wanda proposes to buy a property to live in and wants the trustees to rent out the former family home. She will not benefit from first time buyers' relief because she is treated as the owner of the trust property, with the result that the transaction is subject to the higher rates.

4.10   ANTI-AVOIDANCE

Financial planning is concerned with maximising the wealth (capital and income) of the individual. Estate planning is concerned with the passing on of that wealth within the family.

This can be achieved by lifetime transfers or by will or a combination of the two. Each client is unique and requires a personal plan. The task of the solicitor is to identify the possibilities for estate planning. However much the solicitor believes in a course of action, the decision whether or not to take it is the client's alone.

Tax avoidance through the use of available reliefs and exemptions as in the previous paragraphs is a legitimate activity. However, some schemes designed for taxpayers by their advisers have been so contrived, and the potential savings so great, that legislation has been enacted to combat their effectiveness. The Revenue has successfully challenged some schemes in the courts (see, for example, *Ingram and Another (Executors of the estate of Lady Ingram, deceased) v Inland Revenue Commissioners* [2000] 1 AC 293).

4.10.1 The general anti-abuse rule (GAAR)

FA 2013 (Pt 5 and Sch 43) introduced a general anti-abuse rule (known as GAAR), which is supplemented by Revenue guidance. The rule is aimed at 'tax advantages arising from tax arrangements that are abusive'. Section 207(2) of the Finance Act 2013 defines 'abusive' arrangements as follows:

> Tax arrangements are abusive if they are arrangements the entering into or carrying out of which cannot reasonably be regarded as a reasonable course of action in relation to the relevant tax provisions, having regard to all the circumstances including—
>
> (a) whether the substantive results of the arrangements are consistent with any principles on which those provisions are based (whether express or implied) and the policy objectives of those provisions,
>
> (b) whether the means of achieving those results involves one or more contrived or abnormal steps, and
>
> (c) whether the arrangements are intended to exploit any shortcomings in those provisions.

If tax arrangements are abusive and are successfully challenged under GAAR, such adjustments are to be made as shall be 'just and reasonable'. This may be the disallowance of a loss or may result in the arrangement being ignored altogether (as will be the case with circular self-cancelling arrangements).

In determining any issue concerning GAAR, a court or tribunal must take into account the GAAR Guidance and the opinions of the members of the Advisory Panel about the tax arrangements in question. It must also take account of other materials in the public domain at the time when the arrangement was entered into (including ministerial statements) and evidence of Revenue practice (for instance, had it accepted the scheme in question).

4.10.2 The Disclosure of Tax Avoidance Scheme (DOTAS) Regulations

A further weapon is available to HMRC in the form of the Disclosure of Tax Avoidance Scheme (DOTAS) Regulations. These have been introduced gradually in relation to different taxes since 2004. As the name suggests, the Regulations require those devising new tax avoidance schemes (called 'promoters') to send details of the schemes to HMRC. This gives HMRC early warning of such schemes and an opportunity to consider whether or not new legislation is needed.

The Inheritance Tax Avoidance Schemes (Prescribed Descriptions of Arrangements) Regulations 2011 (SI 2011/170) extended reporting to inheritance tax in very limited circumstances. It was only necessary to report schemes if:

(a) as a result of any element of the arrangements, property becomes relevant property; and

(b) a main benefit of the arrangements is that an advantage is obtained in relation to a relevant property entry charge.

A 'relevant property entry charge' arises when property in excess of the nil rate band is transferred to a relevant property trust. There was no requirement to report new arrangements designed to minimise inheritance tax arising on other occasions, for example on 10-year anniversaries.

In 2014 HMRC announced that it proposed to extend the DOTAS rules in relation to IHT on the basis that the narrow scope of the hallmark meant that very few IHT arrangements were reported.

After a lengthy consultation period (and two sets of draft regulations), the Inheritance Tax Avoidance Schemes (Prescribed Descriptions of Arrangements) Regulations 2017 (SI 2017/1172) came into effect as from 1 April 2018. They replace the old regulations.

There is an 'established practice' exemption designed to remove from the scope of the hallmark established IHT planning schemes whose workings are well understood and agreed by HMRC. 'Established practice' is not defined in the legislation and, therefore, takes its ordinary meaning. The guidance says that it may be demonstrated by reference to published material (whether from HMRC or textbooks or articles in journals) or by other written evidence of what had become a common practice by the relevant time (that is, when the arrangements were entered into). The arrangements actually carried out must be the same as those identified as established practice if the exemption is to apply.

Arrangements which are not within the exception must be notified if it would be reasonable to expect an informed observer (having studied the arrangements and having regard to all relevant circumstances) to conclude that Condition 1 and Condition 2 are met.

Condition 1 is that the main purpose, or one of the main purposes, of the arrangements is to enable a person to obtain one or more of the following advantages in relation to inheritance tax (the 'tax advantage'):

(a)   the avoidance or reduction of a relevant property entry charge;

(b)   the avoidance or reduction of:

(i)   a 10-year anniversary or exit charge (IHTA 1984, ss 64, 65), or

(ii)   exit charges from employee/newspaper trusts (IHTA 1984, s 72), or

(iii)   a charge on a gift made by a close company that is treated as having been made by the participators (IHTA 1984, s 94);

(c)   the avoidance or reduction of a charge to inheritance tax arising from the application of s 102, s 102ZA, s 102A or s 102B of the Finance Act 1986 (gifts with reservation) in circumstances where there is also no pre-owned assets charge to income tax under Sch 15 to the Finance Act 2004);

(d)   a reduction in the value of a person's estate without giving rise to a chargeable transfer or potentially exempt transfer.

Condition 2 is that the arrangements involve one or more contrived or abnormal steps without which the tax advantage could not be obtained.

HMRC promised guidance 'in good time before the hallmark comes into force on 1 April 2018'. It became available via a link in the March 2018 *Trusts and Estates Newsletter* on 29 March 2018.

The guidance contains a number of examples of transactions which do not require disclosure and a much shorter list of transactions which HMRC considers probably do.

Examples of non-notifiable arrangements include:

(1)   *Lifetime gifts to spouses or civil partners and regular gifts out of income.* The guidance states that although Condition 1(d) is met, there is no contrived or abnormal arrangement.

(2)   *Lifetime transfers of value equal to the available nil rate band into a trust, which may be repeated every seven years, and lifetime transfers to a bare trust for a minor beneficiary.* The guidance states that in neither case is Condition 1 met. The estate is reduced but there is a chargeable transfer in the first case and a PET in the second.

(3)   *Executing a will that leaves property to an exempt beneficiary such as a spouse or charity.* The guidance here says:

> Executing a will does not meet any of the elements of condition 1. Although a will may be executed to reduce or avoid the IHT charge on death by use of exemptions, the will does not reduce the person's estate. Rather the will determines how the estate devolves on death and it is this devolution which secures any IHT exemption. As there is no reduction in the person's estate without giving rise to a chargeable transfer, condition 1(d) is not met.

(4)   *Purchase of shares which will qualify for business property relief after they have been owned for two years.* The guidance states that Condition 1 is not fulfilled. The purchase of shares does not reduce the value of a person's estate. Business property relief, if available, only has the effect of reducing the value transferred by a transfer of value; it does not remove the value of the shares from the estate.

The list of arrangements which are likely to be notifiable is short. HMRC says that because all the relevant circumstances of the particular arrangements have to be taken into account, the guidance has to be less definite here. However, it makes the point that arrangements which include multiple steps in order to achieve the intended tax advantage carry an increased likelihood that they may be notifiable.

Included in the examples are arrangements giving shares which qualify for business property relief into trust with a subsequent sale back to the transferor.

The guidance states that, in isolation, the transfer of shares qualifying for relief into a trust, or the sale of trust assets by the trustees, would not meet Condition 1. However, where arrangements are entered into with the intention that all of these steps take place, the arrangements have the effect of placing cash into a relevant property trust, but without incurring a relevant property entry charge.

As one of the main purposes of these arrangements is to reduce or avoid a relevant property entry charge, it would be reasonable to expect an informed observer to conclude that Condition 1(a) is met.

It would not normally be possible to transfer cash into a relevant property trust without incurring a relevant property entry charge, which is what has been achieved. To achieve this outcome and to gain this tax advantage, contrived steps are necessary, that is the transfer of shares qualifying for relief followed by their sale back to the transferor, rather than the simple transfer of cash which would be the non-contrived way of achieving the same result. Without these contrived steps, the tax advantage would not arise. It would therefore be reasonable to expect an informed observer to conclude, considering the arrangements as a whole, that Condition 2 was met.

This can be contrasted to a situation where, for example, family company shares are transferred into trust for succession planning purposes, at which time there is no intention of the trustees selling those shares. If the trustees later took an independent decision to sell the shares, it is unlikely that an informed observer would conclude that these separate steps form part of a single overall arrangement, or to conclude that Condition 1(a) was met.

4.10.3 Associated operations

Where an IHT saving is achieved through a series of artificial steps carried out as a tax-saving measure only, the Revenue may be able to ignore the intervening steps and therefore negate the effect of the scheme (IHTA 1984, s 268).

4.10.4 Conclusion

All practitioners need to be aware of the anti-avoidance legislation and cases (eg, ICTA 1988, s 674A; ITA 2007, Pt 13; IHTA 1984, s 268; and a series of cases beginning with *WT Ramsay Ltd v Inland Revenue Commissioners; Eilbeck (Inspector of Taxes) v Rawling* [1982] AC 300 and *Furniss (Inspector of Taxes) v Dawson* [1984] 1 AC 474) in putting forward tax-saving schemes.

SUMMARY

(1) A client may wish to give away assets during his lifetime for tax reasons, for example:

    (a) to reduce the value of his estate on death;

    (b) to take advantage of the lower income and CGT rates of a spouse or civil partner.

(2) There are numerous exemptions and reliefs available which clients may consider using, and there are some tax pitfalls to be avoided when making outright gifts.

(3) Clients should always consider the practical consequences of making lifetime gifts and not give away anything that they may later regret.

REVIEW ACTIVITY

Question 1

Ed died in July 2020. He made no lifetime gifts, and left a gift of £81,250 to his nephew in his will, and the rest of his estate to his wife, Daisy.

Daisy gave a painting worth £25,000 to her sister in February 2019, but otherwise made no lifetime transfers. Daisy died on 1 March 2022, when the painting was worth £30,000.

Which ONE of the following is CORRECT?

A   Daisy made a PET of £25,000.

B   There will be tapering relief on the PET, reducing the value transferred by 20%.

C   The nil rate band available for Daisy's estate will be increased by £243,750.

D   Daisy made a PET of £30,000.

Answer: C

Daisy made a PET when she gave the painting to her sister. The value transferred can be reduced by use of the annual exemptions. Daisy made no other transfers so the exemption for 2017/18 and for 2018/19 can be deducted. The increase in value of the painting does not matter – it is the value at the date of the transfer that is relevant. The PET has become chargeable but is within Daisy's nil rate band. Although she died between three and four years after the transfer, tapering relief is of no effect because it reduces the tax payable on the PET (here none), not the value transferred. Ed had only used 25% of his nil rate band when he died, so Daisy's estate receives an increase of 75% of the value of the nil rate band in force at the time of her death.

Question 2 (a continuation of Question 1)

Daisy had the following assets on her death on 1 March 2022:

- shares in an unquoted trading company which she inherited from Ed, who had bought them in July 2019
- a life interest in a trust created in 2014 by her grandfather's will (remainder to Daisy's brother) (Trust A)
- a life interest in a trust created in 2005 by her father during his lifetime (remainder to Daisy's brother) (Trust B)
- a life interest in a trust created in 2015 by her mother during her lifetime (remainder to Daisy's brother) (Trust C)
- a remainder interest in a trust created in 2016 by her grandmother's will (life interest is held by Daisy's mother) (Trust D)

Daisy's assets totalled £3 million, after debts. Daisy left a gift of £2,000 to charity and the rest of her estate to her nephew.

Which ONE of the following is correct?

A   The unquoted shares are eligible for business property relief.

B   None of the interests in the trusts form part of Daisy's estate for IHT purposes.

C   Only the interest in Trust A forms part of Daisy's estate for IHT purposes.

D   The gift to charity will be taxed at 36%.

E   If Daisy had given away her interest in Trust D to her nephew before her death, she would have made a PET.

Answer: A

The shares are in an unquoted trading company, and although Daisy did not own them for two years before she died, as she inherited them from her husband she can add his period of ownership to her own, thus allowing them to qualify for business property relief.

The life interests held by Daisy in Trust A and Trust B are qualifying life interests and so treated as part of Daisy's estate. Trust A is a qualifying one because it was created on death, and Trust B is a qualifying interest because, although created by lifetime declaration, it was created before 22 March 2006. The interest in Trust C is not a qualifying one as it was not created on death and created on or after 22 March 2006. It therefore does not form part of Daisy's IHT estate.

The gift to charity is exempt from IHT. The 36% rate only applies to the non-exempt part of the estate and only if a sufficient proportion of the estate is left to charity.

The remainder interest in Trust D is excluded property (as the person with the life interest is still alive). It does not form part of Daisy's IHT estate, and if she had given her interest in this trust away before she died, it would not have been a transfer of value. (For succession purposes the three life interests all end and the capital passes to the remainderman, and not under Daisy's will. When Daisy's mother dies, Daisy's remainder interest in trust D will pass as part of Daisy's estate under her will.)

Question 3

Mel worked for X Co PLC (a confectionary manufacturer) until she retired in January 2020. Since then she has been an employee of her husband's design business, Y Co Ltd.

She makes the following gifts in February 2022:

- £200,000 to her husband
- her shareholding in X Co PLC worth £400,000 (owned for two years, and giving 6% voting rights and entitlement to 6% of distributable profits and assets on winding up) to her son
- her shareholding in Y Co Ltd worth £10,000 (given to her three years earlier by her husband from his existing shareholding, and giving 3% voting rights and entitlement to 3% of distributable profits and assets on winding up) to her daughter

Which ONE of the following is CORRECT?

A   The gift of shares in X Co PLC is eligible for business asset disposal relief and for hold-over relief.

B   The gift of shares in X Co PLC is eligible for hold-over relief.

C   The gift of shares in Y Co Ltd is eligible for business asset disposal relief and for hold-over relief.

D   The gift to her husband is at no gain or loss for CGT purposes.

Answer: B

The gift of shares in X Co PLC is not eligible for business asset disposal relief because, although the company is a trading company, Mel had at least 5% voting rights and had owned them for at least two years before the disposal, she was not also an employee or officer of the company for a year before the disposal. The gift of shares in Y Co Ltd is not eligible because the shareholding gives insufficient rights. (The investment does not fulfil the requirements for investors' relief.)

Both gifts of shares do qualify for hold-over relief under s 165 of the TCGA 1992. The shares in X Co PLC are quoted, but the company is Mel's personal company because she held at least 5% of the voting rights etc. There is no requirement for her to work for the company, or to have held the shares for any length of time. The shares in Y Co Ltd are not quoted and so it does not matter that Mel held less than 5% voting rights.

Disposals of chargeable assets by one spouse to another are at no gain or loss, but here the asset transferred is cash and so CGT is not relevant.

INTRODUCTION TO SETTLEMENTS

LEARNING OUTCOMES

After reading this chapter you will be able to:

- explain what the term 'settlement' means
- identify the different types of settlement and when they are used
- explain the tax consequences of creating a lifetime settlement.

5.1 INTRODUCTION

The term 'settlement' has a variety of meanings depending upon the context in which it is used. It is important to understand what private client lawyers mean when they talk about 'settlements'. In the private client department, the term is commonly used to include any arrangement whereby an individual 'settles' property of any kind upon trust for a beneficiary or group of beneficiaries. The term 'settlement' refers to the whole arrangement; the 'trusts' are the terms upon which the property is held (although informally many people refer to a settlement as 'a trust').

Contrast the following statutory uses of the term:

(a) Under the SLA 1925, a 'settlement' or 'strict settlement' is a trust of land where no trust for sale is imposed. Under the SLA 1925 a beneficiary who has the right to enjoy the land (the tenant for life) has many of the powers over the property which would normally be vested in the trustees (eg, the power to sell the land). TLATA 1996 prevents the creation of any new strict settlements. (The TA 2000, Sch 2 provides that SLA 1925 investments will be made at the discretion of the trustees and no longer at the direction of the tenant for life.)

(b) In tax statutes, the term 'settlement' is frequently used and is defined in a variety of different ways, often very widely. For example, a parental 'settlement' for income tax purposes includes not only a settlement upon trust, but also an outright gift (see **4.6.4.1**).

In this chapter we look at the main types of lifetime settlement and explore:

(a) what can be achieved by a settlement; and

(b) the taxation cost to the settlor,

with a view to being able to help a client select the appropriate type of settlement for his particular purpose.

Different considerations apply to the creation of settlement by will, so apart from a very brief overview, this topic is dealt with separately in **Chapter 12**.

5.1.1 Trusts background – some reminders

5.1.1.1 Fixed interest trusts

When an individual ('the settlor') settles property upon trust, he may wish to determine the precise extent to which his chosen beneficiaries are to enjoy the settled property in the future. He may, for example, divide their enjoyment of the property by creating successive interests, or he may prevent beneficiaries from obtaining access to the capital before a certain age by giving them contingent interests.

Where capital or income is to be divided between a group of individuals, the settlor may determine the extent of each beneficiary's share. It is possible to define beneficiaries by reference to a description rather than by naming them (eg, my grandchildren), provided that the description is sufficiently clear to enable the beneficiaries to be identified with certainty.

The settlor who creates such a trust gives fixed equitable interests to the beneficiaries. Each beneficiary has a bundle of rights resembling an interest in property which he may sell or give away (provided that any such assignment complies with s 53(1)(c) of the LPA 1925).

If the beneficiaries are between them entitled to the whole equitable interest and are all of full age and capacity, they may by agreement put an end to the trust, calling for the trustees to distribute the capital between them in such shares as they may agree (the rule in *Saunders v Vautier* (1841) 4 Beav 115 – see **10.2.3**).

Under TLATA 1996, s 19, such beneficiaries can require the existing trustees to retire and appoint specified new trustees to replace them. This procedure is often preferable to bringing the trust to an end as it avoids the potential CGT liability which arises when a trust ends.

Neither option is available if any beneficiary is a minor, or if there are potential beneficiaries who may be born in the future, although the court has power to consent on behalf of such beneficiaries under the VTA 1958 (see **13.3.4.1**).

The period during which the settlor may dictate how the property is to be held is limited by the rule against remoteness of vesting; interests which do not vest within the perpetuity period will fail (see **6.9**). If the trusts in the settlement should fail for this or any other reason, the property will revert to the settlor (or his estate if he is dead).

5.1.1.2 Discretionary trusts

A settlor may not wish to determine in advance the precise extent of each beneficiary's entitlement. In such a case, he may nominate a category of beneficiaries and give his trustees the power to determine how much (if anything) each potential beneficiary should receive.

The trustees' discretion may simply concern the distribution of income. If the trustees are obliged to distribute the income each year, the trusts are said to be 'exhaustive'. Alternatively, the settlor may widen the trustees' discretion to allow them to retain or accumulate the income as they think fit ('non-exhaustive' trusts). The period during which a power to accumulate income may continue is limited by the rule against accumulations in the case of settlements not governed by the Perpetuities and Accumulations Act 2009 (PAA 2009). In the case of settlements governed by the PAA 2009, trustees can accumulate throughout the lifetime of the settlement unless the settlor has provided otherwise (see **6.10**).

A discretion over the distribution of income may be combined with fixed interests in capital. A common example is to leave capital 'to such of my children as reach the age of 25 equally if more than one', with a direction that the trustees can apply income arising before the capital vests as they see fit.

Alternatively, the trustees' discretion may extend to capital as well as income, giving the trustees the power to distribute capital to one or more of the designated class of beneficiaries at any time (and thus, if they think fit, bring an end to the trust).

A beneficiary under a discretionary trust cannot claim any property as of right. He has only a hope that the trustees will exercise their discretion in his favour.

The extent of the interest of a discretionary beneficiary was recently considered (albeit *obiter*) by Matthews J in *Smith and another v Michelmores Trust Corp Ltd* [2021] EWHC 1425 (Ch), who concluded that a member of a discretionary class has various rights which may be vindicated by court action, for example the right to be considered by the trustees and the right to restrain by injunction a threatened breach of trust. That bundle of rights constitutes the beneficiary's or object's interest, which, according to Matthews J, is something which the beneficiary can choose to disclaim.

Although in principle the rule in *Saunders v Vautier* would allow all the potential beneficiaries to end the trust by agreement, this is unlikely to be possible in practice as the class will be too widely drawn for all the potential beneficiaries to be ascertained and of full age and capacity.

Any discretion over income or capital must be limited to the perpetuity period in order to comply with the rule against remoteness of vesting. A fixed period, called the 'trust period', is usually specified in the trust instrument and the trustees will normally distribute the whole fund within that period. See **6.9** below.

If, however, all members of the class of beneficiaries should die before the trustees have distributed the capital, the trusts will fail. The property will pass to the beneficiary entitled in default if the settlement has been drafted to include one. If no default beneficiary is named, the property will revert to the settlor (or his estate, if he is dead) on a resulting trust. For tax reasons, it is important to avoid any possibility of 'reverter to settlor' in a lifetime trust (see **6.15**) and so an 'ultimate default' provision, usually in favour of a charity, is included (see **6.15.4**) to ensure that the property cannot revert.

There is a difficult distinction between a power of appointment and a discretionary trust or 'trust power'. A trust power arises where the settlor's overriding intention is to benefit a particular class of beneficiaries, giving a power of selection to his trustees. A power of appointment involves no such overriding intention: if the power is not exercised, the property will pass in default of appointment. The distinction was once important because there was a different test for certainty of objects. However, the tests are now the same (*McPhail and Others v Doulton and Others* [1971] AC 424) and the distinction is largely academic. In practice, the trustees' power of selection is commonly expressed as a widely drawn power of appointment enabling them not only to give capital outright to a beneficiary, but also to resettle it on new trusts for the benefit of particular members of the class (see **Chapter 9** and **Appendix 3**, clause 6.2).

5.1.2 Settlements in practice

There are many rules of equity and statutory provisions which have a practical effect on the creation and use of settlements. The most important of these are the tax provisions which govern the treatment of the settlement for tax purposes on its creation, during its life and when it comes to an end.

The FA 2006 introduced substantial changes to the way in which settlements are treated for IHT purposes. Inevitably this has complicated matters, as it means that there are pre- and post-2006 rules to get to grips with.

This chapter is mainly concerned with the taxation implications of the lifetime creation of settlements.

5.2   INHERITANCE TAX AND SETTLEMENTS

5.2.1   The significance of 22 March 2006

22 March 2006 was Budget Day. Without any warning or consultation, the Chancellor introduced huge changes to the way in which trusts were to be treated for IHT purposes. The Treasury had formed the view that settlements were being used primarily to escape IHT and was determined to make them less attractive. The intention was to encourage people to make outright gifts rather than to use trusts. There was concerted opposition from professional advisers and the press, who pointed out that trusts are used for all kinds of tax-neutral reasons. The Treasury backed down to some extent in relation to settlements created on death, but made very few concessions in relation to lifetime settlements. The date, therefore, remains a significant watershed in the tax treatment of settlements.

In the case of trusts created before 22 March 2006, the crucial question is whether or not the settlement has an interest in possession (see **5.2.2** below). This is because the IHT treatment of pre-22 March 2006 settlements with and without interests in possession is entirely different. It makes no difference whether the settlement is created by lifetime transfer or on death. Trusts for a disabled beneficiary were treated as if they had an interest in possession for IHT purposes provided they fulfilled certain criteria.

In the case of settlements created on or after 22 March 2006, the main question is whether the settlement is created by a lifetime transfer or on death. With an exception for settlements for disabled beneficiaries, all lifetime settlements are treated in the same way irrespective of whether or not a beneficiary has an interest in possession. Settlements created on death on or after 22 March 2006 have some special rules, which we shall look at in **Chapter 12**.

This chapter deals with the tax implications of creating *lifetime* settlements. However, for completeness, there is a brief summary of the rules applying to settlements created on death at **5.2.5**.

5.2.2   What is an interest in possession?

An 'interest in possession' was defined in *Pearson and Others v IRC* [1980] 2 All ER 479 as 'a present right to the present enjoyment' of income or assets. Put more simply, it means that the trustees have to pay the annual trust income to a beneficiary, or allow the beneficiary to have the use of assets.

The simplest example of an interest in possession is a life interest.

> **EXAMPLE**
>
> Adam gives £100,000 to trustees to hold on trust for Brenda for life with the remainder to Colin. Brenda has an interest in possession. She is entitled to all the income generated by the trust fund of £100,000. The trustees must pay that income to her.

The purpose of this type of settlement is to provide successive interests. There are various reasons for doing this:

(a)   The settlor may want to benefit several people, one after the other.

> **EXAMPLE**
>
> Dipika wants to benefit her son and daughter-in-law by giving them extra income. She also wants to benefit her grandson. She might set up a trust giving:
>
> (i)   the income to her son for life; and on his death
>
> (ii)   the income to her daughter-in-law (if still living) for life; and on the death of the survivor of her son and daughter-in-law
>
> (iii)   the capital to the grandson absolutely.

(b)   The settlor may wish to give one person the right to income for a given time and then the capital to somebody else.

> **EXAMPLE**
>
> Eashan wants to provide finance for his granddaughter while she studies to be an architect. He thinks she will need his support for about eight years, but ultimately he wants all his money to go to his favourite charity. He might set up a trust giving:
>
> (i)   the income to his granddaughter for eight years or until she qualifies as an architect, whichever is the shorter period; and then
>
> (ii)   the capital to the charity absolutely.

(c)   The settlor may want to stagger a beneficiary's entitlement to property.

> **EXAMPLE**
>
> Fred wants to give a substantial sum of money to his grandson George, who is 19. George is in urgent need of some money, but Fred does not want him to receive everything immediately. Fred might set up a trust giving:
>
> (i)   the income to George until he is 25 years of age; and then
>
> (ii)   the capital to George absolutely.

Note: If the trustees have the power to decide whether or not to pay income to a beneficiary, it is not an interest in possession trust. However, if the trustees are given an overriding power to terminate a beneficiary's right to income, the trust is an interest in possession trust, unless, and until, the trustees exercise the power of termination.

5.2.3   Settlements created before 22 March 2006

As we have already seen in the diagram at **5.2.1,** it is essential from an IHT point of view to determine whether or not a settlement created before 22 March has an interest in possession. Settlements that do have such an interest are subject to a different IHT regime from those that do not.

A beneficiary with an interest in possession in settled property created before 22 March 2006 is treated as beneficially entitled to the property in which the interest subsists (IHTA 1984, s 49(1)). This means that the beneficiary is treated as the owner of the underlying trust property, with important IHT consequences:

(a)   on creation; and

(b)   on termination of the beneficiary's interest in possession.

Interests in possession in existence on 22 March 2006 are often referred to as 'qualifying' interests in possession. It makes no difference whether the settlement was created by lifetime transfer or on death.

Where no beneficiary has a qualifying interest in possession the trust itself is taxed. Again, it makes no difference whether the settlement was created by lifetime transfer or on death.

Settlements created for the benefit of disabled beneficiaries are often created without an interest in possession. These settlements receive special IHT treatment, which means they are taxed as if there was an interest in possession. This special treatment continues after 22 March 2006.

5.2.3.1   Settlements with an interest in possession created before 22 March 2006

Inheritance tax on creation

The settlor's transfer to the settlement is a PET in so far as not exempt (IHTA 1984, s 3A). It might be exempt because an annual exemption is available, or because the beneficiary is a spouse or civil partner of the settlor.

Where a settlor dies within seven years of creating the settlement, the PET becomes chargeable. The trustees will pay the tax from the settlement funds.

EXAMPLE

On 1 March 2006 Harriet transfers £340,000 in cash and shares to a settlement for her brother for life, remainder to her nephew. She has already made chargeable transfers which exhausted her nil rate band and has no annual exemptions available.

The lifetime transfer to the settlement is a PET under IHTA 1984, s 3A, so no IHT is paid at the time of the transfer. If Harriet survives seven years, the PET becomes fully exempt and has no IHT implications. If she dies on 8 February 2013 with assets of £130,000 which she leaves to her sister, the PET becomes chargeable. Taper relief applies as Harriet died more than six years but less than seven years after the PET.

	£
Value transferred	340,000
IHT on £340,000 @ 40%	136,000

20% of £136,000 is payable because of taper relief, ie £27,200.

The tax is due six months from the end of the month in which Harriet died and must be paid by the trustees from the trust fund, so reducing the present value of the trust fund by £27,200. The whole of her death estate will be taxed at 40% as the transfer to the trust has exhausted her nil rate band.

Harriet could avoid the fund being reduced by the tax chargeable on her death by insuring her life for seven years and writing the policy in trust for the trustees of the settlement. The trustees would receive the proceeds of the policy as additional trust property after her death.

She could direct that the tax on lifetime transfers is to be paid from her free estate.

Inheritance tax on termination of the beneficiary's interest

A beneficiary with a qualifying interest in possession is treated as the owner of the trust property so:

(a)   if the beneficiary dies, the trust property is aggregated with his death estate; and

(b)   if the interest terminates in any other way (eg by surrender or assignment), the beneficiary is treated as making a transfer of value.

Note: All interests in possession in existence on 22 March 2006 continue to be taxed in this way.

Transitional serial interests

The FA 2006 contains provisions relating to 'transitional serial interests'. In certain circumstances an interest in possession which arises after 22 March 2006 but which follows a qualifying interest in possession in existence on that date is treated for IHT purposes as if it had been created before 22 March 2006.

One example is a surviving spouse taking an interest following the death of his or her spouse.

Note that a transitional serial interest does not arise if the spouse's successive interest follows a lifetime termination of the interest in possession.

EXAMPLE

Saira created a settlement in February 2000 for 'my daughter for life, remainder to her husband for life, remainder to her children absolutely'. The daughter dies in 2028; her husband is still alive; he is treated as if he had a pre-22 March 2006 interest in possession.

However, if during the daughter's lifetime trustees had used their powers to terminate her life interest and accelerate her husband's life interest, he would not be treated as having a pre-22 March 2006 interest in possession.

Another example of a transitional serial interest occurs where an interest in existence on 22 March 2006 ended in the period between 22 March 2006 and 1 October 2008 and was replaced by a further interest in possession.

We do not consider transitional serial interests further in this book. The relevant legislation is IHTA 1984, ss 49B–49E.

5.2.3.2   Settlements without an interest in possession created before 22 March 2006

No beneficiary is treated as owning the underlying trust property so there are no charges to IHT when a beneficiary dies, or when one beneficiary's interest terminates and is replaced by another. Instead the property held in the settlement is subject to an entirely different IHT regime. This regime is sometimes referred to as the 'relevant property' regime, because IHTA 1984, s 58 refers to property in which there is no qualifying interest in possession and which does not qualify for privileged IHT treatment as 'relevant property'.

Inheritance tax on creation

The settlor's transfer to the settlement is a lifetime chargeable transfer in so far as not exempt. Annual exemptions may be available, but there can be no spouse exemption even if one of the beneficiaries is the settlor's spouse.

At the time of the transfer IHT is charged at half the death rates. If the settlor dies within seven years of creating the settlement, the transfer becomes chargeable at the full death rates, although credit is given for any IHT already paid.

Let us consider the Harriet example from **5.2.3.1** on the basis that the trust created is a discretionary settlement for the benefit of her brother and his children rather than a life interest settlement.

EXAMPLE

On 1 March 2006, Harriet transfers £340,000 in cash and shares to a discretionary settlement for her brother and his children. She had already made chargeable transfers which had exhausted her nil rate band and had no annual exemptions available.

The initial transfer is charged at half the death rates.

Assume that the IHT is paid from the funds transferred to the trustees, so there is no need to gross up the transfer. (If Harriet agreed to pay the IHT, it would be necessary to gross up the transfer.)

	£
Value transferred	340,000
IHT on £340,000 @ 20%	68,000

If Harriet survives seven years, the chargeable transfer drops out of cumulation and has no IHT implications. If she dies on 8 February 2013 with a death estate of £130,000 which she leaves to her sister, the lifetime transfer will become chargeable at the full death rates, although credit will be given for the IHT already paid. Taper relief will be available as she has died more than six years but less than seven years after the transfer.

	£
Value transferred	340,000
IHT on £340,000 @ 40%	136,000
20% of £136,000 is payable because of taper relief	27,200
Less the IHT already paid	(68,000)
IHT to pay	none (but no refund available)

Had tax been due, it would have been payable six months from the end of the month in which Harriet died and would have been paid by the trustees from the trust fund.

The whole of her death estate of £130,000 will be taxed at 40% as the transfer to the trust has exhausted her nil rate band.

Charges to IHT after creation

No beneficiary is treated as owning the underlying trust property and so there are no charges to tax when a beneficiary dies, or when one beneficiary's interest terminates and is replaced by another. Instead, the settlement itself pays a charge to tax every 10 years (often called an anniversary charge) and there is also an exit charge when property leaves the settlement. The calculation of these charges is dealt with at **10.2** below.

5.2.4 Lifetime settlements created on or after 22 March 2006

All lifetime settlements created on or after 22 March 2006 (with the exception of those for disabled beneficiaries considered at **5.2.4.1** below) are treated in the same way irrespective of whether or not there is an interest in possession. They are all subject to the relevant property regime mentioned at **5.2.3.2** above.

5.2.4.1 Lifetime settlements for a disabled beneficiary

Settlements which fulfil the conditions contained in IHTA 1984, s 89 are discretionary in form but are treated as if they created pre-2006 qualifying interests in possession.

The transfer into the settlement will be a PET, in so far as not exempt, if, and only if, it is created for:

(a) the benefit of a beneficiary who is 'disabled' within the meaning of the Finance Act 2005, Sch 1A; or

(b) the settlor's own benefit at a time when the settlor is suffering from a condition that it is reasonable to expect will lead to the settlor becoming 'disabled' within the meaning of IHTA 1984, s 89.

In addition, the terms of the settlement must ensure that:

(a) during the life of a disabled person, no interest in possession in the settled property subsists; and

(b) if any of the settled property or income arising from it is applied during the disabled person's life for the benefit of a beneficiary, it is applied for the benefit of the disabled person.

Note, therefore, that the trust is discretionary in nature; it is not necessary for the disabled person to receive either income or capital which can be retained within the settlement. However, if either or both is applied, then it must, under subsection (b), be used for the benefit of the disabled person during their lifetime and not for anyone else.

The settled property will be treated as part of the beneficiary's IHT estate so there may be a charge to IHT on death, depending on the value of the settled property at that date. The trust itself is not taxed so there are no ongoing anniversary or exit charges.

Trusts for the disabled are beyond the scope of this book and are not considered further.

5.2.4.2 All other lifetime settlements

Inheritance tax on creation

The creation of a lifetime settlement will be a lifetime chargeable transfer. It is irrelevant whether the settlement created is discretionary, has contingent interests or has an interest in possession. All lifetime trusts (except those qualifying as disabled trusts) are subject to the relevant property regime mentioned at **5.2.3.2**.

Let us consider the way in which the Harriet example from **5.2.3.1** will be treated if the transfer takes place on or after 22 March 2006.

The settlement will be subject to the relevant property regime.

EXAMPLE

On 31 March 2015, Harriet transfers £340,000 in cash and shares to a settlement for her brother for life with the remainder to her nephew. She had already made chargeable transfers which had exhausted her nil rate band and had no annual exemptions available.

The initial transfer to the settlement is charged at half the death rates.

Assume that the IHT is paid from the funds transferred to the trustees, so there is no need to gross up the transfer. (If Harriet agreed to pay the IHT, it would be necessary to gross up the transfer; see **5.2.8.1**.)

	£
Value transferred	340,000
IHT on £340,000 @ 20%	68,000

If Harriet survives seven years, the chargeable transfer drops out of cumulation and has no IHT implications. If she dies on 8 February 2022 with a death estate of £130,000 which she leaves to her sister, the lifetime transfer will become chargeable at the full death rates, although credit will be given for the IHT already paid. Taper relief will be available as she has died more than six years but less than seven years after the transfer.

	£
Value transferred	340,000
IHT on £340,000 @ 40%	136,000
20% of £136,000 payable because of taper relief	27,200
Less IHT already paid	(68,000)
IHT to pay	none (but no refund available)

As at **5.2.3.1**, had tax been payable, it would have been due six months from the end of the month in which Harriet died and must be paid by the trustees from the trust fund.

The whole of her death estate will be taxed at 40% as the transfer to the trust has exhausted her nil rate band.

If the settlor has annual exemptions available, the value transferred by the lifetime chargeable transfer will be reduced appropriately. If the trust property is held for the settlor's spouse for life, no spouse exemption is available because the spouse is not treated as beneficially entitled to the settled property.

Inheritance tax treatment during the lifetime of the trust

No beneficiary is treated as owning the underlying trust property so there are no charges to tax when a beneficiary dies, or when one beneficiary's interest terminates and is replaced by another. Instead the trust itself pays a charge to tax every 10 years and there is an exit charge when property leaves the settlement. The calculation of these charges is dealt with at **10.3.3** below.

5.2.5 Settlements created on death on or after 22 March 2006 qualifying for special IHT treatment

We look in detail at settlements created on death in **Chapter 12**. However, for completeness it is useful to know that there are three types of settlement which qualify for special IHT treatment:

(a)   *Trusts for the disabled*

There are no anniversary or exit charges. Instead the beneficiary will be treated as beneficially entitled to the underlying trust assets. The settled property will be aggregated with the disabled beneficiary's own property when the beneficiary dies.

(b)   *Immediate post-death interests*

These are settlements where a beneficiary of an estate has an immediate interest in possession, eg 'to Fred for life'. The beneficiary will be treated as beneficially entitled to the underlying trust assets. The settled property will be aggregated with the beneficiary's own property when the beneficiary dies or when the interest terminates (eg by surrender or assignment). In other words, the beneficiary has a 'qualifying' interest in possession.

(c)   *Trusts for bereaved minors and young people*

Settlements for the benefit of a parent's own child contingent on reaching an age not greater than 25 will not be subject to anniversary charges provided the requirements of IHTA 1984, s 71A or s 71D are satisfied.

If settlement property is paid to the child at or before 18, there will be no exit charge (s 71A and s 71D).

If settlement property is paid to the child after 18 and before 25, there will be an exit charge calculated on the length of time the property has remained in the settlement since the child's 18th birthday(s 71D).

5.2.6 Special IHT treatment for settlements without an interest in possession created for young people before 22 March 2006

Before 22 March 2006, certain settlements without an interest in possession were singled out for privileged IHT treatment. These settlements were called 'accumulation and maintenance' settlements. It did not matter whether the settlement was created by lifetime transfer or on death.

To qualify the settlement had to meet the conditions set out in IHTA 1984, s 71. Broadly, the beneficiaries had to become entitled to income or capital at or before age 25. For example, a settlement 'for my daughter contingent on her reaching 18' would qualify. Lifetime transfers to accumulation and maintenance settlements were PETs and not lifetime chargeable transfers, and there were no anniversary or exit charges.

No new accumulation and maintenance settlements can be created on or after 22 March 2006, and existing settlements lost their privileged status on 6 April 2008 unless they complied with stringent conditions. (This is true for all accumulation and maintenance settlements, whether initially created by lifetime settlement or on death.) See **Chapter 8.**

5.2.7 Settlements and inheritance tax planning

There is now a tax disincentive for taxpayers to create lifetime settlements. The creation of any lifetime settlement will be a lifetime chargeable transfer and will give rise to an immediate charge to IHT unless:

(a) the amount transferred is within the settlor's nil rate band or is exempt, for example because of the annual exemption or normal expenditure out of income exemption; or

(b) the assets transferred attract 100% business or agricultural property relief.

Moreover, there will be a continuing cost as, after creation, there will be anniversary and exit charges to pay to the extent that the trust assets exceed the level of the nil rate band.

Some taxpayers may prefer to make outright gifts to beneficiaries, which will be treated as PETs and give rise to no further IHT liability provided the transferor survives for seven years after making the gift.

5.2.8 Further inheritance tax points on settlements

5.2.8.1 Inheritance tax and grossing up

Where a settlor transfers funds to a lifetime settlement and IHT is payable on that transfer, he can either:

(a) allow the tax to be paid from the sum transferred, in which case the settlement will receive less; or

(b) provide additional funds to meet the tax, in which case the settlement will receive more.

Inheritance tax is calculated on the loss to the transferor, so if the settlor provides additional funds to cover the charge to IHT, there is a greater loss and more IHT will be payable. When calculating the IHT liability it will be necessary to gross up.

In the Harriet example at **5.2.4.2**, we assumed that the trustees paid the IHT due from the funds transferred by Harriet, and we said that there was no need to gross up. However, if Harriet felt more generous and was willing to transfer £340,000 to the settlement *and pay the*

IHT *due as well*, grossing up would be required. She will lose not just the £340,000, but also the amount required to pay the tax.

EXAMPLE

Harriet had already made chargeable transfers which had exhausted her nil rate band and had no annual exemptions available.

She wants the full £340,000 to go into the discretionary trust. The £340,000 is net of 20% IHT. Inheritance tax on the gross gift will be calculated as follows:

Gross up the value transferred at the appropriate tax rates:

Net		Gross equivalent
£		£
340,000	$\times \dfrac{100}{80}$	425,000

The settlement receives £340,000.

The Revenue will receive IHT of £85,000 from Harriet (£425,000 – £340,000 = £85,000).

Any charge which arises as a result of Harriet's death within seven years will be based on a value transferred of £425,000.

5.2.8.2 Cumulation

Because of the way cumulation works, a taxpayer who makes a lifetime chargeable transfer (eg settles property on discretionary trusts before 22 March 2006, or on any trusts on or after that date) may have to survive for 14 years before it ceases to have any impact.

EXAMPLE

May 2014:   Jake, who is divorced, settles £200,000 on discretionary trusts.

May 2018:   Jake makes a gift of £125,000 to his sister Susan.

May 2020:   Jake makes a gift of £200,000 to his granddaughter.

January 2023:   Jake dies.

Ignore annual exemptions and assume rates and bands are the same as in 2022/23 throughout.

Step 1

The transfer to the 2014 discretionary settlement was a lifetime chargeable transfer (LCT) made more than seven years before death and so no further tax is due on it. However, as we shall see, it remains relevant to the calculation of IHT on the transfers in 2018 and 2020.

Step 2

The gift in 2018 was made less than seven years before death and so the PET becomes chargeable. Look back seven years from that transfer to see if there are any chargeable transfers. If so, they must be cumulated. The existence of the 2014 LCT reduces the nil rate band available when calculating IHT on the 2018 transfer.

	£	£
2018 transfer – PET now chargeable		125,000
Cumulative total – LCT	200,000	
Nil rate band (part)	200,000	
Nil rate band (balance)		125,000
		nil

IHT on failed PET – nil

Step 3

The 2020 gift was a PET when made but has also become chargeable. It must be cumulated with all chargeable transfers made in the preceding seven years. In this case, the cumulative total of chargeable transfers is £325,000 (the 2014 LCT and the 2018 PET which is now treated as chargeable) and so exhausts the nil rate band.

	£	£
2020 PET now chargeable		200,000
Cumulative total – the failed PET and the LCT	325,000	
Nil rate band	325,000	
Nil rate band (balance)		nil
		200,000

IHT on £200,000 @ 40% payable by the trustees. Taper relief is not available as three years have not elapsed since the gift.

Step 4

Jake's estate on death is cumulated with chargeable transfers made in the previous seven years, ie the gifts in 2018 and 2020 which are now treated as chargeable.

As these together give a cumulative total of chargeable transfers of £325,000, Jake's estate is prima facie taxable at 40%. The LCT to the discretionary settlement was made more than seven years ago and drops out of cumulation for the death estate.

5.2.8.3   Order of gifts and same day transfers (IHTA 1984, ss 62, 66 and 68)

As we saw at **4.6.2**, where a client is proposing to create a lifetime settlement (for example, a discretionary settlement) and to make a PET, there is an advantage to the later taxation of the settlement in making the discretionary settlement before the PET. If the PET comes first and later becomes chargeable, it will be taken into account when calculating IHT payable by the trustees during the lifetime of the discretionary settlement. See **Chapter 10**.

5.3   CAPITAL GAINS TAX AND LIFETIME SETTLEMENTS

5.3.1   Capital gains tax on creation

The basic CGT treatment of disposals to settlements is not affected by the type of settlement involved. However, on certain disposals a settlor may claim hold-over relief under TCGA 1992, s 165 or s 260 (see para **5.3.2** below).

The transfer of property by a settlor to trustees is a disposal (TCGA 1992, s 70). If chargeable assets are settled, a chargeable gain (or allowable loss) may result. The gain (if any) will be the settlor's, and he will bear the tax unless there is an agreement to the contrary.

EXAMPLE

In December 2022, Ilyana (a higher rate taxpayer) settles her quoted shares worth £38,300 (acquired for £6,000) and cash of £30,000. She has made no other disposals in that tax year. The beneficiaries are her daughter for life, with remainder to her grandchildren. She has no available losses.

Calculate the CGT on the disposal.

Cash is exempt.

Shares:	£
Market value at disposal	38,300
less: acquisition cost	(6,000)
	32,300
less: annual exemption	(12,300)
Chargeable gain	20,000

CGT @ 20% on £20,000 = £4,000

Calculate the cost of the settlement to Ilyana.

	£
Value of shares	38,300
Cash	30,000
CGT	4,000
	72,300

The acquisition cost of the shares to the trustees for the purpose of any future capital gains on a disposal by them is £38,300.

The creation of this settlement is also a lifetime chargeable transfer for IHT purposes of £62,300 (ie, £30,000 plus £38,300 minus 2 × £3,000 annual exemptions). As a result of IHTA 1984, ss 5(4) and 164, the reduction in Illyana's estate caused by the payment of CGT (and any disposal costs involved in the transfer) is ignored for IHT purposes, ie this reduction in value of the estate is not included when calculating the amount of IHT payable.

Capital gains tax on subsequent disposals by the trustees

Once the settlement has been created, any sale of trust assets by the trustees (see **14.5.1**) or a transfer of the trust fund, or part of it, to a beneficiary (see **10.1.4.2**) will be a disposal by the trustees giving rise to a CGT charge.

From 6 April 2016, CGT on any gains made on disposals by trustees is paid at 20%, except for gains made on residential property which are taxed at 28%. (Between 23 June 2010 and 5 April 2016 the rate was 28%; between 6 April 2008 and 22 June 2010 the rate was 18%; between 6 April 2004 and 5 April 2008 the rate was 40%; between 6 April 1998 and 5 April 2004 it was 34%; and for earlier years the rate depended on the type of settlement.)

Trustees have an annual exemption of half that available to an individual, ie £6,150 per annum in the tax year 2022/23 (frozen until 5 April 2026). Where a settlor has created more than one settlement, the annual exemption is divided between them.

EXAMPLE

Albert creates two separate settlements. Each settlement will have an annual exemption of £3,075 (£6,150 ÷ 2) in 2022/23.

There is, however, a minimum exemption per settlement of £1,230.

5.3.2 Capital gains tax and hold-over relief on creation of lifetime settlements (TCGA 1992, s 165 and s 260)

The lifetime disposal of property by a settlor into a settlement post 22 March 2006 is a chargeable event for CGT (unless the asset being settled is cash).

Where a settlor disposes of business assets (see **4.4.5**) to a settlement, he can claim hold-over relief under s 165 (unless the anti-avoidance provisions apply – see **5.5** below). Only the settlor need elect for s 165 hold-over relief.

Hold-over relief is also available on transfers chargeable to IHT under TCGA 1992, s 260:

(a)   irrespective of the nature of the asset being settled, therefore including land and quoted shares; and

(b)   even if the transfer is chargeable at 0% or exempt (see Example 2 below).

Only the settlor need elect for s 260 hold-over relief.

EXAMPLE 1

In January 2023 Lesley settles her country cottage, which she bought for £50,000 and which is now worth £280,000, on her adult children. She has made no previous transfers apart from using her annual exemptions.

The transfer is chargeable to IHT, but at 0% because the £280,000 falls within Lesley's nil rate band.

Lesley has made a gain of £230,000 but can claim CGT hold-over relief. If she claims the relief, the trustees will acquire the cottage at £280,000 less Lesley's chargeable gain, ie an acquisition value of £50,000. If Lesley had incurred allowable expenditure of £5,000, her gain would be £225,000 and the trustees would be treated as acquiring the property for £280,000 less £225,000 = £55,000.

EXAMPLE 2

In January 2023 Morris settles quoted shares purchased for £1,000 and now worth £100,000. He has made no other transfers, apart from using his annual exemptions, but has made chargeable gains this tax year of £12,300 on disposals of other assets.

The transfer to the discretionary settlement is a chargeable transfer.

CGT hold-over relief is available because the transfer was chargeable even though no IHT was payable.

Since 10 December 2003, hold-over relief is not available if the settlor or his spouse, or his minor children who have neither married nor entered into a civil partnership, have an interest in the settlement (see **4.4.5.2** and **5.5.2**).

Sales by the trustees after the settlement has been created will be subject to CGT, depending on the availability of the trustees' exemptions and reliefs. Transfers of capital from the trust fund to a beneficiary may also attract CGT, although hold-over relief may then be available (see **10.2.4.2**). Trustees pay a flat rate of 20% (28% on residential property) on gains irrespective of the level of income of the settlement.

5.4 INCOME TAX AND SETTLEMENTS

The creation of a settlement should have no income tax consequences for the settlor (other than saving of income tax on any actual loss of income, unless the settlor or spouse has retained an interest (or the parental settlement rules apply), when the settlor will continue to be assessed to income tax on the income).

Once the trust is established the trustees will have an income tax liability in relation to the trust income. The income tax rules which apply depend on whether the beneficiaries have a right to income, or whether the trustees have a discretion. This is so, no matter when or how the settlement is created.

5.4.1 Trusts where the beneficiaries have a right to income

The trustees pay income tax at basic rate (20%) and dividend ordinary rate (8.75%), depending on the type of income.

5.4.2 Trusts where the beneficiaries have no right to income

The usual rate of income tax on all trust income for 2022/23 over £1,000 is a single flat rate of 45% (or 39.35% on dividends). The trustees pay income tax at basic rate on the first £1,000.

Note that for the tax year 2009/10 the usual rate of income tax on trust income was 40% (and 32.5% on dividends). For the tax years 2010/11–2012/13 the rate was 50% (and 42.5% on dividends). For the tax years 2013/14–2014/15 the rate was 45% (and 37.5% on dividends).

5.5 ANTI-AVOIDANCE PROVISIONS

There are anti-avoidance provisions in all three taxes, designed to prevent taxpayers purporting to give away property while continuing to derive a benefit from it.

5.5.1 Inheritance tax

Property will continue to be treated as part of a settlor's estate if he is not excluded or virtually excluded from benefit.

5.5.2 Capital gains tax

If the settlor, or his spouse or civil partner, or the settlor's minor unmarried child has an 'interest in the settlement', it is not possible to claim hold-over relief on creating the settlement (see **5.3.2**).

5.5.3 Income tax

Trust income applied for the settlor's minor unmarried children will be taxed as the settlor's, as will income which could be applied for the benefit of the settlor, his spouse, or civil partner.

5.6 CHOICE OF SETTLEMENT

Any settlor who is thinking of creating a settlement should consider the tax implications before taking any final step.

Prior to 22 March 2006, a settlor who wanted to create a lifetime settlement would have had his choice of settlement influenced by the fact that different types of settlement were treated in different ways for IHT.

On or after 22 March 2006, the type of settlement is neutral from an IHT point of view. The decision for the settlor will be whether or not he wants a settlement at all in the light of the tax consequences.

A settlor is likely to consider three options:

(a)   making an outright gift;

(b)   transferring assets to a lifetime settlement;

(c)   retaining assets and leaving them by will.

If the taxpayer concludes that a lifetime settlement is desirable, the decision as to what type of settlement to choose will not be influenced by IHT considerations as all lifetime settlements are treated in the same way (apart from settlements for the disabled). Instead, the decision will depend on what the taxpayer wants to achieve.

The following points will be relevant:

(a) Discretionary trusts are useful for making long-term provision for a class of beneficiaries, where the settlor is unsure which beneficiaries will turn out to have the greatest needs.

The settlor identifies the beneficiaries whom he wishes to benefit, but leaves it to the trustees to select which of these beneficiaries is to benefit and how and when. Discretionary trusts are the most flexible type of settlement because the decision as to beneficial entitlement can be deferred and does not have to be determined at the time the trusts are created. The trustees will normally have a discretion over both the capital and income of the trust fund.

EXAMPLE

Barry wishes to benefit his grandchildren, Cora, Doris and Edward. All three are under 5 years of age, and he does not know how they will develop and whether their needs will be the same. He settles £150,000 on discretionary trusts.

Twenty years later Cora has just qualified as a lawyer; Doris is a hairdresser and single parent; Edward is a bank clerk and physically disabled as a result of an accident several years ago. The trustees may well decide to distribute the money unevenly between the three beneficiaries.

(b) A settlement with successive interests is useful where a settlor wants to make income provision for one beneficiary while preserving the capital for others. The trustees will hold the income for one beneficiary and the capital for another.

EXAMPLE

Hari's first wife died five years ago and he has just married again. He wants to make sure that his second wife has income from a gift of property, while preserving the capital for the children of his first marriage. He will give the property to trustees to hold for his wife for life, remainder to his children.

Often a settlor creating successive interests will also give the trustees a discretion to allow them to appoint capital in case of need either to the life tenant or to the remaindermen. The additional flexibility is useful, but means that the settlor will be less certain of what will happen after establishing the settlement.

(c) Where a settlor wishes to make fixed provision for young children, a settlement with contingent interests is likely to be appropriate. The children will not be entitled to the capital unless and until they reach the specified age. The trustees will normally have a discretion as to how they deal with income, although the terms of the settlement may provide that the beneficiary becomes entitled to income at a specified age. The trustees may also be given a discretion to advance capital at an earlier age in case of need.

EXAMPLE

Saleena transfers £200,000 to trustees to hold for such of her four children as reach 21, equally if more than one. The trust provides that the trustees have a discretion as to whether to use income from each child's presumptive share for maintenance or to accumulate it until each beneficiary reaches 18; thereafter the child has a right to receive the income from their share.

SUMMARY

(1)   The creation of a lifetime settlement has both IHT and CGT consequences. The IHT consequences differ depending on whether the settlement was created before or on or after 22 March 2006. The tables below set out the IHT and CGT treatment of the transfer of assets to a lifetime settlement.

Lifetime settlements created before 22 March 2006

	IHT	CGT
Interest in possession	PET	Disposal – hold-over relief TCGA 1992, s 165 only
Discretionary	LCT: 0% and/or 20%	Disposal – hold-over relief available (TCGA 1992, s 260 and s 65)

Lifetime settlements created on or after 22 March 2006

	IHT	CGT
Settlement for a disabled beneficiary	PET	Disposal – hold-over relief TCGA 1992, s 165 only
Any other settlement	LCT: 0% and/or 20%	Disposal – hold-over relief available (TCGA 1992, s 260 and s 165)

(2)   A beneficiary with a pre-22 March 2006 interest in possession is treated as beneficially entitled to the trust capital for IHT purposes, as, irrespective of the date of creation, is a beneficiary with a disabled person's interest, a transitional serial interest or an immediate post-death interest.

(3)   Trusts created on death giving an immediate interest in possession are treated in the same way as pre-22 March 2006 interests in possession.

(4)   Trusts created on death for the deceased's own children have a special charging regime if they comply with the requirements of the IHTA 1984, s 71A or s 71D, as do 'accumulation and maintenance' settlements created before 22 March 2006 which comply with the requirements of the IHTA 1984, s 71.

(5)   All other settlements are subject to the IHT relevant property regime which imposes anniversary and exit charges.

REVIEW ACTIVITY

Question 1

Which ONE of the following statements is WRONG?

A   A beneficiary with an interest in possession is always treated as entitled to the underlying trust capital for IHT purposes.

B   Beneficiaries with interests in possession created before 22 March 2006 are treated as entitled to the underlying trust capital for IHT purposes.

C   Beneficiaries with interests in possession, created on death after 22 March 2006 and which take effect immediately on death, are treated as entitled to the underlying trust capital for IHT purposes.

D   A person who takes an interest in possession after 22 March 2006 following the death of a spouse who had an interest in possession created before that date is treated as entitled to the underlying trust capital for IHT purposes.

Answer: A

Beneficiaries with an interest in possession in lifetime settlements created on or after 22 March 2006 are not treated as entitled to the underlying trust capital for IHT purposes (unless the settlement qualifies as a disabled person's settlement).

Question 2

In relation to a lifetime settlement created on or after 22 March 2006, which ONE of the following statements is WRONG?

A   A settlement for the settlor's spouse for life, remainder to the settlor's children is a relevant property settlement, so IHT is payable on creation to the extent that the transfer exceeds the settlor's available nil rate band.

B   A discretionary settlement for the benefit of the settlor's spouse and issue is a relevant property settlement, so IHT is payable on creation to the extent that the transfer exceeds the settlor's available nil rate band.

C   A settlement for the settlor's children contingent on reaching 18 is a relevant property settlement, so IHT is payable on creation to the extent that the transfer exceeds the settlor's available nil rate band.

D   A settlement for the settlor's spouse for life, remainder to charity is not a relevant property settlement, so IHT is not payable on creation even if the transfer exceeds the settlor's available nil rate band.

Answer: D

All lifetime settlements created on or after 22 March 2006 (except those qualifying as disabled person's settlements) are relevant property settlements, and all transfers to such settlements are lifetime chargeable transfers giving rise to a charge to IHT at half the death rates on everything in excess of the settlor's available nil rate band.

CHAPTER 6

LIFETIME SETTLEMENTS: SOME COMMON DRAFTING POINTS

LEARNING OUTCOMES

After reading this chapter you will be able to:

- explain the structure of a lifetime settlement
- identify clauses which are generally required in any kind of lifetime settlement.

6.1 INTRODUCTION

We saw in **Chapter 5** that settlements differ depending on what the settlor is trying to achieve. They may have fixed interests, for example 'To X for life and then to Y absolutely' or 'to such of my children as reach 25', or the capital and income may be held at the discretion of the trustees to apply as they see fit amongst a class of beneficiaries. Some settlements are a mixture, giving beneficiaries fixed interests but allowing the trustees overriding discretions to alter those fixed interests by terminating interests and/or advancing capital to beneficiaries early.

However, all settlements follow the same general structure, and in this chapter we look at that general structure and some particular drafting points.

As each client is unique, the available 'standard' precedents may not be appropriate for that client's requirements. When modifying an existing deed or drafting from scratch, you must be aware of the effect of every clause included and the effect of excluding a particular clause. In addition, you should aim for a consistency of style and not use both 'modern' and 'traditional' styles in the same trust instrument.

The basic structure of a settlement is set out in the following table. It is not a definitive list of what should always be included in a settlement. Some clauses are not required if the settlement is a simple life interest settlement. Where a clause may not be necessary for a particular type of settlement, we have included a note explaining this in the comment column.

To keep the content of this chapter relatively brief, the drafting of the trusts of beneficial interests is dealt with mainly in **Chapter 7**. Additional powers required by trustees and their use are examined in **Chapters 9** and **10**. The administrative provisions are discussed in **Chapter 14** but are broadly similar to those in will drafting (see **Chapter 11**).

Structure of settlement

Clause	Comment
Date	
Parties	
Recitals	
Definitions	
Beneficiaries	A separate clause defining beneficiaries is not always required. Beneficiaries may be defined within the definitions clause or, if there are only two or three, they may be named in the clause setting out the beneficial interests. However, where a settlement has a wide class of beneficiaries, a separate clause is normally included.
Perpetuity period	Not required where all interests are already vested, eg in a life interest trust. Settlements with interests which are not vested, such as discretionary settlements or those with contingent interests, must have a perpetuity period. In the case of settlements not governed by the Perpetuities and Accumulations Act 2009 (PAA 2009), it was important to state the perpetuity period expressly as the settlement would otherwise be subject to the less satisfactory common law rules. In the case of settlements governed by the PAA 2009, the period will be 125 years irrespective of what, if anything, the settlement says (see **6.9**).
Accumulation period	Only required where trustees have power to accumulate income rather than having to pay it out each year. In the case of settlements not governed by the PAA 2009, the accumulation period is limited. In the case of settlements governed by the PAA 2009, there are no statutory limitations and income can be accumulated throughout the life of the settlement with the result that, unless the settlor provides otherwise, there will be no restriction on the power to accumulate (see **6.9**).
Transfer to trustees and direction to hold on trust (for sale)	
Trusts of the beneficial interests	This is the most important part of the settlement as it explains the terms on which the trustees hold the trust property and who is entitled to what.
Trustee discretions in relation to the beneficial interests	In a very simple trust, the interests may be fixed and the trustees may have no discretions. However, this is increasingly rare. Even in a simple life interest trust, it is common to give trustees an unfettered power to give capital to the life tenant or remainderman in case of need and a power to terminate the life interest before death.

Clause	Comment
Administrative provisions	
Identification of person with power to appoint new trustees	It is not necessary to nominate a person to appoint new trustees. If no one is appointed, the continuing trustees, or the PRs of the last surviving trustee, will be entitled to make the appointment under Trustee Act 1925, s 36(1). However, because trustees normally have extensive discretionary powers, settlors may wish to choose a person in whom they have confidence to appoint new trustees.
Exclusion of TLATA 1996, ss 11, 12 and 19	
Exclusion of settlor and spouse from any benefit	
Schedules	Schedules are optional. They can make complex documents more comprehensible by keeping detail away from the main body of the document. Some practitioners consign everything except the clauses directly related to the beneficial interests to a series of Schedules. For example: (1) Definitions; (2) The Trust Property; (3) Administrative Provisions.
Signatures	

6.2 THE DATE AND OPENING WORDS

It is usual for the date on which the settlement was made to be set out at the beginning of the trust instrument. In modern style settlements, this may be preceded by a table of contents. The date may be important to determine whether or not a statute applies, for subsequent time-limits and the chronology of events where a settlor has made more than one settlement. Some settlements are known by titles which include their dates, for example, 'Mrs Brown's Grandchildren Settlement of 4 April 1990'.

Sample clause

> This Settlement is made the   day of   Two thousand and

6.3 PARTIES

The settlor and the initial trustees must be clearly identified. How this and the opening words are set out will also determine the style for the rest of the document, ie is it to be modern (Clauses 1 and 2) or traditional (Clause 3)?

Sample clause 1

> BETWEEN
> (1)   DAVID SMITH of [address] ('the Settlor')
> (2)   TONY STUBBS of [address] and ARSHAD RAHMAN of [address] ('the Trustees') which expression shall where the context admits include the trustee or trustees for the time being of this Settlement

Sample clause 2

> PARTIES:
> (1)   [   ] (the 'Settlor'); and
> (2)   [   ] (the 'Trustees').

Sample clause 3

> Between DAVID SMITH of [address] (hereinafter called 'the Settlor') of the one part and TONY STUBBS of [address] and ARSHAD RAHMAN of [address] (hereinafter called 'the Trustees' which expression shall where the context so admits include the trustee or trustees for the time being of the Settlement) of the other part

The definition of the trustees may instead come later in a clause which collects together all definitions used in the settlement.

6.4 RECITALS

Recitals explain the background to the settlement: why it has been created and the settlor's intentions. One common recital is a statement as to whether or not the settlement is to be revocable. In the absence of an express declaration to the contrary, a settlement is irrevocable.

If the settlement is irrevocable, the settlor cannot subsequently change his mind about having created the settlement and demand his money or property back from the trustees. Whilst revocable settlements are possible, in the UK they are uncommon because of their unfavourable tax treatment as settlor interested trusts. Where there is a power to revoke the trusts, the result is that the fund may revert to the settlor or his spouse. For the avoidance of doubt, it is usual to include an express declaration of irrevocability.

Recitals appear immediately after the parties, and in traditional style settlements are introduced by the word 'Whereas'. The numbers or letters to the recital clauses are normally placed in brackets, which distinguishes them from 'operative' clauses, ie the clauses declaring the beneficial interests.

Sample clause

> Whereas
>
> (1)   The Settlor wishes to make this Settlement and has transferred or delivered to the Trustees the property specified in the Schedule
>
> (2)   It is intended that this Settlement shall be irrevocable.

6.5 TABLE OF CONTENTS, CLAUSE HEADINGS, DEFINITIONS AND SCHEDULES

6.5.1 Table of contents

Because settlements are often long and complex, modern precedents generally start by setting out in a table of contents the constituent parts of the settlement, showing the operative parts separately from the administrative provisions. Whilst a table simplifies the use of the settlement, it is important that a further clause ensures that the use of the table does not affect the meaning of the settlement (see **6.5.2**).

6.5.2 Clause headings

It is common to give each clause a heading, as this enables a person who is reading the trust instrument to see quickly and clearly what each clause concerns. This can be particularly useful once the settlement is in use. For example, a trustee may want to know what powers of investment the trustees have. Rather than having to read every clause until he finds the investment clause, he need only look at the clause headings to identify the one he needs to study. It is a matter of personal preference as to whether or not clause headings are used, but they should either be used for every clause, or not at all. Where headings are used, it should be made clear by an additional clause that they are only for administrative convenience, ie, they do not affect the construction of the trust instrument.

Sample clause

Clause headings

The clause headings are included for reference only and do not affect the interpretation of this Settlement

6.5.3 Definitions

Many descriptions and phrases will need to be repeated, often several times, in drafting a settlement. It is, therefore, convenient to give these descriptions and phrases a 'name' by which they can be identified throughout the trust deed.

EXAMPLE

Adam is settling a house, some cash and several holdings of quoted shares on discretionary trusts.

Reference needs to be made to these assets being held on trust, being available for distribution, being invested and so forth.

Unless a 'name' is used, each time reference is made to them the trust deed will have to read: 'The Trustees shall hold the freehold house known as [address], £x cash, 500 shares in A plc etc upon trust ...'.

It is much neater and simpler to call the combined assets 'the Trust Fund' so that the clause would read: 'The Trustees shall hold the Trust Fund upon trust ...'.

It is good practice to give the first letter of the 'names' a capital letter to indicate to the reader that they are definitions.

There is a choice of where to record the definitions of the 'names':

(a)   Definitions can be dealt with as and when they arise in the body of the deed, for example:

The Trustees shall hold the Trust Fund upon trust for such of them, David, Sue and Charles (hereinafter together called 'the Beneficiaries') as shall attain 18 years of age and if more than one in equal shares

The problem with this approach is finding the definition when subsequently using the trust instrument. For example, Brenda is a trustee of a settlement set up for the settlor's young relatives contingent on their reaching 21. She wants to know if the trustees have a power to apply income for the maintenance of a particular beneficiary. A glance through the clause headings shows her that she needs to study clause 18. In reading this clause, she comes across the expression 'the Accumulation Period'. She has no idea what it means and will have to read all the preceding clauses until she finds where the expression was used for the first time.

(b)   Definitions can be contained in a Schedule to the deed. A person reading the trust instrument who comes across a 'name' such as 'the Beneficiary', will know to turn to the Schedule whenever he meets a 'name'.

(c)   All the definitions can be set out in clause 1 of the trust instrument. This is common practice in modern style settlements. It is helpful to place the definitions alphabetically to make it easier for those using the trust to find what they are looking for.

Sample clause

(1)   Definitions

In this deed where the context so admits

(a)   'the Beneficiaries' shall mean ...

(b)   'the Trust Fund' shall mean ...

6.6   IDENTIFYING THE BENEFICIARIES

6.6.1   Need for clarity

Every settlement needs to identify the beneficiaries. In the case of a simple life interest trust, there will be only a small number of beneficiaries and this will not be difficult. They may simply be named in the clause setting out the beneficial interests:

Sample clause

> The Trustees shall pay the income of the Trust Fund to [Luc] during [his] life and after his death shall pay the capital to [Jemima]

or defined in the Definitions clause and then referred to by reference to that definition:

Sample clause

> The Trustees shall pay the income of the Trust Fund to the Life Tenant during [his] life and after [his] death shall pay the capital to the Remainderman

6.6.2   Identification by description

It is not possible to name all the beneficiaries where there is a class which includes unborn or unascertained individuals. This is commonly the case for discretionary settlements or settlements with contingent interests. Here the beneficiaries must be identified by description, and it is vital that the class is described with sufficient clarity to enable the trustees to say with certainty whether or not a particular individual is within the class of beneficiaries, eg 'the children of my niece, Sally'.

Sample clause

> 'The Beneficiaries' shall mean the following persons (whether now in existence or who come into existence during the Trust Period): the Settlor's children and remoter issue and the spouses, widows and widowers (but not such widows or widowers as have remarried) of such children and remoter issue

---

EXAMPLE

Twenty years ago, Aisha created a settlement, which is still continuing, and she used the above clause. When she set up the trusts, she had three adult children, Ben, Cora and Deirdre, and one grandson, Edwin. The trustees wish to know who are the current beneficiaries.

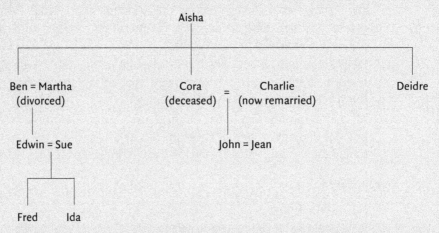

The beneficiaries are:

(a)   Ben, Deirdre, Edwin, John, Fred and Ida because they are the issue of the settlor; and

(b)   Sue and Jean because they are the spouses of the settlor's issue.

> Martha and Charlie have been within the class of beneficiaries, but are now excluded. Martha's divorce from Ben means she is no longer his spouse; although Charlie was the spouse and then widower of the settlor's child, he has remarried.

If a person who was within the class of beneficiaries is subsequently excluded because of a change in status, he does not have to pay back to the settlement any previous benefit he may have received from it.

> **EXAMPLE**
>
> The facts are the same as in the previous example. After Cora's death the trustees gave Charlie £5,000. Charlie remarried two years later. He does not have to repay the £5,000 but cannot receive anything more from the settlement.

It is common to give trustees power to add people to and exclude them from the class of beneficiaries.

6.6.3 Particular points on contingent interests

6.6.3.1 Include age of living beneficiaries

Where gifts are contingent on reaching a specified age, it is normal practice to include each living beneficiary's date of birth, since this enables the trustees to calculate the beneficiary's age and to know the date when his interest will vest.

Sample clause for a trust with contingent interests

The 'Primary Beneficiaries' shall mean:

(1)   The existing [grand]children of the Settlor namely [   ] who was born on [   ]; [   ] who was born on [   ]; [   ] who was born on [   ]; and [   ] who was born on [   ]; and

(2)   every other [grand]child of the Settlor born after the date of this Deed and before the Closing Date.

6.6.3.2 Include a closing date for a class which is open at the time the settlement is created

A settlor may wish later born beneficiaries to be included in the class, for example where a settlor settles property for 'my grandchildren, contingent on reaching age [   ]' and at the time of creation has only got one or two grandchildren but anticipates further grandchildren. This is perfectly acceptable, but the clause should specify that the class is to close on the date when the first beneficiary attains a vested interest in the capital of the trust fund, ie when the contingency is first satisfied, or at the end of the trust if this is earlier.

This is because the trustees will have to distribute a share of the trust property to the beneficiary who has become entitled; for example, if there are four beneficiaries, they will distribute one-quarter. However, if the class remains open, additional beneficiaries may be added to the class after the distribution date. The trustees will have paid the first beneficiary too much, and this will amount to a breach of trust.

Sample clause

The 'Closing Date' shall mean whichever shall be the earlier of:

(1)   the date on which the first Primary Beneficiary to do so attains the age of 25; and

(2)   the date on which the Trust Period shall determine.

6.6.4 Meaning of 'child'

The expression 'child or grandchild', etc will normally include adopted and legitimated (grand) children, and those whose parents are not married to each other. If the settlor wants to exclude any such person, a clause to that effect (eg, as in the sample clause) should be included.

Sample clause

> References to the children, grandchildren and issue of any person shall include his children, grandchildren and remoter issue, whether legitimate, legitimated [, illegitimate] or adopted [, but shall exclude any illegitimate person and his descendants].

There have been a series of statutes allowing adopted children to be treated as children of the adopting parents for succession purposes, starting with the Adoption of Children Act 1949. That Act did not apply to any disposition made before its coming into force, and subsequent adoption statutes, such as the Adoption Act 1976 and the Adoption and Children Act 2002, contained similar transitional provisions preventing their application to any disposition made prior to the coming into force of the statute in question. The same is true of the statutes dealing with illegitimate children.

There have been several challenges to the rule that adopted children cannot take under wills and trust instruments made before the date of the amending legislation, based on alleged breaches of the European Convention of Human Rights (ECHR), Article 8 (respect for private and family life) and Article 14 (no discrimination on any ground including birth).

A challenge was unsuccessful in *Upton v National Westminster Bank plc* [2004] EWHC 1962 (Ch). The judge held that the current legislation was not discriminatory and there were sound reasons (such as certainty) for not making such legislation retrospective. In *Gregg v Pigott, Re Erskine 1948 Trust* [2012] EWHC 732 (Ch), the challengers had limited success. Mark Herbert QC, sitting as a deputy judge, found that, while s 3 of the Human Rights 1998 is not generally retrospective, it can be in cases where adopted children can be included without unfairness. He concluded that because of a number of special features, without any one of which he would have reached a different answer, the trust in question could be construed to eliminate discrimination against adopted children.

In *Hand v George* [2017] EWHC 533 (Ch), the judge took a much more radical approach. Rose J concluded that the domestic legislation breaches the Convention because it results in adopted (and illegitimate) children having worse succession rights than non-adopted children.

To prevent any unfair interference with pre-existing rights, she suggested that the exclusion of adopted children under dispositions already in existence should be allowed to continue if the beneficiary of the disposition has done something to avail himself or herself of the property right in question before the coming into force of the Human Rights Act 1998.

Beneficiaries of a will or trust have normally done nothing to avail themselves of inheritance rights, so adopted (and illegitimate) children will generally be able to inherit under instruments pre-dating the relevant legislation.

Note that in *PQ v RS* [2019] EWHC 1643 (Ch), Chief Master Marsh, while expressing no view as to the correctness of *Hand v George*, accepted counsel's submission that there was a doubt about whether it would be followed and that the trustees of a very large trust fund should, therefore, take other steps to secure the position of a child born before the marriage of her parents.

The Human Fertilisation and Embryology Act 2008 (HFEA 2008) contains provisions about parenthood where a child is born as a result of certain types of fertility treatment (artificial insemination or placing an embryo or sperm and eggs in a woman). These provisions came into force on 6 April 2009 and affect the meaning of 'children' in wills and trusts, whenever made, where the children are born as a result of fertility treatment received after that date.

The Act does not state that the provisions are subject to contrary intention but settlors are free to include and exclude individuals from the class of beneficiaries as they see fit.

The HFEA 2008 provides as follows:

(a)   The woman who carried the child is treated as the child's mother (s 33).

(b)   If the woman is married at the time of the treatment, her husband is treated as the child's father, unless he did not consent to the treatment (s 35).

(c)   If the woman has a civil partner, the couple will be treated in the same way as married couples. The woman who carries the child will be treated as the child's mother, and her civil partner will be treated as the child's second parent unless she did not consent to the treatment (s 42).

(d)   If the woman is not married or in a civil partnership but has a male partner at the time of the treatment, he is treated as the child's father if the 'agreed fatherhood' conditions are satisfied at that time provided no other man is treated as the child's father under s 35 and no woman is treated as a parent under s 42. The 'agreed fatherhood' conditions are set out in s 37. Broadly, both parties must have consented in writing to the man being treated as the father and the partners must not be within the prohibited degrees of relationship, which exclude close relatives.

(e)   Similarly if the woman has a female partner at the time of the treatment, that partner is treated as the child's female parent if the 'agreed female parenthood' conditions are satisfied at that time provided no man is treated as the child's father under s 35 and no other woman is treated as a parent under s 42. The 'agreed female parenthood' conditions are set out in s 44. Broadly, both parties must have consented in writing to the woman being treated as the parent and the partners must not be within the prohibited degrees of relationship, which exclude close relatives. No man will be treated as the child's father.

The HFEA 2008 does not affect the position of male civil partners and same-sex couples. A man who is not the child's genetic father will be treated as a second parent only if he adopts the child.

Where there is a surrogacy arrangement, the woman carrying the child remains the mother unless and until a parental order (similar to an adoption order) is obtained.

6.6.5   Meaning of 'spouse'

The expression 'spouse' does not include civil partner unless the trust instrument makes express provision. In *Goodrich and others v AB* [2022] EWHC 81 (Ch) Chief Master Schuman held that discriminating in this way was inconsistent with the European Convention on Human Rights and so the UK was in breach of its obligations. However, it was not possible to read the Civil Partnership Act 2004 in such a way as to remove the discrimination. In *Goodrich* itself the Chief Master did decide that for various fact and context reasons it was possible to interpret the word 'spouse' in the employee benefit trust being considered as including civil partners. However, this will not normally be possible. If the settlor wishes to include civil partners and former civil partners, they must either be added to the class, which is rather clumsy, or a separate clause can be inserted, extending the meaning of spouse.

Sample clause

> In this will, 'marriage' includes civil partnership as defined in the Civil Partnership Act 2004 and 'spouse', 'husband', 'wife', 'widower', 'widow', are to be construed accordingly

In the case of instruments made after the Marriage (Same Sex Couples) Act 2013 came into force, such terms will include both opposite and same sex marriages, unless stated otherwise. In *Goodrich*, Chief Master Schuman held that the position in relation to instruments predating the Act was discriminatory and inconsistent with the European Convention on Human

Rights. The Master directed that 'spouse' should be read as including same sex spouses in all instruments, whenever executed, unless to do so would deprive someone of a right they have done something to avail themselves of. See further **11.1**.

6.7   THE TRUST FUND

The settlement needs some property to be the subject-matter of the trusts from the outset. The settlor may add to the original trust property from time to time, and other people may also transfer property to the settlement in which case they become joint settlors. The original trust property will be described in detail in the Schedule. The definition of the 'Trust Fund' will refer to the property set out in the Schedule plus any additions.

It is common to set up the trust by transferring a small amount of money (typically £10) and then transferring the various assets later. This is administratively convenient when instructions have to be given to a variety of financial institutions to transfer funds. The process is usually referred to as creating a settlement in pilot form.

When property is transferred from the settlor to the trustees, the correct mode of transfer must be used or the transfer will be ineffective. For example, unquoted shares must be transferred by signed stock transfer form and land by deed or transfer of title.

6.8   TRUST OR TRUST FOR SALE?

Before TLATA 1996, it was usual practice for the trustees of lifetime settlements to hold property on an express trust for sale. This ensured that a strict settlement under SLA 1925 could not arise where land was settled property. TLATA 1996 prevents any new strict settlements being created after 31 December 1996 but does not prevent settlements being drafted with an express trust for sale. An express trust will probably be included only where the settlor wishes the trustees to be under a duty to sell. If, instead, a power of sale is considered sufficient, the trustees will be directed to hold the settled property 'on trust' and will be given power of sale in the administrative provisions of the settlement.

If a trust for sale is used, it has five constituent parts, as shown in the sample clause.

Extracts from sample clause – trust for sale

(1)   The Trustees shall hold the Trust Fund upon trust as to investments or property other than money in their absolute discretion to sell, call in or convert into money all or any of such investments or property

(2)   But with power to postpone such sale, calling in or conversion

(3)   To permit the same to remain as invested

(4)   Upon trust as to money with the like discretion to invest the same in their names or under their control in any of the investments authorised by this Settlement or by law

(5)   With power at the like discretion from time to time to vary or transpose any such investments for others so authorised

6.9   PERPETUITY PERIOD

6.9.1   No perpetual trusts

English law does not allow a private trust (as opposed to a charitable trust) to be perpetual. It must come to an end and the capital vest in a beneficiary within a limited period of time. The time from the creation of the settlement to the moment when the capital must vest is called 'the perpetuity period'. Although not necessary, many settlements also have a defined trust period which is the period within which the trustees can exercise their powers. This is usually defined as the same period as the perpetuity period but could be a shorter period.

6.9.2   What is the perpetuity period?

6.9.2.1   Trusts not governed by the PAA 2009

At common law, the perpetuity period is that of a life or lives in being plus 21 years. The life or lives in being could be expressly selected, eg '21 years from the death of my son, John' or, more creatively, '21 years from the death of the last grandchild of Queen Elizabeth II living at my death'. If no life is expressly selected, the relevant life or lives will be identified from the particular disposition. For example, in the case of a gift to 'the first child of X to reach 21', X is the life in being.

The Perpetuities and Accumulations Act 1964 (PAA 1964) allowed settlors to select a fixed period of anything up to 80 years. The trust instrument must state expressly that it selects a particular number of years as the perpetuity period. Where a period is selected, it is defined in the trust instrument as 'the perpetuity period'. If no mention of a perpetuity period is made in the trust instrument, the common law rules apply.

Sample clause – the trust and perpetuity period

> The trust period shall mean the period ending on the last day of the period of 80 years from the date of this Settlement which period shall be the applicable perpetuity period.

6.9.2.2   Trusts governed by the PAA 2009

The PAA 2009 provides a new perpetuity period of 125 years which will apply to lifetime trusts taking effect and will trusts created in wills executed on or after 6 April 2010 irrespective of the terms of the trust instrument. Trusts already in existence at that date or will trusts coming into effect under wills executed before that date are not affected. The new 125-year period will take precedence over whatever the trust instrument may say, and if the trust instrument is silent the perpetuity period will still be 125 years. It is helpful to include an express statement as to the length of the perpetuity period, as in 20 years time lawyers may not necessarily remember the date on which the PAA 2009 came into force.

Sample clause – the trust and perpetuity period

> The trust period shall mean the period ending on the last day of the period of 125 years from the date of the creation of this settlement which period (and no other) shall be the applicable perpetuity period.

The PAA 2009, s 6(2) provides that the perpetuity period for an instrument created in the exercise of a special power of appointment will begin on the date on which the instrument creating the power took effect.

> **EXAMPLE**
>
> A trust created on 1 July 1980 with an 80-year perpetuity period from that date includes a special power of appointment which is exercised after 6 April 2010 to resettle the property on new trusts. The perpetuity period for the new trusts created by the power will be 80 years starting on 1 July 1980.

The PAA 2009, s 12 allows trustees of pre-Act trusts to opt for a fixed period of 100 years from the date the trust commenced in one limited case. This is where the perpetuity period is defined by reference to a life or lives in being and it is difficult, or not reasonably practicable, to ascertain whether the lives have ended. The trustees must execute a deed stating that they believe there is such a difficulty and that the instrument is to be treated as if it had specified a period of 100 years from commencement (no other period is possible).

6.9.3 What does 'vest' mean?

Property does not have to vest *in possession* provided it has vested *in interest* by the end of the perpetuity period.

EXAMPLE 1

Property is settled on Agnes for life with the remainder to Bert. Agnes has an immediate interest in possession (ie, the right to the income) and Bert is guaranteed the capital, although the actual receipt of the capital will be delayed until Agnes dies.

Agnes's interest is vested in possession. Bert's interest is vested in interest.

You will not need to consider the perpetuity rules as the interests are already vested.

EXAMPLE 2

Property is settled on Connie for life with the remainder to the first child of David to attain 25 years of age.

At the time the settlement is created, David has no children, but shortly afterwards he has one child, Edward. Edward will become entitled to the settled property only if he reaches 25. Until then his interest is contingent. Connie's interest is vested in possession. Here it is necessary to consider the perpetuity rules.

6.9.4 Which settlements need a perpetuity period?

As we saw, no perpetuity period is required when all the interests have already vested, as in Example 1. A perpetuity period is required for settlements where the gifts are contingent upon the beneficiaries reaching a specified age, as in Example 2.

A perpetuity period is also required for discretionary settlements. Trustees select the beneficiary from within a class of beneficiaries and decide how much of the trust property to give that beneficiary. They must exhaust the trust fund, ie give a vested interest in the trust property, within the perpetuity period. A failure to do so will render void the trusts over any remaining property.

EXAMPLE

In 2000 £10,000 is settled on discretionary trusts for the children of X.

There are three children: Rose, Arthur and Kate. The stated perpetuity period is 80 years.

If the trustees make the following appointments which exhaust the fund in the sixtieth year, there will be no perpetuity problems.

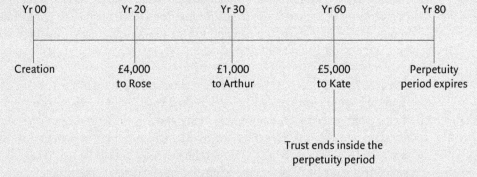

If, at the end of year 80, funds still remained, the trust would become void and the surplus funds would revert to the settlor (unless there was a gift over in default).

When drafting a settlement where there is any possibility that an interest might vest outside the perpetuity period, it is important to include provisions making this impossible rather than simply relying on the trustees to make sure that funds are appointed out before the end of the perpetuity period. As we will see later, in lifetime settlements, the mere possibility of funds reverting to the settlor (however unlikely it is to happen) is enough to produce adverse tax consequences.

To ensure that 'reverter to settlor' can never happen, the settlement should contain an ultimate default trust, ie, a clause directing who should receive any surplus left in the trust at the end of the trust (perpetuity) period.

This ultimate beneficiary must be living or in existence (eg, a charity) and be given a vested interest in the trust fund at the date of the settlement. A settlor will often choose a charity as the ultimate default beneficiary.

Sample clause

> Subject as above and if and so far as not wholly disposed of for any reason whatever by the above provisions, the capital and income of the Trust Fund shall be held in trust for [name] absolutely

---

EXAMPLE

Many years ago, property was settled on discretionary trusts for the settlor's children and remoter issue with a charity as ultimate default beneficiary. The perpetuity period is 80 years. The settlor had one child (Tracy) when the trust was set up. Tracy had two sons, Wayne and Calvin.

Since the settlement was created the trustees have distributed £170,000 of the trust fund, but Wayne died when he was 6 years old, Tracy died three years ago and Calvin has just died having never had any children.

There are no other issue of the settlor and a surplus of £30,000 remains within the trust. The trustees must transfer this to the charity and bring the trust to an end.

6.9.5 Obtaining a new perpetuity period

It is possible to apply to court under the Variation of Trusts Act 1958 for an extension to the perpetuity period. This has become very popular and was done successfully in *Wyndham v Egremont* [2009] WTLR 1473, *Pemberton v Pemberton* [2016] EWHC 2345 (Ch), *Allfrey v Allfrey* [2015] EWHC 1717 (Ch), *A v B* [2016] EWHC 340 (Ch) and *Edward, Duke of Somerset v Fitzgerald* [2019] EWHC 726 (Ch). The court gives its consent to the variation on behalf of minor, unborn, unascertained beneficiaries. Adult beneficiaries must consent for themselves. The court must be satisfied that the change is for the benefit of those on whose behalf it consents. Typically the reason for an application for a new perpetuity period is to avoid inheritance and capital gains tax charges that will arise if the trust terminates.

6.10 ACCUMULATIONS

6.10.1 Meaning of accumulations

In the case of discretionary settlements and those where the interests of the beneficiaries are contingent on reaching a certain age, the beneficiaries will not normally have a right to receive income as it arises. However, the trust property is likely to be earning income all the time. If the trustees choose not to pay it out to a beneficiary, they will retain it within the trust. Such retained income is said to be 'accumulated'.

Historically, there was a fear that allowing income to be accumulated for long periods within settlements would result in such a concentration of wealth in private hands that it might compromise the economic independence of the nation. There have, therefore, been successive statutory provisions limiting the period for which trustees can accumulate income. Once the relevant period expired, the trustees could not accumulate income and had to pay it out.

In recent years, there has been a relaxation in fears of excessive accumulations, and s 14 of the PAA 2009 abolished the statutory rule against excessive accumulations in the case of lifetime trusts created after 6 April 2010 and will trusts created in wills executed after that date. It is therefore possible to accumulate throughout the lifetime of such a settlement. Pre-PAA 2009 trusts will remain bound by the terms of the original instrument.

The PAA 2009 does not override provisions in trust documents, so the unrestricted power to accumulate will be subject to any express provisions in the trust instrument.

6.10.2 Accumulation periods pre-PAA 2009

For trusts not governed by the PAA 2009, there is a limit to the number of years during which income can be accumulated. The PAA 1964 sets out a choice of maximum periods for which income can be accumulated. Most trust draftsmen specified that income could be accumulated for a fixed period of 21 years from the date of the settlement. Although this period was possibly shorter than the maximum achievable under the PAA 1964, a fixed period provided for certainty. The specified accumulation period was not allowed to exceed the perpetuity period applicable to the settlement. At the end of the accumulation period, all income arising in each future year had to be paid out to the beneficiaries, unless the beneficiary was a minor (see **6.10.3**).

However, it is possible for trustees of older trusts to apply to court under the Variation of Trusts Act 1958 for permission to accumulate income even though the accumulation period has expired. Such an application was successful in *Edward, Duke of Somerset v Fitzgerald* (above).

EXAMPLE

Property is settled on discretionary trusts for the benefit of Susan, John and Harry. The accumulation period is 21 years. The trust income is £300 per annum.

		Susan	John	Harry	Accumulated
Accumulation period	Yr 1	100	–	–	200
	Yr 7	–	300	–	–
	Yr 8	100	100	100	–
	Yr 15	–	–	–	300
After accumulation period ends	Yr 22	100	200	–	–
	Yr 23	100	100	100	–
	Yr 24	150	–	150	–

Sample clause

> The Accumulation Period shall mean the period of twenty-one years from the date of this Settlement or the Trust Period if shorter

6.10.3   Extension of accumulation period under Trustee Act 1925, s 31

Where a beneficiary is a minor at the end of the PAA 1964 accumulation period and s 31 of TA 1925 applies to the trust, the trustees can continue to accumulate the income of the minor's share of the trust fund under s 31 until he is 18 years of age.

EXAMPLE

Three brothers were the beneficiaries of a discretionary settlement. The two older boys both died, leaving Adam (aged 16) the only beneficiary. The settlement's accumulation period has just ended. The trustees may accumulate income for a further two years. under s 31 of TA 1925.

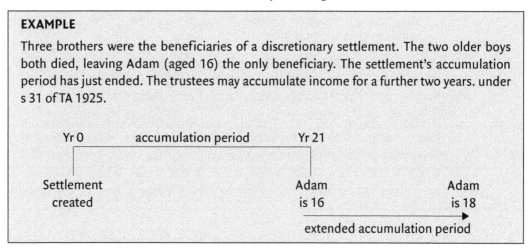

Where the trust instrument substantially modified s 31 of TA 1925, it was usual to limit the alteration to the accumulation period. This was to prevent any suggestion that the statutory provision had been replaced by the express provision.

6.10.4   Perpetuities and Accumulations Act 2009

As explained at **6.10.1** above, s 14 of the PAA 2009 abolished the rule against excessive accumulations for trusts governed by the PA 2009. The abolition is achieved by repealing ss 164–166 of the LPA 1925 and s 13 of the 1964 Act. The result is that trustees are able to accumulate income throughout the lifetime of a trust (which will normally be 125 years – the new perpetuity period).

The PA 2009 does not override provisions in trust documents, so the unrestricted power to accumulate is subject to any express provisions in the trust instrument.

Most settlors want to give their trustees maximum flexibility in relation to accumulating income and so do not want to limit their freedom. The settlement can either be silent as to accumulations, in which case the trustees will be able to accumulate throughout the lifetime of the settlement, or the settlement can define the accumulation period expressly.

Sample clause – the accumulation period

> The accumulation period shall mean the period ending on the last day of the period of 125 years from the date of my death

In the case of settlements not governed by the PA 2009, if trustees use their special powers of appointment to resettle property on new trusts, the old accumulation period will continue to apply to the new trusts (in the same way that such resettlements retain the original perpetuity period).

6.11   TRUSTS OF THE BENEFICIAL INTERESTS

In many ways, this is the most important section of the trust as it sets out the terms on which the trustees are to hold the trust property.

It is important that the whole of the beneficial interest is dealt with. If any of the trust property can revert to the settlor because the trusts are not exhaustive, adverse tax consequences follow.

A simple life interest trust

This will deal first with the payment of income and then with entitlement to capital. It may name the beneficiaries within the clause or may use defined terms.

> The Trustees shall pay the income of the Trust Fund to the Life Tenant during [her] life
>
> Subject to the above the Trustees shall hold the capital of the Trust Fund upon trust for the Remainderman absolutely

Because all the interests are vested, there is no possibility of the Trust Fund reverting to the settlor. If the remainderman dies before the life tenant, the trust capital will be paid to the remainderman's personal representatives and will pass as part of his estate.

Drafting the beneficial trusts where there are discretionary or contingent interests is slightly more complicated. To avoid overcomplicating this chapter, points relevant to drafting these beneficial interests are dealt with in **Chapter 7**. One important point that we will look at there is the importance of including a default beneficiary to take if the main beneficial interests fail. This will prevent the adverse tax consequences that arise if property can possibly revert to the settlor.

6.12 TRUSTEES' DISCRETIONS IN RELATION TO BENEFICIAL INTERESTS

It is common to give settlements creating fixed interests added flexibility by giving trustees additional discretions. A settlor may think that he wants to leave a life interest to his spouse and the capital to his children absolutely and in equal shares, but it is impossible to know what may happen in the future. A spouse may have unexpected need of capital; one child may become very much more wealthy than another.

Flexibility can be provided by making the settlement fully discretionary, but many people prefer to create a settlement with fixed interests and then to give the trustees overriding powers to alter those interests in case of need.

Typical overriding powers would be:

(a)   to appoint trust capital to the life tenant;

(b)   to terminate a life tenant's interest early;

(c)   to advance capital to one or more of the remainder beneficiaries early;

(d)   to distribute the capital to the remainder beneficiaries unequally.

6.13 APPOINTMENT OF NEW TRUSTEES

If a new trustee needs to be appointed because, for example, one of the original trustees has died or wishes to retire, in the absence of anything to the contrary in the trust instrument, the choice and appointment rests with the continuing trustee(s) under TA 1925, s 36.

A settlor who wishes to continue to exercise sole control over the selection of trustees during his lifetime can do so only if the trust instrument gives him the appropriate power (see **14.4.2**).

Sample clause

> During the lifetime of the Settlor the power of appointing new trustees shall be vested in the Settlor

As it is relatively common for settlors to wish to retain control over the appointment of trustees or to nominate close family members to exercise such control, it is important that those advising trustees do not simply assume that the continuing trustees have the power to make new appointments but check the trust instrument. Errors over appointments are amongst the most common of mistakes made in relation to the administration of trusts. They are very serious, as any acts carried out by a person not properly appointed will be invalid.

Some settlements appoint a third party as a 'Protector'. The Protector can perform a variety of roles, but it is common to give the Protector power to appoint and remove trustees.

6.14 EXCLUDING THE EFFECT OF TLATA 1996, SS 11, 12 AND 19

6.14.1 Consultation

Under TLATA 1996, s 11(1), the trustees of a trust of land who are exercising any function relating to the land subject to the trust must consult any beneficiary who is of full age and beneficially entitled to an interest in possession (eg, a co-owner) and, so far as consistent with 'the general interest of the trust', give effect to the wishes of the beneficiary or (in the case of dispute) the majority (according to the value of their combined assets).

Section 11 will not apply if there is a provision to that effect in the trust instrument (s 11(2)). If appropriate, a declaration excluding the s 11 requirement for consultation can be included in the settlement. It is common to include such a declaration.

Sample clause

> The provisions of section 11 of the Trusts of Land and Appointment of Trustees Act 1996 shall not apply so that it shall not be necessary for my Trustees to consult any Beneficiaries before carrying out any function relating to land or for the avoidance of doubt any other property.

6.14.2 Occupation of land by beneficiaries

Section 12 gives a beneficiary who is entitled to an interest in possession (eg, a co-owner) in land, even if not of full age, a right to occupy the land in certain circumstances.

In order to have this right of occupation, a beneficiary must establish either that the purposes of the trust include making the land available for his occupation or that the land is held by trustees so as to be so available.

The trustees have the right to impose conditions on an occupying beneficiary (eg, the payment of outgoings or expenses in respect of the land (s 13)). These conditions may include making payments by way of compensation to a beneficiary whose entitlement has been restricted.

A settlor cannot exclude ss 12 and 13. However, where a settlor does not wish beneficiaries to have a right to occupy, he can include a declaration that the purposes of the trust do not include making land available for occupation.

Sample clause

> The purposes of the trust in clause [   ] do not include making land available for occupation of any Beneficiary.

6.14.3 Right to direct retirement and appointment of replacement trustees

The TLATA 1996, s 19 (unless expressly excluded by the trust instrument) gives beneficiaries who are *sui juris* and entitled to the whole beneficial interest the right to direct trustees to retire and appoint specified replacement trustees (see **14.4.2**).

Settlors can exclude the s 19 right, but beneficiaries who are of full age and capacity and entitled to the whole beneficial interest would still be able to remove the trustees by bringing the trust to an end and then resettling the trust property with different trustees. Ending the trust would be likely to involve a charge to CGT as it will be a disposal. It is likely to be preferable in most cases, therefore, to allow beneficiaries to retain the s 19 right. However, there may be settlors who wish to exclude it.

Sample clause

> Section 19(2)(a) of the Trusts of Land and Appointment of Trustees Act 1996 shall not apply to this trust.

6.15 EXCLUSION OF SETTLOR (AND SPOUSE/CIVIL PARTNER)

To prevent settlors using settlements to obtain an unfair tax advantage for themselves, there are a number of anti-avoidance provisions in the tax legislation. Broadly, these apply where settlors, spouses, civil partners and minor children can benefit from settled property. The most important provisions relating to income tax, CGT and IHT are set out at **6.15.1** to **6.15.3** below.

6.15.1 The general income tax avoidance rules (ITTOIA 2005)

These complex, wide-ranging provisions are intended to prevent a higher rate taxpayer from avoiding income tax on income by transferring the property which produces it to another person, who either pays no income tax or pays at a rate lower than the transferor.

The rules apply to 'settlements'. 'Settlement' is defined very widely (ITTOIA 2005, s 620) to include 'any disposition, trust, covenant, agreement, arrangement or transfer of assets'. They apply to settlements where the settlor retains an interest in the settled property (s 624), but they also apply specifically to settlements by parents for the benefit of their minor unmarried children (s 629; see **4.6.2.3** and **4.6.4.1**).

Under s 624 the income of settled property 'is treated ... as the income of the settlor and of the settlor alone if it arises ... from property in which the settlor has an interest'. Section 625 states that a settlor is treated as having an interest in settled property if there are any circumstances in which the settled property is or may become payable to or applicable for the benefit of the settlor or the settlor's spouse.

Typically (but not exclusively), s 624 will apply where:

(a)   the settled property will revert to the settlor, for example where the property is settled on A for life with the remainder to the settlor. Such a settlement might be considered if a settlor wished to provide an elderly relative with an income but at the same time wanted to ensure return of the settled property when the relative died;

(b)   the settled property could revert to the settlor because the beneficial interests are not exhaustive;

(c)   the settlement contains a power of revocation whereupon the settled property would revert to the settlor or his spouse;

(d)   the settlement contains a discretionary power to benefit the settlor or his spouse or civil partner, ie they are among the objects of the trustees' discretion.

> **EXAMPLE**
>
> Thomas creates a discretionary settlement during his lifetime under which he and his wife Agatha may benefit because they are included in the class of beneficiaries, ie they are among the objects of the trust. Even if neither Thomas nor Agatha actually benefits, for example because the trustees of the settlement accumulate the income or apply all of it for other beneficiaries, all of the income of the settled property will be taxed as though it belonged to Thomas.

Where the rules apply, the income of the property in the settlement is treated as belonging to the settlor for all income tax purposes, although generally he can recover from the trustees any tax he has to pay on the income. This income retains its character in the hands of the settlor, as if it had arisen to him directly. Therefore he will be treated as receiving non-savings income, interest income or dividend income as appropriate (ITTOIA 2005, s 619).

The settlor will also have the benefit of a tax credit of 45% or 38.1% on the trust income attributed to him. In many cases, the settlor will have the same marginal rate of tax as the trustees and so no further adjustment will be necessary. However, if the settlor's income (including the trust income attributed to him) is less than £150,000, some of the tax paid by the trustees will be repaid.

Settlors who receive tax repayments because their marginal tax rate is less than the trustees' rate are required to pass such repayments to the trustees (ITTOIA 2005, s 646). Any such payments will be disregarded for IHT purposes.

6.15.2 CGT where the settlor has an interest in the settlement

Prior to changes to the rates of capital gains tax made in the Finance Act 2008, the gains arising in a settlor interested trust were charged on the settlor rather than the trustees. This legislation has now been repealed, as the rules are no longer necessary due to the increase in the rate of CGT paid by trustees.

The only remaining capital gains tax provisions applying to settlor interested trusts relate to the availability of hold-over relief.

Since 10 December 2003, the settlor cannot claim hold-over relief under TCGA 1992, ss 165 or 260 on a transfer into a settlement in which he, his spouse or his unmarried minor child is interested (see **4.4.5.2**). Hold-over relief already claimed will be clawed back if the settlement becomes settlor interested within six years of the tax year of creation.

6.15.3 Reservation of benefit and IHT

Although the phrase 'an interest in the settlement' is not found in FA 1986, s 102, none the less the concept lies behind the reservation of benefit provisions. These have been discussed at **4.6.5**. If settled property is subject to reservation of benefit for the settlor, s 102 will apply, with the result that the property is still within the settlor's estate for IHT. Note that the rules apply only where the *settlor* derives a benefit. They do not apply if the settlor's spouse or unmarried minor child benefits.

6.15.4 Drafting the settlement

Because of the adverse tax consequences that will follow if the settlor, spouse or minor unmarried child of the settlor can benefit from the trust, it is important to include provisions to ensure that this does not happen. Civil partners are subject to the same anti-avoidance provisions as spouses and so must also be excluded from benefit.

It is important that beneficial interests are drafted to ensure that there is no possibility of property reverting to the settlor. In discretionary and contingent settlements, where the interests are not immediately vested, an ultimate default clause will always be included.

In addition to the default clause, a settlement with discretionary powers will normally contain two references to the exclusion of the settlor, spouse and minor unmarried children; the first, in relation to the power to add new beneficiaries and the second in relation to the exercise of the administrative powers (see **Appendix 3**, clauses 3(3) and 14).

(1)   The trust instrument may give the trustees very wide powers and discretions over the trust fund (see **Chapter 9**). For example, if the trustees can use their powers to benefit the settlor, his spouse or minor unmarried children, even though the power is never used, the settlor is deemed to have an interest in the trust property.

(2)   A clause should be included in the settlement deed to the effect that the settlor, his spouse or minor unmarried child cannot and must not benefit from the trust. This clause serves as a prohibition against trustees ever exercising a trust power in favour of the settlor or his spouse.

Sample clause

> No discretion or power conferred on the Trustees by this Settlement or by law shall be exercised and no provision in the Settlement shall operate, directly or indirectly so as to cause or permit any part of the capital or income of the Trust Fund to become in any way payable to or applicable for the benefit of the Settlor or the spouse [or civil partner] or minor unmarried children of the Settlor

6.16   STAMP DUTY AND STAMP DUTY LAND TAX

It is not uncommon for a settlor to transfer shares into a settlement. Where shares are transferred for no consideration the document transferring them is exempt from stamp duty if the transaction falls within the schedule to the Stamp Duty (Exempt Instruments) Regulations 1987 (SI 1987/516) (see **4.9**). If, very unusually, the settlement deed is the document making the transfer of shares to the trustees it should contain a certificate that the transaction does come within these regulations.

Sample clause

> It is hereby certified that this instrument falls within Category L in the Schedule to the Stamp Duty (Exempt Instrument) Regulations 1987

Category L is 'a conveyance or transfer of property operating as a voluntary disposition inter vivos for no consideration in money or money's worth nor any consideration referred to in section 57 of the Stamp Act 1891 (conveyance in consideration of a debt etc)'.

However, it is much more likely that the transfer to the trustees will be by separate stock transfer form, and it is this document that should contain this certificate.

Stamp Duty Land Tax is payable where an interest in land is transferred for consideration. No consideration is provided where a settlor settles land, so no tax is payable. However, the settlor must provide a separate certificate to the effect that a stamp duty land tax return is not required.

6.17   SIGNATURES

A trust instrument is a deed and must be signed as such by the settlor, and by the trustees as well to show their acceptance of the trusts. One witness is required to each signature.

Sample clause

> Signed as a deed and delivered
> by [name of Settlor]
> in the presence of

SUMMARY

(1)   There are many different types of settlements, for example settlements with fixed vested interests, discretionary settlements and settlements with contingent interests.

(2)   However, all lifetime settlements have many elements in common.

(3)   They all need to appoint trustees, define the trust property, declare the beneficial interests and exclude the settlor, spouse, civil partner and minor unmarried children from benefit to avoid adverse tax consequences.

REVIEW ACTIVITY

Which ONE of the following statements is CORRECT?

A   Since the Civil Partnership Act 2004 came into force, a reference to a spouse in a settlement will be construed as including a civil partner.

B   A settlement created in 2012 for Ann for life, remainder to Ben for life, remainder to Claude absolutely, will be void for perpetuity if Claude has not taken possession of the trust assets within 125 years.

C   In the case of settlements created after the Perpetuities and Accumulations Act 2009 came into force, income can always be accumulated throughout the lifetime of the trust.

D   In the case of settlements created before the Perpetuities and Accumulations Act 2009 came into force, income can be accumulated beyond the end of the accumulation period for the benefit of a minor beneficiary if s 31 of the Trustee Act 1925 applies to the settlement.

Answer: D

Although pre-2009 Act settlements have only limited accumulation periods, s 31 of the Trustee Act 1925 does allow additional accumulation for the benefit of minor beneficiaries.

There are no statutory limits on accumulations in post-2009 settlements, but express provisions can be included to limit accumulations (although this would be unusual).

CHAPTER 7

DRAFTING BENEFICIAL INTERESTS

LEARNING OUTCOMES

After reading this chapter you will be able to:

- explain what needs to be included when drafting beneficial interests for a discretionary settlement
- explain what needs to be included when drafting beneficial interests for a settlement with contingent interests.

7.1 INTRODUCTION

We looked in **Chapter 6** at points which are generally relevant when drafting settlements. In this chapter we shall look at points which are relevant when drafting the beneficial interests in discretionary settlements and settlements with contingent interests. In both types of settlements, the beneficial interests tend to be more complicated than in a fixed interest trust where, typically, property is held for a small number of beneficiaries in succession.

Both these forms of settlement commonly give trustees extensive discretions and it is, therefore, desirable that the settlor prepare a letter of wishes indicating the factors which the settlor would like the trustees to take into account. Such a letter is not binding on the trustees but it will be helpful for them to know what the settlor regarded as important. It will normally set out the settlor's views on matters such as the appropriate age for receiving capital, what sort of things capital should be provided for, and the extent to which the trustees should strive for equality between the various beneficiaries.

7.2 SETTLEMENTS CREATING DISCRETIONARY TRUSTS

The discretionary trusts apply to both income and capital of the trust fund. There are separate clauses for each. The component parts of these clauses are discussed at **7.2.1** and **7.2.2**. A full precedent of the clauses is found in **Appendix 3**.

7.2.1 Discretionary trusts of income

7.2.1.1 The primary trust

The primary trust enables the trustees to decide how to distribute the income of the trust fund amongst the beneficiaries.

Sample clause

> The Trustees shall pay or apply the income of the Trust Fund to or for the benefit of such of the Beneficiaries as shall for the time being be in existence, in such shares and in such manner generally as the Trustees shall in their discretion from time to time think fit

The clause gives trustees the choice not only of which beneficiaries to benefit, but also how to provide that benefit.

> **EXAMPLE**
>
> Property is settled on discretionary trusts for the settlor's two grandchildren, Adam and Debbie. The annual income is £1,000 net. Adam is at university, reading medicine; Debbie is 16, at school and wants to be an actress.
>
> For the last two years the trustees have paid all the available income to Adam as he is finding it difficult to manage financially on the amount available from other sources.
>
> This year the trustees decide to buy one year's membership to the local theatre club for Debbie at a cost of £80 and pay the insurance premium (£20) on the bicycle she has bought herself to save bus fares. They give the balance to Adam.

7.2.1.2   Power to accumulate income

Settlors do not usually want to compel trustees to pay out all the trust income every year. It is normal to allow them to accumulate trust income if they think it appropriate.

Sample clause

> The Trustees may at any time in their discretion accumulate the income by investing it in any investments authorised by this Deed or by law and shall hold such accumulations as an accretion to capital.

We saw at **6.10** that, in the case of settlements not governed by the PAA 2009, the trustees cannot accumulate income indefinitely. The PAA 1964 limits the length of time that income can be accumulated. The accumulation period selected must be stated in the settlement but there is no need to grant an express power to accumulate. Once the accumulation period is selected, the trustees have power to retain income during the selected period.

At the end of the accumulation period, the trustees lose the power to retain income (apart from the power conferred by s 31 of the Trustee Act 1925 to accumulate during the minority of a beneficiary) and must pay out the trust income every year.

In the case of settlements governed by the PAA 2009, trustees can accumulate throughout the life of the settlement (unless the settlor has imposed limitations) so the issue of the accumulation period expiring before the end of the trust period will not arise.

7.2.1.3   Power to use accumulated income

As a general rule, income received during the accumulation period and accumulated becomes part of the capital of the trust fund and so unavailable as income of future years. However, the settlor may wish to give the trustees more flexibility.

Sample clause

> The Trustees may under sub-clause [   ] apply the whole or any part of the income accumulated as if it were income arising in the then current year.

The effect of this clause is that any income retained from previous years can be made available to increase the income available in the current year.

EXAMPLE

Property is settled on discretionary trusts for Gail and Martin. The accumulation period is 21 years and the annual income £100 net.

	Gail	Martin	Accumulate	Total of income available for distributions
Year 1	75	25	–	nil
Year 2	–	–	100	100
Year 3	90	–	10	110
Year 4	60	60	–	90
etc				

7.2.1.4 Accumulated income at the end of the accumulation period

Where the accumulation period is shorter than the trust period, the settlement will direct what is to happen to any undistributed income at the end of the accumulation period.

Extract from clause

> ... and subject to sub-clause [ ] shall hold such accumulations as an accretion to capital

Any accumulated income which has not been spent by the end of the accumulation period is added to the capital of the trust fund.

EXAMPLE

In 2008 £5,000 is settled on discretionary trusts for Penny and Nick. The accumulation period is 21 years and the annual income £100 net.

	Penny	Nick	Total of accumulated income	Capital
Year 20	90	–	320	5,000
Year 21	100	100	220	5,000
Year 22	60	40		5,220
Year 23	50	50		5,220
etc				

7.2.2 Discretionary trusts of capital

The trusts over capital enable the trustees to decide how, when and to which beneficiaries to distribute the capital of the trust fund. The trustees will give effect to their decision by the exercise of a power of appointment. Powers of appointment are dealt with more fully in **Chapters 9** and **10**.

7.2.2.1 The primary trust

Sample clause

> The Trustees may pay or apply the whole or any part of the capital of the Trust Fund to or for the benefit of all or such of the Beneficiaries, eg, in such shares and in such manner generally as the Trustees shall in their discretion think fit

---

EXAMPLE

£100,000 is settled on discretionary trusts for Alice and Bertram. Each year, the trustees pay all available income to the beneficiaries. So far as capital is concerned:

Year 1:   Trustees decide not to pay out any capital.

Year 2:   Bertram is buying a car and the trustees decide to give him £12,000.

Year 15:   For 13 years the trustees exercised their power by not distributing any capital but this year gave £10,000 to Alice to help towards the cost of looking after her new baby and £50,000 to Bertram for alterations to his house.

Year 16:   The trustees decide that the costs of running the settlement outweigh its benefits and so bring it to an end by giving the remaining £28,000 equally to Alice and Bertram.

The settlor should leave a letter of wishes to help the trustees decide how to exercise their discretion.

7.2.2.2 Transfers on to other trusts

Sample clause

> The Trustees may, subject to the application (if any) of the rule against perpetuities pay or transfer any income or capital of the Trust Fund to the trustees of any other trust, wherever established or existing, under which any Beneficiary is interested (whether or not such Beneficiary is the only object or person interested or capable of benefiting under such other trust) if the Trustees in their discretion consider such payment or transfer to be for the benefit of such Beneficiary

The trustees may feel it appropriate to benefit a particular beneficiary by 'resettling' property on new trusts of which he (and perhaps other members of his family) is a beneficiary.

A general power to apply capital for the benefit of beneficiaries might be worded sufficiently widely to allow capital to be transferred to an entirely new trust, but trustees are cautious people and it is preferable to have a clause which specifically allows a transfer to a new settlement.

The exercise of such a power is considered in **Chapter 10**.

7.2.2.3 Ultimate default trusts

As we saw in **Chapter 6** it is important that there is no danger of property reverting to the settlor at the end of the perpetuity period.

All the capital and income of the trust fund must be fully distributed or be subject to vested interests by the end of the trust (perpetuity) period so that the trusts are not void for perpetuity. If for any reason the trustees have not distributed everything, the property remaining in the trust fund will revert back to the settlor. Even though in practice this never happens because the trustees do distribute fully, the fact that it could happen means that the settlor has an interest in the settlement and suffers adverse tax consequences (see **6.15**).

7.3 SETTLEMENTS WITH CONTINGENT INTERESTS

The principal trusts

This clause will state the primary intention of the settlor, namely that the trustees will hold the capital of the trust fund for the beneficiaries until they attain the specified age.

Sample clause

> The Trust Fund shall be held upon trust for such of the Primary Beneficiaries as:
>
> (a)   attain the age of 25 before the end of the Trust Period; or
>
> (b)   are living and under that age at the end of the Trust Period
>
> and, if more than one, in equal shares absolutely.

Commentary on the clause: capital provision

Perpetuity rules

To comply with the perpetuity rules, the contingent interests must vest within the perpetuity period applying to the trust; this will normally be a period of 80 years or 125 years, depending on whether the settlement is governed by the PAA 1964 or the PAA 2009.

This trust provides contingent gifts which are to vest in beneficiaries at the age of 25 years. Any beneficiary attaining that age within the trust period, ie the perpetuity period of the trust, will have a vested entitlement. Any beneficiary who is still under the age of 25 years when the trust period ends will immediately acquire a vested entitlement to a share of the trust fund.

It is of course possible that by the end of the perpetuity period no beneficiaries have or can take a vested interest.

EXAMPLE

Fred creates a lifetime settlement for such of his grandchildren as reach 25. At the time the settlement is created he has one grandchild aged two. This grandchild is killed in a climbing accident, aged 24. No further grandchildren are born. At the end of the perpetuity period there are no beneficiaries who can take a vested interest. The property will revert to the settlor unless the settlement includes an ultimate default clause.

As we saw in **Chapter 6**, adverse tax consequences follow if there is any possibility of property reverting to the settlor, so settlements creating contingent interests should, like discretionary trusts, always include an ultimate default clause. This will give someone (typically, a charity) a vested interest subject to the preceding contingent interests.

Right to capital to vest at 25 years

The sample clause above provides that a beneficiary's entitlement to capital will vest at or before the age of 25. However, as we have seen, it is equally possible to give a beneficiary a right to income contingent on reaching a certain age and leave the entitlement to capital to the trustees' discretion (subject to vesting within the perpetuity period).

Trustee Act 1925, s 32

Section 32 of TA 1925 gives the trustees power to apply capital for the advancement or benefit of a beneficiary who has an interest in the capital of the settlement. The power may be exercised where the beneficiary has a contingent interest even though the beneficiary may never satisfy the contingency, for example, because he dies before the age stipulated for the vesting of the capital. In the absence of contrary provision, s 32 will automatically apply to a settlement with contingent interests.

As originally drafted, the section enabled trustees to advance up to one half of a beneficiary's presumptive, ie contingent, entitlement to capital irrespective of the age to which the right to the capital has been delayed by the terms of the settlement. The statutory power was commonly modified when drafting the settlement to enable the trustees to advance up to the whole of a beneficiary's presumptive entitlement in the same way as the power is often extended when drafting a will.

The Inheritance and Trustees' Powers Act 2014 (ITPA 2014) came into force on 1 October 2014. The Act removes the one half limit from s 32, so that trustees are able at their discretion to pay out up to the whole of a beneficiary's prospective share of capital. This change applies in relation to all trusts created or arising on or after 1 October 2014. See **9.4.4** for further discussion of the changes.

Commentary on the clause: income provision

Income entitlement at 18 years

This clause contains no express reference to income. In particular, the clause does not vary the implied provisions of s 31 of TA 1925 by substituting a later age of up to 25 years for the statutory age of 18 years. Income entitlement of the primary beneficiaries and the trustees' duty to accumulate surplus income is, therefore, determined in accordance with s 31 of TA 1925.

Trustee Act 1925, s 31

Unless expressly excluded, s 31 of TA 1925 will automatically apply to the settlement.

The statutory power gives beneficiaries with a contingent interest a right to income at 18 if the interest is still contingent at that point. When drafting settlements with contingent interests, it is common to defer the entitlement to income to an age exceeding 18. The trustees' discretion then continues until the specified age. However, when deferring entitlement to income, it is important to check the length of the accumulation period. Trusts created before the Perpetuities and Accumulations Act 2009 came into force will always have a limited accumulation period. Those created afterwards may have limitations imposed by the settlor (although this would be unusual) (see **6.10**).

As originally enacted, s 31 contained two restrictions on the way trustees could exercise their powers to apply income, which are commonly removed in well-drafted trusts. The restrictions were:

(a)   Section 31(1)(i) stated that the power was exercisable in respect of such income 'as may, in all the circumstances, be reasonable', which imposed an objective standard on trustees.

(b)   The proviso to s 31(1):

    (i)   listed factors to which the trustees were to have regard in exercising their discretion – the beneficiary's age and requirements, and the circumstances generally; and

    (ii)   imposed a specific restriction on the amount of income which could be paid out where the trustees had notice that the income of one or more other trust funds was also applicable for the maintenance, education or benefit of the beneficiary.

The ITPA 2014 removes both of these restrictions entirely. These changes, like the removal of the one half restriction in s 32, apply in relation to trusts created or arising after the statute came into force.

SUMMARY

(1)   Unless the settlement is a simple one where all interests are vested and the trustees have no discretions, they will need in addition:

    (a)   an ultimate default clause to make sure that there cannot be funds left over at the end of the perpetuity period which would revert to the settlor; and

    (b)   in the case of settlements not governed by the PAA 2009, a clause selecting the perpetuity period and a clause selecting the accumulation period.

(2)   If the trustees have any discretions, the settlor should prepare a letter of wishes to help the trustees exercise their discretions.

REVIEW ACTIVITY

Which ONE of the following statements is WRONG?

A   It is possible to give trustees power to use accumulated income as if it is income of the current year.

B   In the absence of express provision to the contrary, accumulated income becomes part of the settlement's capital.

C   In the case of both discretionary settlements and settlements with contingent interests, it is important to include default provisions to ensure that property cannot revert to the settlor.

D   Discretionary settlements and settlements with contingent interests which do not include default provisions to ensure that property cannot revert to the settlor are invalid.

Answer: D

The inclusion of a default clause is necessary to ensure that adverse tax consequences do not arise, but failure to include such a provision does not mean that the settlement is invalid.

Accumulation and Maintenance Settlements

LEARNING OUTCOMES

After reading this chapter you will be able to:

- identify an accumulation and maintenance settlement meeting the requirements of IHTA 1984, s 71 as amended
- explain the tax treatment of such settlements.

8.1 INTRODUCTION

Individuals often want to provide funds for the benefit of young people but do not necessarily want the young people to have free access to those funds until they are sufficiently mature. Creating a settlement is useful as it allows the trustees to control the availability of funds.

Before 22 March 2006 a particular form of settlement created for young people, called an accumulation and maintenance (A & M) settlement, attracted privileged tax treatment. No new settlements of this type can be created on or after 22 March 2006, but settlements in existence on that date continue to attract privileged tax treatment provided they comply with certain conditions.

You will continue to meet such settlements from time to time, although they are becoming much less common.

Clients wishing to create lifetime settlements for young people on or after 22 March 2006 will have to create relevant property settlements (unless the beneficiary is disabled). The terms of the settlement are immaterial and there are no tax advantages available.

A transfer to a relevant property settlement will be immediately chargeable to IHT, but there will be tax to pay only to the extent that the transfer exceeds the settlor's nil rate band. A married couple can therefore settle £650,000 between them without an immediate charge to IHT. For those wanting to give away more, the immediate charge to tax is a disincentive to creating a settlement.

8.2 WHAT ARE A & M SETTLEMENTS?

Accumulation and maintenance settlements were originally settlements created before 22 March 2006 which fulfilled the requirements of IHTA 1984, s 71. They received IHT privileges (see **8.3**).

On 6 April 2008 existing A & M settlements lost their privileged status unless they fulfilled the requirements of s 71 as amended by FA 2006.

8.2.1 The requirements of the original s 71

The original s 71 laid down the following three requirements, all of which had to be satisfied:

(a) One or more beneficiaries will, on or before attaining a specified age not exceeding 25, become beneficially entitled to the settled property or to income from it.

(b) No interest in possession subsists in the settled property and the income from it is to be accumulated so far as it is not applied for the maintenance, education or benefit of such a beneficiary.

(c) Either:

(i)   not more than 25 years have elapsed since the day on which the settlement was made; or

(ii) all the beneficiaries are grandchildren of a common grandparent, or are children, widows or widowers, or surviving civil partners of such grandchildren who were themselves beneficiaries but died before becoming entitled as in (a) above.

8.2.2 The requirements of the amended s 71

Accumulation and maintenance settlements in existence on 22 March 2006 continued to qualify for privileged IHT treatment until 6 April 2008.

On 6 April 2008 an amended s 71 came into effect, and existing A & M settlements only qualify for IHT privileged treatment if they satisfy the requirements of the amended s 71.

The second and third requirements (see **8.2.1**) are unchanged, but the first requirement is substantially amended as from 6 April 2008 as follows:

> One or more beneficiaries will, on or before attaining a specified age not exceeding 18, become beneficially entitled to the settled property.

The reduction of the age of entitlement to 18 and the requirement that beneficiaries must become entitled to capital and not merely income at 18, meant that many settlements ceased to qualify as A & M settlements on 6 April 2008.

Section 71D of IHTA 1984, introduced by FA 2006, provides for limited IHT privileges for certain types of settlements for young people created on death. It also provides that any A & M settlement in existence on 22 March 2006 may qualify for the same limited privileges from 6 April 2008. To qualify, the settlement must provide that the beneficiaries will become entitled to capital at or before 25, and satisfy certain other requirements set out in s 71D. See **Chapter 12** for details of the IHT treatment of s 71D settlements. Broadly, there will be no anniversary charges but there will be an exit charge when a beneficiary becomes entitled to capital, calculated on the length of time property remains settled after the beneficiary's 18th birthday. (Settlements that fulfil the even more restrictive requirements of s 71A will qualify as s 71A settlements, but this will be unusual.)

Settlements which meet neither the amended first requirement of s 71 nor the requirements of s 71D (or s 71A) are converted into relevant property settlements on 6 April 2008 without any charge to IHT.

During the period 22 March 2006 to 6 April 2008, trustees had to review the terms of their settlements to decide what would happen in 2008. Some trustees allowed their settlements to be converted into relevant property settlements. Some used powers of appointment or advancement to distribute all the capital to the beneficiaries before 6 April 2008, thus bringing the settlement to an end, or to resettle the property on different trusts. Others applied to court to vary the terms of the settlement to allow them to retain their status as A & M settlements.

Because some settlements still qualify as A & M settlements under the amended s 71, we shall look briefly at each of the three requirements. Some of the points made are also relevant to s 71A and s 71D settlements as we will see in **Chapter 12**.

8.2.3 The three elements of the amended s 71

8.2.3.1 At least one beneficiary will become entitled to the trust property on or before his 18th birthday

The requirement is that a beneficiary will become entitled to the capital of the trust fund or a portion of it at or before age 18.

The requirement that a beneficiary 'will' become entitled does not require absolute certainty. Death can always prevent entitlement but the possibility does not mean that this requirement is unsatisfied. It should be read as meaning 'will become entitled, if at all, at or before the age of 18'.

Section 71(4)(b) provides that tax will not be charged on the death of a beneficiary below the specified age. Therefore, the death of all the intended beneficiaries before the specified age does not prevent the settlement being an A & M settlement (see further *Inglewood (Lord) and Another v IRC* [1983] STC 133).

EXAMPLE

Sam settles £10,000 in 2001 on trust for Adam if he attains 18 years of age.

If Adam reaches 18 years (ie, satisfies the contingency) the trustees must give him the £10,000.

If Adam dies, say, aged 15 years, the trust will fail. The £10,000 will not form part of Adam's estate.

The existence of powers which, if exercised, could result in property vesting beyond the specified age or being appointed to a non-beneficiary will, however, prevent a settlement having A & M status.

EXAMPLE

Shazia settles property on Bindi in 2005 contingent on her reaching 18, but the settlement gives the trustees power to appoint the trust property to Shazia's husband if they see fit. This settlement is not an A & M settlement, as it is not possible to say that Bindi *will* become entitled.

8.2.3.2 No beneficiary may have an interest in possession and any income not applied must be accumulated

There are two elements to this requirement:

(a)   no interest in possession; and

(b)   income must be accumulated to the extent that it is not applied for beneficiaries.

Both are normally satisfied while the beneficiary is a minor as a result of the effect of s 31 of TA 1925 (or equivalent express powers).

8.2.3.3 The trust must not have lasted for more than 25 years unless all the beneficiaries have a common grandparent, etc

Where the beneficiaries do not share a common grandparent, the settlement can have A & M status for only 25 years. If it continues as a settlement after the expiry of 25 years, a charge to IHT may then arise.

The grandparent must be common to all the beneficiaries, but need not have any blood tie to the settlor.

EXAMPLE

(1)   In 2004 Sam set up a settlement for the children of his friend, Frances. The beneficiaries have a common grandparent so, if the other requirements of s 71 are satisfied, the settlement can qualify as a s 71 settlement for more than 25 years.

(2)   In 2004 Sam set up a settlement for the children and grandchildren of his friend, Frances. The beneficiaries are from different generations and so do not have a common grandparent. If the other requirements of s 71 are satisfied, the settlement can qualify as a s 71 settlement, but only for 25 years.

This requirement is designed to prevent more than one generation from benefiting from A & M status. Even so, a second generation can benefit in some cases, as the provisions permit substitution where an original beneficiary has died.

EXAMPLE

Sherman died in 2002 and in his will left property to his children, with a substitutional gift to children of any child who predeceased him. One of his children predeceased him, leaving two children who were substituted as beneficiaries. Despite the fact that there is no common grandparent, the settlement can qualify as a s 71 settlement for more than 25 years provided the other requirements are satisfied.

8.3   TAXATION OF EXISTING A & M SETTLEMENTS FROM 6 APRIL 2008

8.3.1   Inheritance tax

Accumulation and maintenance settlements were treated very kindly from an IHT point of view. Be aware of the following points:

(a)   The lifetime creation of an A & M settlement was a PET (IHTA 1984, s 3A), so if the settlor died within seven years of the transfer, IHT would become payable. Tapering relief was available after three years.

(b)   Settlements which retain A & M status have no anniversary or exit charges (unless a settlement created for beneficiaries without a common grandparent lasts for more than 25 years, at which point there will be an exit charge). This means that these settlements defer the beneficiaries' entitlement to capital without incurring any IHT charges for the settlement.

8.3.2   Capital gains tax

There is only one special CGT advantage for A & M settlements. Hold-over relief is available when a beneficiary of an A & M settlement becomes absolutely entitled to capital assets. See **4.4.5.2**.

8.3.3   Income tax

There are no special income tax provisions relating to A & M settlements. The normal income tax rules applying to settlements apply. See **Chapter 14**.

SUMMARY

(1)   A & M settlements had important IHT benefits. Lifetime creation was a PET and they were not subject to anniversary or exit charges.

(2)   These benefits continued until 6 April 2008 for all A & M settlements in existence on 22 March 2006.

> (3) At that date an A & M settlement lost its privileged status and the property within it became subject to the relevant property regime *unless* the settlement satisfied certain conditions, in particular that the beneficiaries are entitled to capital:
>
>   (a) at age 18; or
>
>   (b) at or before age 25.
>
> (4) Settlements which fulfilled the conditions on 6 April 2008 retained their privileged IHT status. They are not subject to the relevant property regime, which means that there are no anniversary or exit charges payable.

REVIEW ACTIVITY

Which ONE of the following statements is CORRECT?

A   It is no longer possible to create accumulation and maintenance settlements qualifying for privileged inheritance tax treatment under IHTA 1984, s 71.

B   All accumulation and maintenance settlements lost their privileged inheritance tax treatment under IHTA 1984, s 71 on 6 April 2008.

C   All accumulation and maintenance settlements lost their privileged inheritance tax treatment under IHTA 1984, s 71 on 22 March 2006.

D   Accumulation and maintenance settlements cannot have beneficiaries from different generations if they are to qualify for privileged inheritance tax treatment under IHTA 1984, s 71.

Answer: A

Privileged settlements retained their status until 6 April 2008 *and thereafter*, provided they complied with the requirements of the redrafted s 71. Such settlements can always have beneficiaries of different generations, although the privileged status will then be limited to 25 years – unless there has been a substitution for a deceased primary beneficiary in which case the 25-year limitation does not apply.

TRUST ADVANCES AND APPOINTMENTS

LEARNING OUTCOMES

After reading this chapter you will be able to:

- identify the differences and similarities between advances and appointments
- explain the effect of the statutory power to apply capital and common modifications to it
- draft a power to appoint capital.

9.1 INTRODUCTION

No one can foresee the future and so it is desirable that trustees have power to override the terms of the settlement if circumstances require it. For many years there has been a statutory power to apply capital for the advancement or benefit of beneficiaries with an interest in capital (currently Trustee Act 1925 (TA 1925), s 32). In addition, modern settlements are drafted to incorporate as much flexibility as possible by giving trustees overriding powers to modify the terms on which the funds are held by using powers of appointment.

This chapter looks at the similarities and differences between the two types of power and at points to bear in mind when drafting express powers. Whenever exercising an overriding power, it is essential to understand the tax implications of the exercise. This is a big topic and is dealt with separately in **Chapter 10**.

9.2 WHAT ARE ADVANCES AND APPOINTMENTS?

The exercise of a power to apply capital for the advancement or benefit of a beneficiary and a power to appoint capital on different terms from those set out in the trust instrument have similar effects. Both normally result in beneficiaries having access to capital at a time or in a way that they would not otherwise have. The property will either become the absolute property of a beneficiary, ie it ceases to be subject to the trusts of the settlement, or it will remain settled property subject to the trusts of the original settlement, as varied by the appointment, or of a new settlement. The trustees' powers may be sufficiently wide for them to 'declare new trusts' over some part of the trust property. The taxation implications of the exercise of these powers are discussed further in **Chapter 10**.

There is a statutory power to apply trust capital (under TA 1925, s 32) for the advancement or benefit of beneficiaries with a vested or presumptive entitlement to capital. The statutory power may be extended or modified by provision in the trust instrument.

People often think that 'advancement' involves giving a beneficiary capital early, but this is not necessarily the case.

According to Lord Radcliffe in *Pilkington v IRC* [1964] AC 612, the word 'advancement' means the establishment in life of the beneficiary who was the object of the power. In the nineteenth century this meant something like buying an apprenticeship, or the purchase of a commission in the army or an interest in business. In the case of women, there could be advancement on marriage. Advancement, therefore, has a limited range of meaning since it conveys the idea of some step in life of permanent significance.

To introduce flexibility, it became common for those drafting trusts to add words such as 'or otherwise for his or her benefit'. It was always recognised that these added words were 'large words' (see Jessel MR in *Re Breeds' Will* (1875) 1 Ch D 226).

In *Pilkington*, Lord Radcliffe said the expression 'advancement or benefit' meant 'any use of the money which will improve the material situation of the beneficiary'. He also said that the word 'advancement' does not carry with it the idea of paying money to a beneficiary early. That is often the result, since the funds advanced come from property in which the beneficiary does not yet have an absolute entitlement, but in some cases the advancement might actually defer the vesting of the beneficiary's absolute title.

For example, a beneficiary may have an interest which is contingent on reaching 21. As he approaches 21, it may become apparent to the trustees that he cannot be trusted to deal sensibly with the capital at such a young age. The trustees may decide to use their statutory powers of advancement to resettle the capital on further trusts, perhaps giving the beneficiary a right to income at 25 but deferring his entitlement to capital.

Powers of appointment can exist only as express powers. The extent of the trustees' powers of appointment depend entirely on the terms of the power. A power may be drafted to be as wide as, or wider than, the statutory power of advancement, or it may be much more limited. In the absence of clear words, a power of appointment only allows trustees to modify the terms of the existing settlement, not to appoint the capital out freed from the terms of the existing settlement. Modern settlements, however, are normally worded to allow the widest possible application. For a fuller discussion of the differences, see **9.3.2** below. Modifying the statutory power of advancement by express provision and the drafting of express powers are considered at **9.4.3** and **9.5**.

9.3 SIMILARITIES AND DIFFERENCES

9.3.1 Similarities

Powers to apply capital and powers of appointment are fiduciary and are dispositive in nature. Either can be exercised to create new beneficial interests for the beneficiaries of the trust (provided the express power is drafted sufficiently widely). Generally, the powers are exercisable by the trustees for the benefit of beneficiaries who have been selected by the settlor of the settlement.

The initiative for the exercise of the power will generally come from one or more of the beneficiaries, normally because they need money. The trustees must, on each occasion, consider whether they have adequate powers to satisfy the beneficiary's request and, if so, whether they wish to exercise those powers.

Any exercise of a power pursuant to such a request will have taxation implications. These should be fully considered before any power is exercised. Taxation aspects of the exercise of powers are considered in **Chapter 10**.

Sometimes, the trustees rather than the beneficiaries will take the initiative and suggest the exercise of the power. This often happens where the trustees foresee a tax problem which they can avoid by using their powers. These aspects of the use of the trustees' powers are considered further in **Chapter 10**.

The exercise of either power may cause settled property to cease to be subject to trusts. In such cases the trustees will need to transfer the trust property out of their names and into the name of the person next entitled, normally a beneficiary; however, if property becomes subject to new trusts, the trustees of the original settlement may need to transfer the property to the trustees of the new settlement. The manner of vesting trust property in beneficiaries or new trustees is considered at **14.4.3**.

9.3.2 Differences

There are differences which relate to the existence of the powers and the manner of their exercise.

9.3.2.1 Existence of the powers

Only the power of advancement is statutory. Section 32 of TA 1925 will be implied into every settlement where a beneficiary has a vested or presumptive entitlement to capital. However, its effect may be extended or restricted by express provision in the settlement depending on the instructions given by the settlor at the time the settlement was created. Section 32 of TA 1925, and its possible modification, are considered at **9.4.3**.

A power of appointment can exist only if there is an express provision in the trust instrument creating it. A power which is widely drafted may permit advancements of the type permitted by s 32 and so render that provision superfluous. Drafting powers of appointment is considered further at **9.5**.

9.3.2.2 Exercise of the powers

Power of advancement

When trustees exercise a power of advancement, they apply capital for the benefit of a beneficiary. For example, they may hold the trust property for a beneficiary contingently on his attaining 25 years. If the trustees exercise the power in TA 1925, s 32 (or an equivalent express power) and give capital to the beneficiary when he is aged 21 to buy a flat, this is an advancement. The trustees may use the power to transfer property to another settlement for the benefit of the beneficiary.

Power of appointment

A power of appointment in a settlement allows trustees to grant a beneficiary income or capital from the settlement, or change the terms on which property is held. Such powers are typically (but not exclusively) found in discretionary settlements. For an example of such a power in a will creating interest in possession trusts, see **12.7.2**.

The exercise of a power of appointment may make capital available to a beneficiary absolutely in the same way that the exercise of a power of advancement can. Alternatively, the exercise of the power of appointment may change the beneficial entitlement to the trust property while leaving the property subject to trusts, for example giving a beneficiary a right to income or changing the age at which beneficiaries become entitled to capital. Those trusts may be the trusts established in the original trust instrument, or they may be new trusts specifically created by the instrument which exercises the power.

EXAMPLE

Trustees are holding property on trust for the settlor's grandchildren. There is a wide power of appointment over the settled property and its income, enabling the trustees to appoint the property among the beneficiaries at such times and in such proportions and for such purposes as they think fit. In default of appointment, the trust property will pass equally to such of the settlor's grandchildren living at the date of the settlement who attain 18.

The trustees may exercise a power of this nature in any of the following ways:

(a)   To provide capital for the absolute benefit of any single beneficiary, or group of beneficiaries, even before the age of 18 years. They must exercise their powers in proper manner having regard to their fiduciary nature.

(b)   To provide capital for one or more of the beneficiaries on their attaining 21 years, ie, the power of appointment is executed to create new trusts in favour of beneficiaries selected from the class beneficiaries. If the power is exercised in this way, care must be taken to observe the perpetuity period applicable to the original settlement (see **6.2.7**).

(c)   To give one or more of the beneficiaries a right to income. This could be for a stated period or until the trustees decide to revoke the appointment.

9.3.3   General and special powers of appointment

Powers of appointment are generally characterised as either special or general powers of appointment.

9.3.3.1   General powers

These powers permit the trustees to appoint to any person they may choose, including themselves, and are, therefore, uncommon. The settlor will generally wish to select the class of beneficiaries among whom the trustees may exercise the power. For this reason most settlements contain special powers of appointment.

9.3.3.2   Special powers

These permit the trustees to appoint to beneficiaries within a class chosen by the settlor. Two areas in particular require prior consideration before the trustees exercise a special power of appointment.

The objects of the power

No power may be exercised in a manner which exceeds any limitations laid down by the settlor in the settlement. The exercise of the power of appointment must, therefore, be for the benefit of a member or members of a class of beneficiaries selected by the settlor. If trustees exercise a power of appointment in favour of a beneficiary knowing that the beneficiary will make the funds available to a non-beneficiary, this is usually a breach of trust known as a 'fraud on the power'. See *Re Pauling's Settlement Trusts No 1* [1964] Ch 303. For a more recent example, see *Smith and another v Michelmores Trust Corp Ltd* [2021] EWHC 1425 (Ch), where the trustees proposed to appoint capital to a bankrupt beneficiary in order to benefit his creditors.

However, it is permissible to make funds available to assist a beneficiary to discharge their obligations: for example if a parent was a beneficiary of a trust fund and wished to pay for school fees for their children, this would be a legitimate exercise of the trustees' discretion: see *Re Hampden's Settlement Trusts* [2001] WTLR 195.

Although the settlor and his spouse can be included within the class of beneficiaries, generally they will be excluded for tax reasons. Minor unmarried children will normally be excluded if the settlor wishes to benefit from holdover relief. See **4.6.2.3** and **6.15**.

The perpetuity period

The property must vest in interest in the beneficiary in whose favour the power is to be exercised before the perpetuity period relevant to the settlement expires. In the case of special powers, this period is the period established by the settlement and which starts to run from the date of creation of the settlement (see **6.9**).

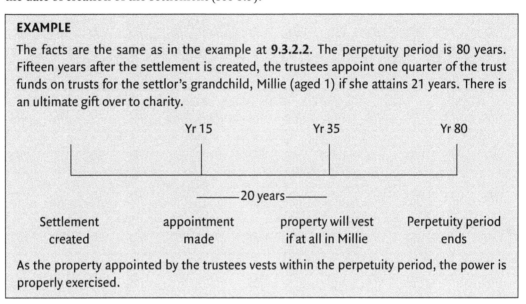

> **EXAMPLE**
>
> The facts are the same as in the example at **9.3.2.2**. The perpetuity period is 80 years. Fifteen years after the settlement is created, the trustees appoint one quarter of the trust funds on trusts for the settlor's grandchild, Millie (aged 1) if she attains 21 years. There is an ultimate gift over to charity.
>
> | Yr 15 | Yr 35 | Yr 80 |
> |---|---|---|
>
> ————20 years————
>
> | Settlement created | appointment made | property will vest if at all in Millie | Perpetuity period ends |
> |---|---|---|---|
>
> As the property appointed by the trustees vests within the perpetuity period, the power is properly exercised.

9.3.4 Formalities

The terms of a power of appointment normally require formalities such as the use of a deed or obtaining the consent of a specified person. Failure to comply with the required formalities will render the exercise of the power void.

See, for example, *Smith v Stanley* [2019] EWHC 2168 (Ch), where, amongst a catalogue of errors, the trustees purported to exercise a power of appointment informally when the trust instrument required the use of a deed.

The statutory power of advancement has no particular formal requirements (although anyone with a prior interest, such as a life tenant, must consent). However, trustees will normally record their decisions in writing and in the case of large amounts may decide to use a deed.

9.4 THE STATUTORY POWER OF ADVANCEMENT

9.4.1 The power of advancement

Section 32 of TA 1925, as originally drafted, allowed trustees to advance up to half of a beneficiary's vested or presumptive entitlement. The Inheritance and Trustees' Powers Act 2014 amended the section in relation to trusts created or arising on or after the Act comes into force to remove the one-half limit so that trustees can advance the whole of a beneficiary's vested or presumptive entitlement. If a trust is created by will, it is the date of death not execution that is significant

Minor amendments were made to make clear that trustees have power to advance assets, not merely cash. This amendment was intended to put the existing case law position on a statutory footing and these amendments, therefore, apply to all trusts whenever established.

The section is now as follows:

(1)   Trustees may at any time or times pay or apply any capital money subject to a trust, or transfer or apply any other property forming part of the capital of the trust property, for the advancement or benefit, in such manner as they may, in their absolute discretion, think fit, of any person entitled to the capital of the trust property or of any share thereof, whether absolutely or contingently on his attaining any specified age or on the occurrence of any other event, or subject to a gift over on his death under any specified age or on the occurrence of any other event, and whether in possession or in remainder or reversion, and such payment, transfer or application may be made notwithstanding that the interest of such person is liable to be defeated by the exercise of a power of appointment or revocation, or to be diminished by the increase of the class to which he belongs:

Provided that—

(a)   property (including any money) so paid, transferred or applied for the advancement or benefit of any person must not, altogether, represent more than ... the presumptive or vested share or interest of that person in the trust property; and

(b)   if that person is or becomes absolutely and indefeasibly entitled to a share in the trust property the money or other property so paid, transferred or applied shall be brought into account as part of such share; and

(c)   no such payment, transfer or application shall be made so as to prejudice any person entitled to any prior life or other interest, whether vested or contingent, in the money or other property paid, transferred or applied unless such person is in existence and of full age and consents in writing to such payment, transfer or application.

(1A)   In exercise of the foregoing power trustees may pay, transfer or apply money or other property on the basis (express or implied) that it shall be treated as a proportionate part of the capital out of which it was paid, transferred or applied, for the purpose of bringing it into account in accordance with proviso (b) to subsection (1) of this section.

(2)   This section does not apply to capital money arising under the Settled Land Act 1925.

(3)   This section does not apply to trusts constituted or created before the commencement of this Act.

9.4.2   Commentary on the statutory power

9.4.2.1   The power is discretionary: the trustees 'may'

Beneficiaries cannot compel trustees to exercise the power. Before exercising this power, the trustees must ensure their intended use of the power is for a legitimate purpose. If not, it will be an improper exercise of the power which will be invalid, and which may cause the trustees personal liability for loss suffered by the trust fund.

9.4.2.2   Interest in capital of the trust fund (or part)

Only beneficiaries with an interest in the capital may benefit from the exercise of the power. However, the interest may be any of the following:

(a)   absolute or contingent (on attaining any age or on any other event occurring);

(b)   in possession, remainder or reversion.

It does not matter that a beneficiary's interest is liable to be defeated or diminished by the occurrence of a future event, for example because the beneficiary may die at a young age and never reach the age at which the interest vests.

> **EXAMPLE**
>
> Trustees are holding £30,000 on trust for Saul contingent upon his attaining the age of 25 years (if he dies under the age of 25 the money is to go to charity). On his 18th birthday, the trustees advance £12,000 to enable Saul to go to university. This is a proper exercise of the power even though Saul may die before his 25th birthday.

Beneficiaries of a discretionary trust do not have an interest in the capital of the settlement. They have a mere hope of benefiting if the trustees exercise their discretion in their favour. While their interest is discretionary, they cannot benefit from s 32.

9.4.2.3 Limitations on the exercise of the power

The trustees may exercise their power only where it is for 'the advancement or benefit' of the beneficiary. As we saw at **9.2**, 'advancement' is normally considered to cover capital payments designed to 'set the beneficiary up in life (often in a business)' or payments made on the occasion of marriage. 'Benefit' has a particularly wide meaning. It has been held in *Pilkington and Another v Inland Revenue Commissioners and Others* [1964] AC 612 to have a meaning wide enough to permit the trustees to exercise their power of advancement by creating trusts for new beneficiaries if such is for the benefit of the beneficiary (a '*Pilkington* advance').

> **EXAMPLE**
>
> Trustees are holding £100,000 on trust for Martha contingent on her reaching 25 years. She is now aged 24, is wealthy and has two children aged 1 and 3 years. She would prefer the funds to be transferred to trustees for her children so that IHT may be avoided if she should die soon after her 25th birthday. The trustees may exercise their power and advance some of the settled funds into a settlement for Martha's children.

Courts have held the following to be for the 'benefit' of beneficiaries:

(a) a settlement on the beneficiary's children relieving him of the 'considerable obligation in respect of making provision for their future' which he would otherwise have owed (*Re Hampden's Settlement Trusts* [1977] TR 177);

(b) a transfer from a substantial trust fund to a family charitable foundation discharging the moral and social obligations felt by the beneficiary (*Re Clore's Settlement Trusts* [1966] 1 WLR 955).

However, an advance to a beneficiary, knowing that the money was to be given to someone else who was not within the class of beneficiaries, is likely to be void as a fraud on the power unless the trustees can demonstrate that the advance was genuinely for the benefit of the beneficiary.

The statutory power limits the trustees to paying, transferring or applying up to the amount of a beneficiary's presumptive or vested share. If the power is exercised, the amount paid, transferred or applied must be 'brought into account' if the beneficiary later becomes entitled to a share in the trust property. The advance will normally be brought into account on the basis of its value at the time of the advance. However, the trustees can stipulate that it is to be brought into account as a proportion of the value of the trust fund. See **9.4.2.5** below.

9.4.2.4 Prior life or other interests

The statutory power can be exercised only if consent is obtained from a beneficiary with a prior interest. For example, if property is held on trust for a beneficiary for life and then for other beneficiaries in remainder, the trustees could not exercise their power in favour of the remaindermen without the consent of the life tenant.

9.4.2.5 Basis on which advances brought into account

The Inheritance and Trustees' Powers Act 2014 inserted a new subsection (1A) into s 32 to confirm that a trustee may advance trust assets on the basis (express or implied) that the advance represents a proportionate part of a beneficiary's future entitlement for the purpose of taking it into account at the time when the beneficiary becomes entitled, rather than at its nominal value at the time of the advance.

The reason for the amendment is that accounting at the nominal value can give the beneficiary who receives the advance a disproportionate benefit if the remaining trust assets increase in value.

EXAMPLE

Suppose that a trust fund is held for the settlor's four children equally at age 21. When the trust fund is worth £400,000, the trustees advance £50,000 to the eldest, A. The trustees later distribute the remainder of the trust fund, now worth £1,400,000, to the four beneficiaries.

If the trustees made the advance to A requiring it to be brought into account:

*   **on the nominal value basis**, the nominal value of the advance is added back into the current value of the trust fund (£1,450,000). A is then entitled to one-quarter of that value less the advance, that is, £312,500. The other beneficiaries will each receive £362,500. If A's advance has grown in value at the same rate as the trust fund, it will now be worth £200,000 and he will have received £512,500 in total;

*   **on the proportionate basis**, it represents half of A's share at the time of the advance. Therefore, the trust fund is now held as to one-seventh for A and six-sevenths for the other three beneficiaries. A is now entitled to £200,000 and the other beneficiaries to £400,000. If A's advance has grown in value at the same rate as the trust fund, all the beneficiaries will have received £400,000 in total.

The amendment (which applies to all trusts whenever created) does not change the case law position which, according to *Re Leigh's Settlement Trusts* [1981] CLY 2453, [2006] WTLR 485, is that trustees can choose the basis on which they make an advance.

9.4.3 Modifying the statutory power

Normally, only minor amendments, as discussed below, need to be made to the statutory form of the power of advancement. They are similar to those made when drafting a will for a testator. As mentioned at **9.2**, it is often the case that a settlement contains a wide power of appointment. If so, the trustees may prefer to exercise this power rather than the statutory power, even in modified form.

Before the Inheritance and Trustees' Powers Act 2014, it was standard practice to vary the statutory power to remove the one-half limitation and allow the trustees to pay or apply up to the whole of a beneficiary's vested or presumptive share. This is no longer necessary.

It is, however, still necessary to vary the section as follows if the other two limitations are not wanted:

(a)   to remove the requirement that the distribution must be brought into account;

(b)   to remove the requirement for a person with a prior interest to consent to the advance.

It is unnecessary to consider extending the circumstances in which the statutory power can be exercised by the trustees. The phrase 'advancement or benefit' is generally considered sufficient, especially in view of the particularly wide meaning of the word 'benefit'.

9.5 DRAFTING POWERS OF APPOINTMENT

As there is no statutory power of appointment, all powers must be drafted as express powers in a trust instrument. The precise form which the power takes will depend upon the particular settlement which is to be drafted.

It is usually helpful to give trustees two separate powers in relation to capital: one allowing them to modify the terms on which property is held within the settlement (a narrow power);

and one allowing them to transfer it out of the settlement completely on new trusts (a wide power). This is not necessary as a wide power can be used in a narrow way: *Swires v Renton* [1991] STC 490. However, having two separate powers helps the trustees focus on what they are doing and may assist in dealings with HMRC. Transferring property out of the settlement will normally be a disposal and have capital tax consequences (see **9.6** and **Chapter 10**), and in some cases HMRC and the trustees may disagree over whether the terms of the existing settlement have merely been varied or completely new trusts created. It will help trustees argue that they have merely modified the existing trusts if they have stated that they used a narrow power.

9.6 TAXATION ASPECTS OF THE EXERCISE OF POWERS OF ADVANCEMENT AND APPOINTMENT

As each power is exercisable in relation to the trust capital, ie, the property in the settlement, it follows that the IHT and CGT aspects of the exercise of the power need be considered by the trustees before the power is actually exercised. These are discussed in **Chapter 10**, but normally there will only be IHT or CGT consequences if property leaves the settlement as opposed to being retained within the settlement on different trusts.

SUMMARY

(1) Section 32 of the Trustee Act 1925 is implied into all settlements unless excluded and gives trustees power to advance up to half or the whole of a beneficiary's vested or presumptive entitlement to capital, depending on whether the settlement came into effect before or on or after 1 October 2014.

(2) Almost all settlements give trustees additional powers to alter the beneficial interests.

(3) There are two types of additional power: powers of appointment and powers of advancement.

(4) The extent of a power of appointment depends entirely on how it is drafted. It is usual to require it to be exercised by deed.

(5) A power of advancement is normally modelled on the statutory power and can generally be exercised informally without a deed.

REVIEW ACTIVITY

Which ONE of the following statements is WRONG?

A   For trusts created or arising on or after 1 October 2014, the statutory power of advancement allows the application of the whole of a beneficiary's presumptive entitlement to capital.

B   Exercising a power of advancement does not necessarily mean that beneficiaries become entitled to capital early.

C   It is not possible to use a power of advancement to defer a beneficiary's right to receive capital.

D   Trustees can use a power of appointment to appoint capital on entirely new trusts only if the power authorises them to do this.

Answer: C

A power of advancement can be used in any way which is for the benefit of the beneficiary. It may be beneficial to defer entitlement to capital. So far as D is concerned, express powers can only be used to modify the terms on which income and capital are held within the settlement unless, as is usually the case, the power states that appointments can be made freed from the original trusts.

CHAPTER 10

THE EXERCISE OF POWERS OF ADVANCEMENT AND APPOINTMENT

LEARNING OUTCOMES

After reading this chapter you will be able to:

- identify the inheritance tax implications of the exercise by trustees of powers of appointment and advancement
- identify the capital gains tax implications of the exercise by trustees of powers of appointment and advancement.

10.1 INTRODUCTION

There are a variety of reasons why the trusts on which capital of a settlement is held may be varied. For example, a life tenant and the beneficiary entitled to the remainder interest may agree that they want to end the settlement and divide the capital between themselves; a beneficiary with a contingent or deferred interest may ask the trustees to exercise a power of advancement or appointment in his favour; a member of a discretionary class of beneficiaries may ask the trustees to exercise a power of appointment in his favour.

In all these cases there will be inheritance tax and capital gains tax consequences because there is a change in the way in which the capital is held.

This chapter looks at the consequences of varying trusts in relation to a variety of different types of settlement.

10.2 EXERCISING POWERS IN RELATION TO INTEREST IN POSSESSION SETTLEMENTS CREATED BEFORE 22 MARCH 2006 OR ON DEATH

At **10.2** et seq we will look at the taxation of interests in possession created by lifetime transfer before 22 March 2006 or on death at any time. In both of these cases the person with the interest in possession is treated as beneficially entitled to the underlying trust capital. Such interests are often referred to as 'qualifying' interests in possession.

Interests in possession can be created by lifetime transfer after 22 March 2006, but the person with the interest in possession will not be treated as beneficially entitled to the underlying trust capital for IHT purposes.

10.2.1 The nature of the trusts and the powers

Settlements with an interest in possession are usually created because the settlor or the testator is seeking to provide one person (often a spouse) with an income for life while controlling the ultimate devolution of the capital. They are often created by will.

After the trust comes into effect, the trustees may be asked by beneficiaries to exercise their powers to apply capital.

Since the introduction of TLATA 1996, it is usual for trustees of interest in possession settlements to hold the settled property 'on trust' and have an appropriate power of sale among the administrative provisions of the settlement. The beneficial trusts provide the life tenant with an income for life and the remainderman with an interest which vests in possession on the life tenant's death. Until then, it is vested in interest only.

> **EXAMPLE**
>
> Trustees hold settled property currently worth £200,000 on trust to pay the income to Aida for life, thereafter for Carmen in remainder. Aida has an interest in possession, ie the right to income produced by the trust property. Carmen has the right to receive the trust property when Aida dies.

Carmen's interest, in the example, is an interest in remainder but is often called (albeit incorrectly) 'a reversionary interest'. It is an asset which can be professionally valued, ie a value can be placed on Carmen's right to receive the trust property when Aida dies. Since Carmen has the right to receive the trust property only when Aida dies, the value of the interest in remainder may be significantly less than the current value of the settled property. The value will be influenced (inter alia) by the prospective life expectancy of Aida. Carmen's interest in remainder is an asset which she may consider selling or possibly giving away as part of her estate planning arrangements (see **4.6.2**).

> **EXAMPLE**
>
> If Carmen waits until Aida dies, she will receive the full trust fund (currently valued at £200,000). Carmen, however, is in need of some money immediately and decides to sell her interest in remainder to David.
>
> (a) Assuming Aida is 84 years old, David might pay Carmen £175,000 for the right to receive the trust fund when Aida dies.
>
> (b) Assuming Aida is 35 years old, David might pay Carmen £40,000 for that right.
>
> If Carmen's sale is for full market value, no IHT or CGT would be payable by her. If, instead, she gave her interest in remainder to David, no tax would be payable (see 4.6.2) because:
>
> (a) her interest in remainder is 'excluded property' for IHT purposes, ie, it is not in Carmen's 'estate' and so may be given away free of IHT; and
>
> (b) as a beneficial interest in settled property acquired without any payment by Carmen, it is exempt from CGT on a disposal whether by sale or gift.

The trustees' power to advance capital to the remainderman in s 32 of TA 1925 applies to an interest in possession settlement, although it may have been modified by express provision in the trust instrument. Any exercise of the statutory power to pay or apply trust property would, unless also suitably modified, require the prior consent of the life tenant. See **9.4** for details of the s 32 power of advancement.

10.2.2 Provision of capital for the beneficiaries of an interest in possession settlement

There are three methods of providing the beneficiaries with capital from the trust:

(a) By the exercise of an express power of advancement or appointment.

Only if the trust instrument contains express provision can the trustees apply capital to or for the benefit of the life tenant.

(b)   By the exercise of the statutory power in s 32 of TA 1925 in favour of the remainderman (with consent of the life tenant, unless the power has been modified).

The decision to exercise either of these powers is a matter for the trustees. Their decision will generally follow an approach by the beneficiary with a request for the advance of some money. The trustees' decision should be formally recorded either:

(i)   by a minute in the trustees' minute book for the trust (if any); or

(ii)   by signing a separate notice to the effect that, in exercise of a power contained in the settlement or in s 32 of TA 1925 certain property is advanced from the settlement to a named beneficiary. This notice should be retained with the trust instrument and records.

(c)   By partitioning the trust fund by agreement between the life tenant and the remainderman (see **10.2.3**).

10.2.3   Partitioning the trust fund

In the absence of an express power to advance capital to a life tenant, capital may be provided by 'breaking the trust' under the rule in *Saunders v Vautier* (1841) 4 Beav 115. 'Trust busting' under this rule allows beneficiaries who are of full age and capacity and together entitled to the whole beneficial interest in the trust fund to bring the settlement to an end and to direct the trustees to transfer the property as they wish.

If the beneficiaries decide to end the trust in this way, they will need to reach agreement as to the value of their respective beneficial interests, ie, a value needs to be placed on the life tenant's right to receive income for life and on the remainderman's right to receive the capital of the trust on the life tenant's death. Agreement may be reached informally between the beneficiaries or by formal valuation by an actuary instructed to act on their behalf.

EXAMPLE

Trustees hold £10,000 on trust for Lana for life, remainder to Ron. Lana and Ron agree that their respective interests are worth 40% and 60% of the settled property. They may direct the trustees to sell the trust property and to divide the sale proceeds between them in the agreed proportions.

Instead of directing the trustees to sell the trust property as in the example, the beneficiaries may prefer to direct the trustees to divide the assets between them so that each beneficiary receives the appropriate proportion of the trust fund. This method of division will require each asset to be valued separately. It may be necessary for the trustees to use cash to achieve exactly the correct proportions of the funds for each beneficiary.

EXAMPLE

The facts are the same as in the previous example. The £10,000 trust fund is made up of shares in A plc valued at £5,000, shares in B plc valued at £4,000, and £1,000 cash.

Ron will receive:

£3,000 A plc shares;

£2,400 B plc shares;

£600 cash.

> Lana will receive:
>
> £2,000 A plc shares;
>
> £1,600 B plc shares;
>
> £400 cash.

Before the settled property is actually distributed among the beneficiaries, the trustees must first consider the taxation implications.

10.2.4 Taxation implications of provision of capital for the beneficiaries

The exercise of the statutory or express power of advancement has capital tax implications which the trustees must consider before releasing the formerly settled property from their control. The trustees will often become personally liable for tax as a result of the exercise of a power. They should retain some of the trust property in their own names until all liabilities have been discharged.

10.2.4.1 Inheritance tax

A person with a qualifying interest in possession (created by lifetime transfer before 22 March 2006 or on death at any time) is treated as beneficially entitled to the property in which he has an interest (IHTA 1984, s 49).

> **EXAMPLE**
>
> Trustees of a will trust hold a fund of £50,000 for Leonard for life, remainder for his daughter, Rachel. Leonard has assets of his own which amount to £100,000. His estate for IHT purposes will be valued at £150,000.

The lifetime termination of a qualifying interest in possession in a will trust or pre-22 March 2006 lifetime trust is a transfer of value by the life tenant.

If the property is then held for one or more of the beneficiaries absolutely, ie the settlement comes to an end, the transfer will normally be a PET.

If, however, the property is held by the trustees for a spouse or civil partner of the life tenant absolutely, the transfer will be exempt. Tax (calculated in the normal manner where there is a 'failed' PET) will be payable only if the former life tenant dies within seven years of termination of the settlement (IHTA 1984, ss 52(1) and 3A).

If an interest in possession is terminated to create a further trust, there will be a lifetime chargeable transfer by the life tenant. See *Smith v Stanley* [2019] EWHC 2168 (Ch) where trustees did not appreciate that terminating the life interest and accelerating discretionary trusts would trigger a large and immediate inheritance tax liability. Fortunately, the court agreed to allow equitable rescission of the termination on the basis of mistake.

Inheritance tax may, therefore, become payable where a power is exercised to provide capital to beneficiaries, depending on what exactly the trustees do (see the three methods set out below). If IHT is payable, it is the trustees of the settlement who must pay it to the Revenue and who should therefore reserve funds for the purpose.

Method 1: Express power to appoint capital to life tenant

If the trustees of a qualifying interest in possession trust exercise a power to advance some or all of the capital to the life tenant, his interest in possession in the capital advanced will end. However, no IHT will be payable on the advance. This is because there is no fall in the value of his estate, since for IHT purposes he is deemed already to own that property which is actually being advanced (IHTA 1984, s 53(2)).

> **EXAMPLE**
>
> Assume that in the previous example the trustees advance the whole fund to Leonard.
>
> Before the advance:
>
> | Leonard's estate | £100,000 | |
> |---|---|---|
> | Trust fund | £ 50,000 | |
> | | | £150,000 |
>
> After the advance:
>
> Leonard's estate £100,000 + £50,000 advanced = £150,000.

Method 2: Statutory power of advancement to remainderman

If the trustees of a qualifying interest in possession trust exercise their power to advance the capital to the remainderman absolutely, the life tenant's interest in possession ends in that part of the settled property. The life tenant makes a PET which becomes chargeable only if he dies within seven years of the advance (IHTA 1984, ss 3A and 52(1)). The tax is paid by the trustees. However, the failed PET has implications for the life tenant too, as it enters their cumulative total and reduces the nil rate band available to their death estate.

> **EXAMPLE**
>
> Assume that the trustees holding the trust property for Leonard for life, remainder to Rachel, had advanced £10,000 to Rachel. Leonard is treated as making a PET. If it becomes chargeable, any IHT payable on the £10,000 (ie, the value of the property in which Leonard's interest in possession has ended) is payable by the trustees from the trust fund.

Note: The statutory power requires the life tenant's consent, although the need for consent can be removed in the trust instrument.

Method 3: Partition of the trust fund

If, by agreement, the fund is partitioned, the life tenant's interest in possession ends in the trust property which passes to the remainderman. This too is a PET made by the life tenant. Inheritance tax is payable by the trustees on that portion of the trust fund if the life tenant dies within seven years of the partition (IHTA 1984, s 52(2)).

> **EXAMPLE**
>
> Assume that Leonard and Rachel in the previous example agreed to partition the £50,000 fund between them in proportions of 30:70. Leonard makes a PET of £35,000 (£50,000 – £15,000 = £35,000). If Leonard dies within seven years of the PET, IHT is payable by the trustees of the partitioned trust fund (which they should remember). They may wish to insure the life tenant's life for seven years.

10.2.4.2 Capital gains tax

Liability to CGT occurs only if there is a disposal of chargeable assets. Disposals may be actual or deemed. Actual disposals by trustees are considered in **Chapter 14**. Deemed disposals are considered below.

Deemed disposals (TCGA 1992, s 71, as amended by FA 1999, s 75)

A deemed disposal occurs when an individual becomes 'absolutely entitled' to settled property against the trustees, for example on any of the occasions mentioned in **10.2.2**. The trustees are deemed to dispose of each item of settled property at its market value and to re-acquire it immediately at the same value as nominees for the beneficiary, ie they continue to hold the property in their names as bare trustees for the beneficiary. The property is no longer settled property but belongs to the beneficiary whose acquisition cost of the property is the market value when the re-acquisition occurred.

EXAMPLE

Trustees appoint 1,000 ABC plc shares worth £20,000 to Leonard, the life tenant of an interest in possession settlement. The shares were worth £2,000 when the settlement was created. No reliefs or exemptions are available. A deemed disposal occurs at the date of the appointment.

Value at deemed disposal	£20,000
Less: acquisition cost	£2,000
Chargeable gain realised by trustees	£18,000

Leonard's acquisition cost of the shares is £20,000.

Reliefs, exemptions and rate of tax

If any CGT is due, it is calculated in 2022/23 at 20% of the gain (28% if residential property is disposed of) and is payable by the settlement trustees. As their deemed disposal gave rise to the gain, any tax is their liability. They pay the tax from the settled funds. If a loss occurs, the trustees can claim relief for it by setting the loss against their gains on other disposals of trust assets in the same or future tax years.

Before calculating their liability to tax, the trustees may deduct an annual exemption (£6,150 in 2022/23), ie, one half of the exemption available to individuals.

On the joint election of the trustees and beneficiaries, hold-over relief will be available when assets leave a settlement if:

(a)   the settled property comprises business property (see **4.4.5.2**); or

(b)   the occasion is chargeable to IHT, ie, it is not a PET.

If they claim hold-over relief, the annual exemption will not be available.

In very limited circumstances, business asset disposal relief (formerly entrepreneurs' relief) may be available (see **4.4.5.3**).

Beneficiaries' and trustees' losses

If a loss arises on the deemed disposal, the trustees may claim relief for it by deducting it from:

(a)   gains which accrued to the trustees on disposals in the same tax year as the deemed disposal; or

(b)   gains accruing on the deemed disposal, ie, gains on the assets to which the beneficiary is entitled.

If the trustees can make no use of the loss (because they have insufficient gains), the loss may be transferred to the beneficiary. The beneficiary is only able to use the loss to offset future gains made on the disposal of assets received from the settlement only. In other words, the loss is not generally available to offset gains on disposals of his other assets.

10.2.5   Drafting a deed of partition

Heading and date

Sample clause

> DEED OF PARTITION
> DATE: [   ]

Parties

Normally, there will be three parties:

(a)   the life tenant (who gives up the right to income in part of the trust fund); and

(b)   the reversioner (who gives up the right to part of the capital of the trust fund); and

(c)   the trustees.

Sample clause

(1)   [name and address] ('the Life Tenant');

(2)   [name and address] ('the Reversioners'); and

(3)   [name and address] ('the Trustees')

Recitals

The recitals will explain the background circumstances giving rise to the partition.

Sample clause

RECITALS

(A) This Deed is supplemental to the settlement ('the Settlement')

[and to the other documents and events] specified in the First Schedule.

(B) The Trustees are the present trustees of the Settlement.

(C) Under and by virtue of the Settlement and in the events which have happened, the Life Tenant is entitled to the income of the Trust Fund for life and, subject thereto, the capital and income of the Trust Fund is held upon trust for the Reversioners [in equal shares] absolutely.

(D) The Trust Fund presently consists of the property described in Parts 1 and 2 of the Second Schedule.

(E) It has been agreed between the Life Tenant and the Reversioners that the Trust Fund shall be partitioned so that [   ] per centum as described in Part 1 of the Second Schedule ('the Life Tenant's Share') shall be held for the Life Tenant absolutely and the balance remaining being [   ] per centum as described in Part 2 of the Second Schedule ('the Reversioners' Share'), shall be held for the Reversioners in equal shares absolutely.

(F) The Trustees have agreed, following the joint request of the Life Tenant and the Reversioners, to release the Trust Fund to the parties respectively entitled under the above agreement.

[(G) This partition is carried out following and in accordance with actuarial advice.]

The clauses assume that there is more than one reversioner and that the reversioners agree to divide their share equally between them. They will need amendment if there is only one reversioner. If the parties did not obtain actuarial advice, delete clause G.

The operative part

Normally, there will be two clauses, one each for the life tenant and the reversioner, whereby they respectively assign and surrender to the other their interest in the income or capital of the trust fund. The consequence is that the trust property is freed from the trust and may be transferred by the trustees in accordance with the arrangement mentioned in the recitals.

Sample clause

OPERATIVE PROVISIONS

1. Definitions and construction

In this Deed, where the context admits, the definitions and rules of construction contained in the Settlement shall apply.

2. Assignment by Life Tenant

The Life Tenant hereby assigns [his/her] interest in the Reversioners' Share to the Reversioners in equal shares absolutely, to the intent that such interest shall merge and be extinguished in the reversion and that the Reversioners shall become entitled to the Reversioners' Share [in equal shares] absolutely.

3. Assignment by Reversioners

The Reversioners hereby assign their respective interests in the Life Tenant's Share to the Life Tenant absolutely, to the intent that the life interest and the reversion shall merge, the life interest shall be enlarged and the Life Tenant shall become entitled to the Life Tenant's Share absolutely.

4. Payment of tax

Without prejudice to the provisions contained in clause 5, it is hereby agreed and declared that any inheritance tax occasioned by the partition in respect of the Reversioners' Share shall be borne by that share and any capital gains tax occasioned by the partition shall be borne by the Life Tenant and the Reversioners in the same proportions as they become absolutely entitled to the Trust Fund.

5. Trustees' lien

Nothing in this Deed shall prejudice or impair in any way any lien to which the Trustees are entitled in respect of any claim for costs, charges or expenses or in order to protect themselves against any tax liabilities.

Clauses 4 and 5 above deal with liability to IHT and CGT which may arise following the partition and the position of the trustees who are liable for that tax. This was considered at **10.2.4**.

Schedules

The First Schedule will give details of the settlement which is to be ended, ie the date and parties to it. A Second Schedule will detail the division of the trust property between the life tenant and the reversioner in accordance with the agreement stated in the recitals.

10.3 EXERCISING POWERS IN RELATION TO RELEVANT PROPERTY SETTLEMENTS

Relevant property settlements are those without a qualifying interest in possession. They may be discretionary settlements, settlements with a contingent interest or settlements with an interest in possession created by lifetime transfer on or after 22 March 2006.

10.3.1 The nature of the trusts and the powers

In the case of discretionary settlements and settlements where the beneficiaries have merely contingent interests, while it is in principle possible for the beneficiaries to divide up capital by consent under the rule in *Saunders v Vautier*, it is not normally practically possible for the following reasons:

(a)   some of the beneficiaries may not be of full age;

(b)   there may be an enormous number of beneficiaries potentially within the class so that it is impossible to identify them all;

(c)   it will be difficult for a large number of beneficiaries to agree on the correct basis of distribution.

Drafting the dispositive provisions of a discretionary settlement is considered in detail in **Chapter** 7. Generally, the trusts are drafted in as wide a form as possible. Such wording permits maximum possible flexibility for the trustees, who can then pick and choose between beneficiaries. They have power to appoint absolute interests or to make trust appointments, ie, to create new trusts in favour of the beneficiaries. Unless and until this power is exercised, the trust fund and its income will be subject to default provisions.

In the case of settlements where the beneficiaries have contingent interests, it is normal to give the trustees wide powers to advance capital to the beneficiaries. Even if the trustees have no express powers, they will normally have the statutory power to advance capital implied under the TA 1925, s 32, although this will be limited to half the beneficiary's vested or presumptive entitlement for trusts created before 1 October 2014.

In the case of settlements created by lifetime transfer on or after 22 March 2006 where a beneficiary has a right to income, the same powers to appoint capital, advance it or partition the trust that we looked at in relation to settlements with a qualifying interest in possession at **10.2.4.1** exist. However, the IHT implications are different, as we will see at **10.3.3** below.

10.3.2 Taxation implications of exercising the power of appointment

The exercise of the power will affect the capital of the settlement. Before exercising it, the trustees must consider the IHT and CGT implications. Having done so, additional clauses may be inserted in the deed of appointment dealing with the payment of the tax (see **10.3.8**).

10.3.3 Inheritance tax

All relevant property settlements are subject to the same IHT regime, no matter what the nature of the beneficiaries' interests. The settlement is a taxable entity in its own right.

A beneficiary may have a right to receive income, but this does not mean that the beneficiary is treated as beneficially entitled to the underlying trust assets. Trustees can, normally, give beneficiaries rights to income and remove those rights without any IHT implications. The only occasion when the trustees' action will give rise to a charge to IHT is where the trustees appoint capital out of the settlement (or, in the case of a will trust, the trustees give a beneficiary a right to income within two years of death – the appointment is read back to the date of death under IHTA 1984, s 144 and will automatically create a retrospective immediate post-death interest; see **Chapter 13**).

The regime charges IHT on the value of 'relevant property', ie settled property in a settlement in which there is no qualifying interest in possession. Rates of tax are limited to half the rates applicable on death, ie a maximum rate of 20% applies, although tax is often charged at rates considerably less than 20% (see **10.3.4**).

There are two types of charge to IHT on relevant property settlements (in addition to the charge which may have arisen when the settlement was created, see **Chapter 5**). These are a periodic charge on each 10-year anniversary of the creation of the settlement and a distribution (exit) charge.

The starting date of a settlement is defined by IHTA 1984, s 48A as the date when property first became comprised in it. In the case of trusts created by will, IHTA 1984, s 83 provides that the starting date is the date of death. The term 'anniversary' means the recurrence of a particular date, so that, for example, if the first property to be transferred into a settlement was transferred on 16 June 1992, the 10-year anniversaries of that settlement are 16 June 2002, 16 June 2012, etc.

The Finance (No 2) Act 2015 has slightly simplified the rules for calculating both 10-year anniversary charges and exit charges arising on or after 10 November 2015 by removing the need to consider non-relevant property held in settlements when calculating charges – even so, no one could describe the rules as simple. The earlier rules are not considered in this book.

10.3.3.1 The periodic charge

This is an anniversary charge at 10-yearly intervals on relevant property in the settlement valued immediately before the 10th anniversary of creation.

> **EXAMPLE**
>
> A discretionary settlement is created on 1 July 2000 when the first assets are transferred to it; the first 10-year anniversary charge falls on 1 July 2010 and the second on 1 July 2020, etc.

10.3.3.2 The distribution (exit) charge

A charge also arises when certain events occur, ie, when property ceases to be 'relevant property' by leaving the settlement, for example, on the exercise of a power of appointment by the trustees.

This charge is a proportion of the rate charged on the previous 10-year anniversary. The proportion is calculated by reference to the number of complete quarters (periods of three months) the property has been in the settlement since its creation or the previous periodic charge. There are 40 quarters in a 10-year period. If property has been in the settlement for five years, 20 quarters will be used to calculate the charge. The proportionate rate is applied to the value of the property leaving the fund. The charge can be likened to a rent payable in arrear for any period during which the property is held in trust without a qualifying interest in possession.

There are special rules for calculating exits in the first 10 years of a settlement's life because there is no previous anniversary charge on which to base the calculation (see **10.3.4** below).

There is no distribution charge, however, if the date when the property ceases to be relevant property is within three months after the creation of the settlement, or within three months after any 10-year anniversary of the creation of the settlement because there is no complete quarter (IHTA 1984, s 65(4)).

10.3.4 Calculating the distribution (exit) charge before the first 10-year anniversary

In the case of distributions of capital made before the first 10-year anniversary, there has to be a special rule for calculating the rate of tax. This is because there has been no previous anniversary and therefore no previous anniversary rate to take a proportion of.

To calculate the liability to IHT, it is necessary to calculate a rate of tax for the settlement (the settlement rate) and then to apply that rate to the value of the trust fund property leaving the settlement. It is necessary to follow five steps.

Step 1: Ascertain the value of a hypothetical chargeable transfer

This is done by adding together:

(a)   the value of the relevant property in the settlement on creation; and

(b)   the value of relevant property added to the settlement after its creation, if any (using the value of the property when added); and

(c)   the value of relevant property in any related settlement at the date of creation (ie, any other settlement created by the settlor on the same day). The inclusion of the value of relevant property in a related settlement is an anti-avoidance provision; and

(d)   for settlements created or added to on and after 10 December 2014, the value of any 'same day addition' unless the settlement is a 'protected settlement' (see **10.3.7.2**). A 'same day addition' arises where a settlor makes transfers of value which increase the value of one or more settlements containing relevant property on the same day (IHTA 1984, s 62A). The inclusion of same day additions is an anti-avoidance measure.

Both of the anti-avoidance provisions are designed to prevent settlors obtaining a full nil rate band for a number of settlements. See **10.3.7** below.

Step 2: Ascertain the tax on this hypothetical chargeable transfer

The rate of tax to be used on the hypothetical chargeable transfer is ascertained from the current table of rates. Tax is calculated at 0% or 20%, ie, half the death rate, even if the discretionary settlement was created by will. The table of rates is joined at the point reached immediately before creation by the settlor's chargeable transfers in the previous seven years. This means that if the settlor had made no chargeable transfers in the seven years before creating the settlement, the settlement has the benefit of the settlor's full nil rate band. (If the settlor adds funds to the settlement after creation at a time when he has used some or all of his nil rate band so that his available nil rate band is reduced, the settlement's nil rate band is similarly reduced.)

Hence, provided the settlor's nil rate band is unused at creation (and also at the time any later funds are added), the settlement enjoys a full nil rate band throughout its life.

Step 3: Ascertain the settlement *rate* of tax

The tax calculated in Step 2 is converted to an estate or average rate.

The rate at which tax is then charged, 'the settlement rate', is 30% of this rate. Thus the maximum rate (only payable where no nil rate band is available) is 30% × 20% = 6%.

Why 30% of the estate rate? The idea is to try to replicate the level of tax charged on an individual. The thinking is that tax might be collected from individuals on death every 30–40 years. Charging 30% every 10 years is a rough approximation.

Step 4: The charge to IHT

Inheritance tax is charged on the fall in value of the trust property, as a result of the exercise of the power of appointment, at the rate of one-fortieth of the settlement rate for each complete quarter (three months) between the setting up of the settlement and the event giving rise to the liability. If an appointment occurs within the first quarter, there is no liability.

Step 5: Paying the IHT

If the tax is paid from the amount to be distributed there is no grossing up and the amount calculated at Step 4 is paid. If the tax is paid from the balance of the trust fund, it is necessary to gross up the distribution to calculate the tax payable.

EXAMPLE 1

A settlor settles £100,000 on discretionary trusts on 1 July 2020. On 1 February 2023 the trustees appoint £50,000 to a beneficiary.

Assume that at the time the settlement was created the settlor had made no previous transfers, ie, he had no cumulative total, no property has been added and there were no related settlements or same day additions.

Step 1:	Find value of hypothetical chargeable transfer	
	No relevant property added or related settlements or same day additions, therefore just the original valued settled	£100,000
Step 2:	Ascertain tax on hypothetical chargeable transfer	
	The settlor made no chargeable transfers in the 7-year period before 1 July 2020 and so there is a full nil rate band available	
	Portion of nil rate band available	£100,000
	IHT	nil
Steps 3–5	Need not be made	
	The charge to IHT is nil on the £50,000 appointed	

EXAMPLE 2

As above, but assume that the settlor's cumulative total of chargeable transfers was £235,000 when the settlement was created.

Step 1:	Find value of hypothetical chargeable transfer	
	No property added or related settlements or same day additions, therefore just the original valued settled	£100,000

Step 2:   Ascertain tax on hypothetical chargeable transfer

The settlor has made chargeable transfers totalling
£235,000 in the 7-year period before 1 July 2020

Balance of nil rate band remaining	<u>£90,000</u>
Portion of hypothetical chargeable transfer taxed at 20%	£10,000

IHT @ 20% × £10,000 = £2,000

Step 3:   Ascertain settlement rate

First find the Average Rate of tax by dividing the tax by the value
of the hypothetical chargeable transfer:

$$\frac{£2,000}{£100,000} \times 100 = 2\%$$

Then convert to the Settlement Rate which is 30% of the Average Rate:

30% × 2% = 0.6%

Step 4:   Ascertain the charge to IHT

Apply the Settlement Rate to the number of complete quarters which
have occurred in the period between the date the settlement was created
and the date of the appointment, divided by 40
(1 July 2020–1 February 2023 = 10 complete quarters) and apply this to the
value by which the trust property has fallen as a result of the appointment

IHT on the appointment of £50,000 is

$$0.6\% \times \frac{10}{40} \times £50,000 = £75$$

Step 5:   Paying the IHT

If the beneficiary pays, the IHT will be £75

If the trustees pay, grossing up applies.

EXAMPLE 3

As above but the settlor had a cumulative total of £325,000, ie, his nil rate band was
already exhausted when the settlement was created.

Step 1:   Find value of hypothetical chargeable transfer

No property added or related settlements or same day additions, therefore just the original valued settled	£100,000

Step 2:   Ascertain tax on hypothetical chargeable transfer

The settlor has made chargeable transfers totalling
£325,000 in the 7-year period before 1 July 2020

As there is no available nil rate band the whole of
the hypothetical chargeable transfer is taxed at 20%

IHT @ 20% × £100,000 = £20,000

Step 3:   Ascertain settlement rate

First find the Average Rate of tax by dividing the tax
by the value of the hypothetical chargeable transfer:

$$\frac{£20,000}{£100,000} \times 100 = 20\%$$

Then convert to the Settlement Rate which is
30% of the Average Rate:

30% × 20% = 6%

> Step 4:   Ascertain the charge to IHT
>
>   Apply the Settlement Rate to the number of complete
>   quarters which have occurred in the period between the
>   date the settlement was created and the date of the
>   appointment, divided by 40
>   (1 July 2020–1 February 2023 = 10 complete quarters)
>   and apply this to the value by which the trust
>   property has fallen as a result of the appointment
>   IHT on the appointment of £50,000 is
>
> $6\% \times \dfrac{10}{40} \times £50,000 = £750$
>
> Step 5:   Paying the IHT
>
>   If the beneficiary pays, the IHT will be £750
>   If the trustees pay, grossing up applies

The effect of the settlor's cumulative total of chargeable transfers

If the settlor has made no chargeable transfers before making the settlement – as in Example 1 (and had created no related settlement, nor added any relevant property to the discretionary settlement, nor made any same day additions) – then a full nil rate band is available to the trustees. Thus, if the hypothetical chargeable transfer in Step 1 (the value of the property at the start of the settlement) does not exceed £325,000, the rate of tax established in Step 3 on *all* exit charges before the first 10-year anniversary will be 0%.

Increases in the value of the trust fund after creation and before the first 10-year anniversary do not increase the rate of tax charged. Earlier transfers from the settlement in the first ten years are also irrelevant. The rate in this period is calculated only by reference to the settlor's cumulative total and the value of the trust property at creation.

Trustees of a discretionary settlement not yet 10 years old can take advantage of this nil rate to distribute all the settled property without liability to IHT, no matter how much it has increased in value. This is an important planning point for the trustees.

10.3.5   The first 10-year anniversary charge

This charge is on the value of the property in the settlement (including any accumulated income) immediately before the anniversary of the creation of the settlement.

The Revenue became concerned that many trusts had large amounts of undistributed income which the trustees claimed had not been formally accumulated and which therefore were not capital for this purpose. Consequently, in FA 2014 a deeming provision was introduced: income that has remained undistributed for more than five years at the date of the 10-year anniversary will be treated as if it were part of the trust capital for the purposes of the 10-year anniversary charge. The Revenue says that it will accept a first-in-first-out approach for income, giving the taxpayer the greatest benefit at the 10-year anniversary.

The original proposal was that income would be deemed to be capital for the purposes of the exit charge as well as the anniversary charge. However, taxpayers objected, pointing out that this would be unfair as it would deny trusts the benefit of the income tax credit available when income is distributed (see **14.5.2.2**). The Revenue accepted this objection, and the deeming provision applies only for the purposes of the anniversary charge.

Step 1: Ascertain the value of a hypothetical chargeable transfer

This is done by adding together:

(a)   the current value of the relevant property in the settlement; and

(b)   the value at creation of any relevant property in a related settlement (if any); and

(c)   for settlements created or added to on and after 10 December 2014, the value of any 'same day addition' unless the trust is a 'protected settlement' (see **10.3.7.2**)

Items (b) and (c) are anti-avoidance provisions and will rarely apply. Thus, any charge will usually relate only to the current value of the settled property. For this purpose income will be included as relevant property once it has been accumulated. Income is accumulated for this purpose when the trustees take an irrevocable decision to accumulate, or are subject to the deeming provision contained in the FA 2014, referred to above

Step 2: Ascertain the tax on this hypothetical transfer

The tax is ascertained from the table of rates. Two cumulative totals are relevant to this:

(a)   the settlor's cumulative total of chargeable transfers in the seven years before the settlement was created, and

(b)   the settlement's own cumulative total of chargeable transfers made in the first 10 years.

(If the settlor adds funds to the settlement after creation at a time when he has used some or all of his nil rate band so that his available nil rate band is reduced, the settlement's nil rate band is similarly reduced.)

Tax is calculated at 0% or 20%, ie, half the death rate (even if the settlement is created by will).

Step 3: Ascertain the settlement rate of tax

The tax calculated in Step 2 is converted into an estate or average rate. The settlement rate is 30% of this rate.

Step 4: The charge to IHT

Inheritance tax is charged at the settlement rate applied to the property in the settlement at the anniversary date.

Step 5: Paying the IHT

The trustees will pay the tax from the trust fund.

EXAMPLE 1

On 1 July 2020 a settlor settled £100,000 on discretionary trusts. The first 10-year anniversary charge falls on 1 July 2030 when the trust fund is worth £140,000 as a result of sound investment by the trustees. All income has been distributed.

Assume that the settlor had a cumulative total of nil when he created the settlement and no appointments have been made.

Step 1:   Find value of hypothetical chargeable transfer

No related settlements or same day additions,
therefore just the value of relevant property
at the date of the first 10-year anniversary   £140,000

Step 2:   Ascertain tax on hypothetical chargeable transfer

The settlor made no chargeable transfers in the
7-year period before 1 July 2020 and there have
been no chargeable transfers out of the settlement
in the 10 years since creation, so there is a full nil rate
band available

Portion of nil rate band available   £140,000

IHT   nil

Steps 3–5: Need not be made

EXAMPLE 2

As above, but assume that in 2020 the settlor had a cumulative total of £235,000 from an earlier transfer of value.

Step 1:	Find value of hypothetical chargeable transfer	
	No related settlements or same day additions, therefore just the value of relevant property at the date of the first 10-year anniversary	£140,000
Step 2:	Ascertain tax on hypothetical chargeable transfer	
	The settlor has made chargeable transfers totalling £235,000 in the 7-year period before 1 July 2020	
	There have been no chargeable transfers out of the settlement in the 10 years since creation	
	Balance of nil rate band remaining	<u>£90,000</u>
	Portion of hypothetical chargeable transfer taxed at 20%	£50,000
	IHT @ 20% × £50,000 = £10,000	
Step 3:	Ascertain settlement rate	
	First find the Average Rate of tax by dividing the tax by the value of the hypothetical chargeable transfer:	
	$\dfrac{£10,000 \times 100}{£140,000} = 7.14\%$	
	Then convert to the Settlement Rate which is 30% of the Average Rate:	
	30% × 7.14% = 2.14%	
Step 4:	Ascertain the charge to IHT	
	Apply the Settlement Rate to the value of relevant property at the date of the first 10-year anniversary	
	IHT on the first 10-year anniversary is 2.14% × £140,000 = £2,996	
Step 5:	Paying the IHT	
	The trustees pay the IHT from the trust fund.	

EXAMPLE 3

As above, assume that the settlor had a cumulative total of £235,000 in 2020, but that during the first 10 years of the settlement the trustees made an appointment of £50,000 to a beneficiary.

Step 1:	Find value of hypothetical chargeable transfer	
	No related settlements or same day additions, therefore just the value of relevant property at the date of the first 10-year anniversary	£140,000

Step 2:   Ascertain tax on hypothetical chargeable transfer

The settlor has made chargeable transfers totalling £235,000 in the 7-year period before 1 July 2020

There has been a chargeable transfer of £50,000 out of the settlement in the 10 years since creation

The cumulative totals of the settlor and the settlement are together £235,000 + £50,000 = £285,000

Balance of nil rate band remaining   £40,000

Portion of hypothetical chargeable transfer taxed at 20%   £100,000

IHT @ 20% × £100,000 = £20,000

Step 3:   Ascertain settlement rate

First find the Average Rate of tax by dividing the tax by the value of the hypothetical chargeable transfer:

$$\frac{£20,000}{£140,000} \times 100 = 14.29\%$$

Then convert to the Settlement Rate which is 30% of the Average Rate:

30% × 14.29% = 4.29%

Step 4:   Ascertain the charge to IHT

Apply the Settlement Rate to the value of relevant property at the date of the first 10-year anniversary

IHT on the first 10-year anniversary is 4.29% × £140,000 = £6,006

Step 5:   Paying the IHT

The trustees pay the IHT from the trust fund.

The effect of cumulative totals of chargeable transfers of the settlor and the settlement

Transfers by the settlor and by the trustees reduce or extinguish the nil rate band available to the settlement on the occasion of the anniversary charge. Uniquely, the settlor's own cumulative total at the time he made the settlement remains relevant to IHT calculations for as long as the settlement continues. It does not 'drop out' in the way it does for an individual after seven years.

The settlement's own cumulative total ceases to be relevant once an anniversary has passed, although subsequent exits will cause the settlement to acquire another cumulative total which will remain relevant until the next 10-year anniversary charge and so on. These factors are particularly relevant to the trustees when considering whether to make distributions, ie, appointments of settled property or to 'break' the settlement.

10.3.6   Subsequent distribution and anniversary charges

Later distribution (exit) charges are brought about by the same events as discussed previously (see **10.3.3**). Inheritance tax is charged on the fall in the value of the settled property at a rate based on the rate at the previous 10-year anniversary charge. The number of quarters (periods of three months since then) will be relevant.

EXAMPLE 3 (CONTINUED) – EXIT CHARGE

A discretionary settlement created on 1 July 2020 had a settlement rate of 4.29% on its first 10-year anniversary (1 July 2030). On 1 January 2033 (10 quarters later) the trustees appoint £40,000 to a beneficiary. The rate will be one-fortieth of the settlement rate for each complete quarter since the first 10-year anniversary.

> The rate of IHT will be 4.29% × $\frac{10}{40}$ = 1.07%
>
> IHT payable will be £40,000 × 1.07% = £428

Later anniversary charges are calculated in the same way as the first anniversary charge. Any cumulative total of chargeable transfers of the settlor before he created the discretionary settlement (or when he added any property to the settlement) are taken into account but only exits since the last anniversary charge will be relevant.

EXAMPLE 3 (CONTINUED) – ANNIVERSARY CHARGE

The facts are the same as in the previous example. To calculate the anniversary charge in 2040 when the value of the trust fund has increased to £190,000:

Step 1: Find value of hypothetical chargeable transfer

No related settlements or same day additions, therefore just the value of relevant property at the date of the second 10-year anniversary   £190,000

Step 2: Ascertain tax on hypothetical chargeable transfer

The settlor made chargeable transfers totalling £235,000 in the 7-year period before 1 July 2020

There has been a chargeable transfer of £40,000 out of the settlement in the 10 years since the previous 10-year anniversary

The cumulative totals of the settlor and the settlement are together £235,000 + £40,000 = £275,000

Balance of nil rate band remaining   £50,000

Portion of hypothetical chargeable transfer taxed at 20%   £140,000

IHT @ 20% × £140,000 = £28,000

Step 3: Ascertain settlement rate

First find the Average Rate of tax by dividing the tax by the value of the hypothetical chargeable transfer:

$\frac{£28,000}{£190,000}$ × 100 = 14.74%

Then convert to the Settlement Rate which is 30% of the Average Rate:

30% × 14.74% = 4.42%

Step 4: Ascertain the charge to IHT

Apply the Settlement Rate to the value of relevant property at the date of the second 10-year anniversary

IHT on the second 10-year anniversary is 4.42% × £190,000 = £8,398

Step 5: Paying the IHT

The trustees pay the IHT from the trust fund.

10.3.7 Anti-avoidance and same day additions

The requirement in s 62A of IHTA 1984 that same day additions are included in the calculation of the hypothetical chargeable transfer for settlements created or added to on and after 10 December 2014 is an anti-avoidance provision. The intention is to combat the use of so-called 'pilot trust planning' which allowed taxpayers, by careful exploitation of the rules, to secure multiple nil rate bands for any number of settlements.

10.3.7.1 How pilot trust planning worked

Before the changes, a settlor with a full nil rate band available would create a number of settlements on different days and transfer a nominal amount, say £1, into each. Because they were created on different days the settlements were not related to each other. The initial transfer would fall within the settlor's annual exemption, and so each settlement inherited the settlor's full nil rate band.

Later, on one day (often on death) the settlor would transfer funds up to the level of the nil rate band to each settlement. Because all funds were transferred on the same day, the settlor's cumulative total immediately before each transfer remained at zero. Each settlement therefore had funds up to the level of the nil rate band inherited and a full nil rate band.

This technique meant that substantial funds could be held in settlements without payment of anniversary or exit charges.

EXAMPLE

George, a fond grandfather, wants to leave £600,000 to a settlement for his grandchildren. He has made no lifetime chargeable transfers and has a full nil rate band available. If he leaves £600,000 to one settlement, there will inevitably be exit and anniversary charges.

Before s 62A was inserted into IHTA 1984, if George created two pilot trusts during his lifetime and then by will left £300,000 to each, each settlement would have a full nil rate band and there would have been no anniversary or exit charges.

When s 62A applies, the hypothetical chargeable transfer for each settlement will be increased by the £300,000 of relevant property added to the other settlement. This means that the rate of tax will be increased, so there will be anniversary and exit charges.

10.3.7.2 Settlements not subject to the same day addition rule ('protected settlements')

(1) Pre-10 December 2014 settlements

Settlements created before 10 December 2014 are not subject to the same day addition rule unless funds are added after that date. In the previous example, provided George added his £300,000 to the pilot trusts before that day, his tax planning continues to work and the hypothetical chargeable transfer is not increased by the same day addition.

(2) Protected settlements

HMRC was concerned that there would be criticism if people who had created pilot trusts and made wills leaving property to the trusts died after 10 December 2014 without having time to review their tax planning. They would have lost the benefit of the multiple nil rate bands they would have been entitled to under the old rules.

The legislation, therefore, introduced a protection period. Same day additions are not included when calculating the hypothetical chargeable transfer where:

- death occurs before 6 April 2017, and
- additions are made to trusts created before 10 December 2014, under '*provisions of the settlor's will that at the settlor's death are, in substance, the same as they were immediately before 10 December 2014*' (IHTA 1984, s 62C).

This allowed a period of time for those affected to change their will to take into account the new rules. Wills could be altered so long as the provisions relating to the pilot trusts remained substantially the same.

EXAMPLE

In January 2014 Sam created three pilot discretionary trusts on consecutive days (so they are not related settlements), each receiving £10. Sam had a full nil rate band available. At the same time he made a will leaving £250,000 to each settlement.

(1) Sam dies in January 2017 with his will unchanged and £250,000 is transferred to each settlement.

In January 2024 the first anniversary charge has to be calculated.

On that date the value of the settled property in each settlement is £325,000 and the nil rate band has remained at £325,000.

Same day additions do not have to be included, so the hypothetical chargeable transfer for each settlement is £325,000.

All three settlements have a full nil rate band available so the anniversary rate of tax on each is nil.

(2) If Sam dies in January 2020, with his will unchanged, when the anniversary charge is calculated in 2024, same day additions will be included in the calculation of the hypothetical chargeable transfer for each settlement.

For each settlement the hypothetical chargeable transfer will consist of the value of the relevant property in the settlement on the anniversary plus the value of any relevant property added to the other two settlements on the same day.

This will be £325,000 + £250,000 + £250,000.

The anniversary rate for each settlement is calculated on a hypothetical chargeable transfer of £825,000.

There is a full nil rate band available to each settlement so 20% is charged on £500,000 = £100,000.

This is an average rate of £100,000/£825,000 x 100 = 12.12%. The settlement rate actually charged is 30% of that, so 3.6%.

Note that, where asset values rise, there is still a benefit to using three settlements rather than putting the whole lot into one big settlement.

If Sam had used one settlement, the rate of tax would have been calculated on a hypothetical chargeable transfer of £975,000. One nil rate band would have been available so tax at 20% would be charged on £650,000 = £130,000.

This is an average rate of £130,000/£975,000 x 100 = 13.33%. The settlement rate actually charged is 30% of that, so 3.9%.

10.3.8 Capital gains tax

As in the case of interest in possession settlements, a deemed disposal by the trustees will occur on their exercise of a power of appointment whereby someone becomes 'absolutely entitled' to the settled property against the trustees.

10.3.8.1 Deemed disposals

Deemed disposals have been considered at **10.2.4.2** in relation to interest in possession settlements. The principles discussed apply equally to appointments by trustees from discretionary trusts in favour of individuals.

If the appointment by the trustees creates new trusts of which there are new trustees, these new trustees may become absolutely entitled to the settled property as against the 'old' trustees. If so, the old trustees will make a deemed disposal to the new trustees. However, if the property appointed remains subject to some of the original trusts and trust instrument, there will be no deemed disposal.

There is often a fine line between the two situations. This is considered further at **10.5**.

10.3.8.2 Reliefs, exemptions and rates

The rate of CGT for all trustees for disposals on or after 6 April 2016 is 20% (unless residential property is disposed of when it is 28%) of the net chargeable gains. An annual exemption of £6,150 is available to the trustees in 2022/23.

Hold-over relief will generally be available when assets leave a discretionary settlement (see **10.2.4**). The relief can be claimed, inter alia, if the occasion which gives rise to the disposal is also an occasion of immediate liability to IHT. The relief will be available even if the rate at which IHT is charged is at 0% – for example, because the transfer is within the nil rate band.

However, because s 65(4) of IHTA 1984 provides that there is no charge to IHT if assets leave the relevant property settlement within three months after the date of creation, or three months after the date of any 10-year anniversary, hold-over relief is not available if the exit occurs during this time (unless the assets qualified as business assets under s 165 of TCGA 1992).

If the trustees and the beneficiaries agree to claim hold-over relief, it is convenient to add an appropriate clause to the deed of appointment containing their hold-over election. As a joint election of the beneficiaries and the trustees is required, they should all be made parties to the deed of appointment. If preferred, the election can be contained in a separate document.

EXAMPLE

Trustees of a relevant property settlement appoint 5,000 DEF plc shares worth £20,150 to Johan in August 2022. The shares were worth £4,000 when they were acquired two years ago. There are no other disposals in the tax year.

Disposal consideration	£20,150
Less: Acquisition cost	£4,000
Chargeable gain	£16,150

(a)   No hold-over relief election:

Trustees pay tax on £16,150 – £6,150 (annual exemption) = £10,000 @ 20% = £2,000. Johan acquires the shares with an acquisition value of £20,000.

(b)   Hold-over relief election:

There are two consequences:

(i)   the trustees pay no CGT

(ii)   Johan's acquisition cost is reduced

Market value of shares at appointment	£20,150
Less: held-over gain	£16,150
Johan's acquisition cost	£4,000

Johan does not benefit from the trustees' annual exemption.

Note that on the facts of the above example the trustees could make two separate disposals of shares. They can then have the benefit of the annual exemption on one disposal and claim holdover relief on the other.

10.3.9 Drafting a deed of appointment

It is good practice for trustees to make all appointments by deed even though an absolute appointment may be made less formally by the trustees making a memorandum note in their records if the trust instrument permits. However, making the appointment by deed has the advantage of providing all the relevant details in a clear form which can be referred to easily in subsequent documents.

Heading and date

Sample clause

> DEED OF APPOINTMENT
>
> DATE: [   ]

Parties

There will be two parties to a deed if an absolute appointment is intended:

(a)   the appointors, sometimes defined as 'the trustees'; and

(b)   the beneficiary.

If an appointment on further trusts with the same trustees is to be made, the deed will normally be made by the appointors alone.

Sample clause

> BETWEEN
>
> (1)   [name and address] ('the Appointors')
>
> (2)   [name and address] ('the Beneficiary')

Recitals

The recitals should explain the circumstances surrounding the exercise of the power. They will be confined to a brief statement that the trustees intend to exercise their power of appointment under the settlement in the manner indicated in the operative part of the deed.

Sample clause

> RECITALS
>
> (A) This Deed is supplemental to the settlement ('the Settlement')
>
> [and to the other documents and events] specified in the [First] Schedule.
>
> (B) The Appointors are the present Trustees of the Settlement.
>
> (C) [   ] is a member of the class of Beneficiaries.
>
> (D) The Appointors wish to exercise their power of appointment under clause [   ] of the Settlement in the following manner.

The operative part

Sample clause

> OPERATIVE PROVISIONS
>
> 1.   Definitions and construction
>
> In this Deed:
>
> 1.1   'the Appointed Fund' shall mean [that part of] the Trust Fund [specified in the Second Schedule]; and subject thereto,
>
> 1.2   where the context admits, the definitions and rules of construction contained in the Settlement shall apply.
>
> 2. Appointment
>
> The Appointors, in exercise of the power of appointment conferred by clause [ ] of the Settlement and of all other relevant powers, hereby [ir]revocably appoint and declare that the Appointed Fund shall henceforth be held upon trust for [   ] absolutely.
>
> [3. Application of Settlement provisions
>
> The trusts, powers and provisions contained in the Settlement shall continue to be applicable to the Appointed Fund so far as consistent with the provisions of this Deed.]

[4. Payment of tax and expenses

Any inheritance tax or capital gains tax and all other costs, expenses and other liabilities occasioned by the appointment contained in this Deed shall be borne by [the Appointed Fund] [the balance of the Trust Fund.]

5. Trustees' lien

Nothing in this Deed shall prejudice or impair in any way any lien or charge to which the Trustees are entitled in respect of any tax and other liabilities whatever for which they are or may become accountable.

[6. Capital gains tax hold-over relief

The parties claim relief under the provisions of s [165] [260] of the Taxation of Chargeable Gains Act 1992 in respect of the appointment contained in this Deed.]

[7. Power of revocation

The Trustees shall have power, at any time during the Trust Period, by deed or deeds wholly or partly to revoke the appointment contained in this Deed.]

Clause 3 will not be required if the appointment is both irrevocable and gives the beneficiary an absolute interest. If the appointment is onto trusts, clause 3 can be used to indicate that the powers under the original settlement are to apply to the Appointed Fund (where those powers are considered suitable). Clause 3 will also be required where the appointment is revocable. Clause 4 deals with the division of capital tax liability where part only of the trust fund is appointed. If the whole fund is appointed, it can be omitted.

Clause 6 is a claim by the parties for hold-over relief on the basis that the appointment is an occasion of charge to IHT (s 260). An equivalent claim could be made under TCGA 1992, s 165 if the assets appointed from the settlement were business assets. Hold-over relief is considered at **4.4.5.2**. Clause 7 will not be required if, as is usual, the appointment is irrevocable.

Schedules

Schedules will give details of the settlement under which the appointment is made and of the trust fund (or part) which is being appointed.

10.4 EXERCISING POWERS IN RELATION TO TRUSTS FOR BEREAVED MINORS AND BEREAVED YOUNG PEOPLE

10.4.1 The nature of the trusts and the powers

These are settlements created on death for the deceased's own children. To qualify as a settlement for bereaved minors, children must become entitled to capital at or before the age of 18; and to qualify as a settlement for bereaved young people, they must become entitled at or before 25. These settlements are considered in detail in **Chapter 12**.

As we will see, trustees of these trusts are allowed only limited powers of appointment if the trust is to qualify for privileged tax treatment. They can have the statutory power of advancement under s 32 of TA 1925, or an express power in the same terms. For trusts created before 1 October 2014 (the date on which the Inheritance and Trustees' Powers Act 2014 came into force), it was permissible to widen the express power to allow trustees to advance up to the whole of a beneficiary's capital entitlement. There must be no possibility of using the power to appoint capital away from the deceased's children to others, eg the deceased's spouse, or the settlement will not qualify. However, the power of advancement can be used to settle property on further trusts provided it is for the benefit of the same beneficiary.

10.4.1.1 Inheritance tax

These settlements have IHT advantages when it comes to capital entitlement. An appointment from a relevant property settlement gives rise to an exit charge. If the trustees use the power of appointment to give a beneficiary of one of these trusts capital at or before

18, there will be no exit charge. If the power is used to give a right to capital after 18, there will be a charge to IHT but only for the period from the beneficiary's 18th birthday.

EXAMPLE

Trustees of a trust created on death by Sunita's will hold £100,000 for her two children, contingent on their reaching 25. The children are aged 6 and 4.

The trustees appoint £50,000 to one child on her 18th birthday. There is no charge to IHT. They appoint the remaining £50,000 to the other on her 21st birthday. There will be a charge to IHT for the three years that have elapsed since her 18th birthday.

10.4.1.2 Capital gains tax

A deemed disposal will occur when a beneficiary of either settlement becomes absolutely entitled to the trust property as against the trustees.

Deemed disposals

The principles discussed at **10.3.8.1** in relation to relevant property settlements apply equally to appointments by trustees from settlements for bereaved minors or bereaved young people.

Reliefs, exemptions and rate

The rate of CGT is 20% (unless residential property is disposed of in which case it is 28%) of any net chargeable gain for disposals on or after 6 April 2016. An annual exemption is available to the trustees (£6,150 in 2022/23). Holdover relief is available under TCGA 1992, s 260 when beneficiaries of either type of trust become absolutely entitled as against the trustees. Relief is available under TCGA 1992, s 165 if the assets qualify as business assets (see **4.4.5.2**).

EXAMPLE 1

Trustees of a trust for bereaved minors hold property for Rajid contingent on reaching 18. He does so in June 2022. The settlement ends and Rajid becomes absolutely entitled to the settled property. Any gain made by the trustees on the deemed disposal may be held over on an election being made by the trustees and Rajid.

EXAMPLE 2

Trustees of a trust for bereaved young persons hold property for Amy contingent on reaching 25. In June 2022 the trustees appoint all the assets to Amy on her 21st birthday. The settlement ends and Amy becomes absolutely entitled to the settled property. Any gain made by the trustees on the deemed disposal may be held over on an election being made by the trustees and Amy.

10.5 EXERCISING POWERS IN RELATION TO ACCUMULATION AND MAINTENANCE SETTLEMENTS

10.5.1 The nature of the trusts and the powers

As we saw in **Chapter 8**, A & M settlements are a particular type of settlement without an interest in possession, created before 22 March 2006 and complying with the requirements of the amended s 71(1) of IHTA 1984. Beneficiaries must become entitled to capital at or before 18.

A power of appointment may be inserted in an A & M settlement. There must be no possibility of using the power to prevent beneficiaries becoming entitled to income or capital at age 18 or the settlement will not qualify as an A & M settlement.

10.5.1.1   Inheritance tax

An appointment from an A & M settlement to a beneficiary will not give rise to an exit charge. There are no anniversary charges.

10.5.1.2   Capital gains tax

A 'deemed' disposal will occur when a beneficiary of an A & M settlement becomes 'absolutely entitled' to the trust property against the trustees.

Deemed disposals

The principles discussed in **10.3.8.1** in relation to discretionary settlements apply equally to appointments by trustees from A & M settlements.

Reliefs, exemptions and rates

The rate of CGT for A & M trustees is 20% (or 28% on disposals of residential property) of any net chargeable gain. An annual exemption of £6,150 is available to the trustees in tax year 2022/23.

Hold-over relief is available under TCGA 1992, s 260, or if the assets disposed of are business assets (TCGA 1992, s 165) – see **4.4.5.2**.

10.6   EXERCISING POWERS IN RELATION TO RESETTLEMENTS

10.6.1   Absolute entitlement for CGT?

So far, this chapter has concentrated upon deemed disposals where an individual has become absolutely entitled to settled property against the trustees. Modern settlements are drafted in flexible form and usually include fiduciary powers for the trustees to 'declare new trusts' in relation to some or all of the settled property. The possibility of exercising a power either of advancement or appointment in this way is mentioned in **Chapter 9** (see **9.2**). Although the statutory power of advancement (TA 1925, s 32) is generally used to give an individual absolute entitlement to property freed from any continuing trusts, it has been held that the section may also be used to create trust advances, ie, to advance property in such a way that it is to be held in trust for a beneficiary, see *Pilkington and Another v Inland Revenue Commissioners and Others* [1964] AC 612 where a settled advance was for a beneficiary's 'benefit' within s 32 (see **9.4.2.3**). An express power of appointment can be used in the same way if it gives the trustees power to resettle (see **9.5**).

The phrase 'absolutely entitled against the trustees' does not mean 'absolutely and beneficially entitled'. It is therefore possible that one set of trustees (whether they are the same people or not) may, following the exercise of a fiduciary power, become absolutely entitled against another set of trustees. However, this does not necessarily mean that there will be a separate settlement. If there is not, then the usual rule in TCGA 1992, s 69 that the trustees are a single and continuing body of persons will apply, ie, there will be no deemed disposal and so there can be no question of liability to CGT arising.

If trustees propose exercising their power to declare new trusts, they need to consider whether or not the exercise of the power will amount to a deemed disposal. This is an area of some uncertainty, although clarification was provided through the Inland Revenue Statement of Practice (SP 7/84) following the decision in *Bond (Inspector of Taxes) v Pickford* [1983] STC 517 (see **10.6.2** and **10.6.3**).

10.6.2   A separate settlement or not?

In *Roome and Another v Edwards (Inspector of Taxes)* [1982] AC 279, the leading case in this area, Lord Wilberforce suggested that the existence of separate trustees, trusts and trust property was not necessarily conclusive as to the existence of a separate settlement. In the following extracts from the judgment, he draws a distinction between a special power of appointment (its exercise being unlikely to create a separate settlement) and the exercise of a wider form power which is more likely to create a separate settlement because property may be removed from the original settlement and subjected to other trusts:

> [T]rusts declared by a ... special power of appointment are to be read into the original settlement ... If such a power is exercised, whether or not separate trustees are appointed, I do not think that it would be natural ... to say that a separate settlement had been created, still less so if it were found that provisions of the original settlement continued to apply to the appointed fund, or that the appointed fund were liable, in certain events, to fall back into the rest of the settled property.

> If such a [wider form] power is exercised, the natural conclusion might be that a separate settlement was created, all the more so if a complete new set of trusts were declared as to the appropriated property, and if it would be said that the trusts of the original settlement ceased to apply to it. There can be many variations on these cases each of which will have to be judged on its facts.

In *Bond (Inspector of Taxes) v Pickford*, there were three relevant powers in the settlement whereby the trustees could:

(a) pay or apply funds to or for the benefit of the beneficiaries;

(b) allocate funds to beneficiaries either absolutely or contingently on attaining a specified age;

(c) resettle funds for the benefit of the beneficiaries.

What was the effect of an allocation of funds for named beneficiaries on attaining 22 years of age under (b) above: did it create a separate settlement? The Court of Appeal held that a new settlement had not been created, and in doing so distinguished between powers in the 'narrower form' and powers in the 'wider form'. The former do not permit property to be freed from the original settlement; the latter do permit this. It is not so much the description given to the power in the trust instrument which is significant, it is what it permits the trustees to do. The Court of Appeal held that the power in (b) above was a narrower form power in that it permitted a reorganisation internally within the original settlement and not the removal of funds from the settlement.

The manner of exercise of any given power is crucial. The mere fact that a wider form power may be exercised to free property from the original settlement does not necessarily mean it has been exercised in this way. It will be a matter of intention; the trustees may decide to exercise it in a narrower form way. If they wish to avoid a separate settlement, and the associated deemed disposal for CGT, they will exercise the power in a narrower way; the property will remain subject to the original trusts. See *Swires v Renton* [1991] STC 490.

10.6.3 Inland Revenue Statement of Practice (SP 7/84)

This Statement of Practice followed the Court of Appeal decision in *Bond (Inspector of Taxes) v Pickford* and contains the following:

> [T]he Board considers that a deemed disposal will not arise when ... [powers in the wider form, which may be powers of advancement or certain powers of appointment, are] ... exercised and trusts are declared in circumstances where:
>
> (a) the appointment is revocable, or
>
> (b) the trusts declared of the advanced or appointed funds are not exhaustive so that there exists a possibility at the time when the advancement or appointment is made that the funds covered by it will on the occasion of some event cease to be held upon such trusts and once again come to be held upon the original trusts of the settlement.

> Further, when such a power is exercised the Board considers it unlikely that a deemed disposal will arise when trusts are declared if duties in regard to the appointed assets still fall to the trustees of the original settlement in their capacity as trustees of that settlement ... Finally, the Board accepts that a power of appointment or advancement can be exercised over only part of the settled property and that the above consequences would apply to that part.

By this Statement of Practice, the Revenue accepts that a new settlement can be created only if a wider form power is exercised. There are, however, limitations when a new settlement would not be created, ie, where the exercise is revocable, the trusts are not exhaustive in the sense that some of the property could again become subject to the original trusts and where the trustees of the original settlement have continuing duties in relation to the settled property.

10.6.4   Drafting the trustees' power of appointment

Powers of appointment given to trustees should be drafted as separate clauses in such a way as to make it abundantly clear whether they are wider form or narrower form powers. Trustees, having considered the effect of the exercise of their powers fully (including the CGT consequences) can then specifically exercise by deed a narrower or a wider form power. By so doing, difficulty of construction and effect for CGT of the deed of appointment should be avoided.

10.6.5   The CGT consequences of a separate settlement

If a separate settlement is created by the exercise of the power of appointment, the new trustees become absolutely entitled against the old (whether they are the same people or not) so that there is a deemed disposal for CGT. The calculation of the gain (or loss) follows normal principles (including the deduction for the trustees' annual exemption). The trustees pay any tax due from the settled property.

If cash is appointed, no liability to CGT will arise. Otherwise, hold-over relief may be available to the trustees under TCGA 1992, s 165 or s 260 depending on the circumstances, but if holdover relief is claimed, the annual exemption will not be available.

10.6.6   The documentation if a separate settlement

In addition to a deed of appointment drafted in the manner discussed earlier, the trustees of the old settlement will need to sign stock transfer forms to transfer the settled stocks and shares to the new trustees (unless the shares are held by a nominee). If they are the same people, stock transfer forms will still be required but it may be sensible specifically to designate the transferees as trustees of the newly created settlement so as to avoid confusing the share certificates in their own names for the investments in the new settlement with those belonging to them as trustees of the original settlement.

10.6.7   Summary

Tax on exercise of powers of appointment and advancement

Settlement	IHT	CGT
Qualifying interest in possession	PET or LTC depending on whether entitlement is absolute or trusts continue (except to the extent the life tenant benefits)	Deemed disposal No hold-over relief (unless business assets)
Discretionary	Exit or periodic charge	Deemed disposal (if absolute entitlement) Hold-over relief available

Settlement	IHT	CGT
Bereaved minors or young people	No exit or periodic charge	Deemed disposal (if absolute entitlement) Hold-over relief available
Accumulation and maintenance	No exit or periodic charge	Deemed disposal (if absolute entitlement) Hold-over relief available

REVIEW ACTIVITY

Question 1

Lauren's husband died in November 2022 and left his estate on trust for Lauren (aged 50) for life, remainder to Rafael, their son (aged 22), absolutely. The will did not vary s 32 of the Trustee Act 1925 and contains no other powers allowing the trustees to apply capital. The trust fund is currently worth £750,000.

Which ONE of the following statements is CORRECT?

A   Lauren and Rafael can agree to divide the capital between themselves in whatever proportions they wish.

B   If Lauren takes £350,000 and Rafael takes £400,000, Lauren will be treated as making a lifetime chargeable transfer of £400,000 to Rafael.

C   If Lauren takes £350,000 and Rafael takes £400,000, Lauren will be treated as making a potentially exempt transfer of £350,000 to Rafael.

D   The trustees can use their s 32 power to appoint £750,000 to Lauren.

Answer: A

The settlement is created on death so Lauren has an immediate post-death interest and is treated for IHT purposes as entitled to the underlying trust capital. Rafael is entitled to the reversionary interest which is excluded property for IHT purposes.

Between themselves, they are entitled to the whole beneficial interest and can do as they wish.

B and C are wrong as Lauren is treated as entitled to the whole of the capital for IHT purposes and will therefore make a PET of £400,000 to Rafael. D is wrong as s 32 can only be used to apply capital for beneficiaries with an interest in capital.

Question 2

On 1 June 2022, Sam settled £625,000 on discretionary trusts for the benefit of his children and grandchildren. He had made no lifetime chargeable transfers although he always uses his annual exemption on 6 April each tax year.

Which ONE of the following statements is WRONG?

A   Sam's cumulative total at the date the settlement is created will be relevant to the calculation of exit and anniversary charges throughout the life of the settlement.

B   There is an anniversary charge every 10 years calculated on the value of the relevant property in the settlement immediately before the 10-year anniversary.

C   When calculating an anniversary charge, transfers made from the settlement in the previous 10 years affect the rate of tax charged.

D   When calculating an anniversary charge, all transfers made from the settlement affect the rate of tax charged.

Answer: D

Transfers from the settlement cease to be cumulated once an anniversary charge has been calculated (unlike the settlor's cumulative total before creation of the settlement which remains relevant throughout the life of the settlement).

Question 3

In which ONE of the following cases will the hypothetical chargeable transfer on the first 10-year anniversary be £600,000?

A   On 1 October 2013 Scott created two discretionary settlements and immediately transferred £200,000 to each. The value of the property in each settlement on the 10th anniversary is £600,000.

B   On 1 October 2013 Scott created one discretionary settlement, transferring £10 and on the following day he created a second discretionary settlement, also transferring £10. On 1 October 2014, he transferred £200,000 to each settlement by a lifetime transfer. The value of the property in each settlement on the 10th anniversary is £300,000.

C   On 1 October 2013 Scott created one discretionary settlement, transferring £10 and on the following day he created a second discretionary settlement, also transferring £10. On 1 October 2016, he died and left £200,000 to each settlement by will executed in 2001. The value of the property in each settlement on the 10th anniversary is £300,000.

D   On 1 October 2013 Scott created one discretionary settlement, transferring £10 and on the following day he created a second discretionary settlement, also transferring £10. On 1 October 2018, he died and left £200,000 to each settlement by will executed in 2001. The value of the property in each settlement on the 10th anniversary is £400,000.

Answer: D

The settlements in A are related settlements so the hypothetical chargeable transfer (HCT) for each settlement includes the value of the relevant property settled in the second settlement (£600,000 + £200,000).

The settlements in B are not related settlements as they were created on different days. They were neither created nor added to on or after 1 December 2014 so same day additions are not included in the HCT which will be £300,000 for each.

The settlements in C are not related settlements as they were created on different days. They were added to after 1 December 2014 but by will and within the protection period so same day additions are not included in the HCT, which will be £300,000 for each.

The settlements in D are not related settlements as they were created on different days. They were added to after 1 December 2014 and outside the protection period so same day additions are included. The HCT for each settlement will be £400,000 + £200,000.

BASIC WILL DRAFTING

LEARNING OUTCOMES

After reading this chapter you will be able to:

- explain the basic clauses which should be included in a will
- draft a simple will.

This chapter deals with the basic content of a will, and the typical provisions likely to appear in all types of will. The next chapter deals with the special provisions required for the creation of different types of trust within a will. For further exploration of the subject, refer to practitioners' books such as Withers, *Practical Will Precedents* (Sweet & Maxwell), *Williams on Wills*, *Wills Probate and Administration* (LexisNexis Butterworths).

It is important to be aware that, since the House of Lords' decision in *White v Jones* [1995] 1 All ER 691, will drafting is a growing area for negligence claims against solicitors. Many firms prohibit anyone who is not a specialist from attempting it.

11.1 PRELIMINARY MATTERS

A solicitor taking instructions for a will should be aware of the need for the testator to have the requisite capacity and intention. This is considered in LPC Guide, **Legal Foundations**.

Solicitors should also be aware of the tax consequences of the testator's instructions, and be able to advise on tax savings where possible. Inheritance tax on death is considered in LPC Guide, **Legal Foundations**, para 4.3, and general tax planning is considered in **Chapter 4** above.

Solicitors should also be aware of relevant issues of professional conduct. For example, they must comply with Principles 4, 5 and 7 and act with honesty, integrity and in the best interests of clients. Paragraph 3.1 of the SRA Code of Conduct for Solicitors, RELs and RFLs requires:

> You only act for clients on instructions from the client, or from someone properly authorised to provide instructions on their behalf.

In the case of a will, solicitors should not take instructions from anyone but the client as the dangers of misunderstanding or deceit are obvious. It would not be in the best interests of the client to take instructions from an intermediary.

Paragraph 6.1 requires:

> You do not act if there is an own interest conflict or a significant risk of such a conflict.

Hence, solicitors should not prepare a will giving significant amounts to themselves, spouses, civil partners or family members unless the client has obtained independent advice.

SRA Ethics guidance, 'Drafting and preparation of wills', issued on 6 May 2014 and updated on 25 November 2019 states:

> If you draft a will where the client wishes to make a gift of significant value to you or a member of your family, or an employee of your business or their family, you should satisfy yourself that the client has first taken independent legal advice with regard to making the gift.
>
> This includes situations where the intended gift is of significant value in relation to the size of the client's overall estate, but also where the gift is of significant value in itself. Paragraph 6.1 of each of the Codes requires you not to act if there is an own interest conflict or a significant risk of an own interest conflict. In a situation like this, you will usually need to cease acting if the client does not agree to taking independent legal advice.
>
> There may be some exceptions where you can continue to draft the will even if the client has not received independent legal advice for example, if you draft wills for your parents and the surviving parent wishes to leave the residuary estate to you and your siblings in equal shares.
>
> However, whether it is appropriate to do so will depend upon the specific circumstances of each situation, and in each case you should consider whether your ability to advise, and be seen to advise, impartially is undermined by any financial interest or personal relationship which you have.

Civil partners

The Civil Partnership Act (CPA) 2004 came into effect on 5 December 2005. It has important implications for will drafting. The CPA 2004 originally allowed same sex couples not closely related to each other to register a civil partnership. At the end of 2019, amendments were made to allow opposite sex civil partnerships. The Civil Partnership (Opposite-sex Couples) Regulations 2019 came into force on 2 December 2019, allowing the formation of new opposite sex civil partnerships from 31 December 2019 onwards. See **4.1** above.

Persons who have registered a civil partnership are, for many purposes, treated as spouses for the purposes of succession to property. Basically the provisions of the Married Women's Property Act 1882, s 11, and enactments relating to wills and administration of estates, and the Inheritance (Provision for Family and Dependants) Act 1975 are amended to apply in relation to civil partnerships as they do to marriages.

The main provisions relating to wills and administration that are amended are:

(a)   revocation by marriage/civil partnership unless a will is made in expectation of marriage or civil partnership;

(b)   gift in will to former spouse/civil partner treated as lapsed where divorce/dissolution of civil partnership occurs;

(c)   gifts attested by spouse/civil partner are void;

(d)   entitlement on intestacy including rights to take 'matrimonial home' in or toward satisfaction of absolute entitlement on intestacy; and

(e)   civil partners have same rights as spouses to make applications under the Inheritance (Provision for Family and Dependants) Act 1975.

However, in private legal documents, a civil partner is not the same thing as a spouse. Hence a gift to a class of beneficiaries including 'spouses' will not include civil partners unless the document includes a definition clause giving 'spouse' an extended meaning. As explained at **4.1**, in *Goodrich and others v AB* [2022] EWHC 81 (Ch) Chief Master Schuman held that UK legislation was discriminatory in this regard and conflicted with the European Convention on Human Rights. She said it was impossible to read the legislation in a way which would remove the discrimination. However, in *Goodrich* itself she was able to interpret the word 'spouse' used in an employee benefit trust as including civil partners. She made it clear though that this was for reasons specific to that trust.

Marriage (Same Sex Couples) Act 2013

This Act permits same sex couples to marry under the law of England and Wales. Its main provisions came into effect on 13 March 2014, enabling the first same sex marriages to take place on 29 March 2014. Same sex couples are generally treated in the same way as couples in opposite sex marriages.

In relation to the drafting of private legal documents, such as wills, Sch 4 of the Act states that documents made before the Act came into force are unaffected. This means that (unless there is any express provision to the contrary in the document) references in these documents to terms such as 'husband', 'wife', 'widow', etc refer only to persons in an opposite sex marriage.

In relation to private legal documents made on or after 13 March 2014, unless they contain express provision to the contrary, references to marriage or to a spouse include both opposite and same sex marriages and spouses. For example, 'husband' also means a man married to another man, 'wife' also means a woman married to another woman and 'widow' also means a woman whose wife has predeceased her, and so on. As explained at **4.1**, in *Goodrich and others v AB* [2022] EWHC 81 (Ch) Chief Master Schuman held that UK legislation was discriminatory in relation to private instruments executed before the Act came into force and conflicted with the European Convention on Human Rights. She said it was possible to read the legislation in a way which would remove the discrimination. She considered that the limitation contained in Sch 4 should apply only to 'an instrument which settles property in so far as (i) it contains a disposition of property, and (ii) the beneficiary of the disposition has done something to avail himself or herself of the property right in question before the coming into force of the Human Rights Act 1998'.

It remains good practice, when drafting, to avoid doubt and argument by defining terms used to make clear what the intentions of the testator were.

European Succession Regulation 650/2012 ('Brussels IV')

This Regulation forms part of a series of regulations on conflict of laws (or private international law (PIL)) issues within the EU. It is often referred to as 'Brussels IV'. The Regulation affects the succession to assets on deaths occurring on or after 17 August 2015. Although the UK (together with Ireland and Denmark) opted out of the Regulation when it was introduced, and is no longer a member of the EU, the Regulation continues to have an impact on UK practitioners advising on wills and estate planning in various circumstances. These include where a UK national wishes to make a will and that person lives in or owns property in an EU State which is bound by the Regulation. Many EU States have forced heirship rules (particularly in relation to land) which are not usually in line with the wishes of UK nationals. It is therefore important to have an awareness of where the Regulation may be relevant and its effect and, where necessary, obtain specialist advice about relevant foreign law.

The aim of Brussels IV is to reduce the expensive and time-consuming legal procedures that can arise in determining questions of succession to property on death where the laws of more than one State may be relevant and they conflict. This could happen, for example, where a person residing in one State has died owning property located in a different State. In the UK there is significant testamentary freedom to leave property to whomever the testator chooses, but in a number of EU States there are 'forced heirship' rules which require some or all of a person's assets to pass to particular family members.

The position is complex because, in addition to a State having its own domestic laws of succession, it also has PIL rules to determine whether to defer to the other State's rules on the matter. It can mean that succession to some assets in a person's estate is governed by one law and other assets by a different law. The UK, for example, considers that succession to land is governed by '*lex situs*', that is the law of the State in which land is located (this is sometimes known as 'renvoi'), but succession to all other assets is governed by the law of the State in which the deceased was domiciled at death.

Other States consider that the law of nationality or the law of habitual residence governs succession.

Very broadly, in States which have adopted the Regulation, Brussels IV provides that the law of only one State applies to determine succession (via will or intestacy) to all of a person's assets on death, wherever these may be located. The Regulation does not therefore deal with lifetime gifts or other methods of property passing, such as survivorship.

Under Brussels IV the law that will apply to determine succession to all of a person's estate is the law of the State in which the deceased was habitually resident at death, unless (i) the person was 'manifestly more connected' with another State, or (ii) the person has chosen the law that is to apply. This chosen law must be the law of a State of which the person was a national, either at the time of making the choice or at death.

There may be possible uncertainty as to where a person is regarded as habitually resident or 'manifestly more connected'. Therefore it is important to make a choice.

The law that applies, whether by choice or by default, can be the law of a State that is not a signatory (Article 20), so nationals of non-EU States and EU States that have not signed up to the Regulation can choose the law of their nationality to govern their succession as opposed to the law of the country in which they are habitually resident at death.

Article 34(1) provides that in relation to 'Third States', the rules that will be applied are its rules of private international law insofar as those rules require a renvoi (the application of the law of another State). Third States were originally intended to be States that are not EU Member States (which now includes the UK). Although the final version of the Regulation does not deal with EU States that have not adopted the Regulation, it seems to be accepted that the non-signatory EU States (Ireland and Denmark) are Third States.

Article 34(2), however, provides that no renvoi will be applied where a person has chosen the law of his nationality.

There is an argument that where a national of a country that is not a signatory to the Regulation chooses the law of their nationality, the law chosen is the country's PIL, not its domestic law. In the case of the UK, this would mean that, for land, *lex situs* would apply, which in many cases would mean forced heirship rules would apply. However, the effect of Article 34 as a whole is not entirely clear. Most people take the view that where a choice of national law is made, the effect is that a State's domestic law applies, not its PIL rules.

Where no choice is made, the effect of Article 34(1) is that States will accept a renvoi.

Clients who own property in the EU States should include a choice of national law as this is likely to be successful and cannot do any harm, although it also remains important for clients to take local advice.

EXAMPLE

Emma is domiciled and habitually resident in England and Wales and has a house in Germany and a house in Italy and bank accounts in each country. Under the law of England and Wales, succession to the bank account is governed by the law of England and Wales, but succession to the house is governed by the laws of Germany and Italy. If Emma has made no choice of national law, German and Italian law will govern succession to the houses (including forced heirship rules). If Emma has chosen the law of her nationality, the law of England and Wales would apply.

At the time of writing, there is a particular problem in relation to France. The French are very attached to the forced heirship rules contained in articles 912 et seq of the French Civil Code which give fixed inheritance rights to the deceased's children and in some cases the surviving spouse. There was some unhappiness at the way in which the EU Succession Regulation could erode these rules. Article 35 allows states to refuse to give effect to any part of the Regulation which is 'manifestly incompatible with the state's public policy'. In 2017, the French Cour de Cassation (the Supreme Court) held in relation to the estate of Maurice Jarre (who had been resident in California for many years before his death) that excluding the forced heirship portion, pursuant to the foreign law designated by the conflict-of-law rule, 'was not, in and of itself, contrary to French international public order policy'.

However, a new law, adopted by the French Parliament on 24 August 2021(Loi no. 2021-1109 du 24 aout 2021 confortant les principes de la République), which came into force on 1 November 2021, amends articles 913 and 921 of the French Civil Code by providing for an increased protection of the rights of protected heirs in situations where the deceased or one of their heirs is either from a Member State of the European Union or a habitual resident of a Member State of the European Union. French notaries will be under an obligation before distributing the estate to inform those forced heirs whose rights may be affected by the provisions of the testator's will of their entitlement under the new law.

> **EXAMPLE**
>
> A UK national with two children who dies while habitually resident in France would be subject to the forced heirship rules.

This new law conflicts not only with the EU Succession Regulation but also with the decision of the Cour de Cassation and so is likely to be challenged in the French courts. Until then, however, it is unclear whether any elections for national law in wills of UK nationals who fall within the terms of articles 913 and 921 will be effective.

Where a person has assets in different jurisdictions anywhere in the world, it is sensible to make separate wills to deal with these assets under the law of the relevant jurisdiction (although care must be taken with the revocation clauses: see **11.2.2**). Where any of these jurisdictions are EU States bound by Brussels IV, it will be important to ensure that there is consistency in stating in all the wills which law is to apply to the assets.

(It is also important to consider the impact of Brussels IV when advising a non-UK national who owns property in or lives in the UK but has links with EU States bound by the Regulation.)

11.2 BASIC CONTENT OF A WILL

All wills should contain the following:

(a)   opening words or commencement;

(b)   revocation clause;

(c)   date;

(d)   appointment of executors;

(e)   legacies and/or gift of residue;

(f)   attestation clause.

Although these provisions may be sufficient for a very simple will, most wills require additional provisions. For example, if any of the legacies is to a charity, it is desirable to make provision for the possibility that the charity may amalgamate or cease to exist. If any of the legacies give rise to a continuing trust, it may be necessary to supply express trust administration powers for the trustees.

11.2.1 Opening words or commencement

The main purpose of this clause is to identify the testator and the nature of the document.

The full name and address of the testator should be stated. If the testator holds property in any other name, it will be helpful when the application for the grant of representation is later made if the will also states this other name and indicates that the testator is also known by it. Details of the testator's occupation may also be included as further identification.

A statement that the document is the 'last will' or 'last will and testament' (there is no legal difference between these phrases) should be included. This helps demonstrate that the testator had an intention to make a will, which is a legal requirement.

Where a person has made or will make a will to deal with assets located outside the UK, it is important to make clear to which assets this will relates. Where appropriate, a statement as to the choice of law governing succession to assets, for the purposes of Brussels IV, can be included.

The date may appear within the commencement or at the end of the will. A space should be left as the will is dated on execution.

A testator who intends to marry or form a civil partnership in the near future and who wants the will to continue to be valid should include a statement that the will is made in expectation of the marriage or civil partnership and is not to be revoked by that marriage or civil partnership taking place. In the absence of such a statement, the will is automatically revoked by subsequent marriage or formation of a civil partnership.

The Marriage (Same Sex Couples) Act 2013 (Consequential and Contrary Provisions and Scotland) (No 2) Order 2014 and the Marriage of Same Sex Couples (Conversion of Civil Partnership) Regulations 2014 came into effect on 10 December 2014. These provide for civil partners to convert their civil partnership into a same sex marriage, and that the conversion from civil partnership to same sex marriage will not automatically revoke or otherwise affect an existing will. There are, at present, no provisions allowing spouses of opposite sex marriages to convert to opposite sex civil partnerships.

11.2.2 Revocation clause

The purpose of this clause is to indicate that all earlier wills and codicils are expressly revoked. Any later will impliedly revokes earlier wills and codicils, but only to the extent that the later will is inconsistent with the earlier provisions. An express revocation avoids the risk of an earlier will or codicil not being wholly revoked by the implied revocation. Where a person has made another will or wills dealing with assets located outside the UK, it is important to consider whether these are to be revoked. If they are not, the revocation stated in this will must make this clear.

The revocation clause may appear by itself, but it is also commonly incorporated into the commencement. It should appear near the beginning of the will.

11.2.3 Appointment of executors (and trustees)

The purpose of this clause is to appoint the persons that the testator has chosen to administer his estate (the executor(s)). If the testator does not take the opportunity to name his own choice, the Non-contentious Probate Rules 1987 (SI 1987/2024) will govern who may act as administrator (see LPC Guide, **Legal Foundations**).

It is sometimes sensible to create an express trust of the estate (see below for where this is the case). Where this happens, the testator should appoint persons to be trustees. It is often convenient to name the same people as both executors and trustees, although it is not essential. Such people will act as executors while they collect in the estate, pay debts and distribute the estate. When they have completed that stage, they will transfer the property that is to be held on trust to themselves to hold in the new capacity of trustee.

11.2.3.1   How many executors?

In principle there is no maximum number of executors that can be named in the will. However, as only a maximum of four can apply for the grant of probate to the same assets, there is little point in naming more than four.

It is possible to limit the appointment of executors to particular parts of the estate. For example, a testator may appoint specialists to deal with his business assets or literary effects and members of his family to deal with his general assets. In such a case each appointment can be of up to four people.

The minimum number is one, and this will often be sufficient for a small, simple estate where the executor is the sole or main beneficiary. (A sole executor can give a good receipt for the proceeds of sale of land held in the estate.) However, there is a risk that the sole executor may pre-decease the testator or be unable to act for some other reason. For example, the effect of a divorce on a will is that the spouse is deemed to have died at the date of the divorce, so that any appointment of the spouse as executor will not take effect (Wills Act 1837, s 18A). The dissolution of a civil partnership has the same effect. It is therefore prudent to appoint at least two persons, or name a substitute for a sole executor.

If the executors will also be trustees, it is sensible to appoint at least two so that they can give a good receipt for the proceeds of sale of any land held in the trust.

11.2.3.2   Whom to choose?

The testator may appoint any combination of:

(a)   individuals who are not professionals (eg, family or friends);

(b)   solicitors or other professionals (as individuals or as a firm);

(c)   banks or other trust corporations.

A testator may ask for advice on the type of person he should appoint and the solicitor should therefore be able to discuss the relevant considerations allowing the testator to make an informed choice.

11.2.3.3   Non-professional individuals

Choosing family members or close friends whom the testator can trust will have the advantage of ensuring that persons familiar with the testator and his affairs will deal with the estate. A further advantage is that such persons are unlikely to want to charge the estate for their time spent in dealing with it. However, this advantage may be more apparent than real. If the estate is other than straightforward, it is likely that the individuals will lack the expertise necessary to complete the administration and will have to employ a solicitor. The costs of this will be paid from the estate.

Naturally the testator should only choose those responsible enough to deal with the estate, and should not appoint anyone barred from taking out a grant of probate (such as a minor) or a person who has already proved untrustworthy with money (such as someone convicted of an offence of dishonesty).

11.2.3.4   Solicitors or other professionals

Choosing a solicitor or other professional will mean that the executor will have the necessary expertise to administer the estate. Family and friends will be spared the burden at a time when they may be grieving. However, the professional executor will expect to be paid not just for expenses incurred but also for the time spent doing the work.

An individual solicitor may be appointed, but there is a risk that this person may die or retire. To avoid this possibility the firm of solicitors can be appointed.

If the testator decides to appoint a firm of solicitors there are some drafting considerations:

(a)   The firm, being a partnership, has no legal identity and so cannot be appointed. Instead the appointment is of the partners in the named firm. As these will change from time to time it is important to specify that it is the partners in the firm at the date of death who are appointed. Otherwise the appointment will be of those at the date of the will. It is usual to express the wish that only two partners will take the grant and act in the administration.

(b)   The firm may change its name, amalgamate or become a limited liability partnership (LLP) between the date of the will and the date of death, and it is sensible to provide for this. Usually the testator will indicate that the appointment is of the partners in the new or amalgamated firm. To allow for a firm becoming a LLP there should be a reference to the solicitors who are the directors or members of, or beneficial owners of shares in, a firm that has become a LLP.

Many wills were drafted before it became possible for a firm to become a LLP, and so the clause appointing the partners in a firm merely refers to the substitution of *partners* in any new or amalgamated *firm*. For a while Probate Registrars took the view that such clauses did not provide for the appointment of solicitors in a LLP, which was a different legal entity. This approach was tested in the case of *Re Rogers (Deceased)* [2006] EWHC 753, where it was held that Probate Registrars should recognise members of an LLP as successors to the original firm, thus saving the need for existing wills to be re-drafted when a firm became a LLP. The judge emphasised that in any firm it is only the profit-sharing partners (as opposed to the salaried partners) who are true partners, although a testator is free to choose a salaried partner to act as an executor if he wishes. Firms where salaried partners are in the habit of taking grants of probate may widen the meaning of 'partner' in wills by including a statement that 'in this will "partner" includes a salaried partner'.

Professional conduct issues

The SRA published 'Ethics guidance: Drafting and preparation of wills' on 6 May 2014 (updated 25 November 2019).

In relation to the appointment of a firm or individual fee earners as executors, it says:

> Your client might decide to appoint you, your business or other people in your business as executors in the will you are drafting for them.
>
> However, you must not exploit a client's lack of knowledge by leading them to believe that appointing a solicitor as an executor is essential or that it is the default position for someone making a will.
>
> Principle 7 of the Principles requires you to act in the best interests of each client. In this context this means not encouraging clients to appoint you or the business you work for as their executor unless it is clearly in their best interests to do so.
>
> In some cases it might be beneficial for a client to appoint a solicitor to act as an executor – for example, if their affairs are complex, or there are potential disputes in the family. However, in other cases there may be little or no advantage to the client – for example, if their estate is small or straightforward. A professional executor is likely to be more expensive than a lay person and the client should be advised about this.
>
> Before drafting a will which appoints you or your business (or someone else in the business) as the executor(s), you should be satisfied that the client has made their decision on a fully informed basis. This includes:
>
> •   explaining the options available to the client regarding their choice of executor;
>
> •   ensuring the client understands that an executor does not have to be a professional person or a business, that they could instead be a family member or a beneficiary under the will, and that

lay executors can subsequently instruct a solicitor to act for them if this proves necessary (and can be indemnified out of the estate for the solicitors' fees);

• recording advice that is given concerning the appointment of executors and the client's decision.

The Law Society has issued a Practice Note, 'Appointment of a Professional Executor Practice Note' (updated 3 September 2020), available on its website. This deals with the information on charging that should be provided and the matters a firm should take into account when deciding how to respond to a request from the beneficiaries that the firm should renounce the appointment.

11.2.3.5 Banks or other trust corporations

A testator may consider appointing a bank as executor. Most high street banks have a trustee department, and it is able to act via the mechanism of a trust corporation. Appointing this type of executor has some similar advantages to appointing a firm of solicitors: the corporation will not die or retire, and there should be financial and some legal expertise. Disadvantages include the fact that the corporation may seem large and impersonal to the family. The charging methods of banks may also be disadvantageous, as they usually charge a percentage of the value of the estate, which can be a significant expense.

11.2.3.6 Charging provisions

Whether an individual professional or a firm is appointed, there will be a need to consider the charging arrangements. An executor or trustee is a fiduciary and unable to profit from his position, unless authorised.

The Trustee Act (TA) 2000, s 29 allows the payment of reasonable remuneration to a trustee for time spent and work done (even if such work could have been done by a lay person), but only if the trustee is either:

(a) a trust corporation; or

(b) a trustee 'acting in a professional capacity', but who is not a sole trustee and who has got the written consent of all his co-trustees.

'Acting in a professional capacity' means acting in the course of a profession or business which involves providing relevant services to trusts. Trustees may only charge for services carried out after 1 February 2001, although the provision applies to all trusts unless excluded.

An express charging provision will always be required to allow any trustee who does not fall within s 29 to charge for time spent and work done. It may also be desirable to include express provisions allowing:

(a) a trust corporation to be paid in accordance with its standard terms and conditions; and/or

(b) a trustee to retain remuneration he has received for services given as a director of a company in which the trust holds shares.

It is usual in any express charging clause to state that the solicitor or other professional may charge for work done, even though it could have been done by a non-professional. Again, the TA 2000 now provides for this, but it is better to have clear express drafting within the will.

Where an express charging provision is included it may appear early on together with the clause appointing the executors, or later among the administrative provisions. It does not matter which approach is used.

Until the TA 2000 came into force, a charging clause was treated as a legacy in the will. Under s 15 of the Wills Act 1837, beneficiaries lose their entitlement under a will if they, or their spouse (or civil partner), witness the will. Therefore, in the past if a will had a charging clause, it could not be witnessed by the individual solicitor appointed or any of the partners in the firm appointed, or any spouses or civil partners. The TA 2000 now provides that a charging clause does not qualify as a legacy for these purposes. (However, the TA 2000 only operates for this purpose on wills where death occurred after 1 February 2001.)

Where a charging clause authorises an executor to charge 'reasonable remuneration', this will be objectively assessed. Professionals cannot necessarily charge at their normal charge-out rate: see *Pullan v Wilson* [2014] EWHC 126 (Ch).

In *Da Silva v Heselton* [2022] EWCA Civ 880 the Court of Appeal held that a charging clause authorising a person 'engaged in any profession or business [to] charge and be paid (in priority to all other dispositions herein) all usual professional and other fees' was limited to charges for work done as part of their usual business. For example, a builder, surveyor or accountant who provided services of the appropriate type to the estate would clearly be able to charge for those services but could not charge for other work done during the administration.

11.2.4 Non-residuary gifts

A testator may wish to make gifts of specific assets or of money. Traditionally, a gift of personalty is called a 'legacy' and a gift of land is called a 'devise'. The term 'gift' applies to either. There are various types of gift.

11.2.4.1 Specific gifts

This is a gift of a specific item or items or specific piece of land which the testator owns, for example, 'I give my diamond engagement ring to my daughter'. If the testator does not own the specific item or property at death, the gift fails ('adeems'). The beneficiary gets nothing in place of the gifted item unless the will expressly provides for substitution.

11.2.4.2 General gifts

This is a gift of an item corresponding to a description. If the testator does not own this item at death, it must be obtained using funds from the estate, for example, 'I give 100 shares in Z plc to my son'. If the testator does not own 100 such shares then they must be purchased.

Note: Where there are insufficient assets in an estate to pay all debts and expenses and pay the legacies in full, legacies will be reduced ('abate') proportionately. General legacies will be reduced first, and only if they are insufficient will specific legacies be taken.

11.2.4.3 Demonstrative gift

This is a gift that is general in nature but is directed to be paid from a specific fund, for example, 'I give £500 to X to be paid from my Nationwide savings account'. If the account exists at the date of the death and contains £500 or more, the legacy is paid from the account and is classified as specific. If there is no account (or if it contains less than £500), the legacy is paid, in whole (or in part), from the rest of the estate and to that extent is classified as general.

11.2.4.4 Pecuniary gift

This is a gift of money. This gift will usually be general, but could be demonstrative, or possibly even specific, for example, 'I give the £100 held in the safe in the study'.

Where a testator wishes to include non-residuary gifts, there are a number of matters to consider and upon which instructions should be obtained.

11.2.4.5 The beneficiary

Identification

Beneficiaries must be clearly identified in the will, otherwise the gift will fail for uncertainty. Accurately stating the name and address is important, and including the relationship to the testator will also help. Where the gift is to a person, rather than a group, it is unwise only to describe that person by relationship, for example, to 'my nephew', because there may be more than one person answering that description. A gift to 'my nephews', though, will not suffer this problem.

A gift to '*my nephews and nieces*' will normally be construed as a gift to the children of the testator's own siblings. However, testators may use the term loosely to refer to children of their spouse's siblings or to the spouses of their nephews and nieces. See *Wales v Dixon* [2020] EWHC 1979 (Ch) where, although the will referred to 'my' nieces and nephews, there was abundant evidence from earlier wills that the testator had intended to include his wife's nephews and nieces as well as his own. Master Teverson was scathing about the way in which instructions were taken:

> The striking feature of the communications between the Deceased and [the will drafter] is the lack of any focus by the Deceased on clause 7 (as opposed to the money bequests under clause 4) and the complete lack of any attempt to establish by name or parent who was intended to receive a share of residue.

> This illustrates graphically the dangers of taking instructions by telephone from an elderly widower without sight of his prior will or knowledge of his family tree. Clause 7 of the Will is badly drafted. It contains grammatical and punctuation errors. It fails to identify by name or parent or family the intended recipients of the gift. The manner in which the Deceased's instructions were taken and the poor quality of clause 7 enhances the scope for giving the words an extended meaning when interpreted against the surrounding circumstances known to the Deceased.

Where the identity of the person who fits the description changes, it is the person who fits that description at the date of the will who is construed as the beneficiary. For example, a gift to 'my son's wife' will mean his wife at the date of the will, even if by the date of death he is married to someone else. See **11.1** above on the effect of the Marriage (Same Sex Couples) Act 2013.

For the meaning of 'children' and 'grandchildren', see **6.6.3.3**.

Gender Recognition Act 2004

The Gender Recognition Act 2004 came into force on 4 April 2005. It provides complete legal recognition for transgender individuals who have obtained a full gender recognition certificate.

The effect of legal recognition is that, for example, a male-to-female transgender individual will be legally recognised as a woman in English law for all purposes (s 9(1)). However, s 15 provides that a change of gender does not affect the distribution of property under a will or other instrument made before 4 April 2005.

For wills or other instruments made on or after that day, the general principle stated in s 9(1) will apply. For example, if a will made on or after 4 April 2005 refers to the 'eldest daughter', and a person who was previously a son becomes the 'eldest daughter' following the issue of a full recognition certificate, that person (subject to s 18) will inherit as the 'eldest daughter'.

A gift to a person by name is a gift to that person even if they change their name, so a gift to 'John' will take effect even if John has become Joanna at the date of death.

Under s 18 the court has power to make orders to deal with the situation where the devolution of property under a will or other instrument is 'different from what it would be but for the fact that a person's gender has become the acquired gender under this Act'.

If, for example, a will left property to 'eldest daughter' of X, and there is an older brother whose gender is recognised as female under the Act, then the person who was previously the 'eldest daughter' may cease to enjoy that position. A person who is adversely affected by the different gender can apply to the court.

The court, if it is satisfied that it is just to do so, may make such order as it considers appropriate in relation to the person benefiting from the different disposition of the property.

Vested or contingent?

Where the testator wishes to benefit persons who may be minors, or relatively young, he should consider whether he wishes to make outright or contingent gifts.

A vested gift imposes no conditions, and the beneficiary will be immediately entitled to it merely by outliving the testator. For example, 'I give £10,000 to my grandson, Oliver'. If Oliver is over 18 at his grandfather's death, he receives his gift straight away. If he is under 18, the £10,000 will be held on a bare trust for Oliver until his 18th birthday. Unless the will provides otherwise, his parents or guardians can give a good receipt and will hold as bare trustees until Oliver is 18. If he dies under age 18, the money forms part of his estate.

A contingent gift imposes conditions to be satisfied before the gift can vest. The most common contingency is to require the beneficiary to reach a certain age, for example, 'I give £10,000 to my grandson, Oliver, provided he reaches the age of 25'. Only if Oliver reaches 25 will he be entitled to the £10,000. If he is under 25 when his grandfather dies, the money will be held on trust until he reaches 25. If he were to die under age 25, his estate will not be entitled to the cash, which will instead pass to the person(s) expressed to be entitled in default or, if none, with the residue of his grandfather's estate.

The testator must decide how he will make the gift and, if contingent, the nature of the contingency. For further discussion of this topic see **12.6**.

Lapse

A beneficiary who predeceases the testator is not able to take a legacy. The legacy will normally fail or 'lapse' and will pass with residue unless the will provides for a substitute beneficiary.

The Wills Act 1837, s 33 provides a limited exception to the doctrine of lapse. It provides that where a gift to the testator's child or remoter descendent fails because that person predeceases the testator, but he or she leaves issue living at the testator's death, then those issue will take the gift.

EXAMPLES OF EFFECT OF WILLS ACT 1837, s 33

Fred leaves his estate to 'such of my children who survive me'.

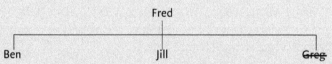

Ben and Jill survive Fred. Greg predeceases him. If Greg has no issue alive at Fred's death, the estate will be split equally between Ben and Jill. However, if Greg has issue who survive Fred, the one-third share which he would have taken will be divided among his issue.

Nobody can take an interest under s 33 if he has a parent alive.

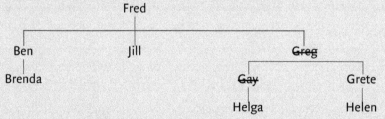

Brenda takes nothing because her father is alive. Greg's one-third share is divided into two. Helga takes the one-sixth her mother, Gay, would have taken. Grete takes the other one-sixth. Helen takes nothing as her mother, Grete, is still alive.

The section can be excluded by contrary intention expressed in the will. It is usual to include an express substitution provision rather than to rely on the implied provisions.

In *Naylor v Barlow* [2019] EWHC 1565 (Ch), two firms of solicitors dealing with the administration of an estate initially overlooked the fact that s 33 applied, and as a result the daughters of the testator's deceased son were entitled to replace their father. Had there been an express substitution clause, this could not have happened.

The section applies unless there is contrary intention in the will. In *Hives v Machin* [2017] EWHC 1414 (Ch), a gift was to such of the testatrix's sons as were 'living at her death'. It was held that those words did not amount to a contrary intention. The words gave no indication of an intention that the deceased beneficiary's issue (as distinct from the deceased beneficiary) should be excluded from taking under s 33. The 'default setting' is that the section applies. There has to be an express exclusion of the statutory substitution.

The Estates of Deceased Persons (Forfeiture Rule and Law of Succession) Act 2011 inserts a new s 33A into the Wills Act 1837. This provides that where a person entitled under a will disclaims his entitlement or forfeits it by killing the testator, 'the person is, unless a contrary intention appears by the will, to be treated *"for the purposes of this Act"* as having died immediately before the testator.'

EXAMPLE

Mother
|
Son
|
Grandson

Mother has made a will leaving her entire estate to her son. If the son kills his mother, he forfeits any entitlement to her property. However, for the purposes of the Wills Act 1837, he is treated having predeceased her. As a result, he can be replaced by his son under s 33 of the Act.

Burden of tax and debts charged on assets

It is important to consider where the burden of any tax or debts charged on the gifted property may fall.

So far as IHT is concerned, IHTA 1984, s 211 provides statutory rules which apply unless the will varies them. Under s 211, tax is a testamentary expense if it is attributable to UK property vesting in the PRs and not comprised in a settlement immediately before death; in other cases the tax is borne by the beneficiary. Hence, in the absence of contrary intention, tax on the following will not be a testamentary expense:

- foreign property,
- lifetime gifts,
- property passing by survivorship,
- trust property in which the deceased had a qualifying interest in possession.

The tax on property passing under the will is a testamentary expense and therefore, in the absence of a direction to the contrary, will be paid from undisposed of property (if any) or from residue.

So far as debts charged on specific assets are concerned, the legatee will take the asset subject to the debt charged on it unless the will declares otherwise. A contrary intention can be shown in the specific gift itself, for example, 'I leave my house to [X] free of mortgage', or by directing that debts be paid from residue, but in this case it is necessary to include an express reference to debts charged on particular assets. In the absence of such an express reference, the direction will be construed as applying only to unsecured debts.

It is important to vary the rules expressly if the testator does not want them to apply, and, even where he does, it is usual to state what is to happen expressly so that the testator is made aware of the position.

The most common concern is usually whether the IHT attributable to the gift should be borne by the residue (in which case the gift should be stated to be 'free of tax') or by the beneficiary of the gift (in which case the gift should be stated to be 'subject to tax'). Where gifts are expressed to be 'free of tax', the burden of tax falling on residue may significantly reduce the benefit taken by a residuary beneficiary. The testator should be made aware of the consequences of the different wording. In particular, in certain circumstances, it can make a difference to the overall amount of tax payable on the estate. This is the case where a partially exempt transfer occurs (see **11.3**).

11.2.5 Drafting considerations for certain types of beneficiary

11.2.5.1 Gifts to a class of beneficiary

Where the testator does not name his beneficiary but makes a gift to a class which could continue to grow after his death, it is sensible to impose a closing date for entry to the class. For example, a gift of '£20,000 to my nephews and nieces' would apparently include those alive at the death of the testator and those later born, which would make the gift very inconvenient to administer. A sensible closing date would be the death of the testator, for example, 'to my nephews and nieces alive at my death'. However, if the will is silent there are a number of class closing rules which may apply to close the class at an artificially early date. In the example just given, the class closing rules would close the class at death provided there was at least one member; if there was no nephew or niece living at that date, the class would remain open until all possible members were ascertained. However, stating the position in the will expressly makes it more likely that the testator will understand what will happen and may head off arguments after death with disappointed individuals.

11.2.5.2 Gifts to charitable bodies

It is important to identify the charitable body accurately. To avoid argument later, the solicitor should include the address and registered charity number of the body for identification.

A further issue to consider is how the executors will obtain a receipt from the charity for the gift. Without express provision stating otherwise, all members of an unincorporated association would have to sign a receipt. To avoid this, it is normal to authorise the executors to accept the receipt of an authorised officer of the charity. The clause should provide that the receipt of the person who appears to be the treasurer or other proper officer of the organisation will be sufficient. This avoids the need for the executors to check the constitution of the body to establish the identity of the proper officers.

A further problem to consider is that the charitable body may dissolve, amalgamate or change its objects before the date of death. It is useful to state that the gift is to the body 'for its general charitable purposes'. This may help establish that the gift has not failed, because those purposes can continue to be performed by another organisation, or help establish that the testator had general charitable intention and so allow the gift to be applied cy-près to a similar charity. A further option is to provide in the will that the executors may choose a similar charity to pay to, if the original recipient charity has ceased to exist. The Charities Act 2011, s 311 provides a statutory substitution where a charity merges with another between the date of the will and death, but it is preferable to make express provision for this possibility.

Where 10% or more of an estate (after deduction of nil rate band, exemptions and reliefs) is given to charity, the rate of IHT on the chargeable part of the estate is reduced to 36% (FA 2012, s 209 and Sch 33). It is impossible to predict the size of legacy required at death to meet the 10% requirement. Therefore, where a client is anxious to get the reduced rate, the legacy should not be drafted as a fixed sum but as a legacy of the amount required to get the benefit of the reduced rate. See further **4.8.1** and **13.3.3**.

11.2.5.3 Will for spouse and children

We saw at **4.5.3.3** that, until the introduction of the transferable nil rate band between spouses and civil partners, it was efficient from an IHT perspective for the first spouse to die to leave assets up to the limit of the available nil rate band to his children and the balance to the spouse.

Provided the estate of the survivor will not exceed the taper threshold for the purposes of the residential nil rate band, many spouses will choose to leave everything to the other either absolutely or on a terminable life interest (see **12.7** for discussion of terminable life interests). However, some may be uncertain about the wisdom of passing everything to the spouse and may prefer the flexibility of a nil rate band legacy.

One aim of a will containing a nil rate band legacy is that there will be no IHT payable as a result of the testator's death. Such wills must give the residue to an exempt beneficiary. This is usually a spouse or civil partner, but could be a charity. The legacy to non-exempt beneficiaries must not be of an amount that will cause IHT to be payable. The difficulty is how best to draft such a legacy. It is not possible to word the legacy as a gift of a fixed amount for two reasons: first, the testator will not know what the level of the nil rate band will be at death, eg because of changes in the law or availability of an increased nil rate band; and, secondly, the testator may not have a full nil rate band available at death, for example because he made transfers after the date of the will which have become chargeable.

It is therefore important to word the legacy as a 'formula' to ensure that the appropriate amount passes under the legacy. A simple example of this would be to word the gift as 'the maximum amount that can pass on the testator's death without attracting inheritance tax'.

Some clauses set out expressly all the things that will have to be taken into account when calculating the amount payable under such a clause. These are:

(a)   lifetime chargeable transfers;

(b)   property passing on death to non-exempt beneficiaries under the will, the intestacy rules or by survivorship;

(c)   settled property passing to a non-exempt beneficiary where the deceased was treated as beneficially entitled to the underlying trust assets;

(d)   property given to a non-exempt beneficiary during the deceased's life but included in the deceased's estate under the reservation of benefit rules.

However, it is not necessary to list these things expressly. It is sufficient to state that the amount payable is the maximum which can be paid without incurring a liability to inheritance tax.

EXAMPLE

Freda makes a will giving her goddaughter jewellery worth £10,000, her sons a legacy equal to the greatest amount that can pass without attracting IHT, and the residue to her husband. She dies when the nil rate band is £325,000. Her estate is £1m.

Freda always gave £1,500 to each of her two sons on 6 April to make use of her annual exemption, but two years before her death she also gave her grandson £45,000.

> The legacy to her sons will be calculated as follows:
>
> | | £ |
> | --- | --- |
> | Nil rate band at date of death | 325,000 |
> | Less | |
> | Lifetime chargeable transfer | (45,000) |
> | Property passing by will to goddaughter | (10,000) |
> | | 270,000 |
>
> The maximum amount that can pass to the sons without attracting IHT is £270,000, so that is the amount they will take under the legacy.

It is important to make clear to clients that the amount passing under such a legacy may be reduced to zero if other gifts have exhausted the nil rate band. See *Royal Commonwealth Society for the Blind v Beasant and Another* [2021] EWHC 2315 (Ch) where exactly this happened. The will left specific assets and gifts of cash to non-exempt beneficiaries the value of which at the date of death exhausted the testatrix's nil rate band.

Testators whose main concern is to provide adequately for their spouse (or civil partner) need to think carefully before leaving assets away from the spouse. A reduction in the size of residue is particularly significant at present due to the low interest rates available. A surviving spouse may find it difficult to manage on what is left after the deduction of a nil rate band legacy. There could also be a problem where the estate includes property eligible for business or agricultural property relief (see **4.3.6**). A formula clause passing the maximum available nil rate band amount may mean that little is left for the surviving spouse. Where the estate could include such assets, care is needed to word the legacy to achieve the client's aims.

Another matter that may concern testators is that the nil rate band may increase to such an extent that too little of the estate will be left to make adequate provision for the surviving spouse. One of the policies proposed by the Conservative Party at its Conference in October 2007 was the introduction of a nil rate band of £1m for everyone.

The introduction of the transferable nil rate band in October 2007 has increased the amount that can pass under nil rate band legacies and, therefore, caused decreases in the amount received by spouses, civil partners and charities.

> **EXAMPLE**
>
> Edith made a will in June 2002 leaving the largest amount she could pass without payment of IHT to her godson and the balance of her estate to her favourite charity. At that time the nil rate band was £250,000. She died in November 2017 with the benefit of a nil rate band transferred from her husband who had died some years earlier leaving everything to Edith. Edith's estate was £1m. The godson receives £650,000 and the charity £350,000. This may or may not be what Edith would have wanted.

Where the testator may have the benefit of transferred nil rate band on death, it is important to establish whether he intends that increased nil rate band amount to be gifted, and draft accordingly. The Revenue has given some examples of the type of formula wording that will and will not achieve this. The point was at issue in *Woodland Trust v Loring* [2014] EWCA Civ 1314, where a testatrix had left 'an aggregate value equal to such sum as is at the date of my death the amount of my unused nil-rate band for inheritance tax' to her issue and residue to charity. The court interpreted this wording to include the additional nil rate band amount that the testatrix acquired from her husband. This was because the wording of the legislation makes it clear that where a person has the benefit of transferred nil rate band, the effect is to increase the amount of their personal nil rate band.

An example given by HMRC where it considers that transferred nil rate band would not be included is a gift of 'such sum as I could leave immediately before my death without IHT becoming payable'. This is because any nil rate band that might be transferred is not available immediately before the death.

The transferred nil rate band is only available if claimed by the personal representatives. For the avoidance of doubt, it is sensible to direct the personal representatives to claim it (assuming the testator wants to pass the maximum possible).

If the deceased disposed of residential property before death and has the benefit of a downsizing allowance, the same principle applies. The amount of the downsizing allowance increases the amount that can pass without tax but has to be claimed. The will should therefore direct the personal representatives to claim any downsizing allowance available.

If the testator wants to make a more limited provision, it is possible to include a maximum limit on the amount payable to the non-exempt beneficiaries under the legacy. This can be achieved by specifying a figure or by leaving a legacy *'equal to the upper limit of the nil per cent band in the table of rates of tax applicable on my death in schedule 1 to Inheritance Tax Act 1984 after deduction of any amounts chargeable to inheritance tax in my estate'*.

Rather than giving an outright legacy to the children, it is common for testators to leave the nil rate sum on discretionary trusts for issue and spouse. See **12.6.1.1**.

11.2.5.4   Impact of the residence nil rate band

The residence nil rate band is available when a residence or interest in a residence is inherited by a lineal descendant of the deceased (see further **4.3.1**). Obviously those wishing to save inheritance tax will want to obtain the benefit of the residence nil rate band, if possible.

There is no requirement to make a specific gift of the residence. It is sufficient to leave 'my estate' or 'my residue' provided the assets include a residence or an interest in a residence. If the gift is divided between a lineal descendant and a non-lineal descendant, the value of the residence is divided proportionately.

HMRC's IHT Manual has an example at IHTM 46027 of Simon who leaves half of his estate to his grandson. The estate includes a residence, and the grandson is treated as inheriting 50% of the value of the residence.

Married couples (or civil partners) with children should consider the following points when deciding how best to leave their assets:

(1)   Normally the first spouse to die will want to leave everything to the survivor. This will not waste the residence band of the deceased as, like the ordinary nil rate band, it can be transferred to the survivor.

(2)   If the survivor's estate is likely to exceed the taper threshold of £2m, at which point the residence nil rate band starts to be withdrawn, the couple should consider other options:

(a)   The first to die could leave assets to the value of their available ordinary nil rate band to a discretionary trust for the benefit of the survivor and issue.

(b)   If the estate of the survivor is still likely to exceed the taper threshold, the first to die will need to consider leaving an interest in a residence to lineal descendants in order to get the benefit of the residence nil rate band on the first death. It is possible to use a formula clause, 'an interest in any residence I own at the date of my death, equal to the value of my available residence nil rate band'.

(c)   Advisers normally discourage clients dividing ownership of the family home between surviving spouse and children as it will cause difficulty if the children run into financial problems. However, the family may have a second home. The residence nil rate band is available on any property which has been used as a residence during the period of ownership. It is not limited to the main residence. There is less cause for concern if the children are given an interest in a second home.

(d)   Alternatively, to protect the home in the event of the children encountering financial problems, the interest of the children could be left on immediate post-death interest trusts with power for the trustees to appoint an interest in capital at their discretion. The residence nil rate band is available where property is left in this way as well as when it is left absolutely.

(e)   If the couple do not want the complication of share of a property held on trust, the survivor can consider making lifetime gifts to reduce their estate below the taper threshold.

11.2.6   The subject matter of the gift

It is essential that the property which is the subject matter of the gift is clearly identified. This is particularly important for non-pecuniary gifts. There are several drafting considerations for specific gifts.

11.2.6.1   Ademption

A general problem is ademption. This is the failure of the gift because the specific item described no longer exists within the testator's estate at death. A testator should be alerted to the fact that this could happen. For example, a gift of 'my gold and ruby necklace' could fail because during the testator's lifetime the testator gives it to someone else, sells it or loses it in a fire or burglary. This is the case even if the testator has bought another similar necklace to replace it. This is because the 'my' indicates that the testator is referring to the specific item in his possession at the date of the will and not to whatever item matching that description he happens to own at death. If the testator wants the beneficiary to have a substitute benefit if the original gift adeems, the will should provide for a replacement or substitute or word the legacy in more general terms.

11.2.6.2   Burden of costs

There may be costs associated with the packing or transport of the specific gift. Unless the will provides otherwise the beneficiary will bear these costs. The testator should consider if these costs will be too great for the beneficiary and if so provide that the gift is free of these costs. If such words are included, the costs will be paid from the residue of the estate.

11.2.6.3   Gift involving selection

The testator may leave a gift to several people inviting them to select an item from the estate. To prevent argument, the testator should indicate the order of choosing or provide for a means of resolving any dispute. It is normal to provide that the decision of the executors will be final. It is also wise to require the selection to be done within a time-limit to avoid delays in the administration.

11.2.6.4   Gifts of specific company shares

These are especially susceptible to ademption, not just because the owner may buy and sell shares on a regular basis, but also because the company may be renamed or taken over, and the will should provide for this. Shares may also be subject to a charge secured on them. The rule is that the beneficiary will take subject to this charge unless the will provides otherwise.

11.2.6.5   Gift of specific land

Again this type of gift is susceptible to ademption. A gift of the testator's main residence at death will avoid some problems but will not provide for situations where the testator owns no residence at all, for example because the testator has sold up and gone into residential accommodation. A house or flat is also likely to be subject to a mortgage. As with gifts of shares it is necessary to expressly provide for a gift of land to be free of a mortgage charged on the land if the testator does not want the beneficiary to pay the mortgage. Alternatively, if the testator has taken out a mortgage protection policy to cover the debt, the will can leave the benefit of the mortgage insurance policy to the beneficiary too.

11.2.7 Gift of the residue

It is important that the will contains a gift of the residue and that care is taken to ensure that it does not fail, as the result would be a partial intestacy.

11.2.7.1 Is a trust required?

Where the testator wishes to leave the residue on trust of some kind (for example, a life interest trust) then clearly there will be a trust expressly declared in the will. However, a trust may arise in less obvious circumstances. Where any of the beneficiaries is under 18 years at the death of the testator and the testator does not want the minor's parent or guardian to give a receipt on his behalf, there will need to be a trust of that person's entitlement until he reaches 18 and can give a good receipt. Where there is a possibility that this could occur (and even if all the primary beneficiaries are adults there may be a possibility of a substitution being made) it would be preferable to declare a trust expressly in the will and so control the terms and trustees.

It is also desirable to declare a trust where contingent gifts are made, so that property can be properly dealt with until the contingency is satisfied (or fails). A simple contingent pecuniary legacy does not carry with it the right to receive intermediate income produced by the amount given or capital growth. This is not normally what testators want.

> **EXAMPLE**
>
> Theo gives £100,000 to his granddaughter, Grazia, contingent on her reaching 25, and the residue to his children. Grazia is 5 when Theo dies.
>
> Theo's PRs will put funds aside to meet the legacy, but in the meantime any interest earned or income produced will be paid to Theo's children as residuary beneficiaries. By the time Grazia reaches 25, inflation will have eroded the value of the legacy, but she is only entitled to the amount stated in the will. Any capital growth will be paid to the children.
>
> Had these problems been explained to Theo, he would probably have opted to create a trust of the £100,000, giving the trustees full powers to apply income and capital for Grazia's benefit.

Where the residue is passing outright to adult (or charitable) beneficiaries, there is no need for an express trust. Note, however, that if a trust created by will is still in existence two years after the death, details of the beneficial owners of the trust will have to be registered on the Trust Register as a result of the Money Laundering, Terrorist Financing and Transfer of Funds (Information on the Payer) Regulations 2017 (SI 2017/692). Further, it is not unusual to create a trust of the residue in these circumstances as it does no harm.

Whether or not the residue is left on express trust, there should be an express direction for the payment of all debts, expenses and legacies to be made from the residue before it is distributed to the beneficiaries. In the absence of such a direction, the statutory order set out in the AEA 1925 will apply, and this can lead to problems.

11.2.7.2 Avoiding partial intestacy

If a gift of residue fails, the property will pass under the intestacy rules. The testator may be happy with this, but it is preferable to include substitutional gifts to cover the possibility of the primary gift failing. For example, where the residue is left to the testator's niece, there could be an express substitution of children of the niece. It is also worth considering a 'longstop' beneficiary to inherit if all the intended arrangements fail. Although this could be another person, it is also worth considering charitable bodies as there is little possibility of such a gift failing. The testator may prefer to benefit a favourite charity in preference to distant relatives or the Crown as *bona vacantia*.

A gift of the residue to more than one person also raises some drafting issues. For example, assume that the testator has three children, A, B and C and wishes to leave them an equal share. He could leave one-third to each named child. This carries risks. He may have more children before he dies who will be excluded. Also any or all of the children may predecease him. If this were to happen, Wills Act 1837, s 33 would provide for the failed one-third share to pass to any child of the dead child; but if there were none, the failed one-third share would pass on intestacy.

Therefore, it is wiser to omit names and specific shares in the residue, and refer only to any children the testator may have at the date of death. Using the phrase 'for such of my children as survive me and if more than one in equal shares' will ensure that there will be a partial intestacy only if all children predecease the testator. The testator will normally want to provide that the share of a child who predeceases should pass to his or her own children, if any.

The testator may desire to establish a trust rather than make an outright gift of the residue. Various types of trust that can be useful in a will are considered in **Chapter 12**.

11.2.8   Directions and declarations

It is common to include declarations of the testator's wishes. Examples of such declarations are set out below.

11.2.8.1   Survivorship

Unless a will states otherwise, a beneficiary only has to be alive at the death of the testator to acquire a vested interest. This may have an unfortunate effect where the beneficiary dies a very short time after the testator. This can happen where, for example, members of the same family are involved in a common accident.

The testator's property will pass in accordance with the will or intestacy provisions of the deceased beneficiary, which may mean passing to a person the testator would not want to inherit.

> **EXAMPLE**
> Tarala leaves property to her married son. She dies and her son dies a week later. He leaves everything to his wife. Tarala might well have preferred her assets to pass to beneficiaries of her own choice rather than to her son's wife.

There will also be the burden and expense of the property being part of the administration of two different estates. Lastly, there may be adverse IHT consequences. For example, suppose Mildred leaves her estate of £300,000 to her divorced daughter, Diana, who has £300,000 of her own assets. Diana dies a week after Mildred, leaving everything to her son, Sam. Both Mildred and Diana have full nil rate bands available but do not have the benefit of any transferable nil rate band. Diana's estate now includes her mother's property and so IHT will be payable on the amount which exceeds Diana's nil rate band. Had Mildred left her estate directly to Sam, no IHT would have been payable as both estates would have been within the nil rate band.

To avoid unnecessary IHT and give the testator more control over the destination of his property, a survivorship clause may be used. This usually directs that the beneficiary must survive the testator by a minimum period of time. The time usually chosen is about a month, stated either as a calendar month, or as a period of 28 or 30 days. Using a longer period may lead to delays in the administration of the estate. The period should not exceed six months or the gift will be treated as creating a settlement without an interest in possession.

The testator may declare that a general survivorship period is to apply to all gifts in the will, or only to certain of the gifts.

There are two situations, in the case of spouses and civil partners, where including a survivorship clause can increase the amount of IHT payable. The first is where spouses (or civil partners) die in quick succession and the assets of the first spouse or civil partner exceed the nil rate band while the survivor's do not.

EXAMPLE

Harry and Wanda are married. Harry has assets worth £425,000. On 1 June 2022 Harry dies with an estate of £425,000 and a full nil rate band. One week later his wife, Wanda, dies with assets of £200,000 and a full nil rate band.

(1)   *If Harry includes a survivorship clause*

Harry leaves his estate to Wanda but includes a survivorship clause giving the property to their children if Wanda fails to survive by 28 days. Harry's estate, therefore, passes directly to the children and IHT will be payable on £100,000. Wanda's estate passes to the children without any IHT as her estate falls within the nil rate band.

(2)   *If Harry does not include a survivorship clause*

Harry leaves his estate to Wanda absolutely. No IHT is payable on his death as the spouse exemption applies. Wanda has the benefit of the transferable nil rate band so the combined estates of £525,000 will fall within her enhanced nil rate band.

There is administrative inconvenience in passing assets from one estate to another and no way of knowing which spouse or civil partner will die first, so it may be more satisfactory to redistribute family assets so that each spouse or civil partner has sufficient to take advantage of a full nil rate band.

The second is where spouses (or civil partners) die in circumstances where it is uncertain which died first. In such cases, s 184 of the LPA 1925 applies and the elder is deemed to have died first. Section 4 of the IHTA 1984 provides that a person's IHT estate does not include property inherited under s 184. However, the younger spouse (or civil partner) still inherits the unused nil rate band of the elder (see IHTM43040). The result is extremely beneficial in IHT terms.

EXAMPLE

Horsa and Wakita, a married couple, die in circumstances where the order of deaths is uncertain. Horsa is older than Wakita. Each has an estate of £650,000. They each leave their estate to the other without a survivorship clause.

Horsa's £650,000 passes to Wakita and is exempt from IHT.

Wakita's estate (£1.3m) passes to the children as Horsa is deemed to have predeceased her. For IHT purposes her estate is only £650,000 as it does not include the property she inherited from Horsa. As she has the benefit of Horsa's transferred NRB, no IHT is payable on her estate.

Had Horsa's will included a survivorship clause with a gift in default to the children, there would have been IHT on £325,000 payable from his estate. Wakita would not have had any transferred nil rate band so there would have been IHT on £325,000 payable from her estate too.

It is possible to provide that the survivorship clause does not apply where there is uncertainty as to the order of deaths.

The decision in *Jump v Lister* [2016] EWHC 2160 (Ch) illustrated another problem: the inclusion of a survivorship clause may result in double payment of pecuniary legacies where there are mirror wills and the testators die within the survivorship period.

Mr and Mrs Winson (both in their 80s) were found dead of natural causes at their home in circumstances where it was impossible to determine which of them had died first. Mr Winson was three years younger than his wife so he was deemed to survive her.

The couple were childless. Mr Winson left everything to his wife, and if the gift failed he made a number of substantial pecuniary legacies and left the residue to two nieces. As his wife was deemed to have predeceased him, the gift to her failed and the substitutional gifts took effect.

Mrs Winson's will was a mirror image of her husband's. Hence, if the gift to her husband failed, the same pecuniary legacies were payable.

Both wills contained a general survivorship clause providing that 'My estate is to be divided as if any person who dies within 28 days of my death had predeceased me.'

Hence, under the terms of Mrs Winson's will, her husband Mr Winson was to be treated as having predeceased her. The result was that the legacies were payable twice, thereby reducing the amount available for the residuary legatees.

The residuary gifts should not have been made subject to the general survivorship clause.

11.2.8.2 Directions concerning the body

Some testators wish to include directions concerning how their body is to be disposed of, for example cremation, woodland burial or donation for medical research. The testator should be aware that such directions have no legal effect. Testators should ensure that their close family and friends are aware of their wishes.

In England and Wales and Scotland, there is now an 'opt-out' system of organ and tissue donation, otherwise known as 'deemed consent'. This means that all adults are considered to have agreed to be an organ and tissue donor when they die, unless they have recorded a decision not to donate or are in one of the excluded groups. The law does not apply to people that die under the age of 18. Northern Ireland still has an 'opt-in' system.

11.2.9 Administrative provisions

Personal representatives (PRs) and trustees have a number of statutory administration powers. The AEA 1925 gives certain powers to PRs, and the TA 1925 and TA 2000 give powers to both trustees and PRs. However, it is usual to extend or modify some of these statutory powers where they are not regarded as sufficient. Even where the statutory powers are adequate, it is common to put in an express provision on the basis that it makes the will easier to construe.

A will which might give rise to a trust (for example, because there is a substitutional gift to children of a primary beneficiary who predeceases the testator) will benefit from the inclusion of extensive express administrative provisions. However, even a simple will leaving everything to adults or to a charity will benefit from some express provisions.

We have divided the administrative provisions below into those that should be considered for inclusion in any will irrespective of whether or not it might give rise to a trust, and those which should be considered only if a trust might arise.

11.2.9.1 Administrative provisions to consider in relation to all wills

Power to charge

We have already dealt with this at **11.2.3.5**. If the testator wishes to give the executors (and trustees) power to charge, the power can either be included as part of the appointment clause or with the other administrative provisions. When drafting such a clause it is important, in the light of the Court of Appeal decision in *Da Silva v Heselton* [2022] EWCA Civ 880, to be clear whether a person engaged in *any* profession or business can charge for time spent on the administration (for example, a brain surgeon) or whether *only* a person whose profession involves administering estates and trusts can charge (for example, a solicitor or accountant).

Power for trust professional to charge

> Any Trustee who acts in a professional capacity may charge reasonable remuneration for any services provided to the trust.
>
> For this purpose a Trustee acts in a professional capacity if he acts in the course of a profession or business which consists of or includes the provision of services in connection with the administration or management of trusts.

Power for any business person to charge

> Any Trustee who is engaged in a profession or business may charge reasonable remuneration for any services provided to the trust.

Extended power to appropriate assets without consent of legatee

The AEA 1925, s 41 gives PRs the power to appropriate any part of the estate in or towards satisfaction of any legacy or any interest in residue provided that the appropriation does not prejudice any specific beneficiary. Thus, if the will gives a pecuniary legacy to a beneficiary, the PRs may allow that beneficiary to take chattels or other assets in the estate up to the value of his legacy, provided that these assets have not been specifically bequeathed by the will. The section provides that the legatee (or his parent or guardian if he is a minor) must consent to the appropriation.

It is common to remove the need for the legatee's consent.

Express amendment

Specimen clause

> Power to exercise the power of appropriation conferred by section 41 of the Administration of Estates Act 1925 without obtaining any of the consents required by that section.

This provision is commonly included in order to relieve the PRs of the duty to obtain formal consent. Nevertheless, the PRs would informally consult the beneficiaries concerned.

Power to insure assets

The statutory power to insure assets of the estate conferred by TA 1925, s 19 was inadequate and it used to be necessary to extend it. However, TA 2000 substituted a new s 19 which is much more satisfactory. It gives PRs and trustees power to insure assets against all risks, to the full value of the property, and to pay premiums out of income or capital.

It is no longer necessary to amend the statutory provision. However, including an express provision makes life easier for lay PRs who will be able to see from the will itself exactly what they can do. The following is a typical provision.

Specimen clause

> Power to insure any asset of my estate on such terms as they think fit and to pay premiums at their discretion out of income or capital and to use any insurance money received either to restore assets or as if it were the proceeds of sale.

Power to accept receipts from or on behalf of minors

Under the general law, an unmarried minor cannot give a good receipt for capital or income. A married minor can give a good receipt for income only (LPA 1925, s 21). Parents and guardians used not to be able to give a good receipt on behalf of minors unless specifically authorised to do so in the will. This meant that without such authority the PRs would have to hold onto a legacy until the minor reached 18 and was able to give a good receipt. The AEA 1925, s 42 gives PRs the power to appoint trustees to hold a legacy for a minor who is absolutely entitled under the will. The receipt of the appointed trustees (who could be the child's parents or guardians) discharges the PRs from further liability. This power does not apply where the child has a contingent interest.

The Children Act 1989 provides that parents with parental responsibility have the same rights as guardians appointed under the Act. These rights are set out at s 3 and include the right to receive or recover money for the benefit of the child. Therefore, since the Children Act 1989, parents and guardians have been able to give a good receipt to PRs.

There are often tensions within families and a client may not be happy for a parent or guardian to give a good receipt for a legacy. In such a case, the will should be drafted to leave a legacy to trustees to hold for the benefit of the minor rather than to the child directly. Alternatively, the will may include a clause allowing the PRs to accept the receipt of the child himself if over 16 years old. The provision may be incorporated into the legacy itself or may be included in a list of powers in the will.

Power to continue a sole trader's business

Personal representatives have power only to carry on a business for the purpose of selling it as a going concern. When doing this, they have power to indemnify themselves from the assets of the estate for liabilities they incur.

It is helpful to authorise the PRs to postpone the sale of the business if they so wish and to carry on the business in the meantime. The clause should make clear which assets of the estate can be used in the business. The PRs will be able to indemnify themselves from those assets.

In practice few PRs are going to want to get involved in running a business. Professional trustees will normally refuse to take a grant in such cases. It is preferable to appoint the person(s) taking the business under the will as special executors limited to dealing with the business.

Note: A testator who is a member of a partnership should check that the partnership agreement deals adequately with arrangements for the death of a partner. The PRs of a deceased partner have no implied rights to take part in the running of the business.

A testator who runs a business through the medium of a limited company should also consider what will happen after death. The company will continue as a separate legal entity, but is there anyone in place who will be able to carry on the business?

Removing need to comply with the Apportionment Act 1870

Section 2 of the Apportionment Act 1870 provides that income such as rent and dividends is to be treated as accruing from day to day and apportioned accordingly. Thus, where assets in the estate produce income (such as bank or building society interest or dividends) which is received after death but which relates to a period partly before and partly after death, the income must be apportioned. The part accruing before death is a capital asset of the estate. The part accruing after death is income relating to the particular asset.

Unless the Act is excluded, s 2 will have to be complied with where a will creates a trust which gives capital to one person and income to another. It also has to be complied with where there is no trust but a will gives an income-producing asset to one person and residue to another. If the Apportionment Act applies, it is necessary to apportion the income between the two beneficiaries.

> **EXAMPLE: APPORTIONMENT ACT NOT EXCLUDED**
>
> John's will gave 'my ABC Co shares to Fred and my residue to Graham'.
>
> ABC Co declares a dividend of £12,000 three months after John's death. The dividend is expressed to cover the previous 12 months.
>
> Three-quarters of the dividend relates to the pre-death period and is regarded as capital forming part of the residue of the estate. It will pass to Graham.
>
> One-quarter of the dividend relates to the post-death period and is regarded as income passing with the shares to Fred.

This calculation is time-consuming, but if the Act is excluded all the income will pass with the income-producing asset. In the example above, this would mean that Fred would receive the whole dividend.

Power to employ agents

The TA 2000, ss 11–15 replace in similar but clearer terms the provisions of TA 1925, s 23(1) by allowing non-charitable trustees to delegate to agents any or all of their 'delegable functions'. Functions personal to the trustees which cannot be delegated include:

(a)   decisions on distributing trust property to beneficiaries;

(b)   allocation of fees or payments to income or capital;

(c)   appointment of trustees;

(d)   appointment of nominees or custodians of trust assets.

Only in the case of delegation of their asset management function is agreement in writing required.

A trustee who satisfies the duty of care in TA 2000, s 1 in relation to the appointment and subsequent review of the appointment of an agent is not liable for the acts and defaults of the appointee. Typically, this power will be used by PRs to employ estate agents, stockbrokers or bankers to carry out executive functions in relation to the administration. For example, PRs may instruct estate agents to sell the deceased's house or stockbrokers to value shares for IHT purposes.

Delegation by power of attorney

The TA 1925, s 25, as substituted by Trustee Delegation Act 1999, s 5, allows trustees and PRs to delegate by power of attorney the exercise of any of the powers and discretions vested in them for a period not exceeding 12 months. However, in this case, the PRs remain liable for the acts of the delegate as if they were their own acts.

This provision is often used by PRs who, having obtained their grant, find that they are unable to be involved personally in the administration for some temporary reason, such as absence abroad on business or on holiday. If, before taking out the grant, a long absence is anticipated, the better course of action would be for the PR to renounce his right to a grant or for others to take a grant reserving power to any absentee executor. It is too late to renounce or reserve power if the grant has already been obtained or if an executor has accepted office by intermeddling in the estate.

11.2.9.2   Administrative provisions to consider in relation to wills which may give rise to a trust

Removal of need to comply with apportionment rules

The Trusts (Capital and Income) Act 2013 came into force on 1 October 2013. This Act disapplies most of the apportionment rules for trusts which are created on or after 1 October 2013, subject to contrary provision in the will or trust document. This means that it is not now necessary to expressly disapply the rules of apportionment when drafting a will or trust. However, the information on the rules set out below is of use when interpreting wills and trusts created before the Act came into force.

The Apportionment Act 1870

We have already seen the relevance of this Act where an income-producing asset goes to one person and residue to another, and the importance of excluding its operation.

The same applies:

(a)   where a will creates a life interest trust;

EXAMPLE: APPORTIONMENT ACT NOT EXCLUDED

Tom died in June 2013. His will gave 'my residue to Larry for life, remainder to Rob'.

ABC Co declares a dividend of £12,000 three months after Tom's death. The dividend is expressed to cover the previous 12 months.

Three-quarters of the dividend relates to the pre-death period and is regarded as capital of the estate. It will be held for Larry for life and will eventually pass with the rest of the capital to Rob.

One-quarter of the dividend relates to the post-death period and is regarded as income. It will be paid to Larry.

EXAMPLE: APPORTIONMENT ACT EXCLUDED

The whole of the dividend will be treated as income and paid to Larry.

(b)   where there is a trust with contingent interests. Beneficiaries will fulfil the contingency at different times (or fail to fulfil it) and unless the Act is excluded there will have to be an apportionment of income each time there is a change in beneficial entitlement.

EXAMPLE

In 2012 a trust is created for three children contingent on reaching 18.

When the first child reaches 18 any income will have to be apportioned to the pre- and post-birthday period. The first child will be entitled to one third of the post-birthday income but all of the pre-birthday income will be a trust asset.

If the Act is excluded the first child will be entitled to one third of the whole receipt.

The equitable rules of apportionment

The equitable apportionment rules were designed to deal with trusts where residuary personalty is left to one person for life, remainder to another, in order to achieve a fair balance between the competing interests of the life tenant (who wants high income) and the remainderman (who wants capital growth).

For trusts created or arising on or after 1 October 2013, the Trusts (Capital and Income) Act 2013 disapplies the rules on equitable as well as statutory apportionments.

The rules are included below as they may be relevant to earlier trusts, although professionally drawn wills have almost invariably excluded them for many years.

Under the rule in *Howe v Dartmouth* (1820) 7 Ves 137, trustees had to sell assets which were either wasting (such as copyrights) or non-income producing (such as reversionary interests) and invest the proceeds in authorised investments. If there was a delay in selling, the rule required the trustees pay only 'a fair yield' to the life tenant and treat the rest as capital, using a complicated formula for calculating the fair yield.

Under the rule in *Re Earl of Chesterfield's Trusts* (1883) 23 Ch D 643, where trustees delayed selling a non-income-producing asset, the proceeds of sale had to be apportioned between income and capital, using a formula for the calculation.

Under the rule in *Allhusen v Whittell* (1867) LR 4 Eq 295, debts of the estate had to be treated as paid partly with capital and partly with the income that the capital produced, with the burden apportioned between tenant for life and remainderman.

The expense involved in making the various calculations meant that it was usually considered appropriate to exclude them, particularly as even where the equitable apportionment rules were excluded, trustees still had to strive to achieve fairness between beneficiaries (see **14.3.2**).

Power to appropriate assets

Section 41 of AEA 1925 does not apply to trustees. It is necessary to include an express provision, equivalent to s 41, to permit the trustees to appropriate trust property towards beneficial interests arising under the trust.

Specimen clause

> Power to appropriate assets in or towards satisfaction of any beneficial interests arising under the trust without obtaining the consent of any beneficiary.

The power to invest

The TA 2000 contains a new 'general power of investment' giving trustees power to invest as if absolutely entitled to the trust assets (s 3). This general power does not permit investment in land other than by mortgage. However, s 8 allows trustees to acquire land in the UK for investment or occupation by beneficiary, or for other reasons, which means that all trustees will now have similar powers to a trustee of land with regard to acquiring land.

Trustees exercising any investment power, whether expressly given or under the TA 2000, must comply with various specific requirements, which include reviewing the investments chosen from time to time (s 4), taking proper advice before investing or reviewing the investments (s 5), and having regard to 'the standard investment criteria' which means considering the suitability to the trust of the investment type chosen and considering the need for diversification in so far as is appropriate to the circumstances of the trust (s 4).

Although an improvement on the previous provisions under the Trustee Investments Act 1961 (TIA 1961), it may still be desirable expressly to state the investment powers and make some modifications and additions to the effect of the TA 2000. For example, the trust instrument should contain express permission to:

(a)   purchase foreign investments including land; and/or

(b)   retain or purchase non income-producing investments, such as insurance policies; and/or

(c)   retain investments originally settled, for example, shares in the settlor's family company; and/or

(d)   pursue an 'ethical' investment policy; and/or

(e)   borrow (and use trust property to be charged) for the purposes of investment; and/or

(f)   exclude the obligation to diversify the trust fund.

It is not possible to exclude s 4 (which requires the trustees to have regard to the need for diversification when investing). However, particularly where the trust contains primarily one type of asset and it is intended that the trustees should not sell this (for example, shares in a private company) it is advisable to state this expressly.

The TA 2000 provides that the management of trust assets can now be delegated (s 15) and that trustees may also appoint certain persons as nominees (s 16). Previously an express power was required for these actions. There are a number of special requirements to be observed if a trustee wishes to delegate asset management and investment decisions, for example, the trustee must create a written policy document to guide the delegates and review this from time to time. It is not clear whether this requirement applies to all trustees, or only to those exercising power under the TA 2000. In practice, though, it is usual for trustees to set out the investment aims of the trust when appointing managers to deal with the investment decisions.

See **14.3** for a further discussion of trustee investments.

Power to purchase land

The TA 2000, s 8 gives trustees power to acquire freehold or leasehold land in the UK for 'investment, for occupation by a beneficiary or for any other reason'. When exercising their power, the trustees are given 'all the powers of an absolute owner in relation to the land'.

Specimen clause

> My Trustees may apply trust money in the purchase or improvement of any freehold or leasehold dwelling-house and may permit any such dwelling-house to be used as a residence by any person with an interest in my residuary estate upon such terms and conditions as my Trustees may think fit.

This clause gives trustees an express power to use trust money to buy or improve land for use as a residence by the beneficiaries. It leaves the question of responsibility for the burden of repairs and other outgoings to the discretion of the trustees.

The statutory power does not authorise the purchase of land abroad, nor does it allow trustees to purchase an interest in land with someone else (eg, a beneficiary). An express power will be needed if the trustees are to have such powers.

Power to sell personalty

Trustees holding land in their trust have the power to sell it under their powers of an absolute owner under TA 2000 (see above). However, there is some doubt whether trustees who hold no land and where there is no express trust for sale have power to sell personalty. For this reason, some wills may continue to impose an express trust for sale over residue. The alternative solution is to include power in the will (among the administrative provisions) giving the trustees express power to sell personalty.

Specimen clause

> Power to sell mortgage or charge any asset of my estate as if they were an absolute beneficial owner.

Power to use income for maintenance of beneficiaries

Where trustees are holding a fund for a minor beneficiary, TA 1925, s 31 gives them power to use income they receive for the minor's maintenance, education or benefit. Section 31 also requires that where a beneficiary is 18 but is not yet entitled to the capital of the trust fund, the trustees have a duty to pay the income received from that beneficiary's share of the fund to that beneficiary.

Section 8 of ITPA 2014 makes amendments to s 31 of TA 1925, but only in relation to wills and trusts created after s 8 came into effect on 1 October 2014. It is therefore necessary to have an understanding of the operation of the amended and unamended versions of s 31 for some time to come. However, as the amendments reflect commonly made, expressly drafted amendments, the difference in practical terms will not be very significant.

The position where s 31 of TA 1925 applies to wills and trusts created before 1 October 2014

Section 31 (as amended by TA 2000) states (inter alia):

(1)   Where any property is held by trustees in trust for any person for any interest whatsoever, whether vested or contingent, then, subject to any prior interests or charges affecting that property—

    (i)   during the infancy of any such person, if his interest so long continues, the trustees may, at their sole discretion, pay to his parent or guardian, if any, or otherwise apply for or towards his maintenance, education, or benefit, the whole or such part, if any, of the income of that property as may, in all the circumstances, be reasonable, whether or not there is—

        (a)   any other fund applicable to the same purpose; or

        (b)   any person bound by law to provide for his maintenance or education; and

    (ii)   if such person on attaining the age of eighteen years has not a vested interest in such income, the trustees shall thenceforth pay the income of that property and of any accretion thereto under subsection (2) of this section to him, until he either attains a vested interest therein or dies, or until failure of his interest:

Provided that, in deciding whether the whole or any part of the income of the property is during a minority to be paid or applied for the purposes aforesaid, the trustees shall have regard to the age of the infant and his requirements and generally to the circumstances of the case, and in particular to what other income, if any, is applicable for the same purposes; and where trustees have notice that the income of more than one fund is applicable for those purposes, then, so far as practicable, unless the entire income of the funds is paid or applied as aforesaid or the court otherwise directs, a proportionate part only of the income of each fund shall be so paid or applied.

(2)   During the infancy of any such person, if his interest so long continues, the trustees shall accumulate all the residue of that income by investing it, and any profits from so investing it, from time to time in authorised investments, and shall hold those accumulations ... .

(3)   This section applies in the case of a contingent interest only if the limitation or trust carries the intermediate income of the property ...

Examples of the application of s 31

EXAMPLE: TRUST 1

The trustees of a trust created in 2013 are holding £100,000 for Mary (16) who has a vested interest in the capital. Under s 31(1), the trustees have the power to pay all or part of the income to Mary's parent or guardian or 'otherwise apply' it for Mary's maintenance, education or benefit. This could include paying bills (eg, school fees) directly.

The power is limited to so much of the income as is 'reasonable'. The proviso at the end of s 31(1) (ie from the words 'Provided that ...') directs the trustees to take into account various further points, such as Mary's age and requirements, and whether any other fund is available for her maintenance.

Section 31(2) directs the trustees to accumulate any income not used for maintenance and invest it.

EXAMPLE: TRUST 2

The trustees of a trust created in 2013 are holding £100,000 for Dora (14) who has an interest in capital contingent on reaching 21. They may pay or apply the income for Dora's maintenance, education or benefit in the same way as the trustees of Trust 1.

> The trustees are also holding £100,000 for Charles (19) who has the same contingent interest in capital. Section 31(1)(ii) directs them to pay all the income from his share of the trust fund to Charles until his interest vests (ie, until he is 21), when he will receive the capital, or fails (ie, if he dies before he is 21).
>
> The same will apply to the income from Dora's share from her 18th birthday onwards.

EXAMPLE: TRUST 3

The trustees of a trust created in 2013 are holding £200,000 for Henry for life with remainder to Stephen (10). They have no power to use the income for Stephen's benefit as Henry is entitled to it. If Henry dies while Stephen is still a minor, s 31 will apply to allow the trustees to apply income for Stephen's maintenance etc during the period from Henry's death until Stephen is 18 (when they will transfer the capital to Stephen).

It has always been possible to make express amendments to s 31 when drafting a will or trust. Common examples of this are shown in this specimen clause.

Extending s 31: specimen clause

> Section 31 of the Trustee Act 1925 shall apply to the income of my estate as if the words 'as the Trustees shall in their absolute discretion think fit' were substituted for the words 'as in all the circumstances be reasonable' in paragraph (i) of subsection (1) thereof and the proviso to subsection (1) had been omitted and as if the age of 21 years were substituted for all references to the age of 18 wherever they occur in section 31 (references to 'infancy' being construed accordingly).

The clause begins by removing the 'reasonable' limitation in s 31. It gives the trustees complete discretion over whether to pay or apply income for minor beneficiaries and over how much income they pay or apply. In particular, by removing the proviso trustees are not obliged to consider particular factors when making their decisions, and they are also not obliged to pay only an appropriate proportion of the trust income where they are aware of other trust income available for the beneficiary.

Secondly, the clause removes the right for a contingent beneficiary to receive all the income from the age of 18. The trustees' discretion under s 31 to pay or apply income for maintenance, or to accumulate any surplus will continue until the beneficiary is 21. Thus in Trust 2 the trustees would have a discretion over the payment of income to Charles even though he is over 18.

The position where s 31 of TA 1925 applies to wills and trusts created on or after 1 October 2014

Section 8 of ITPA 2014 amends s 31(1) of TA 1925 in two ways:

(a)   it removes the restriction in s 31(1)(i) that the amount of income applied must be reasonable, by removing the words 'as may, in all the circumstances, be reasonable' and instead inserting 'as the trustees may think fit'.

(b)   it removes the proviso to s 31(1), as explained above.

These amendments therefore reflect those that have previously been commonly expressly included when drafting a will or trust. However, ITPA 2014 does not make any amendments to the age at which there is a right to income under s 31. This remains 18, and so it will still be necessary to amend s 31 expressly on this point when drafting a will or trust, if appropriate.

See **Chapter 7** for further details.

Power to use capital for advancement of beneficiaries

The TA 1925, s 32 allows trustees in certain circumstances to permit a beneficiary with an interest in capital to have the benefit of part of his capital entitlement sooner than he would receive it under the basic provisions of the trust. Section 9 of the ITPA 2014 makes amendments to s 32. One key amendment applies only to wills and trusts created after s 9 came into effect on 1 October 2014. Other amendments apply to wills and trusts whenever created.

As originally enacted, s 32 states:

(1)   Trustees may at any time or times pay or apply any capital money subject to a trust, for the advancement or benefit, in such manner as they may, in their absolute discretion, think fit, of any person entitled to the capital of the trust property or of any share thereof, whether absolutely or contingently on his attaining any specified age ... and whether in possession or in remainder or reversion ...

Provided that—

(a)   the money so paid or applied for the advancement or benefit of any person shall not exceed altogether in amount one-half of the presumptive or vested share or interest of that person in the trust property; and

(b)   if that person is or becomes absolutely and indefeasibly entitled to a share in the trust property the money so paid or applied shall be brought into account as part of such share; and

(c)   no such payment or application shall be made so as to prejudice any person entitled to any prior life or other interest, whether vested or contingent, in the money paid or applied unless such person is in existence and of full age and consents in writing to such payment or application.

Examples of the application of s 32 as originally enacted

EXAMPLE: TRUST 1

Mary has a vested interest in the £100,000 capital. Section 32 allows the trustees to release some of the capital for Mary's benefit. 'Benefit' is widely construed: money could be used to pay educational or living expenses. The amount the trustees may advance is limited to one half of Mary's entitlement, ie, £50,000.

EXAMPLE: TRUST 2

Charles and Dora have contingent interests in the capital, their presumptive shares being £100,000 each. Section 32 applies to allow the trustees to release up to £50,000 for the benefit of either beneficiary. The trustees could give money directly to Charles as he is old enough to give a valid receipt. The power applies even though the interests of Charles and Dora are contingent. If either beneficiary dies before the age of 21 there is no right to recover any advance even though that beneficiary's interest in capital has failed.

Section 32(1)(b) requires advances to be brought into account on final distribution. If the trustees give £50,000 to Charles now, he will receive a lesser amount than Dora when the fund is finally distributed to them.

EXAMPLE: TRUST 3

Henry has only an interest in income and s 32 does not permit the release of capital to him. The section does apply to Stephen's vested interest in remainder, and permits the trustees to apply up to £100,000 (half his interest) for Stephen's benefit.

Such an advance would prejudice Henry since his income would be substantially reduced. Section 32(1)(c) provides that no advance may be made without Henry's written consent.

It has always been possible to make express amendments to s 32 when drafting a will or trust. Common examples of this are shown in the specimen clauses below.

Extending s 32: specimen clause 1

> Power to apply for the benefit of any Beneficiary as my Trustees think fit the whole or any part of the share of my residuary estate to which that Beneficiary is absolutely or presumptively entitled and I leave it within the discretion of my Trustees whether and to what extent the beneficiary shall bring into account any payments received under this clause.

This clause extends the limit in s 32(1)(a) to the full amount of the beneficiary's share. Up to £100,000 could be advanced for Mary (in Trust 1) or for Charles and Dora (in Trust 2). In Trust 3, the whole fund could be advanced for Stephen provided that Henry consents.

The second part of the clause supersedes s 32(1)(b) and means that, if in Trust 2 £50,000 was advanced to Charles, the trustees could on distribution still divide the remaining fund equally between Charles and Dora.

Extending s 32: specimen clause 2

> Power to pay or apply capital money from my residuary estate to any extent to or for the benefit of the Life Tenant.

> Power to advance capital money from my residuary estate to the Life Tenant by way of loan to any extent upon such terms and conditions as my Trustees may in their absolute discretion think fit.

These provisions would permit the trustees of a life interest trust like Trust 3 to give or lend capital from the fund to the life tenant even though he has an interest only in income, not capital. Such a clause may be included to give more flexibility in case the income proves insufficient for the life tenant's needs. The life tenant is dependent on the discretion of the trustees.

Note: Section 31 specifically allows trustees to pay income to the parents or guardian of a minor beneficiary, or 'otherwise apply it' for the minor's 'maintenance, education or benefit'. Similarly s 32 allows trustees to pay or 'apply' capital for the beneficiary's advancement or benefit. Thus, even without express authorisation, the trustees could take a good receipt from parents or guardians.

The effect of s 9 of ITPA 2014

The most significant change made by s 9 of ITPA 2014 applies only to wills and trusts created after the section came into effect on 1 October 2014. This is to remove the restriction in s 32(1)(a) of TA 1925 that only up to one-half of a beneficiary's share of the capital may be advanced. This reflects what has been commonly expressly included when drafting wills and trusts, but the other examples of amendments indicated above (such as enabling trustees to use capital for a beneficiary with no interest in the trust capital) will still have to be expressly included when drafting a will or trust, if appropriate.

Section 9 of ITPA 2014 also makes some other amendments to s 32 that apply to all wills and trusts, whenever created. Some of these are relatively minor and clarify certain matters that have previously been assumed (eg that any advancement for a beneficiary could be by way of transfer of non-cash assets). See **9.4.4** and **9.4.5** for further details of these amendments.

Control of trustees by beneficiaries

Section 19 of TLATA 1996 provides that, where beneficiaries are *sui juris* and together entitled to the whole fund, they may direct the trustees to retire and appoint new trustees of the beneficiaries' choice. This means that in a case where the beneficiaries could by agreement end the trust under the rule in *Saunders v Vautier* (1841) 4 Beav 115, they now have the option of allowing the trust to continue with trustees of their own choice. The provision may be expressly excluded by the testator. If, under the terms of the trust, the position could arise where all the beneficiaries are in existence and aged over 18 but the trust has not ended, the testator may wish to prevent the beneficiaries from choosing their own trustees.

Specimen clause

> The provisions of section 19 of the Trusts of Land and Appointment of Trustees Act 1996 shall not apply to any trust created by this will so that no Beneficiary shall have the right to require the appointment or retirement of any Trustee or Trustees.

Trusts of land

The TLATA 1996 gives special powers (see below) to a beneficiary under a trust of land who has an interest in possession. If, under the terms of the will, a trust with an interest in possession could arise, the will may amend those powers. The Act does not define 'interest in possession', so it presumably has its usual meaning; a beneficiary has an interest in possession if he is entitled to claim the income of the fund as it arises or enjoy an asset as of right (normally either because he has a life interest, or because he is over 18 and entitled to claim income or enjoyment under TA 1925, s 31).

Duty to consult beneficiaries

Trustees exercising any function relating to the land must consult any beneficiary who is of full age and beneficially entitled to an interest in possession in the land and, so far as consistent with the 'general interest of the trust', give effect to the wishes of any such beneficiary (TLATA 1996, s 11). The duty to consult may be excluded by the will.

Specimen clause

> The provisions of section 11 of the Trusts of Land and Appointment of Trustees Act 1996 shall not apply so that it shall not be necessary for my Trustees to consult any Beneficiaries before carrying out any function relating to land.

Beneficiary's rights of occupation

A beneficiary with a beneficial interest in possession, even if not of full age, has the right to occupy land subject to the trust if the purposes of the trust include making the land available for occupation by him or if the trustees acquired the land in order to make it so available (TLATA 1996, s 12). There is no power to exclude s 12, but a declaration that the purpose of the trust is not for the occupation of land may be included in the will.

Specimen clause

> The purposes of any trust created by this will do not include making land available for occupation of any Beneficiary [although my Trustees have power to do so if they wish].

11.2.10 Attestation clause

All wills should contain an attestation clause reciting that the formalities required by Wills Act 1837, s 9 have been complied with. The s 9 formalities require the testator to sign or acknowledge in the presence of two witnesses present at the same time and the witnesses to afterwards sign (or acknowledge) in the presence of the testator. An attestation clause raises a presumption of due execution.

Example

> Signed by me [testator's name]
> in our joint presence and then by us in [his/hers] [names of witnesses]

The social isolation resulting from the Covid-19 pandemic meant that some testators had problems with execution. Presence already had an extended meaning so that it was sufficient for there to be a line of sight between the testator and the witnesses, and many wills have been successfully executed in front gardens, on park benches and on the bonnets of cars.

However, on a temporary basis for wills executed on or after 31 January 2020 and on or before 31 January 2022, reg 2 of the Wills Act 1837 (Electronic Communications) (Amendment)

(Coronavirus) Order 2020 (SI 2020/952) provides that 'presence' includes presence by means of video conference or other visual transmission. The closing date of 31 January 2022 was extended to 31 January 2024 by the Wills Act 1837 (Electronic Communications) (Amendment) Order 2022 (SI 2022/18). The Regulations came into force on 28 September and so were retrospective. However, reg 3 provides that the Regulations do not affect any grant made before 28 September 2020 (the date on which the statutory instrument came into force) or anything done pursuant to such a grant. Regulation 3 is designed to cover the following situation:

> **EXAMPLE**
>
> Alf makes a conventional will in 2015. In February 2020 he makes a will which is witnessed remotely. He dies in April 2020. At that time the advice was that 'presence' required physical presence so, believing the 2020 will to be invalid, the executor of the 2015 will obtained a grant of probate in June 2020. The statutory instrument prevents the grant of probate being overturned.

Regulation 3 refers only to grants of 'probate'. The policy intention appears to be that a grant of letters of administration on intestacy granted before 28 September will be overturned by a valid remotely witnessed will, but a grant of probate will not. The status of a grant of letters of administration with will annexed obtained before 28 September 2020 is unclear. On a literal reading of reg 3, such a grant will be overturned by a valid remotely witnessed will, but, if this is the intention, the logic is hard to follow.

Where a will is virtually witnessed, the witnesses must sign the document that the testator has signed, so the will has to be taken or posted to the witnesses. If the testator (or one of the witnesses) dies before the signatures of the witnesses have been added, the will is invalid.

When the change to the Wills Act 1837 was announced, the government press release said:

> The use of video technology should remain a last resort, and people must continue to arrange physical witnessing of wills where it is safe to do so.

Anyone who can arrange physical witnessing would be better off doing so. Where virtual witnessing occurs, the attestation clause should be amended.

Example

Testator

Signed by me in the joint virtual presence of these two witnesses, who are witnessing me doing this remotely via a video-conferencing link

[signature of testator or testatrix]

[Date]

Witnesses

Signed by me in the virtual presence of [testator/testatrix] and the [actual] [virtual] presence of [other witness] having watched [testator/testatrix] sign remotely via a video conferencing link on [date]

[signature of witness

[Date]

11.3 PARTIALLY EXEMPT TRANSFERS

Sometimes only a part of an estate on death is exempt for IHT purposes and the other part is not exempt. Difficulties may arise in determining how much tax is payable. Any tax relating to the non-exempt part of the estate can affect the calculation of the size of the exempt beneficiary's inheritance. Provisions designed to resolve these difficulties are contained in IHTA 1984, s 38. In general, these provisions apply relatively rarely and give rise to complicated calculations. It is, however, important to understand their effect where there are legacies on which tax is chargeable combined with a gift of residue to an exempt beneficiary. This could happen, for example, where the residue passes to a spouse and there are legacies to children.

EXAMPLE

In her will, Polly gives £358,000 to her son Mark and the rest of her estate to her husband, Harry. Polly has made no lifetime gifts in the seven years preceding her death. Her estate is worth £800,000. The nil rate band available to Polly's estate is £325,000. The legacy to Mark exceeds Polly's nil rate band, and there will be tax to pay. Residue is exempt. The amount of tax payable depends on who is liable to pay the tax.

(a) If Polly's will gives the legacy to Mark 'subject to tax', simply calculate tax on the legacy in the usual way. £

Calculate tax on	£358,000	
	£325,000 @ 0%	Nil
	£33,000 @ 40%	13,200
Distribution:	Tax bill	13,200
	Mark receives legacy (less tax)	344,800
	Harry receives residue	<u>442,000</u>
		<u>800,000</u>

(b) If Polly's will gives the legacy to Mark 'free of tax', the calculation is more complicated. Section 38(3) of the IHTA 1984 provides that the value transferred is the aggregate of the value of the gift and the 'tax which would be chargeable if the value transferred equalled that aggregate'.

The value transferred is, therefore, made up of the £358,000 which Mark takes (the net sum) PLUS the tax attributable to it.

In order to ascertain the value transferred, it is necessary to calculate what sum would, after deduction of tax at the appropriate rate, leave £358,000: ie, the legacy must be grossed up.

		£
Gross up Mark's legacy:		
	£325,000 (grossed up @ 0%)	325,000
	£33,000 (grossed up @ 40%) $33,000 \times \dfrac{100}{60}$	55,000
	Gross gift	380,000
Calculate tax on £380,000		
	£325,000 @ 0%	nil
	£55,000 @ 40%	22,000
Distribution:	Mark receives legacy	358,000
	Tax bill	22,000
	Residue to Harry (after payment of tax)	<u>420,000</u>
		<u>800,000</u>

It is particularly important to be aware of these provisions when drafting a will. If a legacy is given 'free of tax', the tax bill may be considerably higher than if the legacy were given 'subject to tax', but the beneficiary will take more. Compare the tax paid in the example above. The alternatives should be explained to the testator so that clear instructions can be taken and express provision included as to whether the legacy is to be free of tax or subject to tax.

A will may direct that residue is to be divided between an exempt and a non-exempt beneficiary. The share of the non-exempt beneficiary attracts tax whereas the share of the exempt beneficiary does not. The IHTA 1984, s 41 provides that an exempt share of residue shall not bear any part of the tax attributable to the non-exempt share of residue even if the will directs otherwise. The non-exempt share of residue must bear its own tax and the non-exempt beneficiary will receive less benefit from the gift than will the exempt beneficiary.

EXAMPLE

Douglas (who has exhausted his nil rate band) leaves the residue of his estate after payment of debts, expenses and tax to be divided equally between his wife and his son, Henry.

After paying debts, expenses and tax attributable to non-residuary gifts, the residue is £600,000. His wife will receive £300,000. Henry will receive £300,000 less 40% tax ie, £180,000. Tax of £120,000 is paid on Henry's share of residue.

In this example, Douglas may object that he does not want his son to receive less than his wife. He may ask if the tax can be paid first and then what is left be divided into two equal shares. This is not possible because s 41 provides that a chargeable share of residue must bear its own tax and any provision to the contrary in a will is void.

However, he could direct that the residue be divided unequally between his wife and son in such proportions that after the payment of tax attributable to his son's share they each end up with the same amount.

The grossing up calculation is particularly difficult where there are specific legacies given free of tax and residue divided between exempt and non-exempt beneficiaries.

As we know, the tax on the legacies is paid from residue before division into shares, and the tax attributable to the non-exempt share of residue is paid exclusively from the non-exempt share. Unfortunately, the rate of tax at which the legacies are to be grossed up depends on the size of the non-exempt residue which cannot be known until the amount of the gross specific legacies is known.

In order to solve this problem, a two-stage process known as double grossing up is required. The tax free legacies are grossed up once as if they were the only taxable element of the estate; the value of the non-exempt residue is then calculated and the tax-free legacies are then grossed up again taking into account the value of the non-exempt residue. The calculation is lengthy and arithmetically challenging but fortunately there is a grossing up calculator available on the GOV.UK website which will do most of the job for you.

SUMMARY

(1)   All wills contain certain common elements: opening words to identify the document, revocation of previous wills, appointment of executors, legacies (if required) and gift of residue, attestation clause and date.

(2)   It is often appropriate to include additional clauses to deal with particular problems, for example: a survivorship clause and substitutional gift in case a beneficiary predeceases or dies shortly after the testator. In all but the simplest will, it is sensible to include administrative provisions to facilitate the administration of the estate

(3)   The introduction of the transferable nil rate band means that a spouse or civil partner can leave everything to the survivor without the couple suffering an IHT penalty.

REVIEW ACTIVITY

Question 1

Which ONE of the following statements is WRONG?

A   A will does not have to include a revocation clause.

B   A gift of 'my 3-stone diamond ring' will fail if the testator owns no item corresponding to the description at the date of death.

C   A will can only include an appointment of up to four executors.

D   No more than four executors can take a grant in respect of the same assets.

Answer: C

It is desirable that a will contains a revocation clause but not essential. The will can name any number of people as executors, but no more than four can take a grant to the same assets.

Question 2

James died in 2012, leaving his estate on trust for his wife (Ruth) for life and then to his son (Simon) contingent on his reaching age 25, but if not, to charity. Assume that s 31 and s 32 of TA 1925 apply unamended to the trust.

Which one or more of the following statements is/are CORRECT?

A   Ruth is alive and Simon is aged 17. The trustees have no power under s 31 of TA 1925 to use trust income for him.

B   Ruth is alive and Simon is aged 18. The trustees must pay the trust income to Simon until he reaches 25.

C   Ruth has died and Simon is aged 17. The trustees have power under s 31 of TA 1925 to use trust income for him.

D   Ruth has died and Simon is aged 18. The trustees cannot pay Simon any income as he does not yet have a vested interest.

E   Ruth is alive and Simon is aged 18. Under s 32 of TA 1925 the trustees can pay Simon all of the trust capital, provided Ruth consents.

F   Ruth is alive and Simon is aged 18. Under s 32 of TA 1925 the trustees can pay Ruth half of the trust capital.

G   Ruth has died and Simon is aged 18. The trustees cannot pay Simon any capital as he does not yet have a vested interest.

Answer: A, C

While Ruth is alive the income must be paid to her. Once she dies, s 31 applies in relation to Simon, so that there is power to use income for his maintenance, education or benefit while he is a minor, and a duty to pay the income to him when he reaches 18.

As this is a trust to which s 9 of ITPA 2014 does not apply, under s 32 of TA 1925 there is a limit on the amount that may be advanced of up to one-half of a beneficiary's share of the capital being advanced. This will need the consent of the life tenant (Ruth) while she is alive. Trustees may exercise their power under s 32 in relation to a beneficiary who has an interest in the trust capital, whether the interest is vested or contingent. Simon has an interest in the trust capital but Ruth does not.

WILL TRUSTS

> **LEARNING OUTCOMES**
>
> After reading this chapter you will be able to:
>
> - explain the different types of trust that can be created by will and their IHT treatment
> - explain the different methods of introducing flexibility into will trusts
> - explain the use of a flexible life interest
> - explain the effect of the Inheritance Act 1984, s 144.

12.1 INTRODUCTION

The main contents of a will are the dispositive provisions, ie the clauses which actually leave property to the beneficiaries. Testators will frequently want to leave property on trust rather than making outright gifts.

The purpose of this chapter is to consider in more detail the different ways in which a testator may leave his property on trust.

The principles of drafting are identical whether a trust is created on death or by lifetime transfer. However, there are significant IHT differences between lifetime trusts and those created on death, which we shall consider in this chapter. We shall also look at ways of using trusts to provide flexible benefits by will.

12.2 WHY INCLUDE TRUSTS IN A WILL?

Testators may want to provide for beneficiaries in succession. The only way to do this is through a trust. For example, a will may provide that the testator's spouse is to receive income for life, and after their death the capital is to be paid to the testator's children.

Testators are frequently uncertain about the precise nature of the gifts they want to make, because they do not know what the financial and personal position of the people they want to benefit will be at the date of their death and in the years following. Instead of making fixed gifts in the will, testators may prefer to have a will which delays the decision as to who shall benefit on death until a later date. This can be achieved by including trusts in the will and authorising the trustees, or others, to determine the matter after death. These trusts may relate to non-residuary gifts and/or the gift of the residue.

There are a number of possibilities for the testator to consider when planning a will which delays the ultimate choice of beneficiary until after his death. A trust is usually involved, and in each case the succession and taxation implications must be balanced carefully. This chapter discusses each of these matters, as well as the drafting considerations which arise.

12.3   SPECIAL IHT TREATMENT FOR CERTAIN SETTLEMENTS CREATED ON DEATH

Most settlements created on death will be subject to the relevant property regime. However, there are the following exceptions:

(a)   settlements created for a beneficiary who is disabled within the meaning of the Finance Act 2005, Sch 1A;

(b)   immediate post-death interests;

(c)   trusts for bereaved minors;

(d)   trusts for bereaved young people.

12.3.1   Settlements created for a disabled beneficiary

As in the case of lifetime trusts (see **5.2.4.1**), these are settlements fulfilling the qualifying conditions and created for the benefit of a beneficiary who is 'disabled' within the meaning of the Finance Act 2005, Sch 1A.

There are no anniversary or exit charges. Instead the beneficiary will be treated as having a qualifying interest in possession, ie, as beneficially entitled to the underlying trust assets. The settled property will be aggregated with the disabled beneficiary's own property when the beneficiary dies.

12.3.2   Immediate post-death interests

To qualify as an immediate post-death interest (IPDI), a person must have become beneficially entitled to an interest in possession in settled property on the death of the testator or intestate and must have continued to have such an interest at all times since the death (IHTA 1984, s 49A).

A person with an IPDI has a 'qualifying' interest in possession. This means that they are treated as if beneficially entitled to the underlying trust property. There are no anniversary or exit charges. Instead the property is aggregated with the beneficiary's own estate on death.

If the interest comes to an end before death, the beneficiary will be treated as making a lifetime transfer of value. The type of transfer depends on whether the property passes to someone absolutely, in which case there is a PET (to the extent that the transfer is not exempt), or whether the property passes on trust, in which case there is a lifetime chargeable transfer.

> **EXAMPLE 1**
>
> Terri leaves property to Lucy for life, remainder to Rohan absolutely.
>
> If Lucy surrenders her lifetime interest, the property will pass to Rohan absolutely. Lucy will make a PET. If, however, she was married to Rohan, the transfer would be exempt.

> **EXAMPLE 2**
>
> Terri leaves property to Larry for life, remainder to Linda for life, remainder to Rocco.
>
> If Larry surrenders his life interest, he will make a lifetime chargeable transfer, not a PET, because there is no absolute gift.

Linda will not have an IPDI because the life interest is not taking effect immediately on the testator's death. The settlement will, therefore, continue as a relevant property settlement.

In determining whether an interest qualifies as an IPDI, it is irrelevant that trustees may be able to terminate the interest. The settlement will be an IPDI settlement unless and until the interest is ended. If the interest does come to an end at any point, for example as a result of the trustees exercising a right to appoint the property elsewhere, the IPDI ceases. It cannot restart even if the original beneficiary reacquires the interest in possession because it will no longer be 'immediate'.

A survivorship clause of not more than six months is ignored. The dispositions actually taking effect are treated as if they had had effect from the beginning of the period.

12.3.3 Trusts for a bereaved minor

A trust for a bereaved minor (BMT) is a trust which satisfies the conditions set out in IHTA 1984, s 71A. That is:

(a)   the trust must be created by will or on intestacy for the deceased's own child (the bereaved minor);

(b)   the bereaved minor must, on or before attaining 18, become entitled to the settled property, any income arising from it, and any income that has already arisen and been accumulated.

(c)   while the bereaved minor is living and under 18:

    (i)   any capital applied must be applied for the benefit of the bereaved minor,

    (ii)   if any of the income arising from any of the settled property is applied for the benefit of a beneficiary, it is applied for the benefit of the bereaved minor.

The word 'must' in (b) above does not require absolute certainty. Death can prevent the beneficiary taking an interest. The word should be read as meaning 'must, if at all'.

The power to advance capital under s 32 of TA 1925 allows trustees to advance capital for the 'benefit' of a beneficiary. 'Benefit' is a wide word and could include settling it on trusts for the beneficiary and close family members. This would seem to conflict with the requirement in (c) that capital must be applied for the bereaved minor. However, s 71A(4) makes specific provision for this problem. It provides that a settlement can still satisfy the capital condition if s 32 applies, or, in the case of a settlement created before ITPA 2014 comes into force, if the settlement widens the statutory power to allow up to the whole of the beneficiary's interest to be advanced.

In 2012 the Government announced that it wanted to harmonise the wording and requirements of all the settlements providing special tax treatment for 'vulnerable beneficiaries', by which it meant disabled beneficiaries and bereaved minors. As part of this harmonisation, a change was made to the condition relating to the use of capital. A new sub-section (4)(za) was added to s 71A, which provides that a settlement can still comply with the capital requirement while allowing the trustees to pay a limited amount 'otherwise than for the benefit of the bereaved minor'. The amount per tax year is currently fixed at £3,000, or 3% of the maximum value of the settled property during the tax year.

A settlement which satisfies the s 71A requirements will not be subject to the relevant property regime. There will be no anniversary or exit charges.

EXAMPLE

Mandy dies intestate on 5 June 2012, leaving three children aged 4, 3 and 2. The children will be entitled to the capital at age 18. No anniversary charge arises in June 2022, and no charges arise as each beneficiary reaches 18 and becomes entitled to a share of the capital.

Section 71B provides that no IHT is to be payable as a result of the death under age 18 of the bereaved minor.

Notice that these trusts are very restricted:

(a)   A grandparent cannot create a BMT for a grandchild.

(b)   Income and capital must be applied for the beneficiaries for whom the property is held. There must be no overriding powers to appoint elsewhere.

Note, however, that a settlement can be a BMT even if the beneficiary has a right to receive income.

Note also that a s 71A trust does not have to take effect immediately on death. A wife might leave property to her husband for life and then to her children contingent on reaching 18. If the husband dies while the children are under 18, the settlement can qualify as a s 71A settlement.

A will may leave property to the testator's children contingent on their reaching 18, with a substitutional gift to a grandchild if a child predeceases the testator. The trust for the children will be a BMT, but if a grandchild is substituted for a child who has predeceased, that part of the settlement held for the grandchild will be subject to the relevant property regime.

EXAMPLE

Trevor dies with an estate of £600,000 which he leaves on trust for his three children, Ann, Ben and Clare, contingent on reaching 18, with a substitutional gift to children of a child who predeceases also contingent on reaching 18.

On Trevor's death Ann is 24. Ben died, aged 22, but has left a child, Brady, who is aged 2; Clare is 17.

Ann has a vested interest and is immediately entitled to her share; Clare's interest is a BMT; the portion held for Brady is subject to the relevant property regime.

Oddly, IHTA 1984, s 71A provides that where the trusts arise on intestacy, there will be a BMT for a substituted grandchild. Had Trevor died intestate in the above example, there would have been a BMT for Brady.

Section 71A is drafted by reference to a single beneficiary called the bereaved minor, suggesting that each bereaved minor must become entitled to his or her own 'share' of the trust capital and income. If this was the correct interpretation, it would be fatal to the status of the settlement for the trustees to have a power to alter the shares of individual beneficiaries to give more to one than the other. However, the Revenue issued guidance in July 2007 on the section, which said that this was not the correct interpretation. The Revenue considers that is possible to include a power for trustees to apply income unequally and/or to appoint capital in unequal shares, or even all to one at the expense of another.

EXAMPLE

Extract from Trust Deed

> ... to such of my children alive at my death as attain the age of 18 years and if more than one in such shares as the trustees shall from time to time by deed or deeds revocable or irrevocable appoint and in default of such appointment in equal shares absolutely at 18.

Fred died and left £400,000 to trustees to hold for his three children, contingent on reaching 18, and with a power to appoint capital in the above terms. The trustees decide to appoint £300,000 to the youngest child and the rest equally to the two older children. The Revenue's view is that the trust fulfils the requirements of s 71A.

However, according to the Revenue guidance the power must not permit the trustees to vary the share of a child who has *already* reached 18. The Revenue also takes the view that once a child has been excluded from benefit, even revocably, the power cannot afterwards be used to benefit the excluded child. In the Revenue's view it is not possible under the s 71A regime for someone who is not currently benefiting to become entitled in the future. Trustees should therefore consider carefully before excluding a child from benefit or making a revocable appointment of all the trust funds to one child. The mere possibility of trustees exercising the power in this way in the future will not affect the status of the BMT.

To prevent problems the power of appointment should be limited in the following way:

> PROVIDED that no such appointment shall be made and no such appointment shall be revoked so as to either diminish or to increase the share (or the accumulations of income forming part of the share) of or give a new share (or new accumulations of income) to a child who at the date of such appointment or revocation has reached the age of 18 nor to benefit a child who has been excluded from benefit as a result of the exercise of the power.

Note that a BMT attracts no special treatment for CGT or income tax, except that when a beneficiary becomes absolutely entitled as against the trustees, hold-over relief is available under TCGA 1992, s 260.

12.3.4 Trusts for a bereaved young person

As a result of public criticism of the very restricted trusts afforded privileged treatment for IHT contained in the Finance Bill 2006, the Government amended the Bill at a late stage and introduced s 71D into IHTA 1984. This allows some privileged treatment for trusts where entitlement to capital is to be deferred beyond 18.

The following conditions set out in s 71D must be satisfied:

(a)   the trust must be created by will for the deceased's own child (B);

(b)   B must, at or before age 25, become entitled to the settled property, any income arising from it and any income that has already arisen and been accumulated;

(c)   while B is living and under 25:

   (i)   any capital applied must be applied for the benefit of B,

   (ii)   if any of the income arising from any of the settled property is applied for the benefit of a beneficiary, it is applied for the benefit of B.

As is the case for a BMT (see **12.3.3**), the word 'must' does not require absolute certainty. Death can prevent the beneficiary taking an interest. The word should be read as meaning 'must, if at all'.

As is the case for a BMT, a settlement can still satisfy the capital condition if s 32 applies, or if, in the case of a settlement created before ITPA 2014 came into force, the settlement widens the statutory power to allow up to the whole of the beneficiary's interest to be advanced. The power can be used to advance capital on relevant property trusts.

The same amendment was made by the Finance Act 2013 that we saw in relation to s 71A trusts (see **12.3.3** above). The settlement can fulfil the capital requirement despite the fact that the trustees have power to pay limited amounts (£3,000, or 3% of the maximum value of the trust fund each tax year) otherwise than for the benefit of B.

A settlement which satisfies the s 71D requirements will not be subject to the relevant property regime while the beneficiaries are under 18.

There will be an exit charge if a beneficiary becomes entitled to capital after the age of 18. The charge will be calculated on the amount of time the property has remained settled since the beneficiary's 18th birthday. There are no anniversary charges. The calculation of the exit charge is similar to the calculation of an exit charge in the first 10 years of a relevant property settlement (see **10.3**).

Section 71E provides that no IHT is to be payable as a result of the death under 18 of the beneficiary.

Settlements satisfying the s 71D requirements can be created only by parents for their own children.

A settlement can qualify as a s 71D trust a even if the beneficiary has a right to receive income. However, s 71D(5) of the IHTA 1984 provides that a settlement which gives a beneficiary a right to income arising immediately on death will be classified as an immediate post-death interest (IPDI), not a s 71D settlement. (This is not the case for s 71A settlements where a settlement fulfilling the s 71A requirements will be classified as a s 71A settlement even if it gives the beneficiary an immediate right to income.)

As was the case for s 71A trusts, a s 71D trust does not need to take effect immediately on death. Where a life interest terminates on or after 22 March 2006 and is followed by trusts for the testator's children contingent on reaching an age between 18 and 25, these trusts will qualify as s 71D trusts if the children are under the stated age at the time (even if some have attained 18). The fact that the trusts do not take immediate effect on death, but are postponed to another interest, is irrelevant.

Section 71D is drafted by reference to a single beneficiary called 'B'. The Revenue guidance issued in July 2007 takes the same approach in relation to s 71D settlements as to s 71A settlements. Trustees can have a power to apply income and appoint capital unequally amongst the beneficiaries without affecting the status. As with s 71A settlements, the power must not be exercisable in favour of a child who has reached 25 and the trustees must not make an appointment to a beneficiary who has been excluded.

Most people making wills who want to benefit their children with as little IHT as possible will probably choose a s 71D settlement in preference to a s 71A one. The trustees of a s 71D settlement are free to advance the trust funds to the beneficiaries at age 18 if they choose, in which case there will be no charges to IHT. If, however, the beneficiary is too immature to deal with the funds at age 18, the trustees can allow the settlement to continue until age 25. There will be an exit charge at that point.

If the trustees are still doubtful as to the maturity of the beneficiary as 25 approaches, they could use any power of advancement they may have to settle the trust funds on further trusts for the benefit of the beneficiary. The same exit charge will be payable as if the property went to the beneficiary absolutely. There will be subsequent anniversary charges and an exit charge when the property eventually leaves the settlement, but this may be worthwhile if the beneficiary cannot be trusted to deal sensibly with the funds. (Trustees of a BMT can also make use of the power of advancement to settle the trust property on further trusts for the benefit of the beneficiary before his 18th birthday. There will be no exit charge at the time of the advance but, once the property is settled on the new relevant property trusts, there will be subsequent exit and anniversary charges on the property.)

Note that there is no special treatment for CGT or income tax, except that when a beneficiary becomes absolutely entitled as against the trustees, hold-over relief is available under s 260 of the TCGA 1992.

12.4 PRECATORY TRUSTS

12.4.1 Misnomer

A so-called 'precatory trust' arises when a testator gives assets to a beneficiary and expresses a wish that the beneficiary will pass the assets on to others in accordance with an expression of wishes left by the deceased.

There is actually no trust at all. The beneficiary is free to ignore the testator's wishes.

To create a binding trust, there must be certainty of intention, ie the gift must use words which make it clear that there is a binding obligation to hold property 'on trust', together with certainty of subject matter and of objects, ie the beneficiaries. A testator who expresses a 'wish' or a 'hope' is not imposing any obligation. There is simply an expectation that the beneficiary will try to comply with the wish or hope.

12.4.2 Using the clause

Precatory trusts are normally used by testators when disposing of personal chattels, and in particular their jewellery. They are useful where the testator is undecided who should benefit from what on his death, especially in respect of property which may change in extent between the date of the will and the subsequent death. The clause introduces a degree of flexibility, giving the testator the opportunity to change his mind as to his wishes but without needing to change the will by codicil or, possibly, by executing a new will.

12.4.3 Drafting the clause

Sample clause

> I give and bequeath all my personal chattels as defined by section 55(1)(x) of the Administration of Estates Act 1925 to [my wife] for [her] own absolute use and benefit and I express the wish (but without imposing any legal obligation on [her]) that [she] should distribute such assets in accordance with any instructions I communicate to [her] whether orally or in writing at any time and from time to time.

12.4.3.1 Definition of personal chattels

Although it is convenient to adopt the definition used in the AEA 1925 for personal chattels, thought should be given as to whether it is appropriate. For example, if a testatrix wishes to make a gift of jewellery only, the clause should be modified by inserting an appropriate description of the gift in place of the words 'personal chattels as defined by section 55(1)(x) of the Administration of Estates Act 1925'.

12.4.3.2 The nature of the gifts

There is an absolute gift in the sample clause to the testator's wife. She could retain all the personal chattels, but the testator hopes that through the use of the precatory words she will retain only certain chattels and will distribute the rest. Flexibility is achieved since the instruction to the testator's wife can be changed as often as the testator pleases by giving further, non-testamentary instruction.

12.4.4 Taxation implications of the precatory trust

12.4.4.1 Inheritance tax (IHTA 1984, s 143)

The gift takes effect initially as an absolute gift to the beneficiary named in the clause. Inheritance tax is initially calculated on this basis. Thus, under the sample clause, no IHT will become payable because of the spouse exemption. If no exemption is available, IHT may be payable immediately on the testator's death.

Section 143 provides that where the named beneficiary transfers property in compliance with the testator's wish within two years after the death of the testator, 'this Act shall have effect as if the property transferred had been bequeathed by the will to the transferee'. Section 17(b) supports this by stating 'the transfer (by the named beneficiary) shall not be a transfer of value'. The benefit of s 143 is given automatically and does not need to be specifically claimed. Thus the distribution of the property by the named beneficiary in accordance with the 'precatory words' is not a PET by the beneficiary, and so will not attract IHT if the named beneficiary dies within seven years of the distribution.

> **EXAMPLE**
>
> Martha by will leaves her jewellery to her daughter Emma, coupled with the wish that Emma shall distribute some of it to persons named in a letter handed to her before Martha's death. Emma distributes half of the jewellery to members of the family named in the letter and keeps the remainder.
>
> No IHT exemption is available on Martha's death, so tax is payable on the value of the jewellery. No adjustment of the position will be needed when Emma distributes one half of the jewellery (unless some is given to Martha's spouse or civil partner, in which case the spouse exemption will become available on those items given to the spouse or civil partner). Assuming no items are given to a spouse or civil partner, the IHT position on Martha's death will be unchanged, whether Emma keeps the items or distributes them.
>
> Emma makes no transfer of value provided she re-distributes the jewellery within two years of her mother's death.

12.4.4.2 Capital gains tax

There are no CGT provisions equivalent to s 143 of IHTA 1984. The named beneficiary will make a disposal of assets each time property is transferred in accordance with the precatory trust. However, CGT will be payable only if there is a gain on disposal which is beyond any available exemption or relief. In view of the timescale between the death and the later transfer of the property, it is unlikely that any taxable gain will arise.

Even if there are gains, they are likely to fall within the tangible moveable property exemption contained in s 262(1) of the TCGA 1992, which applies to disposals of non-wasting assets where the disposal consideration is £6,000 or less.

12.5 WILLS CONTAINING FLEXIBLE TRUSTS

12.5.1 Why have a flexible will?

A testator cannot anticipate accurately the circumstances prevailing at his death, whether in relation to the extent of his property or his family, and so may decide his will should be drafted in 'flexible' form. Some flexibility is afforded in any event by s 32 of TA 1925, but this is very limited and most testators will want the added flexibility that only express powers can provide.

12.5.2 Two methods of creating flexible wills

There are two ways to draft a flexible will. In terms of flexibility, the choice between the two is a matter of personal preference, since the same result can be achieved using either. In both cases, the flexible gift can be a legacy, the whole residue of the estate or a share of the residue, depending on the testator's wishes.

The two methods are as follows:

(1) The chosen property is left to the executors and trustees on discretionary trusts with wide powers of appointment over the capital and income and a gift over in default of appointment. If the powers of appointment are not exercised by the trustees, the property will pass 'in default of appointment' to beneficiaries chosen by the testator and named in the will.

(2) The chosen property is left to named individuals on immediate post-death interest trusts but subject to the trustees' overriding powers of appointment, for example to a spouse for life with a gift over to children, but with overriding powers for trustees to appoint the trust property to discretionary beneficiaries, thus terminating the spouse's life interest.

A will of either type enables the trustees to take into account the circumstances prevailing at the death of the testator and use the trust property as best suits those circumstances. For example, a testator's spouse may be financially well provided for and so not require any provision from the testator. If so, the trustees could exercise their powers over the income and capital in favour of the testator's children. If the circumstances were different and the spouse was in need of the testator's estate, the whole of it could be made available by exercise of the trustee's power of appointment in favour of the spouse.

Although the two methods are the same from a flexibility point of view, there are tax differences. Where the testator has a surviving spouse or civil partner, there can be an IHT advantage in using the second option. If property is left to the spouse on a terminable life interest, it attracts the spouse exemption and no IHT has to be paid on application for the grant. If the spouse's interest is later terminated in whole or part of the trust fund to give capital to other beneficiaries absolutely, the spouse makes a PET. If the spouse survives seven years, no IHT will be payable.

Compare that result with leaving the whole estate on discretionary trusts: IHT will have to be paid on application for the grant on everything in excess of the nil rate band. However, even this disadvantage can be avoided if the trustees take action before the personal representatives apply for a grant; as we shall see at **12.6.2**, if the trustees make an appointment out of the trust within two years of death, the appointment is written back into the will and IHT is adjusted, if necessary.

EXAMPLE

Ravi dies with an estate of £2 million. He is survived by a wife and children.

If he leaves the whole estate to his wife on a life interest subject to overriding powers, no IHT is payable. If the trustees override part of the wife's life interest to give £500,000 to the children absolutely, Ravi's wife is treated as making a potentially exempt transfer of £500,000.

If he leaves the whole estate on discretionary trusts, IHT is payable on £2 million less the nil rate band.

If the trustees appoint three-quarters of the estate to Ravi's wife and one-quarter to the children within two years of death, the appointment is written back into the will. This means there will be a refund of the IHT attributable to the wife's portion. See **12.6.2**.

12.6   FLEXIBLE WILL USING DISCRETIONARY TRUSTS

Instructions will be required from the testator on various matters before the will can be drafted.

12.6.1   Planning the flexible will using discretionary trusts

12.6.1.1   Legacy or residue on discretionary trusts?

A 'settled legacy', ie a legacy of specific property or cash to be held on discretionary trusts, is often incorporated into a will which then leaves the residuary estate to other beneficiaries absolutely.

Sample clause – settled legacy

(1) I give to my Trustees free of all taxes the sum of [ ] thousand pounds (which said sum and all investments and property for the time being representing the same is hereinafter referred to as 'the Settled Legacy') upon the trusts and with and subject to the powers discretions and provisions contained in the succeeding paragraphs of this Clause

(2) For so long during the period of 125 years from my death (the perpetuity period applicable hereto) as any of the persons hereinafter mentioned is living my Trustees shall have power at

> any time and from time to time if and whenever they shall in their absolute discretion think fit to pay or apply the whole or any part or parts of the income or of the capital or of the income and the capital of the Settled Legacy to or for the benefit of all or any one or more exclusively of the others or other of the following persons that is to say my [spouse and issue] and with power to accumulate any income of the Settled Legacy not so paid or applied and to add any such accumulations to the capital thereof
>
> (3) Subject to the foregoing provisions of this Clause and to any and every exercise of the powers and discretions hereinbefore conferred upon them my Trustees shall hold the Settled Legacy upon trust for such of my [children and grandchildren] ...

If there is no settled legacy, the will may provide absolute legacies, for example to the testator's children, and then leave the residuary estate on discretionary trusts for a class of beneficiaries possibly including the testator's spouse and issue.

If a will contains a relevant property settlement (whether of a legacy or the residuary estate), it is generally inadvisable for the will to create another settlement containing relevant property. This is because s 62 of the IHTA 1984 provides that if two settlements are made on the same day by the same person (the testator on the day he dies), they are 'related settlements'. The value of relevant property comprised in a related settlement, immediately after commencement, is added to the value of the property in the other relevant property trust when calculating the value of the hypothetical chargeable transfer. The effect is that the rate charged will be higher than it would have been had the will made an absolute gift as opposed to creating a related settlement. The problem does not arise if the will contains a relevant property settlement and another type of settlement, such as an immediate post-death interest trust or trusts for a bereaved minor or young person.

12.6.1.2   Duration of the discretionary trust

The settlement, whether a settled legacy or a settlement of residue, may be drafted so as to be capable of lasting for a full perpetuity period. Even if it is drafted in this way, it is unlikely that it will in fact last so long. Trustees will normally exercise their powers of appointment over capital far earlier.

Often, trustees will distribute all or a substantial portion of the assets within two years of death to take advantage of the IHT relief contained in IHTA 1984, s 144 (see **12.6.2.1**).

12.6.1.3   Extent of the property within the discretionary trust

Where the trust is a settled legacy, it may be limited to property to the value of the available nil rate band for IHT at the testator's death. Such 'nil rate band settlements' have the advantage that no IHT is payable when the trustees exercise their discretionary powers. However, there is nothing to prevent the testator leaving the entire estate on flexible trusts.

12.6.2   IHT implications of discretionary trusts in wills

12.6.2.1   IHTA 1984, s 144

Section 144 is specifically designed to permit distribution of property from a settlement without an interest in possession within two years of the testator's death, without liability to IHT. It does not apply where a beneficiary has been given an interest in possession such as a terminable life interest.

The section applies where property is settled by a will if two conditions are satisfied:

(a)   no interest in possession subsists in the settled property; and

(b)   an event occurs in relation to the settled property within the period of two years after the death of the testator which:

    (i)   would otherwise be chargeable to tax, for example the distribution of trust property by the trustees to a beneficiary; or

(ii) causes the property to be held on trusts containing what would have been immediate post-death interests or bereaved minor or bereaved young person interests had they been included in the testator's will.

If the conditions are met there are two consequences:

(a) there is no exit charge to IHT when the property leaves the settlement; and

(b) the will is treated as if it had left the property in the way the trustees have distributed it. A 'writing back' effect is, therefore, achieved in a manner similar to that which occurs with a post-death variation (see **13.2.1.1**).

EXAMPLE 1

Mary by her will creates a discretionary trust of her residuary estate of £575,000. The beneficiaries are her husband, Henry, and their children and grandchildren. She dies in May 2022, having made no lifetime transfers.

Death of Mary: £100,000 IHT is payable (£575,000 – £325,000 = £250,000 @ 40%). The spouse exemption is not available.

Distribution by Mary's trustees in October 2023 (within two years of Mary's death) as follows:

£325,000 to trustees on discretionary trusts for the grandchildren: within nil rate band.

The rest to Henry absolutely: spouse exemption.

No IHT is now payable on Mary's death as the trustees' distributions are 'written back' into Mary's will.

EXAMPLE 2

Maya (who has no transferred nil rate band) by her will creates a trust for her grandchildren contingent on them reaching 25 and varies s 31 of TA 1925 to exclude the right to income at 18 so that the grandchildren's contingent interests continue until 25.

This settlement is a relevant property settlement.

At the date of death Maya's estate is £750,000 and her three grandchildren are 19, 21 and 23. One year after Maya's death, the trustees decide that rather than keeping the trust going, they will advance the whole of each grandchild's share and terminate the settlement.

The advances are 'written back' into the will and no exit charges are payable. Without the 'writing back' effect of s 144 there would have been exit charges.

Had s 31 of TA 1925 not been varied to remove the right to income at 18, s 144 would not have been required, as each grandchild would have had an interest in possession. The advances would have had no IHT implications as each grandchild would already be treated as entitled to his or her share of the capital.

This writing back effect is automatic; no election is required. The IHT paid by the PRs to obtain the grant of probate will be repaid (with interest) by the Revenue. Where (as is often the case) the PRs apply for the grant before the trustees make an appointment, they will have to pay IHT on the basis of there being no spouse exemption. If they make an appointment to the spouse, they will obtain a refund of IHT paid with interest. It is possible for the trustees to use their powers of appointment before the PRs vest assets in them. They will appoint their rights to the property left by the will (for example to a fixed legacy or a share of residue) to the chosen beneficiary. If the beneficiary is a surviving spouse, the spouse exemption will then be available. The Revenue accepts that an early appointment is possible but prefers to see an express power authorising the trustees to use their powers while the administration of the estate is continuing.

Because the writing back effect is automatic, trustees should be careful of taking action within two years of death in case they produce an unwanted result.

EXAMPLE

Fay dies leaving two investment properties on discretionary trusts for the benefit of her husband and issue. Her husband, Sam, wants the income from the investment properties, so nine months after Fay's death, the trustees exercise their discretionary powers to give Sam a right to the income from the properties. The appointment retrospectively creates an immediate post-death interest and Sam's estate will include the investment properties.

This can be unfortunate, for example where the reason for the discretionary trust was to keep Sam's estate below the residence nil rate band taper threshold of £2m.

If the trustees do not wish to create a retrospective immediate post-death interest, they should exercise their discretionary powers to pay income to Sam on an *ad hoc* basis for the two years following death and then award him a right to income. Once the two years have elapsed, appointments of a right to income have no inheritance tax effect.

See *Payne v Tyler* [2019] EWHC 2347 (Ch) for a recent example of trustees overlooking the automatic reading back of s 144 and inadvertently creating an immediate post-death interest.

Distributions after two years from death

Section 144 writing back occurs only for distributions made within the two-year period. Later distributions will be taxable in accordance with normal principles which apply to relevant property trusts (see **10.3**). Will trusts often used to require trustees to distribute within two years of death, but this is now uncommon. It is often appropriate not to appoint all the property out within the first two years but to let the trust continue.

If the trust does continue, it will be treated for tax purposes as an ordinary relevant property trust created at the date of death of the testator.

EXAMPLE

Tom, a widower, dies on 1 September 2020 leaving his entire estate on discretionary trusts for the benefit of his grandchildren. The estate is substantial and the grandchildren are all minors. The trustees decide that there is no need to make any immediate appointments and that they will allow the trust to continue.

The first 10-year anniversary will be 1 September 2030.

The rate of tax charged on distributions made after the first two years and within the first ten years will be calculated using the number of complete quarters that have elapsed since 1 September 2020.

12.6.2.2   Pre-2006 use of nil rate band discretionary trusts

Before the introduction of the transferable nil rate band, many testators who wanted to make use of their nil rate band chose to settle an amount equal to the unexhausted portion of their nil rate band on discretionary trusts and leave the residue to the surviving spouse.

This had a number of benefits:

(a)   no IHT was payable on the death estate;

(b)   the testator made use of his nil rate band, which at that time would have been wasted if all assets were passed to the spouse.

Now that the nil rate band of the first spouse to die can be transferred to the survivor, these benefits can be obtained while leaving the whole estate to the surviving spouse either absolutely or as an IPDI. There are still some continuing tax benefits to using a nil rate band discretionary trust, although these are much reduced. These benefits are:

(a)   There is the flexibility to make funds available to whichever beneficiaries are most in need. The surviving spouse, as well as the children and issue, can be included, so the testator will know that, if required, all the assets of the estate can be made available to the spouse. If the spouse does not need the assets, they can be made available to the children or issue.

However, funds could also be made available to spouse and children by using a terminable life interest – see **12.7**. So a nil rate band discretionary trust is not the only way to get this particular advantage.

(b)   Where a surviving spouse's IHT estate may exceed the taper threshold of £2 million leading to loss of the residence nil rate band, it is helpful to keep funds outside the IHT estate by using a discretionary trust.

(c)   The nil rate band has been frozen at £325,000 for several years, and will not be increased until 6 April 2026 (when it is due to rise in line with the consumer prices index). In a case where there are assets the value of which can be identified as likely to increase at a faster rate than the nil rate band, it is tax-efficient to keep them outside the estate of the survivor by using a nil rate band discretionary trust.

EXAMPLE

Fiona, who was married to Sam, died in July 2018 with a substantial estate. Included in her estate was an investment property worth £325,000 (the value of the nil rate band in 2018/19). The spouse exemption is available on Fiona's death, and Sam's estate will benefit from the transferred nil rate band.

Sam dies in 2025 when the nil rate band is still £325,000 and the investment property has increased to £400,000. His other assets are £1 million.

At the time of Fiona's death, the investment property fell within her nil rate band, but the increase in the value of the property at Sam's death (£75,000) is not matched by an equivalent increase in the nil rate band.

Accordingly, if the investment property is given to Sam and is part of his IHT estate, tax at 40% is charged on the £75,000 increase (a potential tax bill of £30,000).

Had Fiona left the investment property to a discretionary trust, this would have exhausted Fiona's nil rate band, but on Sam's death no IHT would be payable on the value of the property.

Whenever a nil rate band settlement is created, IHT will be charged at 0% during the first 10 years, making it possible to defer final decisions as to distribution, without cost. However, the will must not contain any related settlement holding relevant property, or the rate of IHT will be increased (see **12.6.1.1**).

EXAMPLE

Raymond dies in September 2021 having made PETs of £125,000 which became chargeable on his death. By his will he creates a discretionary trust of the balance of his nil rate band of £200,000 and leaves the residue of his estate to his wife Wendy. The beneficiaries of the trust are Wendy, his children and grandchildren.

(1)   Calculate the IHT on Raymond's death.

No IHT is payable because:

(a)   the funds in the nil rate band discretionary trust are taxed at 0% because the balance of Raymond's nil rate band is available (£325,000 – £125,000 = £200,000);

(b)   the residuary estate has the benefit of the spouse exemption.

(2)   Distribution by the trustees.

Eight years after Raymond's death, when the nil rate band has increased to £400,000, Wendy tells the trustees that she can manage without relying on the nil rate band discretionary trust fund and she asks if they will distribute it to the children. The trustees agree to do so. The value of the trust assets has risen to £450,000. No IHT is payable by the trustees from the discretionary trust. The settlement rate will be nil.

Using the method illustrated in **10.3.4** (exit charge before the first 10-year anniversary), the calculation is:

Step 1:	Hypothetical chargeable transfer	£200,000
	(value of funds settled by will)	
Step 2:	Ascertain tax payable	
	Raymond's cumulative total £125,000	
	Nil rate band (balance)	£200,000
Step 3:	Ascertain settlement rate	nil

Note: the settlement rate will always be nil within the first 10 years so long as the funds entering the discretionary settlement at death are limited to the testator's available nil rate band:

Step 1:	Value of funds	£325,000
Step 2:	Available nil rate band	£325,000
Step 3:	Ascertain settlement rate	nil

The nil rate band discretionary trust also has non-tax benefits which may make it attractive:

- Funds can be made available to any of the beneficiaries who need them. Commonly, the surviving spouse will enjoy the income for some years, and at a later stage the capital will be appointed to issue.

- The surviving spouse cannot deal unilaterally with the settled property, so the capital is protected in the event of the survivor remarrying and wanting to leave assets away from the issue.

- Because the settled property is not owned beneficially by the surviving spouse, it is not included for means testing purposes if the spouse has to go into residential care, nor is it available to a trustee in bankruptcy if the survivor becomes bankrupt.

However, there have always been some practical problems in relation to nil rate band discretionary trusts. Many couples own a valuable house as beneficial tenants in common but have little in the way of cash and investments. When the first spouse dies, the cash and investments in the estate may be far short of the current nil rate band. The PRs can transfer all or part of the deceased's interest in the matrimonial home to the trustees of the nil rate band settlement, but the surviving spouse is often unhappy about losing control of the home, and the arrangement can give rise to CGT problems when the property is sold as half the house belongs to the trust. The solution to the problem is set out at **12.6.2.3** below.

12.6.2.3   Solution to problem of lack of liquid assets – use of a debt or charge

A solution which is commonly adopted where a couple want to create a nil rate band discretionary settlement but lack liquid or easily transferable assets, is for the will creating the nil rate band settlement to give the PRs the right to require the trustees of the nil rate band settlement to accept a debt from the PRs instead of assets.

The PRs normally secure the debt on the assets transferred to the surviving spouse. In such cases the trustees of the nil rate band settlement have the right to enforce the charge against those assets during the spouse's lifetime but normally wait until death. If the spouse wants to sell the property, the charge has to be paid off, but the trustees can lend trust funds to the spouse for the purchase of a replacement property provided the trust instrument gives them suitable powers. The will normally gives the trustees the right to claim interest on the debt or to index link it.

The benefits of this route are:

(a)   the first spouse to die makes use of his or her nil rate band to protect assets and keep them out of the estate of the survivor;

(b)   the surviving spouse has the use of all the assets of the couple free of IHT;

(c)   on the death of the surviving spouse there is a debt which will reduce the IHT value of the estate.

> **EXAMPLE**
>
> Fred and Georgia are married. They own the matrimonial home worth £800,000 as beneficial tenants in common. Fred dies first, and in addition to his half interest in the house he has £50,000 in cash and investments. His will leaves a nil rate band legacy on discretionary trusts for the benefit of Georgia and their children and grandchildren, and the residue to Georgia. The will allows his executors to require the trustees of the nil rate band settlement to accept a debt instead of assets.
>
> The executors transfer all the assets of Fred's estate to Georgia, charged with a debt of £325,000 together with interest. Georgia dies four years later. The trustees will demand repayment of the debt with interest, which will reduce the IHT value of Georgia's estate. The trustees of the settlement can then distribute the settlement funds as they see fit.

12.6.3   CGT implications of discretionary trusts in wills

No special statutory provisions exist for CGT where distributions are made from discretionary trusts created by a will. In particular, there is no writing back effect for CGT corresponding to s 144 of the IHTA 1984. Thus, ordinary principles must be applied to calculate any liability (see further **10.3.7**).

However, the Revenue accepts (see Capital Gains Tax Manual, para 31430) that where the trustees of a settlement without an interest in possession exercise their powers of appointment during the administration period and *before* the PRs have vested assets in them, then the assets should be treated as passing direct to the appointee and never entering the trust at all. The Revenue likes to see an express power authorising the trustees to make an early appointment but no longer regards the inclusion of the power as essential.

The appointee then takes those asset(s) as legatee, and therefore acquires the assets at probate value by reason of s 62(4) of the TCGA 1992. This means that there will be no liability to CGT resulting from the appointment.

This is clearly the best course for the trustees who want to make an appointment. If they wait until the PRs vest assets in them and then make the appointment, adverse tax consequences may follow. The precise consequences depend on whether the appointment is made within or outside the two-year period from death. If the appointment is outside the two-year period, normal CGT principles apply and the position is as follows.

When a beneficiary becomes 'absolutely entitled' to trust property as against the trustees, the trustees are 'deemed to dispose' of the property at its market value and to re-acquire it at the same value as bare trustees, ie it remains in the names of the former trustees but is now the absolute property of the beneficiary for CGT purposes. If the value of the assets comprised in the settlement has increased since the date of death by more than the annual exemption available to the trustees, there will be an immediate liability to CGT. However, normally, hold-over relief is available on deemed disposals. This is because the appointment from the settlement is a chargeable transfer for IHT purposes (see **4.4.5.2**).

However, if the appointment from the settlement is made within two years of death, there is a deemed disposal with a possible CGT liability, but hold-over relief is not available under TCGA 1992, s 260 because the appointment is written back into the will under IHTA 1984, s 144, so there is no chargeable transfer by the trustees. (If the assets are 'business assets', hold-over relief may be available under TCGA 1992, s 165.)

EXAMPLE 1: NIL RATE BAND DISCRETIONARY TRUST – APPOINTMENT OUTSIDE TWO-YEAR PERIOD

A testator's will creates a nil rate band discretionary trust. Three years after death the trustees appoint the trust property to the testator's spouse who thereby becomes absolutely entitled to it. The assets appointed were worth £325,000 at death but are now worth £400,000. The deemed disposal will produce an immediate liability to CGT on £75,000, less any deductible expenses and annual exemption. The beneficiary will acquire the assets at £400,000. (There is no liability to IHT because the appointment out is before the first 10-year anniversary, so assets are not revalued: see Example at **12.5.3.2**.)

If hold-over relief is claimed, there will be no immediate liability to CGT but the beneficiary will acquire the assets at £325,000.

EXAMPLE 2: NIL RATE BAND DISCRETIONARY TRUST – APPOINTMENT WITHIN TWO-YEAR PERIOD

A testator's will creates a nil rate band discretionary trust. The PRs have vested assets in the trustees. The trustees exercise the power of appointment within two years of death so that it is written back into the testator's will. There is no chargeable transfer by the trustees because IHTA 1984, s 144 applies. Thus hold-over relief will not be available under TCGA 1992, s 260. (If the trust property is 'business assets', hold-over relief under TCGA 1992, s 165 may be available.) Assuming no hold-over relief is available under s 165, there will be an immediate liability to CGT on £75,000, less the annual exemption and any deductible expenses. The beneficiary will acquire the assets at £400,000.

Had the trustees exercised their power to appoint the trust assets to the beneficiary *before* the PRs had transferred them to the trustees, the beneficiary would have taken as legatee and there would have been no disposal by the trustees. However, the beneficiary would acquire the assets at their probate value of £325,000.

12.6.4 Income tax implications of discretionary trusts in wills

If no beneficiary has a right to income from a flexible trust (for example a discretionary trust with no appointment of a right to income), income over £1,000 from the settled property received by the trustees will attract tax at the trust rate or the dividend trust rate (Income Tax Act 2007, s 9). This, and the position of the beneficiaries, is considered in **Chapter 14**.

Distributions by trustees from discretionary trusts created by a will do not create settlements which fall within the income tax anti-avoidance provisions discussed at **4.6.2** and **4.6.4**.

EXAMPLE

David appoints his wife, Sheena, as his executor and trustee. His will bequeaths her a substantial legacy and leaves his residuary estate on flexible trusts for Sheena and their children. David dies leaving two young children.

Within two years of David's death, Sheena, as trustee, appoints the residuary estate onto new s 71D trusts for their minor children. Even though the children's trust was created by appointment by their mother, the appointment onto the new trusts is not a 'settlement' by a parent on her child within the income tax anti-avoidance provisions. Sheena creates the new settlement in her capacity as trustee of David's will, not as a parent.

Compare the position in relation to post-death variations (see **13.4.2**), where the income tax anti-avoidance legislation can apply.

12.6.5 Drafting discretionary trusts of residue

The clauses which follow create discretionary trusts and should be inserted into the will after the clauses directing the payment of the testator's debts, legacies, funeral and testamentary expenses and hence establishing the residuary fund to be 'the Trust Fund'. Many of the provisions used to create a discretionary trust by will are similar to those used to establish a lifetime settlement. The comments on the clauses which follow are confined to those relevant only to will trusts. (Remember that an alternative way to achieve flexibility is to leave property on a terminable life interest to the surviving spouse.)

12.6.5.1 Trust definitions

Sample clause

In my Will where the context so admits

(1) 'the Trust Fund' shall mean

   (a) my Estate after the payment of my debts funeral and testamentary expenses and legacies and

   (b) all money investments or other property accepted by the Trustees as additions and

   (c) all accumulations (if any) of income directed to be held as an accretion to capital and

   (d) the money investments and property from time to time representing the above

(2) 'the Trustees' shall mean my Executors or other of the trustees for the time being of the Trust Fund

(3) 'the Trust Period' shall mean the period ending on the earlier of

   (a) the last day of the period of 125 years from the date of my death which period (and no other) shall be the applicable perpetuity period or

   (b) such date as the Trustees shall by deed at any time or times specify (not being a date earlier than the date of execution of any such deed or later than a date previously specified)

(4) 'the Discretionary Beneficiaries' shall mean

   (a) [my wife] [my husband]

   (b) my children and remoter issue (whether living at my death or born thereafter)

   (c) the husbands wives widowers and widows of my children and remoter issue

   (d) any company trust or other body regarded as charitable under the law of England and Wales

(5) 'the Discretionary Period' shall mean [the period of two years (less one day) from the date of my death] [the Trust Period]

Clause (5) contains alternatives. If the period of 'two years (less one day) from the date of death' is selected, the trust will necessarily comply with the provisions of s 144 of IHTA 1984, ie a two-year discretionary trust will have been established.

By limiting the trustees to a period of two years less one day, it is intended to remove uncertainty as to whether the distributions in fact occurred within two years of the testator's death. Difficulties can arise if an exact period of two years is used instead.

It is not necessary to require the trustees to appoint within two years. Many testators prefer to leave the trustees to make their own decision. There may be good reasons for keeping the trust in existence. If the testator wants to give the trustees this flexibility, the second alternative (the 'Trust Period') should be selected. This will allow the settlement to continue as an ordinary discretionary settlement.

12.6.5.2   Nil rate band discretionary trust

The clauses set out above may be used to establish a flexible settlement of the whole of the testator's estate on discretionary trusts after payment of debts, expenses and legacies . If a nil rate band discretionary settlement is to be created, these clauses can be used but the definition of the trust fund must be altered to limit its extent.

Sample clause

'the Trust Fund' shall mean

(1)   the greatest value (if any) which such Trust Fund can have within the nil rate band of inheritance tax applicable at the date of my death which does not cause inheritance tax to be charged (other than at the said nil rate) in respect of my estate as a consequence of my death

(2)   (a)–(d) [as for (1) in the previous clause]

In cases where the testator may be entitled to a transferred nil rate band, it is desirable to include a direction making clear whether the personal representatives must claim it or whether the testator leaves it to their discretion. The Court of Appeal in *Loring v Woodland Trust* [2014] EWCA Civ 1314 indicated that in the absence of any direction in the will, it would be a matter of discretion for the personal representatives.

12.6.5.3   Residuary gift: discretionary trusts

Sample clause

(1)   The Trustees shall hold the capital and income of the Trust Fund upon such trusts in favour or for the benefit of all or such one or more of the Discretionary Beneficiaries exclusive of the other or others of them in such shares or proportions if more than one and with and subject to such powers and provisions for their respective maintenance education or other benefit or for the accumulation of income for any period (including administrative powers and provisions and discretionary trusts and powers to be executed or exercised by any person or persons whether or not being or including the Trustees or any of them) and so that the exercise of this power of appointment may be delegated to any extent and in such manner generally as the Trustees (subject to the application (if any) of the rule against perpetuities) by any deed or deeds revocable during the Discretionary Period or irrevocable and executed during the Discretionary Period shall appoint provided always that no exercise of this power shall invalidate any prior payment or application of all or any part or parts of the capital or income of the Trust Fund made under any other power or powers conferred by my Will or by law and provided further that this power may be exercised whether or not the administration of my Estate has been completed and whether or not a transfer of the Trust Fund has been effected by my Executors under Clause [   ]

All powers and provisions established by the clause are exercisable by the trustees at any point in the administration period – even before the executors transfer the assets remaining in the estate to the trustees. This is almost certainly the position in any event, but the proviso removes any doubt by expressly authorising the trustees to exercise the powers in the way set out in the clause. In particular, the Revenue likes to see this clause, so it is sensible to include it.

Sample clause (continued)

(2) Until and subject to and in default of any appointment under sub-clause (1) the following provisions of this sub-clause shall apply to the Trust Fund during the Discretionary Period

    (a) the Trustees shall pay or apply the income of the Trust Fund to or for the benefit of all or such one or more of the Discretionary Beneficiaries exclusive of the other or others of them as shall for the time being be in existence and in such shares if more than one and in such manner generally as the Trustees shall in their absolute discretion from time to time think fit

    (b) notwithstanding the provisions of sub-clause (2)(a) the Trustees may in their absolute discretion instead of applying all or any part or parts of the income accumulate the same in the way of compound interest by investing or otherwise applying it and its resulting income from time to time in any applications or investments authorised by my Will or by law and subject to sub-clause (2)(c) below shall hold such accumulations as an accretion to capital

    (c) the Trustees may apply the whole or any part or parts of the income accumulated under sub-clause (2)(b) as if it were income arising in the then current year

    (d) notwithstanding the trusts powers and provisions declared and contained in this sub-clause the Trustees may

        (i) at any time or times pay or apply the whole or any part or parts of the capital of the Trust Fund to or for the benefit of all or such one or more of the Discretionary Beneficiaries exclusive of the other or others of them in such shares if more than one and in such manner generally as the Trustees shall in their absolute discretion think fit

        (ii) (subject to the application (if any) of the rules against perpetuities) pay or transfer any income or capital of the Trust Fund to the Trustees of any other trust wherever established or existing under which all or any one or more of the Discretionary Beneficiaries is or are interested (whether or not all or such one or more of the Discretionary Beneficiaries is or are the only objects or persons interested or capable of benefiting under such other trust) if the Trustees shall in their absolute discretion consider such payment or transfer to be for the benefit of all or such one or more of the Discretionary Beneficiaries

(3) At the end of the Discretionary Period and subject to and in default of any appointment under sub-clause (1) the Trustees shall hold the Trust Fund upon trust for ...

If this clause is used to create a nil rate band settled legacy, the ultimate default trusts in clause (3) would generally provide that the property in the settled legacy should pass to the residuary beneficiary under the will of the testator.

12.7 FLEXIBLE WILLS CONTAINING A TERMINABLE LIFE INTEREST

12.7.1 Form of the will

Many testators wish to provide adequately for their surviving spouse and yet wish to incorporate into their wills flexibility whereby other members of the family may benefit should the surviving spouse not require the provision when the testator dies.

Although a will containing discretionary trusts or contingent trusts with overriding powers of advancement and appointment (see **12.6**) may be used to achieve the testator's wishes, the testator may prefer a will which gives his surviving spouse a direct benefit in the form of a life interest (coupled with powers of advancement in her favour over the capital), with 'an overriding power of appointment' allowing the trustees to appoint the property away from the spouse among a class of beneficiaries identified by the will.

There is an IHT advantage to drafting the will trust to leave a terminable life interest to the surviving spouse in that the property in which the spouse has an IPDI will attract the spouse exemption so no IHT will have to be paid on it. See **12.7.3.1** below. In the case of surviving spouses dying on or after 9 October 2007, any proportion of the nil rate band of the first spouse to die unused on his or her death can be transferred to the surviving spouse.

If the property left on IPDI trusts includes the deceased spouse's interest in residential property, 100% of the deceased's residential nil rate band will be transferred to the survivor. Provided the survivor dies on or after 6 April 2017 and their estate does not exceed the taper threshold, two residential nil rate bands will be available on any residential property inherited by lineal descendants. To obtain the residence nil rate band in relation to a residence in which the deceased had an IPDI, lineal descendants of the deceased IPDI beneficiary must be beneficially entitled to the residence (IHTA 1984, s 8J(5)).

EXAMPLE

Fatima dies in 2014. She leaves her estate (value £500,000), which includes her half share of the matrimonial home, on IPDI trusts to her husband, Aru. Her residential nil rate band is unused (naturally as she died before it was introduced). Aru dies in 2022/23, so two residential nil rate bands then amount to £350,000. The house is worth £350,000. He has cash and investments of £1 million. Neither he nor Fatima made any lifetime transfers chargeable to IHT. Compare the following two scenarios.

(1) The terms of the IPDI trust provide that, after Aru's death, the settled property passes to the couple's two children absolutely. Lineal descendants of Aru are beneficially entitled to the half share held on trust, so the residential nil rate band is available against the settled property as well as against Aru's own half share.

(2) The terms of the IPDI trust provide that, after Aru's death, the settled property is held on discretionary trusts for the benefit of the couple's children and grandchildren. In this case, lineal descendants of Aru are not beneficially *entitled* to the half share held on trust, so the residential nil rate band is not available against the settled property, only against Aru's own half share.

On these figures, the couple are losing the benefit of one whole residential nil rate band. During Aru's life, the trustees should review the powers of appointment available to them. If, as will usually be the case, they have wide powers to modify the terms of the trust, they should use those powers to ensure that lineal descendants will become entitled to the residence on Aru's death. It is too late to do this after his death. Section 144 of the IHTA 1984 cannot help as it does not apply where there has been an interest in possession.

12.7.2 Drafting life interest trusts subject to an overriding power of appointment

After the usual provisions dealing with payment of debts, legacies, testamentary expenses etc, and after the residuary fund defined as 'my Trust Fund' has been established, the clauses creating the beneficial trusts should be set out. Extracts of the principal clauses are set out below in the order they usually appear, ie, the life interest for the surviving spouse follows the overriding power for the trustees.

Sample clause

> My Trustees shall hold the capital and income of the Trust Fund upon such trusts in favour or for the benefit of all or such one or more of the Beneficiaries exclusive of the other or others of them in such shares or proportions if more than one and with and subject to such powers and provisions for their respective maintenance education or other benefit or for the accumulation of income … as my Trustees (subject to the application (if any) of the rule against perpetuities) by any deed or deeds … shall appoint …

This clause subjects the whole of the trust fund to a wide power of appointment. It may be exercised by the trustees to create absolute interests or interests under trusts in favour of the beneficiaries who will have been identified earlier in the will in a clause setting out various definitions (see **6.5.3**). Normally, the beneficiaries would include the testator's spouse, children and remoter issue and their respective spouses. The testator's intention would be that the trustees exercise this power only after consulting the surviving spouse (although there is no express provision requiring the consent of the spouse) and after they have taken into account all the circumstances existing at the testator's death. In such circumstances, it would not be unusual for the testator to appoint the surviving spouse as a trustee. The effect of exercising the power is to bring to an end the surviving spouse's life interest (see the following clause) in the whole or part of the trust fund, although if included in the class of beneficiaries, the trustees may appoint capital to the former life tenant.

Sample clause

Until and subject to and in default of an appointment under clause [   ]

(a)   My Trustees shall pay the income of the Trust Fund to the Life Tenant for life [or until remarriage] [if the Life Tenant shall survive me by [   ] days]

(b)   (i)   My Trustees may at any time or times during the Trust Period as to the whole or any part of the Trust Fund in which the Life Tenant has for the time being an interest in possession transfer or raise and pay the same to or for the absolute use or benefit of the Life Tenant or raise and pay or apply the same for the advancement or otherwise for the benefit of the Life Tenant in such manner as my Trustees shall in their absolute discretion think fit

(ii)   In this clause 'interest in possession' shall have the same meaning it has for the purpose of the Inheritance Tax Act 1984 and any statutory modification or re-enactment of such Act

(c)   ...

(d)   ...

This clause gives the spouse the right to receive the income from the fund until such time as the trustees choose to use the overriding power of appointment. It also gives the trustees express power to advance capital to the life tenant (who would also be identified in the definition clause in the will) should his circumstances so require. Sub-clauses (c) and (d) would set out the further trusts in the event of the trustees not exercising their overriding power of appointment.

12.7.3   Terminable immediate post-death interest trusts for lineal descendants

A further use of these trusts has arisen as a result of the residence nil rate band.

Only a limited range of settlements attract the residence nil rate band. Immediate post-death interest trusts do. Those wanting to settle property for the benefit of lineal descendants and to obtain the benefit of the residence nil rate band may consider leaving property on immediate post-death interest trusts with overriding powers allowing the trustees to appoint capital at their discretion. If the client wants to limit the settled property to the value of the residence nil rate band, it is possible to use a formula clause.

> **EXAMPLE**
>
> Grace wants to leave her estate which includes her house on trust for her grandchildren.
>
> If she leaves the estate to her grandchildren contingent on reaching 18 and the grandchildren are under 18 at the date of her death, the trust is a relevant property trust and the residence nil rate band will not be available.

> If she gives the grandchildren a right to the income from her estate and gives the trustees power to advance capital at their discretion, this is an immediate post-death interest and the residence nil rate band will be available.

When drafting an immediate post-death interest for beneficiaries who may be minors at the date of the testator's death, it is necessary to include a clause varying the effect of s 31(2) of the Trustee Act 1925, which will otherwise have a divesting effect and remove the right to income apparently conferred by the will.

Section 31 allows the trustees to apply income or accumulate it for the benefit of minor beneficiaries. Section 31(2) deals with what happens to income which has been accumulated. It provides that a minor with a vested interest in income (such as a right to income) will get the accumulated income if they reach 18, but if they do not, the income will pass with the capital. This means that the minor's interest is merely contingent and the trust will be a relevant property trust, not one creating an immediate post-death interest.

A suitable clause to disapply s 31(2) is as follow:

Sample clause

> If and so long as the Life Tenant is under the age of 18, section 31 of the Trustee Act 1925 shall not apply to the Share. The Trustees may pay or apply any income of the Share to him or for his maintenance or education or otherwise for his benefit as they shall in their discretion think fit. Any balance of the income shall be retained by the Trustees upon trust for the Life Tenant absolutely.

12.7.4 Taxation implications of an overriding power where spouse has a life interest

12.7.4.1 Inheritance tax

Death of the testator

No IHT is payable on the death of the testator since the spouse exemption is available as a result of the qualifying interest in possession given to the surviving spouse. Thus, a grant of probate can be obtained without the need to negotiate a loan to pay any IHT. This is an advantage which is not available where the property is left on discretionary or contingent trusts (see the 'Mary' example at **12.6.2.1**).

Exercise of the overriding power

The spouse has an IPDI. In so far as capital is appointed to the spouse, no IHT will arise.

If the power is exercised in favour of the other beneficiaries, the ending of the IPDI is a transfer of value which may be a PET (if an outright gift) by the life tenant so that IHT is payable only if death occurs within seven years (IHTA 1984, s 52), or may be a lifetime chargeable transfer (if the appointment is on continuing trusts). Thus, in both cases the IHT position is similar to that discussed at **10.2.4.1** in relation to partitioning trust funds.

12.7.4.2 Capital gains tax

If the exercise of the power results in someone becoming 'absolutely entitled' to the settled property against the trustees, there is a deemed disposal by the trustees. Absolute entitlement can occur where property leaves the trust following an outright appointment in favour of a beneficiary, or where the trustees appoint property to trustees to hold on new trusts (see further **10.5**). Either of these methods is possible under the power of appointment set out at **12.7.2**.

The calculation of the trustees' liability, the exemptions, reliefs and rates of tax is also similar to that for lifetime trusts (see **10.2.4.2**).

12.7.5 Drafting the deed of appointment

The drafting of the deed, and its contents, will follow closely the drafting of the deed of appointment discussed at **10.3.9**.

12.8 POSSIBLE INHERITANCE ACT CLAIM BY SURVIVING SPOUSE/CIVIL PARTNER

Testators are free to leave their property as they choose. However, certain categories of person, including surviving spouses and civil partners, are entitled to make a claim under the Inheritance (Provision for Family and Dependants) Act 1975.

Section 3(2) of the 1975 Act requires the court to have regard to the provision which the court would have ordered had the marriage or civil partnership ended in divorce or dissolution rather than death. Since the decision in *White v White* [2001] 1 AC 596, it is at least arguable that the starting point for an ancillary relief order would be an equal division. Thus a surviving spouse or civil partner who does not receive a substantial part of the capital assets but instead gets an entitlement to income, has a good chance of receiving a capital award if he makes an application.

The Court of Appeal made this point in *Berger v Berger* [2013] EWCA Civ 1395 (an application by a widow with only a life interest), although it refused the applicant leave to apply out of time. The delay had been excessive (six and a half years) and there were insufficient grounds to excuse it. In *Cowan v Foreman* [2019] EWCA Civ 1336 (also an application by a widow with no entitlement to capital for leave to apply out of time), the Court of Appeal considered that the surviving widow had a strong arguable case given the size of the estate, the length of the relationship, the fact that Mrs Cowan received only chattels of nominal value outright, she had no autonomy, no security and no direct interest in her home of 20 years.

Testators should be aware of the possibility of an Inheritance Act claim if the surviving spouse is left a terminable life interest.

12.9 IHT TREATMENT OF SETTLEMENTS CREATED ON DEATH ON OR AFTER 22 MARCH 2006

Trusts for testator's own children	Section 71A: Bereaved minor's trust (BMT) (18): • No exit or anniversary charges. • Beneficiary not treated as owning underlying capital. Section 71D: Bereaved young person's trust (18–25): • As above except that there are exit charges once beneficiary reaches 18, calculated on the length of time elapsed since beneficiary reached 18.
Immediate life interest for anyone	Immediate post-death interests (IPDI): • Beneficiary treated as beneficially entitled to underlying trust capital for IHT.
Trust for disabled beneficiary	Although trust is discretionary in form, beneficiary is treated as if he or she had a qualifying interest in possession in the capital of the trust fund.
All other trusts	Relevant property regime, ie exit and anniversary charges. (NB: Section 144 'writing back')

SUMMARY

(1)   Many wills create trusts. The Finance Act 2006 contains special IHT provisions relating to trusts created on death. Four types of trust attract special IHT treatment:

    (a)   immediate post-death interests;

    (b)   bereaved minor trusts;

    (c)   bereaved young person trusts;

    (d)   trusts for a beneficiary who is disabled within the meaning of FA 2005, Sch 1A.

(2)   Testators may not be certain whom they want to benefit and may wish to incorporate flexibility. There are a number of ways of achieving flexibility:

    (a)   precatory trusts;

    (b)   residue left on discretionary trusts. This ensures maximum flexibility;

    (c)   nil rate band discretionary trust for spouse and issue, residue to spouse;

    (d)   terminable life interest for spouse, residue to issue. This gives the surviving spouse a right to the income from the settled property and secures the spouse exemption. However, it gives flexibility as the trustees can terminate the life interest and appoint capital to the spouse or issue depending on their respective needs. If the appointment is to the spouse, there will be no IHT implications. If the appointment is to the issue, the spouse will be treated as making a PET. Such an arrangement may be vulnerable to challenge under the Inheritance (Provision for Family and Dependants) Act 1975 if no capital is made directly available to the surviving spouse.

REVIEW ACTIVITY

Question 1

Which ONE of the following statements is WRONG?

A   Settlements can be created on death which have special IHT treatment which is not available to settlements created by lifetime transfer.

B   If a settlement is to satisfy the requirements of IHTA 1984, s 71D (settlement for bereaved young people), it must be created for the testator's own children.

C   Even if a settlement satisfies the requirements of IHTA 1984, s 71D, there may be IHT exit charges when beneficiaries become entitled to capital.

D   If a settlement is to satisfy IHTA 1984, s 71D, it must not give beneficiaries a right to income.

Answer: D

All that s 71D requires in relation to income is that none is applied for anyone other than the bereaved young person(s). It is irrelevant whether the beneficiary has a right to receive income or whether it can be accumulated.

Question 2

Where s 144 of IHTA 1984 applies, the disposition of an estate on death is effectively rewritten for IHT purposes. In which of the following cases will s 144 NOT apply?

A   Property is settled by will for A for life, remainder to B. Twelve months after death, the trustees exercise an overriding power of appointment to appoint the trust fund to B.

B   Property is settled by will on discretionary trusts for the testator's spouse and issue. Twelve months after death, the trustees appoint the trust fund to the testator's spouse absolutely.

C   Property is settled by will for the testator's two children contingent on them reaching 25, and s 31 of the Trustee Act is varied to exclude the right to income at 18. The children are 23 and 21 at the date of death. Twelve months after death, the trustees exercise an overriding power of appointment to appoint the trust fund to the two children absolutely.

D   Property is settled by will on discretionary trusts for the testator's spouse and issue. Two months after death and before the PRs have vested any property in the trustees, the trustees exercise an overriding power of appointment to appoint their right to the trust fund to the testator's spouse for life.

Answer: A

Section 144 has no effect in A because s 144 applies only where there has been no interest in possession. In B and C there is no interest in possession and so writing back occurs as a result of the appointments. There is nothing to stop the trustees exercising their powers of appointment before completion of the administration (although the Revenue likes to see an express power authorising this).

CHAPTER 13

POST-DEATH ARRANGEMENTS

LEARNING OUTCOMES

After reading this chapter you will be able to:

- understand when it is possible to change the dispositions of an estate post-death and the tax consequences of this
- understand how to draft the appropriate documents to carry out the change.

13.1 INTRODUCTION

Beneficiaries and trustees may wish to rearrange dispositions of property in an estate following a death. Reasons for rearrangements include:

(a) a beneficiary's wish to redirect benefits to other members of the family who are less well provided for, either as a result of the death or generally;

(b) the saving of tax, usually IHT, particularly where the disposition of the estate does not fully utilise the deceased's nil rate band; and

(c) to utilise the lower IHT rate where the proportion of the estate passing to charity is below the required 10%.

There are various ways of redirecting assets, and there are some statutory provisions that allow this to take place in a tax-advantageous way. This chapter focuses on the most common method used – post-death variation – and explores the tax consequences of using this, and how to draft the documentation to carry it out.

The Revenue carried out a consultation on the use of deeds of variation for tax purposes, following the Budget on 8 July 2015. The aim was to assess whether there is any abuse in the way they are used. It concluded that there was no evidence of any such abuse although it said it would continue to monitor their use.

13.2 TYPES OF ARRANGEMENT

Property passing as a result of death may be redirected in a number of ways. The following are the most common examples.

13.2.1 A lifetime gift by the beneficiary of an inheritance under a will or under an intestacy

This may be an outright gift by the beneficiary. If so, it will constitute a PET for IHT and a disposal for CGT by the beneficiary. If instead the beneficiary transfers the property to trustees to hold on trust, it will be a lifetime chargeable transfer (unless it is a trust for disabled persons). For CGT, a gift to individuals will be a disposal, as will a gift to trustees whichever type of trust is selected. Creation of trusts by lifetime gift is considered in **Chapter 5**.

13.2.2 'Precatory trusts' and wills creating two-year discretionary trusts

These are flexible dispositions created by the testator. The exact testamentary effect of the will is, effectively, determined after death by the act of the personal representatives (and in some cases, the beneficiaries), and not by the testator at the time of making the will. Wills containing this type of provision were considered in **Chapter 12**.

13.2.3 Orders made under the Inheritance (Provision for Family and Dependants) Act 1975 and the capitalisation of a life interest on an intestacy

Both of these amount to rearrangements of the disposition of an estate on death. In either case, the estate is treated as if left in accordance with the terms of the rearrangement. This 'writing back' effect will affect the extent of the liability to IHT on the estate on death. (See further LPC Guide, *Legal Foundations*.)

13.2.4 Post-death variations of the dispositions of the deceased's estate

If the variation complies with the statutory requirements, the effect is to write the provisions of the variation back into the terms of the deceased's will or the intestacy law for IHT and CGT purposes. The estate on death is then treated for IHT/CGT purposes on the basis of the amended provisions and the beneficiary suffers no adverse tax consequences. If the writing back effect is not obtained, the beneficiary is left in the position of making lifetime gifts as discussed above.

Note that the writing back effect takes place only for IHT and CGT. For other purposes, such as income tax and the deliberate deprivation rules that apply when a person seeks local authority funding for care home fees, the original beneficiary is treated as making a lifetime gift of the inherited property. See *FSS v LMS (by her litigation friend, the OSS)* [2020] EWCOP 52 where it was accepted that a post-death variation could amount to deliberate deprivation causing loss of means-tested benefits.

An interesting example of the limited effect of writing back occurred in the case of *Barrs Residential & Leisure Ltd v Pleass Thomson & Co* [2020] UKUT 114 (LC). The benefit of a pitch agreement for a mobile home can be transmitted on death to a person entitled to the mobile home by virtue of the deceased's will or on intestacy (Mobile Homes Act 2013, s 3). The deceased's will was varied to give his son the mobile home. The court held that although the variation passed the mobile home to the son, that did not mean that he was a beneficiary under the terms of the deceased's will for the purposes of the Mobile Homes Act. The variation was only to be treated as the deceased's disposition for the purposes of IHT and CGT. Hence, the son acquired no right to the pitch agreement, the benefit of which remained with the executor.

Variations are discussed further at **13.3**.

13.2.5 Disclaimer of benefit

Disclaimers amount to a rejection of the assets inherited under the will or the intestacy law. The disclaimed assets then pass to the person next entitled, usually the residuary beneficiary or, where the gift disclaimed is a residuary gift, the person(s) entitled on intestacy. Disclaimers are, therefore, appropriate for use only if, following the rejection, the property passes to the person whom the original beneficiary intends to benefit. If the disclaimer complies with the statutory requirements, the property is treated as passing from the deceased to the person next entitled under the will or intestacy rules for IHT and CGT purposes.

13.2.6 Variation or disclaimer?

Post-death variations and disclaimers permit alteration of the disposition of property after a death by a beneficiary whether the deceased died testate or intestate. They offer estate planning opportunities for the beneficiary who can afford 'not to receive' property for whatever reason.

Post-death variations operate more flexibly than disclaimers. A variation permits the beneficiary positively to redirect the devolution of the property. This allows the introduction of 'new beneficiaries' into the terms of the deceased's will or the provisions of the intestacy law, and the imposition of contingencies or limitations. If not used to redirect the property among the family, a variation will sometimes be used to provide charitable payments by will attracting the IHT exemption and possibly the 36% IHT rate for the estate. There is no writing back for income tax purposes, so the variation may be subject to the parental settlement rules. See **13.5**.

A beneficiary cannot control the devolution of the property by using a disclaimer. Thus, if the disclaimed property would pass to the 'wrong beneficiary', a variation will be required to redirect its devolution as appropriate. Although a variation will enable the desired rearrangement to be achieved, the lack of 'writing back' provisions for income tax can cause difficulties where the original beneficiary wants to vary in favour of their own minor children. These income tax difficulties are considered at **13.5**. The advantage of redirecting property by disclaimer is that there is no equivalent income tax disadvantage. Thus, where possible, a disclaimer by a parent is the favourable method of effecting a post-death rearrangement in favour of minor children.

There may be excellent non-tax reasons for disclaiming an asset. For example, the asset concerned may be a lease or contaminated land subject to onerous liabilities. Disclaimer allows escape from those liabilities. A variation does not as the person varying is treated, except for the purposes of IHT and CGT, as having accepted the asset and then passed it on.

13.3 POST-DEATH VARIATIONS

13.3.1 The conditions (IHTA 1984, s 142; TCGA 1992, s 62)

13.3.1.1 Inheritance tax

To achieve the desired writing back effect, the beneficiary must enter into the variation, in writing, within two years of the deceased's death. For variations made on or after 1 August 2002, there must be a statement in the instrument of variation, by the persons making it, that IHTA 1984, s 142(1) is to apply to the variation. If the variation will result in additional IHT being payable on the estate of the deceased, the personal representatives must also join in this statement, and they can refuse to do so only if they do not hold sufficient assets to meet the additional tax liability. For deaths on or after 6 April 2012, where a variation involves any redirection of property to a charity, it is also necessary to notify the charity or charities concerned. The writing back effect of s 142 will only apply in relation to the charity exemption if HMRC has confirmation that this has been done.

A further requirement is that the variation must not be made for any consideration in money or money's worth (other than consideration in the form of other variations or disclaimers of the same estate). This is an anti-avoidance measure, illustrated by *Margaret Lau v Revenue and Customs Commissioners* [2009] STC (SCD) 352. In this case the deceased's will gave his children substantial gifts free of tax, and the residue to his wife. As this was a partly exempt estate, the IHT was calculated on grossed up values, significantly depleting the residue. The children varied their gifts with the aim that the whole estate would pass tax free to the deceased's wife, and, in return, she made lifetime gifts to the children. The variation was ineffective for the purposes of writing back under s 142(1) because of the consideration received by the children.

Provided the beneficiary complies with all of these conditions, the variation is not a transfer of value by him and so no IHT will be payable (IHTA 1984, s 17(a)).

13.3.1.2 Capital gains tax

The conditions for CGT are similar to those for IHT: the variation must be in writing, made within two years of the deceased's death and must not be made for any consideration in money or money's worth. For variations made on or after 1 August 2002, there must be a statement in the instrument of variation, by the persons making it, that TCGA 1992, s 62(6) is to apply to the variation. No CGT is payable on the deceased's death in any event so that the substitution of new beneficiaries will not affect the CGT position on the death. However, electing for writing back means that the beneficiary making the variation does not make a disposal.

There is a difference between the IHT and CGT effects of a post-death variation. A variation takes effect for the purposes of the whole of the IHTA 1984 whereas it only takes effect for the purposes of s 62 of the TCGA 1992. Section 62 is the section that deals with the passing of property on death. For other CGT purposes, the original beneficiary makes a disposal. The CGT relief is therefore significantly narrower than the corresponding relief from IHT under s 142.

This means that where the variation creates a settlement for CGT purposes and the benefit of s 62(6) of TCGA 1992 is claimed, the variation itself is treated as being made by the deceased, so that the original beneficiary does not make a disposal. However, the original beneficiary is regarded as the settlor of the settlement that comes into existence as a result of the variation (TCGA 1992, s 68C). This distinction can be significant as highlighted by the decision of the House of Lords in *Marshall (Inspector of Taxes) v Kerr* [1995] 1 AC 148. The deceased was domiciled outside the United Kingdom. A residuary legatee, who was domiciled in the United Kingdom, entered into a deed of variation under which she settled her interest. The House of Lords held that the beneficiary was to be treated as the settlor, not the deceased. The decision in *Marshall v Kerr* was put on a statutory footing by s 68C of the TCGA 1992.

13.3.2 Whether or not to choose the writing back effect

The writing back effect of a variation, unlike that of a disclaimer, is not automatic. The original beneficiary is the person who decides whether to make use of the writing back effect for either or both taxes. His decision will depend on his own tax position and that of the estate. A written statement of intent is required, and may be made for one or both taxes. In the case of a disclaimer, provided it is made in writing, writing back is automatic and no statement of intent need be made.

13.3.2.1 IHT: If the original beneficiary makes no statement that IHTA 1984, s 142(1) is to apply to the variation

For IHT purposes the property is treated as passing to the original beneficiary. He is then treated as making a PET to the new beneficiary (or a lifetime chargeable transfer if the new beneficiary is a trust). If he survives for seven years after making a PET it will become fully exempt; but if he dies within seven years it will become chargeable, thus reducing the nil rate band available for his death estate and possibly giving rise to tax being payable on the PET. (If the original beneficiary makes a lifetime chargeable transfer and dies within seven years the IHT is recalculated at full death rates, but there is no further IHT if he survives seven years.)

13.3.2.2 IHT: If the original beneficiary states that IHTA 1984, s 142(1) is to apply to the variation

There will be no possibility of a charge to IHT so far as the original beneficiary is concerned. He is not treated as having made a transfer for IHT purposes. The property is treated as passing from the deceased to the new beneficiary direct.

The effect on the IHT liability of the deceased's estate will depend on several factors, for example whether the original or new beneficiaries are exempt. There may be no change, there may be a reduction in IHT or there may be an increase in IHT. If there would be an increase, this should be weighed against the benefit to the original beneficiary of avoiding making a PET.

EXAMPLE 1

Jane dies with an unused nil rate band, leaving her £425,000 estate to her nephew, Nick. Nick decides to give this to his adult daughter.

Without a statement that s 142 is to apply:

(a)   IHT on Jane's death is £40,000 (£325,000 @ 0% and £100,000 @ 40%).

(b)   Nick makes a PET. If he dies within seven years, there will be IHT on the transfer and a reduction to his nil rate band.

With statement that s 142 is to apply:

(a)   IHT on Jane's death is the same.

(b)   Nick avoids making a PET.

The writing back effect for IHT should be chosen by Nick.

EXAMPLE 2

Dan dies having used all of his nil rate band, leaving his £500,000 estate to his wife, Shona. Shona decides to give this to their children.

Without statement that s 142 is to apply:

(a)   IHT on Dan's death is nil as the death estate is spouse exempt.

(b)   Shona makes a PET. If she dies within seven years, there will be IHT on the transfer and a reduction to her nil rate band.

With statement that s 142 is to apply:

(a)   Recalculate IHT on Dan's estate of £500,000.

   As there is no nil rate band available, the £500,000 is all charged at 40% = £200,000 tax. (The PRs would need to consent to this variation.)

(b)   Shona avoids making a PET.

In this scenario Shona should not elect for writing back into the will for IHT purposes. It is more tax-efficient for her to make a PET and hope to survive for seven years. She could take out insurance to cover the increased IHT on her own estate if she does not survive the required period.

13.3.2.3   CGT: If the original beneficiary makes no statement that TCGA 1992, s 62(6) is to apply to the variation

The original beneficiary will make a disposal for CGT to the new beneficiary. There may be a gain or a loss if the asset has increased or decreased in value since the date of death. The new beneficiary will be treated as acquiring the asset at market value at the date of the disposal. If the gain is small it may be covered by the original beneficiary's annual exemption. If the original beneficiary has losses available, these will offset the gain. In neither case will any CGT be paid.

13.3.2.4   CGT: If the original beneficiary states that TCGA 1992, s 62(6) is to apply to the variation

There will be no disposal by the original beneficiary and, therefore, no question of any liability to CGT. The asset will be treated as passing from the estate of the deceased to the new beneficiary direct. The new beneficiary will be treated as acquiring it at market value at the date of death.

EXAMPLE

(1)   Assume in Example 2 above that the £500,000 includes quoted shares that have increased in value by £10,000 since death. Shona makes no other disposals in this tax year.

Without statement that s 62(6) is to apply:

(a)   CGT on Dan's death is nil.

(b)   Shona makes a disposal with chargeable gains of £10,000. This is covered by her annual exemption so Shona pays no CGT.

(c)   The children acquire the shares at the higher current value.

With statement that s 62(6) is to apply:

(a)   CGT on Dan's death is nil.

(b)   Shona makes no disposal and pays no CGT.

(c)   The children acquire the shares at the lower value at the date of death.

In this scenario, Shona should not elect for writing back for CGT purposes.

(2)   Assume in the above example that the £500,000 includes quoted shares that have increased in value by £20,000 since death. Shona has already made several disposals realising gains which have exhausted her CGT annual exemption for the tax year.

Without statement that s 62(6) is to apply:

(a)   CGT on Dan's death is nil.

(b)   Shona makes a disposal with chargeable gains of £20,000. This is added to her other gains in the year, and the total exceeds her annual exemption, so she will pay CGT on the £20,000.

(c)   The children acquire the shares at the higher current value.

With statement that s 62(6) is to apply:

(a)   CGT on Dan's death is nil.

(b)   Shona makes no disposal and pays no CGT.

(c)   The children acquire the shares at the lower value at the date of death.

In this scenario, Shona should elect for writing back for CGT purposes.

HMRC accepts that it is possible to vary the disposition of an asset that has already been sold. The variation should state that it applies to the proceeds of sale of the asset left in the will. If the sale produced a CGT liability, the liability will become that of the object of the variation. HMRC says in the CGT Manual at CG31630:

> If the assets have vested in the legatee and the legatee has disposed of the assets before the deed is executed, then the disposal is no longer treated as an occasion of charge for the legatee. Instead it is treated as an occasion of charge for the assignee.

13.3.3   Post-death variations and charity

We have seen in **Chapter 4** that where a person leaves a sufficient amount of his estate to charity, the rest of the estate may benefit from a 36% rate of IHT (see IHTA 1984, Sch 1A). Drafting a will to achieve this requires some sort of formula clause. These can be complex, and the testator may not wish to make a gift where the amount would be so uncertain. An alternative is to redirect an appropriate amount to charity by post-death variation. This means that the surviving beneficiaries, if they are minded to give to charity, can assess how much to give, knowing the precise size of the estate. In some circumstances they may receive more overall, despite giving more to charity.

EXAMPLE

Bradley never married or formed a civil partnership and never made any transfers of value. He died leaving an estate of £500,000, entirely composed of assets in his sole name, and no debts. There are no reliefs available. His will left a gift of £15,000 to charity and the rest to his sister. The gift to charity is not large enough for the estate to qualify for the lower rate of IHT. (After deducting the nil rate band, the charitable legacy is 8.57% of the net estate.) The IHT on the estate is therefore:

£500,000 less £15,000 charity exemption = £485,000. The first £325,000 is taxed at 0% and the remaining £160,000 at 40% = £64,000.

The sister receives £421,000 from the estate.

If she varies her gift so that £18,000 in total is left to charity under the will, the estate will now qualify for the 36% IHT rate. (After deducting the nil rate band, the charitable legacy is 10.28% of the net estate.) The IHT on the estate will now be £56,520 (£500,000 less £18,000 charity exemption = £482,000; £325,000 taxed at 0% and £157,000 at 36%).

The sister receives more (£425,480) from the estate, and the charity also receives more.

In the case of deaths on or after 6 April 2012 new sub-sections 142(3A) and (3B) of IHTA 1984 provide that where property is left to a charity by variation, there is no writing back for IHT purposes unless the taxpayer provides evidence that the charity has been notified of the variation. This amendment was apparently made to deal with suspicions that some taxpayers were varying estates to create charitable legacies, claiming the IHT charity exemption and then never passing on the 'legacy' to the charity.

13.3.4 Capacity to make a variation

An original beneficiary under a will or an intestacy can make a variation in relation to his interest provided he has attained 18 years of age and has mental capacity. A beneficiary with an absolute interest may settle it on trusts for the benefit of others or make an outright gift.

EXAMPLE

David by will leaves £325,000 to John, who wishes to provide for his own child, Carol, now aged 19 years. By post-death variation, David's will is varied, leaving £100,000 in trust for Carol contingently on her attaining 25 and the residue of £225,000 for John.

13.3.4.1 Consent of the court

In some cases, the consent of the court will be needed before a variation can be made. Under the Variation of Trusts Act (VTA) 1958, the court has power to consent on behalf of beneficiaries who cannot consent for themselves, for example beneficiaries who are (inter alia) minors or are unborn or unascertained. The court's powers are wide enough to permit the variation of beneficial interests whether they are vested, contingent or discretionary, but it will exercise the powers only where the proposed arrangement is for the benefit of the beneficiary.

However, VTA 1958 applications to the court are expensive and time-consuming so are only justified if the tax saving to be achieved will be substantial. The Revenue indicates in its Inheritance Tax Manual that it may accept deeds unapproved by the court provided, of course, that they are beneficial to the minor or leave the minor's interest substantially unaffected.

Beneficiaries who lack capacity to manage their own financial affairs ('P') will be represented either by a deputy or by an attorney acting under a lasting power of attorney. As we saw in **Chapter 3**, deputies and attorneys have very limited powers to make gifts on behalf of P. Varying the disposition of an estate is essentially a lifetime gift and will normally be beyond those powers. Hence deputies and attorneys wishing to vary on behalf of P will need to apply to the Court of Protection for authority. The decision will be made by the court in P's best interests.

Problems of lack of capacity to consent generally do not arise in the context of 'flexible' wills containing discretionary trusts or an overriding power of appointment. In these cases, any rearrangement of the deceased's estate after death occurs as a result of the decision of the trustees acting under the terms of the will. The lack of ability of a beneficiary to consent is not crucial to making the proposed arrangement. This feature of flexible wills tends to make them attractive in practice (see **12.4**).

13.3.4.2   Can the estate of a deceased beneficiary be varied?

The Revenue accepts that a variation on behalf of a deceased beneficiary is possible.

Who should make the variation? According to HMRC at IHTM35042, it is the PRs of the deceased beneficiary but with the consent of their beneficiaries. If the beneficiaries are not a party to the deed of variation then HMRC will request other written evidence of their consent. It is not sufficient that the document recites the beneficiaries' consent; separate written signed consent from each beneficiary is required.

Such a variation can often save IHT.

EXAMPLE

Veronica, who is unmarried and has made no lifetime gifts, dies leaving the whole of her estate valued at £325,000 to her brother, Arthur (a divorcee). He dies soon after his sister, leaving his estate of £825,000 (£500,000 of his own plus £325,000 inherited from Veronica) to his child, Damon. Arthur's PRs, with Damon's consent, can make a variation to redirect Veronica's estate directly to Damon to save IHT.

Without variation:

(a)   IHT on Veronica's death is nil

      £325,000 is within her nil rate band

(b)   IHT on Arthur's death

      £325,000 @ 0% = Nil

      £500,000 @ 40% = £200,000

Damon receives £625,000 as a result of the death of his aunt and father.

With variation:

Arthur's PRs (with Damon's consent) make a variation of Veronica's estate to pass all her assets to Damon.

(a)   Recalculate IHT on Veronica's estate of £325,000

      IHT is still nil as the estate value is within her nil rate band

(b)   Recalculate IHT on Arthur's estate of £500,000

      £325,000 @ 0% = Nil

      £175,000 @ 40% = £70,000

As a result of the variation, Damon's total entitlement from his aunt and father is £755,000.

13.4 THE SCOPE OF THE STATUTORY PROVISIONS FOR VARIATIONS AND DISCLAIMERS

It is possible to vary or disclaim 'any of the dispositions (whether effected by will, under the law relating to intestacy or otherwise) of the property comprised in the estate immediately before his death' (IHTA 1984, s 142).

In the application of this provision the following points should be noted.

13.4.1 Interests in joint property

An interest in property held as joint tenants is an asset of the 'estate' of a deceased person for IHT. Although an interest in property held in joint tenancy passes on death by survivorship to the surviving joint tenant, it is nevertheless within the IHT (and CGT) provisions permitting variations and disclaimers following a death. This is because these provisions apply where a disposition on death is effected by will, on intestacy 'or otherwise', ie, by survivorship.

> **EXAMPLE**
>
> Alice and Bill inherited Rose Cottage as joint tenants many years ago. Since then they and their respective families have used the cottage for holidays.
>
> Alice has just died, leaving her estate by will to her only child, Clara, but her share of the cottage passes to Bill by survivorship. Bill feels Clara should have inherited her mother's interest in the cottage.
>
> Bill can effect a variation so that Alice's estate is taxed as if the joint tenancy had been severed before her death and her will had left her half of the cottage to Clara. This will be effective for IHT and CGT purposes provided Bill includes the necessary statements of intent. To complete the gift Bill must convey the legal estate to himself and Clara by a separate deed.
>
> Because writing back is effective for all IHT purposes, Bill is not treated as making a gift and so the gift with reservation of benefit provisions do not apply (see **13.4.3** below).

13.4.2 Interests in property not capable of variation

The 'estate', for IHT purposes, of a deceased person includes, inter alia:

(a)   the property in which the deceased had an interest in possession immediately before death, for example a life tenant under an existing will trust; and

(b)   the property to which the deceased is treated as entitled by application of the 'reservation of benefit' rules (FA 1986, s 102 and see **4.6.5**).

Although both of these interests may attract IHT on death as part of the deceased's estate, it is not possible for either to be the subject of a variation (or disclaimer) for taxation purposes. This is because the definition of 'estate' within the meaning of s 142 of IHTA 1984 specifically excludes each of these interests. This is because in both cases the inclusion of the interests in the IHT estate is a fiction. The property does not 'really' belong to the deceased. The legal title to property subject to a reservation is no longer owned by the deceased. Similarly, property in which the deceased had a qualifying interest in possession is held under the terms of the trust for the remainder beneficiaries.

13.4.3 Do the reservation of benefit rules apply to variations?

Do the reservation of benefit rules apply if a beneficiary (the donor) makes a post-death variation but still continues to enjoy the property? If so, any advantage intended through the post-death variation would be lost.

The IHTA 1984 applies 'as if the variation had been effected by the deceased or, as the case may be, the disclaimed benefit never conferred'. Thus, the effect for all IHT purposes of making use of the writing back effect is that the deceased is to be taken as making the variation and, therefore, is the donor of the gift. The original beneficiary under the will or the intestacy is not the donor. As a consequence, any benefit enjoyed by the beneficiary who made the variation cannot come within these provisions.

EXAMPLE 1

Edha died leaving a will containing a gift of her house to Raj. Raj occupies the house but within two years of Edha's death redirects this gift by post-death variation to his only child Padma. The variation contains the statement that s 142 is to apply. Raj remains in occupation. This will not result in a reservation of benefit to him since the gift of the house to Padma is taken to be by Edha for all IHT purposes. Raj's estate on his death will be taxed on this basis.

EXAMPLE 2

Roger dies leaving a substantial cash legacy to Jo absolutely. Jo redirects this property into a discretionary trust by means of a variation containing the relevant statement. Jo is named as one of the beneficiaries of the discretionary trust. No reservation of benefit for IHT will result as the discretionary trust is taken to be made by Roger. However, there may be income tax consequences as there are no writing back provisions for income tax equivalent to those for IHT and CGT. The result is that Jo, not Roger, will be treated as the settlor for the purposes of the income tax avoidance rules (see **6.2.11.1**).

13.4.4   Can a variation secure the residence nil rate band?

Yes. Because the variation is effective for all IHT purposes, a variation can retrospectively secure the residence nil rate band for an estate.

EXAMPLE

Tariq's will leaves a pecuniary legacy to his adult son and residue including a residence to his cohabitee. The cohabitee and son should vary the disposition of the estate to leave the residence to the son and other assets to the cohabitee.

Although writing back is not available where there has been consideration, the limitation applies only to extraneous consideration brought in from outside the estate. The section specifically allows 'cross-variations' made by beneficiaries. It is, therefore, possible for beneficiaries to agree amongst themselves to vary the disposition of an estate to give themselves different entitlements.

13.4.5   More than one variation?

Sometimes beneficiaries may want to make a number of variations in relation to the same will or intestacy. No difficulty will arise provided each variation deals with a separate part of the estate. Clearly, property given by a legacy in a will and the property in the residuary gift are separate parts each capable of being the subject of a variation. It is also accepted that two or more variations, each relating to separate items of property in residue, can be effective. For example, a residuary beneficiary can validly redirect by variation one half of the residuary property to new beneficiary A and the other half to new beneficiary B, and in each case achieve the writing back effect for IHT purposes (provided the variations contain the relevant statements).

However, the Revenue has stated (inter alia) that in its view 'an instrument will not fall within s 142 of IHTA 1984 if it further redirects any item or any part of an item that has already been redirected under an earlier instrument'. A second variation in relation *to the same property* will, therefore, not be effective for tax purposes. It is, however, possible to vary the disposition of property received following a disclaimer (and vice versa).

Similarly, a s 142 variation can be combined with a s 144 reading back.

> **EXAMPLE**
>
> Take the facts of Example 2 above where Jo varies to create a discretionary trust. If the trustees appoint a right to capital or income within two years of Roger's death, the appointment will be read back under s 144 and treated as Roger's disposition. The trustees should be advised that if they give a beneficiary a right to income within two years of death, it will create an immediate post-death variation. If they do not want to do this, they should wait two years before altering the terms of the trust.

13.4.6 Beneficiaries other than members of the family

Normally, the rearrangement will involve redistribution of the deceased's property among members of the family. However, there is no restriction in the legislation, whether for IHT or CGT, which restricts the introduction of a new beneficiary who is not a member of the family. This opens up the possibility of introducing as a beneficiary the following:

(a) A claimant under the Inheritance (Provision for Family and Dependants) Act 1975. For example, a claim by a person 'maintained by the deceased' under s 1(1)(e) of the Act for reasonable financial provision may be compromised within two years of the death. If the conditions are satisfied, this may take the form of a variation which, provided it contains the relevant statement, will achieve the writing back effect of any other post-death variation and will be effective for both IHT and CGT.

(b) A charity. A charitable donation, within the IHT exemption, can be made from the deceased's estate by introducing a charity as a legatee. If the conditions are satisfied, the terms of the will or of the intestacy law will then be read as if the deceased had made the donation himself to the named charity. There can be a further benefit of obtaining the 36% IHT rate (see **13.3.3** above).

13.4.7 Is it possible to vary a discretionary trust?

In principle this is possible under *Saunders v Vautier*. The beneficiaries must be of full age and capacity and between then entitled to the whole beneficial interest. However, in practice, there are usually minor, unborn and unascertained beneficiaries which make this impossible.

> **EXAMPLE**
>
> Taj created a discretionary trust in his will for the benefit of his wife and two children. At the date of his death the two children are over the age of 18. The three beneficiaries can vary the trust.
>
> However, if the trust was for his wife, children and grandchildren and the grandchildren are minors at the date of death, a variation is not possible.
>
> The inability to vary is not normally a problem because the trustees will have power to make an appointment under IHTA 1984, s 144 which will be written back into the will. This is likely to be easier in practice than a variation (even where a variation is possible) as there will usually be only two trustees whereas there are likely to be several beneficiaries.

13.4.8 Can PRs of a deceased person vary to give up a life interest left to them?

Where a person is left a life interest, the value of the trust property is part of their estate for IHT purposes. If they die within two years of being left the life interest, it would be attractive from an IHT point of view for their PRs to give up the life interest on their behalf to avoid aggregation of the trust property.

> **EXAMPLE**
>
> Callum leaves his estate of £1m to his daughter, Dana, for life, remainder to her children. Dana dies shortly after Callum with an estate of £300,000 and a single NRB.
>
> The £1m trust fund is aggregated with her free estate, and IHT is payable on the total. The IHT is apportioned and the trust bears its share, but Dana's free estate will be reduced by its share of the IHT. Without the trust fund, there would be no tax.

HMRC does not accept that it is possible to vary an interest in possession after the death of the beneficiary as there is nothing left to vary. However, it will accept a disclaimer under IHTA 1984, s 93. See IHTM 35042.

Section 93 of IHTA 1984 provides that:

> Where a person becomes entitled to an interest in settled property but disclaims the interest, then, if the disclaimer is not made for a consideration in money or money's worth, this Act shall apply as if he had not become entitled to the interest.

There is no statutory time limit for disclaimers under s 93, but as a matter of general law, a disclaimer is not possible once any benefit has been taken.

HMRC will investigate the question of benefit carefully. For example, IHTM 35165 says that 'a beneficiary who is given a life interest in the house in which they live would find it difficult to argue that they had not received any benefit from the bequest'.

The section is of general application so, while it applies to interests arising on death, it also applies to interests arising under lifetime settlements. Any kind of interest in settled property can be disclaimed under this provision, including reversionary interests. There was uncertainty as to whether or not a beneficiary had a sufficient interest to allow disclaimer. Matthews J considered this point in *Smith and another v Michelmores Trust Corp Ltd* [2021] EWHC 1425 (Ch) and said (*obiter*) that in his opinion a disclaimer by a discretionary beneficiary was possible. Such a beneficiary has various rights under a trust, including the right to be considered and the right to restrain by injunction a threatened breach of trust by the trustees.

HMRC states that a disclaimer under s 93 should be made by the PRs of the deceased: see IHTM 35164.

13.5   INCOME TAX, TAX AVOIDANCE AND POST-DEATH ARRANGEMENTS

13.5.1   Income before a variation or disclaimer is made

There are no specific income tax provisions equivalent to the IHT and CGT provisions where a variation or disclaimer has been made. Thus, income received before the variation or disclaimer from the property concerned will be taxed as the income of the original beneficiary. This will apply even if the beneficiary has specifically given up all income from the property since the date of death. For example, if the original beneficiary by variation redirects a specific legacy of shares, he remains liable to pay any income tax on dividends paid before the variation.

13.5.2   Income after a variation or disclaimer is made

In most cases, once the rearrangement has been made, the original beneficiary ceases to be liable to pay income tax on income produced after the variation or disclaimer. The new beneficiary becomes liable for income tax on income produced by the property concerned. However, the position will be different where the new beneficiary is the minor child of the original beneficiary. In such cases the parent will remain liable for income tax on the income even though he does not enjoy it or own the property which produces it. The reason is the income tax anti-avoidance provisions discussed at **4.6.2** and **4.6.4**. These are of general application and can apply to pre- and to post-death arrangements.

13.5.2.1 How do the income tax avoidance rules apply to variations?

If the variation creates a settlement for income tax purposes from which the original beneficiary may continue to benefit, he will still be liable to pay income tax on all the settlement income (see **6.15.1**). To avoid this, the variation must be drafted so as to exclude the settlor and spouse from all enjoyment from the property which has been redirected, and from its income.

If the variation creates a settlement for income tax purposes in which the original beneficiary's minor unmarried children may benefit, the position is similar. However, the original beneficiary is only liable to pay income tax on settlement income that is actually paid to or applied for his minor unmarried children, and is not liable in relation to income that is accumulated.

If the anti-avoidance provisions apply, they will cease to do so once the children have reached their majority or have married; from then onwards their parents will no longer be taxed on the settlement income.

EXAMPLE 1

A variation by Hannah (of the estate she inherited from her father) redirects £325,000 absolutely to her adult children. The children will pay income tax on the income of the property.

EXAMPLE 2

A similar post-death variation is made by Ania but her children (the new beneficiaries) are minors. Even though the children have an absolute (vested) entitlement to the £325,000, the income of the property actually paid to or applied for the children is deemed to be Ania's for tax purposes.

13.5.2.2 Disclaimers distinguished

A variation is the positive redirection of benefit by the original beneficiary, whereas a disclaimer is merely the rejection of a benefit. The Revenue does not consider a disclaimer to be a 'settlement' and so to come within the income tax anti-avoidance provisions. The consequence is that income of property which is disclaimed by a parent is not taxed as though it is still his, even if his minor unmarried child inherits the property as a result of the disclaimer. Similarly, any capital gains made would not be taxed as the settlor's. Thus, parents who are considering post-death rearrangements for the benefit of their children should, where possible, use a disclaimer instead of a variation which might fall within the provisions.

13.6 DRAFTING A POST-DEATH VARIATION AND THE STATEMENT OF INTENT

13.6.1 Is a deed required?

Both IHTA 1984, s 142 and TCGA 1992, s 62 require only an instrument in writing, but as a post-death variation is a gratuitous promise to transfer property, it should be by deed to be enforceable. Further, unless it is by deed the deceased's personal representatives may not be prepared to act in accordance with its terms.

13.6.2 The date and opening words

Sample clause

This deed of variation is made the [   ] day of [   ]

Two thousand and ...

13.6.3 Parties

Both IHTA 1984, s 142 and TCGA 1992, s 62 require only 'the persons who benefit or would benefit under the disposition ... to make the written instrument'. However, often there will be three parties:

(a)   the original beneficiaries (who give up the benefit);

(b)   the new beneficiaries (who receive the property and thus will include trustees if the variation creates a trust); and

(c)   the personal representatives of the deceased's estate (who must also join in any statement that s 142(1) IHT is to apply if additional IHT is payable as a result of the variation).

Sample clause

BETWEEN

(1)   [name and address] ('the Original Beneficiary')

(2)   [name and address] ('the New Beneficiary')

(3)   [name and address] ('the Executors')

Personal representatives should be made parties for their own protection when they distribute property in accordance with the post-death variation rather than the will in its original form. It is not essential to join the new beneficiaries in receipt of property as parties, but many practitioners prefer to do so.

13.6.4 Supplemental to the will or intestacy

The deed of variation is made to relate expressly to the deceased's death.

Sample clause

Supplemental to the will [with ... codicil(s)] ('the Will') of [name] ('the Deceased') and to the other documents and events specified in the Schedule

The Schedule will contain details of the will, date of death, grant of probate, etc.

13.6.5 Recitals

Recitals will always be used in the deed to explain the circumstances giving rise to the variation. Usually the recitals are restricted to statements relating to:

(a)   the entitlement of the original beneficiary under the will or the intestacy of the deceased; and

(b)   the wish of the original beneficiary to vary the provisions of the will or the intestacy in the manner stated in the operative part of the variation.

Sample clause

WHEREAS

(A) Under the Will the Original Beneficiary was given [   ] interest ('the Interest') in [all of the] [x% of the] residuary estate of the Deceased

(B) The Original Beneficiary wishes to vary the dispositions effected by the Will in relation to the Interest in the following manner

The interest will be an 'absolute' interest or a 'life interest' and the clause should be completed accordingly, showing whether it relates to the whole or part of the residuary estate.

13.6.6 The operative part

It is often convenient when drafting the operative part of a post-death variation to consider how the will, or a codicil to it, might have been drafted for the testator before his death. This can often give valuable guidance on drafting the post-death variation. For example, in the context of a variation to create a nil rate band legacy for a child, only a short provision is required.

Sample clause

> Now this deed irrevocably witnesses as follows:
>
> By way of variation of the disposition made by the Will the Original Beneficiary declares that the Will shall have effect as if it contained a pecuniary legacy to the New Beneficiary of an amount on which no IHT is chargeable other than at the nil rate on the death of the Deceased such legacy to be discharged from the Interest.

An alternative approach is to draft replacement provisions in full, ensuring that the wording and definitions are consistent with the will.

Sample clause

> By way of variation of the disposition made by the Will the Original Beneficiary declares that the Will shall have effect as if clauses 3 and 4 were omitted and replaced by the following:
>
> '3. I give £10,000 to The Landmark Trust (registered charity number 243312) for its general charitable purposes and I direct that the receipt of a person who appears to be a proper officer of The Landmark Trust shall be a sufficient discharge to my Executors.
>
> 4. I give £100,000 to each of my granddaughters, Bella Jones and Rebecca Brown, free of tax.'

If a legacy is being introduced into the will by the post-death variation, it should be considered whether it is to be a legacy 'subject to' or 'free of' IHT. In the former case, any IHT which does become payable is paid by the legatee. The payment of the legacy will be directed to be made from a particular part of the estate, which normally will be the residue.

If trusts, rather than outright gifts, are to be created by the variation, these may either be set out in a schedule to the deed or it may refer to trusts created by a separate instrument. For example, the original beneficiary may wish to direct that his interest be transferred to the trustees of a settlement created by the deceased during his lifetime for his grandchildren.

13.6.7 Achieving the writing back effect

To achieve the writing back effect for tax purposes, there must be a statement in the written variation by the beneficiaries making the variation that it is intended that IHTA 1984, s 142(1) and/or TCGA 1992, s 62(6) shall apply to the variation.

If the variation causes additional IHT to become payable, for example where a spouse gives up a benefit and the spouse exemption is lost, the PRs must join in the statement. Only if the PRs have no funds available to them for payment of any extra IHT may they refuse to join in the statement. This protects PRs who have already distributed the estate before they become liable to pay the extra IHT resulting from the written variation.

If there will be additional IHT payable as a result of a variation made on or after 1 August 2002, the persons making the variation and the PRs must supply a copy of the variation to the Revenue within six months of the variation being made (IHTA 1984, s 218A (inserted by FA 2002)) or be liable for a fine (IHTA 1984, s 245A (inserted by FA 2002)). If the variation results in less IHT being payable, the PRs will want to supply a copy of the variation to HMRC to explain why less IHT is payable than would appear to be payable on the original disposition of the estate.

Sample clause

> The Parties hereto hereby declare pursuant to section 142(2) of the Inheritance Tax Act 1984 and section 62(7) of the Taxation of Chargeable Gains Act 1992 that section 142(1) of the Inheritance Tax Act 1984 and section 62(6) of the Taxation of Chargeable Gains Act 1992 shall apply to the variation made by this deed

If the variation provides for *any* property to go to charity (whether or not it means the 36% rate applies), the writing back effect for IHT will not apply unless the charity has been notified and HMRC has confirmation of this. It is not necessary to include this in the deed, however, and the notification and confirmation can be carried out by letter.

SUMMARY

(1)   Beneficiaries can redirect property they inherit or acquire as a result of death without tax implications for themselves if they comply with certain statutory requirements. It therefore allows a further opportunity for tax-efficient lifetime giving.

(2)   The most common method is a post-death variation allowing the beneficiary to redirect the property in whatever way he chooses. A disclaimer is a rejection by the beneficiary, and the property then passes in accordance with terms of the will or testacy.

(3)   By including a statement of intent, a beneficiary can have the variation written back, ie treated as if made by the deceased on death, for either or both IHT and CGT purposes. A disclaimer made in writing within two years of death is automatically written back. There is no need for a statement of intent.

(4)   Writing back for IHT:

    (a)   saves the original beneficiary from making a transfer of value;

    (b)   allows the original beneficiary to give away property and continue to use it without it being a gift with reservation of benefit;

    (c)   can allow the reduced IHT rate to apply to the estate;

    (d)   is not usually appropriate if it means more IHT becomes payable on the estate.

(5)   Writing back for CGT:

    (a)   saves the original beneficiary from making a disposal;

    (b)   means that the acquisition value for the new beneficiary is the value at death;

    (c)   may not be necessary if the gain is covered by the original beneficiary's losses and/or annual exemption.

(6)   To achieve the writing back effect, the variation must:

    (a)   be in writing;

    (b)   be made within two years of death;

    (c)   not be for consideration in money or money's worth;

    (d)   contain a statement of intent;

    (e)   (if it involves benefit to a charity) be notified to the relevant charity.

REVIEW ACTIVITY

Question 1

Alison died in February 2022, having used all of her nil rate band in her lifetime. She left her £1 million estate (which included a holiday cottage) to her husband, Bill. Bill has never made any lifetime gifts or disposals for CGT. He wishes to pass the cottage to his niece. It was worth £150,000 at Alison's death and is now worth £200,000. Bill thinks he may still use the cottage occasionally but could afford to pay a market rent. He is 65 and in good health.

Which ONE of the following is most likely to be CORRECT?

A   Bill should make a variation in relation to the cottage and claim writing back for both IHT and CGT purposes.

B   Bill should disclaim his right to the cottage.

C   Bill should make a variation in relation to the cottage and claim writing back for CGT but not IHT.

D   Bill should make a variation in relation to the cottage and claim writing back for IHT but not CGT.

Answer: C

A variation will ensure that the property passes to his niece, whereas this would not necessarily be the case under a disclaimer.

At present there is no IHT payable on Alison's estate as it is all spouse exempt, but she had no available nil rate band. If Bill re-directs the cottage to his niece and claims writing back for IHT, although he will avoid making a gift with reservation of benefit, if he continued to use the cottage, there is the considerable disadvantage that the estate must now pay IHT on £150,000. It would be better for Bill to make a PET to his niece, and he can either not use the cottage or use it and pay a proper fee for his use. (Had he wanted to redirect the cottage to children or grandchildren, the residence nil rate band of £175,000 in 2022/23 would have been available.)

For CGT purposes, if Bill does not claim writing back he will make a chargeable gain of £50,000, and even after use of his annual exemption he will pay tax, unless he has losses available. It will be preferable to elect for reading back. This will avoid an immediate CGT liability. The niece will, however, take the cottage with an acquisition value of £150,000, rather than £200,000.

Question 2

Which ONE of the following correctly completes the sentence? 'A post-death variation is not validly made ...

A   unless the parties include the personal representatives, the original and the new beneficiaries.'

B   unless it is made by deed.'

C   if it deals with property held by the deceased as joint tenant.'

D   unless it is made within 2 years of death.'

Answer: D

The variation must be in writing and made within two years of death. It is usually made in a deed, but does not have to be. The original beneficiary must be a party. It is usual for the executors to be a party also (and they must join in any claim for IHT writing back if it will mean more IHT for the estate). The new beneficiaries are also often included as parties, but need not be. It is possible to vary the disposition of property passing by survivorship.

TRUST ADMINISTRATION

LEARNING OUTCOMES

After reading this chapter you will be able to:

- understand typical management powers available to trustees
- understand how to draft the documents to effect a change of trustee
- understand the tax consequences of trusts receiving income and distributing it to beneficiaries, and of trustees selling trust assets.

14.1 INTRODUCTION

Many aspects of trust administration have been considered in the earlier chapters in this book. Most of these matters have related to the dispositive provisions of the trust instrument, ie the provisions dealing with the beneficiaries and beneficial entitlement, and include the following:

(a) TA 1925, ss 31 and 32 in **Chapters 5** and **10**;

(b) the powers of trustees in **Chapter 11**;

(c) advances and appointments by trustees in favour of beneficiaries in **Chapters 9** and **10**;

(d) capital tax implications of changes in beneficial entitlement arising from (a) and (b).

As well as dealing with the distribution of trust property from time to time, the trustees must also ensure that the day-to-day management of the trust is carried out correctly. This chapter considers some of the more important duties and powers that trustees have in administering a trust. These include:

(a) trustee investments;

(b) the appointment of trustees;

(c) vesting trust property in trustees and in beneficiaries;

(d) taxation liability arising during the trust period, including CGT on sales by trustees on rearrangements of the investment portfolio and the income tax liabilities of the trustees and beneficiaries; and

(e) accounting for the trust assets and income.

14.1.1   International requirements to report information on trusts

Governments are taking steps to promote transparency in relation to the beneficial ownership of funds. The USA was the first to do this with the Foreign Account Tax Compliance Act (FATCA), but other countries swiftly followed. The most important exchange regimes are:

- Foreign Account Tax Compliance Act (FATCA)
- Common Reporting Standard (CRS)
- EU Directive on administrative co-operation in tax matters (DAC)

The UK implemented DAC by means of the CRS which will presumably be applied in the rest of the EU. The USA has not signed up to CRS.

The systems differ slightly but we will look at FATCA by way of illustration. FATCA is a piece of United States legislation which, as a result of intergovernmental agreement, has application to the UK (FA 2013, s 222). The aim of FATCA is to impose a burden on certain persons or bodies who pay monies to US nationals to report this to the US tax authorities. Whilst it is mainly banks and investment management providers who are affected by this, UK non-charitable trusts are also within the ambit of FATCA. This is so even if the trust has no link currently to any US national.

Very broadly, the effect of FATCA upon trustees (and their advisers) is that they must firstly assess the status of the trust. The trust may be categorised as a Non-Financial Foreign Entity or a Financial Institution, depending on several factors connected with the investments held by the trust, how they are managed, and the identity of the trustees. If the trust is a Financial Institution then it must be registered with the US tax authorities and ensure that it reports (via HMRC) any payments to US nationals. Trustees of a trust that is a Non-Financial Foreign Entity do not need to do this, but must review the status of the trust if circumstances change.

There is further detailed guidance in relation to the effect of FATCA upon lawyers and their clients which has been issued jointly by The Law Society, The Institute of Chartered Accountants in England and Wales (ICAEW) and the Society of Trusts and Estates Practitioners (STEP).

14.1.2   Money Laundering, Terrorist Financing and Transfer of Funds (Information on the Payer) Regulations 2017

The Money Laundering, Terrorist Financing and Transfer of Funds (Information on the Payer) Regulations 2017 ('the 2017 Information on the Payer Regulations') (SI 2017/692) came into force on 26 June 2017 and implement the 4th Anti-Money Laundering Directive (2015/849/EU) in the UK. The Directive came into force on 25 June 2015 and Member States were required to implement it by 26 June 2017.

The principle behind the Directive is that anonymous structures (companies and trusts) should be prevented from financing terrorism and laundering money. Therefore, the Directive imposes the following obligations:

- trustees of 'relevant trusts' must keep and provide certain information;
- HMRC must maintain a trusts register of 'taxable relevant trusts';
- trustees of 'taxable relevant trusts' must register information.

The register was originally open only to law enforcement agencies and not to the public. The 5th Anti-Money Laundering Directive (2018/843) was adopted by the European Parliament on 19 April 2018. Member States were required to implement it by 20 January 2020. It requires that the register should be open to those with a legitimate interest and indicates that there should be transparency in the ownership of corporate entities and trusts. This obviously raises serious privacy issues.

Despite Brexit, the Treasury Consultation Paper on the Directive published in April 2019 stated in relation to the Directive that the UK government 'shares the objectives which it seeks to achieve on the prevention of the use of the financial system for the purposes of money laundering or terrorist financing'.

The question of 'legitimate interest' is left to individual States to define, and the Government stated in the Consultation Paper that the UK would be taking a narrow approach. It said at 9.44:

> In this context, the government considers someone who has a legitimate interest in this data will:
> - have active involvement in anti-money laundering or counter-terrorist financing activity
> - have reason to believe that the trust or person that is the subject of the legitimate interest enquiry is involved with money laundering or terrorist financing: in other words, speculative enquiries into all or multiple trusts on TRS will not be deemed legitimate
> - have evidence underpinning that belief.

14.1.2.1   The 4th Anti-Money Laundering Directive

The following is a brief explanation of the main requirements of the 2017 Information on the Payer Regulations under the 4th Anti-Money Laundering Directive. The 2017 Information on the Payer Regulations impose the following obligations:

- trustees of 'relevant trusts' must keep and provide certain information;
- HMRC must maintain a trusts register of 'taxable relevant trusts';
- trustees of 'taxable relevant trusts' must register information.

A relevant trust is defined in reg 42 as a UK trust which is an express trust, or a non-UK trust which is an express trust and receives income from a source in the United Kingdom or has assets in the UK on which it is liable to pay one or more of the taxes specified in reg 45(14) (see below for the taxes specified).

Regulation 45(14) provides that a taxable relevant trust is a relevant trust in any year in which its trustees are liable to pay any of the taxes specified: income tax, capital gains tax, inheritance tax, stamp duty land tax, land and buildings transaction tax, stamp duty reserve tax.

Many trusts will be taxable relevant trusts in one year and not in another. For example, a discretionary trust holding a non-income producing asset such as a residence will have no income tax or CGT liability and in most years will have no IHT liability. However, on 10-year anniversaries, there will be a liability to pay an anniversary charge and the trust will be taxable in that year.

Note that trustees who have mandated income to beneficiaries have no income tax liability, and therefore the trust will not be taxable unless it has a liability for another tax.

Regulation 44(1) provides that trustees of a relevant trust must keep information on the trust and information on the beneficial owners:

(1) Information about the trust:
   (a) a contact address for the trustees; and
   (b) the full name of any advisers who are being paid to provide legal, financial or tax advice to the trustees in relation to the trust.
(2) Information about beneficiaries, trustees, settlor and any protector. Except where there is a class of beneficiaries, not all of whom have been determined, the following is required:
   (a) full name;

(b)   national insurance number or unique taxpayer reference, if any;

(c)   if the individual does not have a national insurance number or unique taxpayer reference, their usual residential address;

(d)   if the address provided under sub-paragraph (c) is not in the UK:

    (i)   passport number or identification card number, with the country of issue and the expiry date of the passport or identification card; or

    (ii)   if the individual does not have a passport or identification card, the number, country of issue and expiry date of any equivalent form of identification;

(e)   date of birth;

(f)   the nature of the individual's role in relation to the trust.

The collection of all this information is obviously burdensome for trustees and may involve people who are very unlikely ever to benefit, for example 'default' beneficiaries. HMRC has recognised this and in its guidance says:

> We want to get an accurate picture of who can benefit from a trust. Some trusts may list named individuals, who only become beneficiaries contingent upon, for example, the death of a named beneficiary or in circumstances where there are no remaining named beneficiaries or beneficiaries in a class. Where this occurs we are content that the individuals are listed as a class of beneficiaries, until such time as the contingent event occurs.

The trustees must disclose this information to law enforcement agencies and to financial institutions or professional advisers who are required to carry out due diligence.

Trustees of taxable relevant trusts have to register the above information together with additional information about the trust. The information must be provided on or before 31 January following the tax year in which the trustees were first liable to pay the UK taxes set out in reg 45(14).

Following registration, the trustees must, in any year in which the trust is taxable, update the register to reflect any changes to the information placed on the register or confirm that there are no changes. In years in which there is no tax liability, there is no requirement to update the register.

Where a trust is liable to income tax or capital gains tax, registration must be completed by 5 October following the end of the tax year in which the liability arises. This is to give HMRC time to issue self-assessment tax returns.

14.1.2.2   The 5th Anti-Money Laundering Directive

The Money Laundering and Terrorist Financing (Amendment) Regulations 2019 (SI 2019/1511) came into force on 10 January 2020. The Regulations implemented the bulk of the 5th Anti-Money Laundering Directive, but they did not include the amendments to the trust registration service.

The Money Laundering and Terrorist Financing (Amendment) (EU Exit) Regulations 2020 (SI 2020/991) (the '2020 Exit Regulations') came into force on 6 October 2020 and finally implement the changes to the Register.

As explained above, the Register must be open to anyone with a 'legitimate interest'. However, the UK is interpreting legitimate interest as confined to those involved in fighting money laundering and terrorist financing. There will be no general access.

Trustees of all UK express trusts (and non-EU resident express trusts that acquire UK land or property or enter into a new business relationship with an entity obliged to do due diligence on or after 10 March 2020) must register those trusts whether or not the trust has incurred a UK tax liability, unless they are excluded from the registration requirement.

The January 2020 technical consultation said that the Government proposed to define the scope of the Regulations in a way that was proportionate to the risk. It therefore proposed that trusts should not be required to register where:

- their purpose and structure meant payments to beneficiaries were predetermined and highly controlled; and
- they were already supervised by HMRC or other regulatory bodies.

The 2020 Exit Regulations insert a new Sch 3A into the Money Laundering, Terrorist Financing and Transfer of Funds (Information on the Payer) Regulations 2017 setting out the UK non-taxable trusts which will be excluded from the registration requirement.

The excluded trusts (so far as is relevant to private client lawyers) are as follows:

(1)   *Legislative trusts*: for example the statutory trust imposed on intestacy or co-ownership of land.

(2)   *Trusts of insurance policies*: Trusts of policies paying out only on the death, terminal or critical illness or permanent disablement of the person assured; or to meet the cost of healthcare services provided to the person assured.

(3)   *Charitable trusts*

(4)   *Pilot trusts* holding property with a value not exceeding £100, and created before the Regulations came into force.

(5)   *Will trusts* where:

    (a)   the trust is holding only the property comprised in a person's estate on death, and

    (b)   less than two years has passed since that person's death.

(6)   *Death benefit trusts* where:

    (a)   the trust is holding only benefits received on the death of the person assured under a policy within para 4, and

    (b)   less than two years has passed since that person's death.

The exclusion for will trusts is very welcome but note that it is limited to two years, so unless the trust is wound up within two years of death, it will have to be registered at the end of that period (or earlier if assets are received from outside the estate). Note that HMRC considers that if a will leaves the estate to trustees on trust to pay debts, legacies and hold the balance for one or more residuary beneficiaries, there is a trust of the entire estate which will have to be registered if the administration of the estate has not been completed within the two year period.

In addition, trusts 'meeting legislative requirements' are excluded. These are:

- trusts for bereaved minors or bereaved young persons (IHTA 1984, s 71A or s 71D)
- heritage funds
- personal injury trusts
- trusts for tenants' service charges
- trusts for a disabled beneficiary.

A number of responses suggested that bare trusts should be exempted on the basis that the risk of money laundering was low. Paragraph 15 of Sch 3A introduces a limited exemption which applies only where a trust is created on the transfer or disposal of an asset in order to hold the legal title to the asset for the person to whom the transfer or disposal is being made until the time when the procedure required by law to effect the transfer or disposal of legal title is completed. This would cover a delay while a transfer of shares was registered but not the situation where one person holds as a nominee for another.

The registration deadlines under the 2017 Information on the Payer Regulations were linked to submitting tax returns. Given that the link to tax no longer exists under the 5th Directive, the Government no longer considered that deadline to be appropriate. Both the 2019 and 2020 consultations accepted that there would have to be a long lead-in period to allow for the huge number of existing trusts that will have to register.

However, the intention is that, once the system is up and running, registration will be part of the creation process, so there will be a very short registration period. Hence, at the end of a transition period, most trusts will be required to register details within 90 days of creation. Will trusts holding only the original assets will have to register within 90 days of acquiring new assets or the end of the two-year period.

The enormous volume of existing non-taxable trusts requiring registration meant that there had to be a lengthy transitional period. Non-taxable trusts in existence when the Regulations came into force had until 1 September 2022 to register. Those coming into existence afterwards had until 1 September 2022 or 90 days whichever was the longer.

A number of responses to the January 2020 consultation made the point that the proposed requirement for non-EEA trusts to register when entering a 'business relationship' with a UK obliged entity went further than the Directive required and would have negative consequences for the UK financial sector due to the requirement for non-EEA trusts that use UK-based advisers to register. These respondents were concerned that the proposals would discourage trustees of non-EEA trusts from using UK based advisers, due to the additional costs of complying with the registration requirements and the potential loss of confidentiality as a result of registration. Respondents felt that it was likely that those trustees would use services outside the UK as a result.

It was suggested that the Government should not require trusts to register if their only connection to the UK is through a service provider such as an investment manager, lawyer or accountant. There was also concern as to when a 'business relationship' is entered into.

The July 2020 summary of responses said (at 2.14) that, for the purposes of the Trusts Register, 'business relationship' means a business, professional or commercial relationship that arises out of the professional activities of the obliged entity and that is expected, at the time the relationship is established, to endure for a period of time – in the Government's view, at least 12 months.

The Government recognised that the registration requirement could have adverse effects on UK business and said (at 2.15) that it was opting 'to take a measured approach and will only require non-UK trusts to register on entering a business relationship with a UK obliged entity if the trust has at least one UK resident trustee'. This means that non-UK trusts will not be required to register if their only link to the UK is through a business relationship with a UK based adviser. The 2020 Exit Regulations amend reg 42(2) of the 2017 Information on the Payer Regulations to achieve this result.

14.2 MANAGEMENT POWERS OF TRUSTEES

When creating a settlement, particularly a discretionary settlement, the settlor will wish to incorporate wide-ranging powers for the trustees covering all aspects of the trust fund and its administration. The settlor must bear in mind the present and future trust property, the wide-ranging nature of the trusts and the wide class of beneficiaries. The trust may continue for many years, so it is necessary to consider all the provisions which may be of assistance to the trustees in the future. It is usual to incorporate these wide powers by inserting them in a schedule to the trust instrument.

14.2.1 Other matters relating to the trustees

Apart from the appointment and retirement of the trustees referred to in **14.4**, express provision in relation to the following will normally be made.

14.2.1.1 Self-dealing

The fiduciary position of the trustees prevents them from purchasing the trust property or entering into any other transaction affecting the trust property where the trustees' duties and personal self-interest are in conflict. Express provision may permit self-dealing by the trustees.

Given that in many smaller family trusts the beneficiaries are also trustees, it is important to include provisions allowing trustees to 'self-deal'. It is also important to review the trust provisions carefully when advising trustees who are also beneficiaries as provisions vary enormously. Some require there to be one independent trustee; others have more complicated requirements.

14.2.1.2 Losses

To protect an honest trustee, the trust instrument will often contain a general indemnity against loss to the trust fund caused by the trustee or an agent (other than where there is wilful fraud or dishonesty of the trustee).

14.2.1.3 Delegation of powers

Trustees cannot delegate their functions as trustee to others unless authorised to do so. The trust instrument may contain express powers to do this, but, if not, there are statutory powers. If the trustees collectively wish to delegate some of their specific functions, for example those concerning investment management, they are permitted to do so by s 11 of TA 2000. This allows trustees to delegate 'delegable functions' to an agent, who can be anyone except a beneficiary. Delegable functions do not include decisions on distributing trust property to beneficiaries, paying fees and appointing trustees. Having made the appointment, the trustee must continue to review it from time to time. It may be desirable expressly to exclude the limitation on a beneficiary being an agent.

Instead of all the trustees wanting to delegate a specific function, one or more of the trustees may wish to delegate all their functions for a period, for example if out of the country for a few months.

Section 25 of TA 1925 (as substituted by the Trustee Delegation Act 1999) permits trustees to delegate by power of attorney any of their powers and discretions for up to 12 months. In addition, s 9 of TLATA 1996 permits trustees of land to delegate by power of attorney their functions in relation to the land, for example their power of sale, to beneficiaries of full age who are beneficially entitled to an interest in possession in the land.

14.2.1.4 Payment of trustees

Trustees are fiduciaries and must not make an unauthorised profit from their position as trustees. Section 29 of TA 2000 provides authorisation for trustees to charge for their time spent and work done, provided a number of conditions are satisfied (see **11.2.3.5**). Payment may also be authorised by the court, and by the beneficiaries of the trust, provided that all the beneficiaries have capacity and all agree. More commonly, though, trust instruments will contain an express provision permitting trustees to charge for their work. Such clauses will vary as to what they permit. Some may allow any trustee to charge for any type of work done, but others may be limited to only allowing trustees who are professionals or are in business to charge (see **11.2.9.1**). Many charging clauses allow a professional trustee to charge 'reasonable' charges. The question of what is reasonable is an objective one. The mere fact that professionals are charging their normal charge-out rate does not mean that the charges are reasonable. See *Pullan v Wilson* [2014] EWHC 126 (Ch). Note that all trustees are entitled to be reimbursed from the trust for out of pocket expenses properly incurred whilst acting as trustees (TA 2000, s 31).

14.3 TRUSTEE INVESTMENTS

14.3.1 Retention of the original trust fund

For a settlement to be effective, it needs property to be subject to the trusts. When a settlement is created the initial trust fund may consist of cash, or assets (eg, shares or land), or a combination of cash and assets. The trustees must decide whether they are permitted to keep the initial trust fund as it is and, if so, whether in fact they should do so.

Problems often arise where the assets settled are shares in a family company. Should the trustees retain the investment as it is, thereby allowing the family to maintain control of the company, or should they sell the shares and diversify? It can be a difficult decision for trustees, particularly as different groups of beneficiaries are likely to have very different views. A vivid example of getting it wrong is *Gregson v HAE Trustees Ltd* [2008] EWHC 1006 (Ch) where the individuals who built up Courts Furniture Stores (in its day a hugely successful high street chain) settled the shares for the benefit of the family. The trustees retained the shares and lost everything when the company went into insolvent liquidation. The beneficiaries were not happy.

Most lifetime settlements and will trusts are drafted by professionals who will ensure that the settlement gives the trustees the widest possible powers of investment and enables them to keep any assets transferred to them by the settlor or from the estate.

The TA 2000 implies similar powers into trusts where there are no express powers, for example, where a statutory trust arises under the AEA 1925 on the death of someone intestate.

14.3.2 Suitable investments

In deciding whether to retain permitted assets, the trustees must consider the suitability of the assets for the aims of the settlement. This is also a governing factor when deciding how to invest any cash that may have been settled.

EXAMPLE 1

A settlement is created for Donna for life with remainder to Nigel. The trustees are faced with competing needs: Donna requires an income from the trust fund whilst Nigel needs the real value of the capital to improve. As a general rule, assets producing a good income return offer lower capital growth, and vice versa.

The trustees need to invest the trust fund in a range of investments which provide overall income and capital growth; perhaps gilts and a National Savings Income Bond for income and quoted shares or unit trusts for growth.

EXAMPLE 2

A settlement is created for Arshad and Badia, 6-year-old twins, contingent as to both capital and income on their attaining 25 years of age. They are unlikely to need any income for at least the first five years of the settlement, and any income accumulated in the settlement will suffer 45% income tax (see **14.5.2**).

As there is no need for income, the trustees can concentrate on improving the capital value of the trust fund, perhaps by investing in quoted shares.

> The trustees should, however, be cautious in their investment strategy. In *Daniel v Tee* [2016] EWHC 1538 (Ch), solicitor trustees were holding £3.4 million for two minors contingent on reaching 25. On the advice of investment managers, they agreed to an investment policy of 85% equities, and 15% bonds and cash. They accepted the advisers were recommending high tech IT and telecom sector equities. The beneficiaries claimed £1.4 million for the loss to the trust caused in 2001 when the 'dot.com' stock market bubble burst. The court found that the policy was one which no trustee, complying with the duty to act prudently, could reasonably have adopted.

Note: There may be circumstances where the settlor does not want the trustees to hold a balance. For example, a testator may leave his property to his elderly wife for life and the remainder to charity. His major concern may be that his wife should be well provided for, and he may not be very concerned as to the amount the charity eventually takes. He can leave a statement of wishes, but the trustees will still be at risk of an action for breach of trust from the remainderman. To protect them, he should include a direction in the trust stating that the trustees are not to be required to invest impartially.

14.3.3   Subsequent changes to the trust fund

Although with an express power of investment the bulk of the fund is likely to be invested in land and/or securities, most trustees should consider retaining a degree of liquidity by holding a small amount of cash in an interest-bearing instant access bank or building society account. This will provide the trustees with cash to meet expenses, such as solicitors' or accountants' fees, and their own out-of-pocket expenses. It will also provide them with the ability to make a new purchase for the trust fund if an opportunity suddenly arises. On occasion, they may also use such an account to retain the proceeds of sale of an investment where there is not to be an immediate reinvestment of the realised fund.

Once a settlement has been created, trustees need to review the trust fund regularly. The TA 2000 imposes a duty to do so, and trustees should ensure that there are minutes of trustees' meetings confirming that review took place. Trustees can make many of the investments which an individual concerned with his personal estate planning might make (see **Appendix 2**). How often trustees review their investments depends on a number of factors, but it should not be less than once a year and may be more frequently. This is to ensure that the fund continues to provide for the aims of the settlement; to minimise the liability to CGT; and to protect the fund against economic forces.

14.3.3.1   Changes to reflect the aims of the settlement

Settlements are designed to last for many years. An investment strategy that was appropriate at the outset may not be appropriate 10 years later; in particular, the beneficiaries needs may have changed or there may be about to be a change in the beneficial interests in the settlement. Trustees may need to alter the investments in the trust fund to reflect these changes.

> **EXAMPLE**
>
> Twelve years ago, Darshan settled £100,000 cash on discretionary trusts for his three grandchildren then aged 5, 4 and 2 years. The children had no immediate need for income and, as all income accumulated within the trust suffers income tax which is non-recoverable, the trustees invested the majority of the trust fund in low income, high-growth shares and unit trusts. The trust fund is now worth £180,000 and produces £3,500 per annum income. The eldest beneficiary intends to start medical school in three months' time, and the trustees have decided to exercise their discretion and pay her £5,000 per annum income from the trust fund.

> The trustees must, therefore, sell some of their investments and reinvest the proceeds to increase the income generated by the trust fund. As a known amount of income is required, the trustees might consider achieving this by investing in gilts or a guaranteed rate building society account.
>
> Note that when rates of income are low, it may not be possible to produce the desired income level. If it is not, the trustees will either pay what income they can to the beneficiary or choose to pay some capital to make up the required amount.

14.3.3.2   Minimising CGT

A large proportion of a trust fund is likely to be invested in assets such as quoted shares which attract a charge to CGT on their disposal. As trustees have only an annual exemption of £6,150 and gains are charged at 20% (28% on residential property) in all settlements, it is sensible (where possible) to manage the fund to minimise the liability. For example, trustees may invest in land to be occupied by a beneficiary under a trust as his residence. If so, any gain on sale by the trustees would qualify for the principal private residence exemption. If such investment and occupation occur within two years of death under the terms of a discretionary trust established by will, this (at least in the view of the Revenue) may amount to giving the beneficiary an interest in possession in the part of the settled property represented by the private residence, retrospectively creating an immediate post-death interest by reason of the writing back effect of IHTA 1984, s 144.

A charge to CGT will arise on two occasions: on a deemed disposal when a beneficiary becomes absolutely entitled to trust property (as we saw in **Chapter 10**); and on an actual disposal when trust property is sold as a result of investment changes (see **14.5**). Trustees should always aim to utilise their annual exemption, as it cannot be carried forward to future tax years or transferred to beneficiaries.

In a year in which a deemed disposal will occur, trustees should consider carefully whether any investment changes need to be made or whether they can leave the changes to the next tax year, so keeping their annual exemption available to set against the charge on the deemed disposal.

14.3.3.3   General reviews

Most investors who invest in the stock market, whether through the direct purchase of shares or via unit trusts, do so to make money rather than as a desire to be part of a particular company. The stock market is divided into sectors with companies predominantly involved in particular activities being grouped together, for example, both WH Smith plc and Marks & Spencer plc are in the 'Retailers General' sector whilst Lloyds plc is in the 'Banks' sector. Trustees, like most individual investors, are looking for a spread of investments, investing in companies from a number of sectors rather than concentrating on companies in one sector. This is because sectors of the economy perform differently depending on different economic factors and, if one sector is suffering, the value of the shares in the majority of companies in that sector is likely to fall. It is unusual, however, for all sectors to be depressed at the same time and the theory of investing in a number of sectors is that the gains and losses should be evened out.

Trustees may be advised to sell their shares in companies in a particular sector and invest the proceeds in a different sector for a while, or to change companies within a sector.

> **EXAMPLE**
>
> The trustees of a discretionary settlement have invested one quarter of the trust fund in gilts and the remainder equally between A plc (an airline company), B plc (a food manufacturer) and C plc (an oil company). Their stockbrokers advise that the airline market is depressed and that the value of their shareholding is falling but that companies in the 'online retail' sector look set to make large profits. The trustees decide to sell their shares in A plc and use the proceeds to buy shares in D plc, an online retail company.

14.4 APPOINTMENT OF TRUSTEES

14.4.1 The original trustees

14.4.1.1 Choice of trustees

The choice of the original trustees of the settlement is made by the settlor at the time he makes a settlement. Their appointment as trustees takes effect immediately the trust instrument is executed. Once appointed, they are in a fiduciary position and so must act with good faith. Their duty is to administer the trust for the benefit of its beneficiaries.

14.4.1.2 Number of trustees

Although every trust must have at least one trustee, it is usual for the settlor to appoint between two and four individuals to act as trustees of his settlement. A maximum of four trustees can be appointed for trusts of land, but at least two trustees (or a trust corporation) are required to give a buyer a valid receipt for the proceeds of sale of land held in a settlement. There is no limit to the number of trustees who can be appointed for trusts of personalty, but the appointment of more than four can cause the trust administration to be unnecessarily cumbersome.

14.4.1.3 Selection of trustees

The settlor should take great care in choosing the original trustees. It is possible to appoint a trust corporation to act as trustee, but most settlors prefer to appoint individuals because of the personal involvement this will bring to the administration of the trusts. The settlor should consider the following.

A professional trustee

It is often helpful to appoint a solicitor or other professional person to be a trustee (often together with member(s) of the settlor's own family). Where a professional is appointed, the administrative provisions of the trust should include a charging clause. Even if a professional is not appointed at the outset, it is a good idea to include a charging clause allowing professionals to charge in case a professional is appointed as a trustee in the future (see **14.2.1.4**).

The settlor as trustee

The settlor may appoint himself to be the sole trustee or one of several trustees of his settlement. This allows him to retain an involvement in the settlement and have some influence over how it is administered, for example he will have a say in whether the trustees should exercise their discretion in favour of a particular beneficiary under a discretionary settlement. If he is appointed a trustee, the settlor must not allow his personal wishes to overshadow his duties as trustee. He should not be paid as this would amount to a benefit from the trust, and the trust would be taxed as a settlor-interested trust.

Instead of being appointed a trustee, the settlor may prefer to exercise some influence over the trustees through the use of a 'letter of wishes' (or a side letter) addressed to the trustees. Clearly, such a letter will have no binding effect on the trustees but, by setting out how he wishes the settlement to be administered in the future, the settlor hopes the trustees will have some regard to his intentions.

A beneficiary as trustee

The settlor may appoint one or more of the beneficiaries to be a trustee of the settlement but this may cause difficulty, for example a conflict of interest may arise between the individual's position as trustee on the one hand and as beneficiary on the other. In view of this, a beneficiary should not be a sole trustee. Two or more trustees provide safeguards in that they must supervise one another, must be unanimous in the exercise of their powers (an important protection for the beneficiaries) and their appointment will ensure a continuing trustee if one were to die or to retire from the trusts. Where a beneficiary is appointed, it is helpful to have a clause expressly allowing the trustee to exercise powers in his own favour. This might be implied from the fact that the settlor made the appointment, but an express clause gives clarity and, if desired, can impose limitations; for example, the clause might require there to be one independent trustee.

14.4.2 Subsequent trustees

A trust may exist for a number of years, and during that time there are likely to be several changes of trustee as new trustees replace those that retire or die. It is vital that the appointment of new trustees is carried out correctly. This involves:

- ensuring that the person with power to appoint (under any express provision in the trust instrument, but if not under statutory power) makes the appointment;
- drafting and executing an appropriate deed;
- transferring the trust property to the new trustees.

14.4.2.1 Appointment by the settlor

Once the original trustees have been appointed the settlor has no statutory power to appoint trustees. If a settlor (who is not also a trustee) wishes to control the selection of trustees during his lifetime, he can do so only if the trust instrument gives him the express power to appoint new trustees.

Sample clause

> During the lifetime of the Settlor the power of appointing new trustees shall be vested in the Settlor.

14.4.2.2 The statutory power of appointing new or additional trustees

If there is no person nominated in the trust instrument (eg, the settlor or a chosen individual), s 36 of TA 1925 provides wide statutory powers for the appointment of new trustees. As a last resort, s 41 of TA 1925 allows the court to appoint new or replacement trustees where it is difficult to do so by other means.

Replacement trustees (TA 1925, s 36(1))

The appointment of a new trustee must be made in writing (but will normally be by deed, see **14.4.4**) by:

(a)   the surviving or continuing trustees (including any retiring or disclaiming trustee if he wishes to join in the appointment: s 36(8)); or

(b)   the personal representatives of the last surviving trustee.

A new trustee can be appointed under s 36(1) to replace, inter alia, a trustee who has died, is incapable of acting, or who retires.

Trustee who has lost capacity

Trustees who lose mental capacity do not cease to hold office. They must be removed. Loss of capacity is a ground for removal under TA 1925, s 36(1).

Trustees must act unanimously, so until the trustee is removed, the administration of the trust is paralysed.

The incapacitated trustee will be removed by the person nominated in the trust instrument for the purpose of appointing new trustees (s 36(1)(a)) or the continuing trustees if there is no such person (s 36(1)(b)).

There is a significant difference between the two subparagraphs. If removal is by the continuing trustees, the consent of the Court of Protection will be required to remove a trustee who has a beneficial entitlement in possession (see s 36(9)). This is not the case if the trust instrument provides for another person to remove and appoint new trustees.

The process for applying to the Court of Protection is detailed in Practice Direction G to Part 9 of the Court of Protection Rules 2007, and is extremely tedious. An extensive list of exhibits is required to accompany the application, including the trust document, conveyancing documents, details of the existing trustee(s) and independent witness statements confirming the suitability of the new trustee, to name but a few. It is worth trying to avoid the need for such an application by use of one of the following methods:

- If possible, get the trustee to retire voluntarily under TA 1925, s 39 while they retain sufficient capacity to do so.
- When drafting trusts:
  – specify a person to appoint new trustees under s 36(1)(a) so that the requirement for court consent does not arise;
  – include a provision that a trustee who loses capacity is to be treated as having died for the purposes of acting as a trustee, thus removing the need for an application to the Court of Protection.

Additional trustees (TA 1925, s 36(6))

The appointment of additional trustees must be made in writing by the continuing trustee(s). The number of trustees after the new appointment is made must not exceed four.

Directions as to trustees by beneficiaries (TLATA 1996, s 19)

If there is no person still alive nominated in the trust instrument to appoint new trustees, the beneficiaries of full age and capacity who together are entitled to the trust property can give written directions to the trustees for the retirement and appointment of a trustee. As it is possible for the trust instrument to exclude s 19, settlors should be invited to consider whether they prefer future control over the appointment and retirement of trustees to remain with the existing trustees or to pass instead to the beneficiaries.

14.4.3 Vesting the trust property in the trustees

14.4.3.1 On creation of the settlement

Once the original trustees have been appointed, the settlor must transfer to them the 'settled property', ie the assets mentioned in the trust instrument as being subject to the trusts of the settlement. It is a duty of the trustees to bring all the trust property under their control.

The settlor will transfer the settled property to the trustees by whatever means of transfer is appropriate to that property. For example, stock transfer forms will be used to transfer shares (unless they are held by nominee); a deed or Land Registry transfer will be used to transfer the legal estate in land.

14.4.3.2 On the appointment of replacement or additional trustees

Following a change in the trustees, the trust property must be vested in the new trustee(s). If the appointment of the new trustee(s) is by deed, s 40(1) of TA 1925 provides that the vesting of the trust property will occur automatically. There are, however, circumstances where s 40(1) does not apply so that formal transfer of the trust property to the new trustee(s) will be required. In particular, there is no automatic vesting of stocks and shares. In these cases, a stock transfer form transferring the shares into the names of all the trustees must be signed by the 'old trustees' and registered with the company (unless the shares are held by a nominee). Although the shares are held by the trustees as trust property, there is no reference to this on the company's membership register. Shares are shown as registered in the individual names of the trustees without reference to their capacity as trustees.

14.4.4 Drafting a deed of appointment of new trustees

14.4.4.1 Heading and date

Sample clause

> DEED OF APPOINTMENT AND RETIREMENT
> DATE: [   ]

14.4.4.2 Parties

Who the parties are will depend on the circumstances giving rise to the appointment of new trustees. The person(s) with the power to appoint will always be parties; so too will the new trustee(s) and any retiring trustee.

Sample clause

> BETWEEN
> (1)   [name and address] ('the Continuing Trustees')
> (2)   [name and address] ('the New Trustee')
> (3)   [name and address] ('the Retiring Trustee')

This example envisages that there is no one expressly authorised in the trust instrument to select and appoint a new trustee. If there was, this person (or persons) would appear as a party and would likely be defined as 'the Appointor'.

14.4.4.3 Recitals

Normally, there will be three or four separate provisions detailing the circumstances giving rise to the change of the trustees.

Sample clause

> RECITALS
> (A)   This Deed is supplemental to the settlement ('the Settlement') [and to the other documents and events] specified in the [First] Schedule.
> (B)   The statutory power of appointment applies to the Settlement and is exercisable by the Continuing Trustees and the Retiring Trustee.
> (C)   The Continuing Trustees and the Retiring Trustee are the present trustees of the Settlement.
> (D)   The Continuing Trustees and the Retiring Trustee wish to appoint the New Trustee to act as a trustee of the Settlement in place of the Retiring Trustee.
> (E)   It is intended that the property now in the Settlement [, details of which are set out in the Second Schedule,] shall be transferred to, or under the control of, the Continuing Trustees and the New Trustee.

Such clauses allow for the retirement of the trustee. If no trustee is retiring, all references to 'the Retiring Trustee' should be deleted from the clauses as well as from 'the parties'.

If there was an express provision conferring power to appoint a new trustee in the trust instrument, Recital B would indicate this, referring to the relevant clause number.

Recital (E) is intended to enable the trust property to be detailed in the schedule to the deed of appointment. It is not an express declaration vesting property in the new trustee.

14.4.4.4 The operative part

By this clause, those with the power to do so make the appointment of the new trustee. This may be the Appointor under a specific power in the trust instrument, or the present trustees under s 36 of TA 1925.

If a trustee is retiring, it is usual to include a statement in the deed confirming that there is no intention for the residence status of the trust to change. Where a trust 'emigrates' (see **Chapter 15**) there is a CGT charge, and this can result in anyone who has been a trustee within the 12 months prior to the emigration of the trust being liable. The statement will help prevent a retired trustee being liable.

Sample clauses

Appointment of New Trustee in place of Retiring Trustee

In exercise of the power of appointment conferred by the Trustee Act 1925 and of all other powers (if any), the Continuing Trustees and the Retiring Trustee hereby appoint the New Trustee as a trustee of the Settlement to act jointly with the Continuing Trustees in place of the Retiring Trustee who hereby retires and is discharged from the trusts of the Settlement.

Declaration as to residence

It is hereby declared that, at the date hereof, there is no proposal that the Trustees of the Settlement might become non-resident in the United Kingdom.

Again, if no trustee is to retire, the references to 'the Retiring Trustee' should be deleted and there is no need to refer to the residence of the trust.

14.4.4.5 Schedules

It is usual to include in the schedules particulars of the settlement to which the deed of appointment is supplemental (together with brief details of any documents or events that have occurred since creation, eg any previous deeds dealing with a change of trustee or appointment of funds to a beneficiary), as well as details of the trust property currently held by the trustees. This list of trust property is useful for the new trustee who must now exercise his duties as trustee in relation to it.

14.5 TAXATION DURING THE ADMINISTRATION OF A SETTLEMENT

The settlor's liability to IHT and CGT on the creation of the settlement is considered in **Chapter 5**, and liability to the same taxes which arises on trust advances and appointments is considered in **Chapter 10**. Broadly, these earlier chapters covered the capital tax position on creation and termination of the settlement. The liability to CGT and income tax arising on the trust capital and its income during the administration of a settlement are considered below; any relevant IHT liabilities during the trust's existence are considered in the chapters referred to above.

14.5.1 Actual disposals: CGT

If the trustees of the settlement rearrange their portfolio of investments, CGT liability may arise on any sales. If so, the trustees are liable to pay the tax and will do so from the settled funds. Sales by the trustees are 'actual disposals' giving rise to CGT liability in a manner similar to disposals by an individual.

> **EXAMPLE**
>
> Trustees are holding 5,000 XYZ plc shares as part of a trust fund. These shares are sold for £30,000 (net of disposal costs) having been worth only £5,000 when they were acquired by the trustees. There were no costs of acquisition.
>
> | | £ |
> |---|---|
> | Disposal consideration | 30,000 |
> | Less: | |
> | Acquisition cost, ie, the value of the shares when they were acquired by the trustees | 5,000 |
> | Chargeable gain | 25,000 |

The calculation is the same as any CGT calculation. It is based on the trustees' disposal consideration and their acquisition cost, ie the value of the shares when transferred to them by the settlor at the time the settlement was created, or the price paid by the trustees when they bought the shares if they were acquired later.

14.5.1.1 Reliefs, exemption and rates of tax

Rates of CGT

The net gains made by trustees on all disposals in a tax year are aggregated, and the annual exemption is deducted. Since 6 April 2016 trustees pay tax at a flat rate of 20% (28% on residential property).

Exemptions

Trustees of any settlement are entitled to an annual exemption of one-half of the exemption for individuals, so £6,150 in the tax year 2022/23. If the settlor has created a number of settlements, the exemption is divided between them with a minimum of £1,230 in each case.

> **EXAMPLE (continued)**
>
> In addition to making the gain of £25,000 on the XYZ plc shares, in the same tax year the trustees sell shares in ABC plc, making a gain of £4,150. The settlor created no other settlements.
>
> | Total gains in the year | £29,150 |
> |---|---|
> | Less: | |
> | Annual exemption | £ 6,150 |
> | | £23,000 |
>
> This is taxed at 20% = £4,600

Reliefs

In limited circumstances, business asset disposal relief (formerly entrepreneurs' relief) may be available where there is an actual disposal of business assets held in the settlement and a number of conditions are met (see **4.4.5.3**).

Hold-over relief is not available on actual disposals. It is available only on deemed disposals by trustees. If hold-over relief is not taken on a deemed disposal then any gain made must be aggregated with gains on actual disposals made in the same tax year, and the CGT calculation proceeds as above.

Losses

Losses realised by trustees on disposals are set against gains in the usual way.

EXAMPLE

Trustees of a discretionary settlement sell the trust's holding of shares in A plc which are now worth £10,000, having been purchased three years ago for £25,000. (Assume no costs of acquisition or disposal.)

	£
Disposal consideration	10,000
Less: Acquisition cost	25,000
Loss (15,000)	

As this loss is incurred by the trustees, they are entitled to claim loss relief. They do so by setting the loss against gains they make on other sales in the same tax year. If there are none, or if there are insufficient gains to absorb the loss, the trustees may carry the loss forward to set against gains made in future years.

14.5.2 Income tax

It is necessary to distinguish the liability of the settlement trustees from the beneficiary's liability.

14.5.2.1 Trustees' liability

The trustees must pay tax on all income produced by the trust assets. In tax years before 2016/17, interest was received net of basic rate tax, and dividends were received with a basic rate tax credit. However, as from 2016/17, banks and building societies ceased to deduct tax from account interest at source (including for personal representatives and trustees), and dividends are paid without a tax credit.

Trustees, therefore, receive all income gross and have to pay tax at the appropriate rate. The rate depends on whether or not the beneficiaries have a right to receive income. Trustees (and PRs) do not qualify for the tax-free savings or dividend allowance, which are available only to individuals.

Settlements where there is a right to income

Beneficiaries may have a right to receive income because the terms of the settlement expressly state this, or because of the operation of s 31 of TA 1925 or because trustees exercise a power giving this right. Where beneficiaries have a right to income, the trustees are only liable for income tax at the basic rate (20%) and dividend ordinary rate (7.5%), depending on the type of income.

EXAMPLE

Trustees of a trust where B has a right to income receive the following income in the tax year 2022/23:

£5,000 gross dividends

£2,000 gross interest

£10,000 gross rental income

The trustees will pay tax as follows:

- dividends

  8.75% x £5,000 = £437.50

- interest
  20% x £2,000 = £400
- rentals
  20% x £10,000 = £2,000

The trustees will give the beneficiary a certificate of deduction of tax showing the amounts paid.

Settlements where there is no right to income

Trustees of trusts where the beneficiaries have no right to receive income must pay 'the trust rate' or 'the dividend trust rate' on income which is to be accumulated or which is payable at their discretion (ITA 2007, s 479). Income which is properly used to pay management expenses is deductible from the income before tax (ITA 2007, ss 484–486).

The trust rate (45%) is paid on non-dividend income and the dividend trust rate (39.35%) is paid on dividend income.

Since 6 April 2005, for trusts where the beneficiaries have no right to receive income, a basic rate band applies. For the tax year 2022/23 it applies to the first £1,000 of income as follows:

(a) non-dividend income within this level that would normally be charged at the trust rate of 45% will instead be charged at 20%.

(b) dividend income that would normally be charged at 39.35% will instead be charged at 8.75%.

This means that a number of trusts do not pay the trust rate on any of their income because their total income falls below the £1,000 threshold.

EXAMPLE 1

Trustees of a discretionary trust receive the following income in the tax year 2022/23:

(a)   £150 gross rental income;
(b)   £100 gross interest;
(c)   £400 gross dividends.

All the gross income falls within the £1,000 band so the trustees will pay tax as follows:

- rentals
  20% x £150 + £30
- interest
  20% x £100 + £20
- dividends
  8.75% x £400 = £35

The trustees will give the beneficiary a certificate of deduction of tax showing the amounts paid.

Where the trustees have annual income above £1,000, the excess will be chargeable at the trust rate, but the basic rate band will still apply to the first £1,000 slice of gross income. The basic rate band is allocated to income in the following order:

(a)   non-dividend income;
(b)   dividend income.

EXAMPLE 2

Trustees of a discretionary trust receive the following income in the tax year 2022/23:

(a)   £300 gross rental income;

(b) £500 gross interest;

(c) £1,000 gross dividends.

The gross income is £1,800. That part of the gross income that falls within the £1,000 band escapes the trust rate (45%) or dividend trust rate (39.35%) so:

(a) The gross rent (£300) is charged at 20% = £60

(b) The gross interest (£500) is charged at 20% = £100

This leaves only £200 of the basic rate band, so:

(a) £200 of the gross dividend income is charged at 8.75% = £17.50

(b) The remaining gross dividend income (£800) is charged at 39.35% = £314.80

(c) Total tax is £492.30

In previous tax years, when interest was received net of basic rate tax and dividends with a basic rate tax credit, trustees of trusts with only a basic rate tax liability had no further tax liability. To keep administration to a minimum, trustees were only issued with a self assessment tax return once every five years.

Now that all income is received gross, all trustees who receive any income will have a tax liability. The Revenue recognises that this will increase administration costs for small trusts. The April 2016 Trusts and Estates Newsletter said it was reviewing arrangements and:

> for the tax year 2016 to 2017 we will not require notification from trustees or personal representatives dealing with estates in administration where the only source of income is savings interest and the tax liability is below £100.
>
> We are currently reviewing the situation longer term and will notify key customers prior to tax year 2017 to 2018 as to the new arrangements.

The effect is that where the income of a trust is limited to a small amount of interest, the trustees do not need to submit tax returns nor pay income tax.

Where income is paid to beneficiaries, they will include it on their tax returns and pay the tax due.

Note that the concession is very limited. If any income is received from other sources, for example dividends, the trustees must complete tax returns.

In its December 2017 Newsletter, HMRC confirmed that it was extending these interim arrangements to tax years 2017–18 and 2018–19 and would continue to review the situation longer term. The August 2019 Newsletter announced an extension to tax years 2019/20 and 2020/21. HMRC say that it will continue to review the situation longer term. In April 2022 the Government issued a consultation and in response announced that it is now proposing to formalise the concession and widen it. The proposal is to allow estates or trusts with income of up to £500 from any source (which is equivalent to an income tax liability of £100 or less) to benefit.

14.5.2.2 The beneficiary's liability

When trust income is paid to a beneficiary, it is added to the beneficiary's other income and the total is assessed to income tax, although the beneficiary will have credit for any tax already paid. There is a difference between the position of a beneficiary who has a right to the income of the settled property and that of other beneficiaries, for example beneficiaries of a discretionary settlement.

Beneficiaries with a right to income

Beneficiaries with a vested entitlement to the settlement income are entitled to receive from the trustees the trust income after deduction of the relevant amount of tax. If it is non-dividend income it is received after tax at 20% has been paid. If it is dividend income it is received after tax at 8.75% has been paid on it. Beneficiaries are liable to tax on this income in the same way as they pay tax on any other income they may have.

Beneficiaries add the various types of income received from the trust (eg interest and dividends) to any other income they receive of a similar type, and then calculate their overall tax position for the year. They may have to pay further tax, or they may be able to reclaim overpaid tax on non-dividend income. As tax at 20% and 8.75% has been paid, the beneficiaries only have a tax liability if they are higher or additional rate taxpayers. If they are non-taxpayers, they can reclaim tax on all income.

The trustees provide beneficiaries with a tax deduction certificate in Form R185 which the beneficiaries will pass on to the Revenue to show that tax has already been paid.

EXAMPLE

Trustees are holding a trust fund in which Tony has a right to income. The trustees' gross dividend income in 2022/23 is £1,000. After payment of the £87.50 tax due on dividends, they pay £912.50 to Tony to whom they give Form R185 showing the payment of tax at the dividend ordinary rate. Tony's gross income from the trust is £1,000, ie, £912.50 + £87.50.

Tony's tax position depends on the amount of his other income:

(a)   If he is an additional rate taxpayer

gross trust dividend income £1,000 × 39.35% =	£393.50
Less tax @ 8.75% credited as paid by the trustees	£87.50
tax due	£306.00

(b)   If he is a higher rate taxpayer

gross trust dividend income £1,000 × 33.75% =	£337.50
Less tax @ 8.75% credited as paid by the trustees	£87.50
tax due	£250.00

(c)   If he is not a taxpayer, he will be able to reclaim the £87.50 tax credit as the income comes from dividends.

(d)   If he pays tax at basic rate, he has no further tax to pay.

Where a beneficiary has a right to income, trustees can instruct those paying income to bypass the trustees and pay the income to the beneficiary. The trustees drop out of the picture and have no liability to pay tax or provide tax returns. The Trusts, Settlements and Estates Manual says at TSEM 3040:

> Sometimes there are instructions or arrangements for income to bypass the trustees of an interest in possession (IIP) trust. If trust income passes directly or indirectly to a beneficiary without going via the trustees, for example income passes through an investment manager to the IIP beneficiary, there is no statutory basis for charging the trustees to income tax in respect of this income, because the trustees are neither entitled to it nor in receipt of it

Arranging direct payment to the beneficiaries obviously greatly reduces the administrative workload for trustees.

Beneficiaries with no right to income

Where no beneficiary has the right to receive the income of the trust property, the trustees may exercise their discretion to pay it to a beneficiary, or they may accumulate the income. If they do pay out income to a beneficiary, they must provide the beneficiary with a Form R185. This states the amount of tax paid on the income by the trustees. The beneficiary will pass it on to the Revenue and will receive a tax credit for the tax paid by the trustees. All income received by the beneficiary is treated as income received net of the trust rate of tax (45%) (ITA 2007, s 494), regardless of the original source of income received by the trust. The beneficiary enters the income on his or her tax return as a new source of income, 'trust income', irrespective of its original nature.

EXAMPLE 1: INCOME ACCUMULATED

The trustees of a discretionary settlement receive in 2022/23 bank interest of £2,000 gross. The income is taxed as follows:

The first £1,000 is taxed at 20% = £200, and the remaining £1,000 is taxed at 45% = £450. There is a total tax liability of £650 which the trustees must pay.

They have no expenses. None of the income is paid to beneficiaries. The trustees accumulate the remaining £1,350 by adding it to the capital of the trust. The £650 tax paid on the gross income of £2,000 cannot be recovered from the Revenue.

Had the £2,000 gross income come from dividends, the trustees' tax liability would have been 8.75% on the first £1,000 = £87.50 and 39.35% on the remaining £1,000 = £393.50. As in the previous example, the tax paid would not have been recoverable from the Revenue.

EXAMPLE 2: INCOME APPLIED

The facts are the same as in Example 1 but the trustees pay £330 of the remaining income to a discretionary beneficiary, Abdul. His income from the trustees is treated as the net amount from which 45% tax (the trust rate) has been deducted. Therefore the gross value of this £330 received by Abdul is £600, and he adds this amount to his other gross income for the year.

Abdul's tax position in relation to the income received from the trust depends on the amount of his other income:

(a)	If he is an additional rate taxpayer	
	tax treated as paid by the trustees at 45%	£270
	tax at additional rate £600 × 45%	£270
	no further tax due	£0
(b)	If he is a higher rate taxpayer	
	tax treated as paid by the trustees at 45%	£270
	tax at higher rate £600 × 40%	£240
	refunded by the Revenue	£30
(c)	If he is a basic rate taxpayer	
	tax treated as paid by the trustees at 45%	£270
	tax at basic rate £600 × 20%	£120
	refunded by the Revenue	£150
(d)	If he is not a taxpayer (ie, he has no other income)	
	tax treated as paid by the trustees at 45% (refunded by the Revenue)	£270

Where beneficiaries are not additional rate taxpayers, the trustees should consider exercising their discretion over the income to pay it to beneficiaries rather than accumulating it. The tax paid by the trustees can then be repaid to the beneficiaries (see Example 2). If the income is accumulated as in Example 1, the tax cannot be reclaimed.

Trustees of settlements who pay income to a beneficiary who has no right to receive it provide the beneficiary with a new source of income for his own tax purposes. The source of the income is the trust, not the underlying companies which pay dividends or banks which pay interest to the trustees. This means that beneficiaries cannot set their dividend or savings allowances against income received from a trust.

The current legislation requires trustees who exercise a discretion to pay income to a beneficiary to provide the beneficiary with a tax deduction certificate at the trust rate of tax (45%) even when, in fact, the trustees have paid at a lower rate (either because the income is within the £1,000 basic rate tax band or because it is dividend income on which the top rate of tax is only 39.35%).

A beneficiary who is not an additional rate taxpayer can reclaim tax from the Revenue. Non-taxpayers can reclaim the whole 45%; basic rate and higher rate taxpayers can reclaim the difference between the 20% or 40% for which they are liable and the 45% tax credit.

This looks as if HMRC is being generous and allowing beneficiaries to claim the benefit of more tax than the trustees actually paid. Sadly, this is not the case. ITA 2007, s 496 provides that any shortfall between tax due at the trust rate (45%) and the rate at which it is actually paid (20% or 8.75% for the first £1,000 income and 39.35% in the case of any other dividend income) will be assessed on the trustees. This creates a problem for trustees, who must retain sufficient income to meet this extra liability unless they are willing to have recourse to capital to cover the additional tax due. (For further discussion of this see, for example, *Revenue Law: Principles and Practice*, 37th edn (Bloomsbury Professional, 2019.)

An alternative (and probably better) approach is for the trustees to give one or more beneficiaries a right to receive the trust income in the short term. They could give a beneficiary a right to receive the income arising in the next 12 months. The settlement will then be treated as one in which the beneficiary has a right to income; the trustees will be liable to basic rate income tax only and the beneficiary will receive a tax credit for the tax actually paid. The income is entered on the beneficiary's tax return and retains its original nature. Hence the beneficiary can make use of any tax-free dividend or savings allowance available.

14.6 DISTRIBUTING THE TRUST FUNDS

14.6.1 Accounting to the beneficiaries

Trustees must prepare capital and income accounts when changes in the beneficial interests under the settlement occur. The most likely occasions of this happening are:

(a)   when a beneficiary becomes entitled to receive settled property from the trustees, for example, following the exercise of a power of advancement under s 32 of TA 1925; or

(b)   when the trustees exercise a power of appointment, for example, when they appoint property to or for a beneficiary.

The accounts will show the investments and any cash in the trust fund together with any income which the trustees hold in their income account. From these accounts the beneficiary can ascertain precisely what his entitlement amounts to. The task of producing these accounts will be much easier if the trustees have kept full and accurate records of all transactions affecting the trust during the period of its administration. These will include records of sales and purchases of investments, advances made to the beneficiaries and any tax liabilities discharged.

14.6.2 Form and content of accounts

There is no prescribed form for trust accounts. The aim is to present clear and concise accounts which can easily be understood by the beneficiaries. Normally, trust accounts are produced in a vertical format showing the trust fund, payments made from it, for example, IHT and solicitors' costs and a balance for the beneficiary. A separate income account will reveal the income available for distribution, less any expenses payable from it, for example, any income tax due to the Revenue. The form of trust account shown in **Appendix 6** adopts this more usual vertical format.

14.6.3 Vesting the trust property in beneficiaries

Once the trustees have paid any tax liabilities and have prepared their accounts, the trust fund (or the appropriate part of it) must be transferred to the beneficiary. The means of vesting property in the beneficiary will depend on the nature of the property. The legal estate in land can be vested in the beneficiary by means of a deed; a stock transfer form will be required to transfer shares. Chattels (if any) pass to the beneficiary by delivery and any remaining cash will be transferred by cheque drawn on the trustee's bank account.

SUMMARY

Trust administration

- Trustees must properly administer the trust, complying with relevant duties and powers.

- Most trusts have express provisions but otherwise statutory provisions (primarily in TA 1925 and TA 2000) are implied for matters such as investment, delegation, change of trustee and payment of trustees.

Retirement and appointment of new trustees

- The appointment of new trustees must be carried out by the person(s) with power to appoint new trustees (either named in the trust instrument or according to s 36 of TA 1925).

- Retirement and appointment is usually carried out by deed.

- The appointment of new trustees must be followed by the transfer of title to trust property to the new trustees.

Tax on trust investments

- Trustees must report and pay any CGT and income tax liability arising from the investment of the trust assets.

CGT

- Sales of trust assets are actual disposals, calculated in usual way.

- All trust gains and losses in the tax year are aggregated.

- The trust annual exemption (half that of an individual) is deducted.

- Gains are taxed at 20% (28% on residential property).

Income tax

- Trustees receive income generated by trust investments.

- They must pay it to any beneficiary who has a right to it, but otherwise may have powers to accumulate or pay it out.

- The tax position of both trustees and beneficiaries depends on whether beneficiaries have a right to the trust income.

Trusts where a beneficiary has a right to income

Income received by trustees

- Trustees are liable at dividend ordinary rate of 7.5% on dividends.

- Trustees pay at 20% on any other income.

Income paid to beneficiary

- The beneficiary adds income from the trust (in its original form) to his other income to establish his personal tax liability.
- Trustees give the beneficiary a certificate to show tax already deducted at source or paid by the trustees.

Trusts where no beneficiary has a right to income

Income received by trustees

- On the first £1,000 of gross income, trustees pay at basic and dividend ordinary rate.
- On other income, trustees pay at the trust rate (45%) or dividend trust rate (38.1%).

Income paid to beneficiary

- Trustees may choose to pay income to beneficiaries.
- The beneficiary receives a new source of income, treated as having suffered tax at 45%.
- The beneficiary may recover the difference between his tax liability and the 45% deemed to have been paid.
- The trustees are liable for any shortfall between the 45% and the tax actually paid by them.

REVIEW ACTIVITY

Question 1

Bob created a trust in his will for his sister (Jill) for life, remainder to such of her children who reach the age of 25, and if more than one in equal shares. The trust has been in existence for two years. The trustees are Tabarak and Tom. The trust fund contains £500,000 in cash and quoted shares, and has produced net income of £12,000 this year. The trust deed states that the appointment of any new trustees is to be carried out by Bob's brother, Alan. Jill is alive and has two children, aged 18 and 12.

Which ONE OR MORE of the following is/are CORRECT?

A   If Tabarak dies, Alan and Tom will appoint a replacement trustee.
B   If Tabarak and Tom would like an additional trustee to act with them, Alan, Tabarak and Tom will choose and appoint someone.
C   The trustees have no further income tax to pay.
D   The trustees must pay income tax at 45% on all the trust income.
E   The trustees must pay income tax at 20% on all the trust income.
F   The trustees must pay the net trust income to Jill.
G   If Jill is a non-taxpayer, she can reclaim 45% tax on the trust income.
H   If the trustees sell some of the shares and make a gain, they can use hold-over relief.

Answer: F

The appointment of new or replacement trustees must be carried out by the person(s) with authority to do so. This will be the person(s) stated by express provision in the trust deed (as here) or, if none, the person(s) indicated by s 36 of TA 1925.

For tax years 2016/17 onwards, interest and dividends are received gross, so trustees have a tax liability on all sources of income. As this is a trust where a beneficiary has a right to income, the trustees will pay basic rate (20%) on everything except dividend income, on which they will pay the ordinary dividend rate (8.75%). Jill is not treated as receiving a new source of income, but as receiving interest and dividends. She therefore reclaims the 20% tax paid on the interest, and the 8.75% paid on the dividends.

The trustees make an actual disposal when they sell the shares and hold-over relief is available only on deemed disposals.

Question 2

Jim died intestate, with a net estate of £300,000. He was divorced and has two children: Kate (aged 14) and Liam (aged 10). The estate (comprising shares in quoted companies) is therefore held on the statutory trusts for Kate and Liam, contingent on their reaching 18 (or marrying or forming a civil partnership before this). There are no express provisions concerning trust income so s 31 of TA 1925 applies. The trustees are Mia and Norris. The trust receives £6,000 net income this year.

Which ONE OR MORE of the following is/are CORRECT?

A   If Mia wants to retire, Mia and Norris will appoint a replacement.

B   Mia is an accountant and is, therefore, entitled to receive payment for the time she spends as trustee.

C   The trustees have no further income tax to pay.

D   The trustees must pay income tax at 39.35% on all the trust income.

E   The trustees must pay income tax at 45% on all the trust income.

F   The trustees do not have to pay any income out of the trust this year.

G   If the trustees pay any trust income for Kate, they will have to pay further tax.

H   If the trustees sell any of the shares, they will have an annual exemption available equal to that of an individual.

Answer: A, F and G

This trust has arisen on intestacy and so there are no express provisions dealing with appointment of trustees or payment of trustees. Under s 36(1) of TA 1925, the power to appoint replacement trustees lies with the continuing trustees (plus the retiring trustee, if willing).

Section 29 of TA 2000 authorises the payment of some trustees for their time and work for the trust. A trustee acting in a professional capacity (as defined in s 28(5) of TA 2000), such as Mia, may receive reasonable remuneration but only if the other trustee consents – she has no right to be paid.

This is a trust where no beneficiary has a right to income: the children have contingent interests in the trust capital. In the absence of any express provisions, s 31 of TA 1925 governs what the trustees do with the trust income. The beneficiaries are under 18 so the trustees may use the income for the maintenance, education or benefit of the beneficiaries, but must otherwise accumulate it. For income tax purposes for such trusts, the first £1,000 gross income is taxed at basic rate and thereafter at the trust rate (or dividend trust rate). As there is only dividend income for this trust, the first £1,000 gross income is taxed at 8.75% and then the rest is taxed at 39.35%. If the trustees do pay or apply any income for a beneficiary, the beneficiary is treated as receiving a new source of income which has had 45% tax paid on it. As this is not so, the trustees have to pay further tax to make up for the tax shortfall.

Trustees have a CGT annual exemption that is half that of an individual.

THE OVERSEAS DIMENSION

LEARNING OUTCOMES

After reading this chapter you will have an understanding, in outline, of:

- the need to identify the residence and domicile of a client
- the principles involved in ascertaining the residence and domicile of a person
- the tax consequences of a person being resident or domiciled in the UK
- when a trust is regarded as non-resident and the tax consequences.

15.1 INTRODUCTION

The previous chapters in this book assume that private clients are UK resident and are domiciled in the UK. It has also been assumed that the property owned by these private clients is situated in the UK. However, the affairs of many private clients have an overseas dimension, for example:

(a) a UK resident and domiciled client is leaving the UK, either to work abroad or to emigrate; or

(b) an individual, while remaining a UK resident, is buying property overseas; or

(c) a foreign national is proposing to come to the UK on a temporary or long-term basis, or intends to invest in the UK.

This chapter considers the impact of a client's affairs having an overseas dimension. The law in this area, in particular concerning taxation and succession to property, is extensive and very complex, so this chapter aims to provide an introduction to some basic concepts, in particular relating to tax, as a basis for further study. A significant concern for such clients is whether and to what extent they are subject to UK taxes, and this largely depends on whether a person is resident or domiciled in the UK. The chapter considers how this is ascertained, and then provides an overview of the tax effects of being non-resident and domiciled. The final part of the chapter provides an introduction to trusts and the overseas dimension. The impact of Brussels IV in relation to will drafting for a person who has links to EU States bound by this Regulation was considered at **11.1**.

15.1.1 The issues involved

There are many practical and legal issues where a client's affairs take on an overseas dimension.

15.1.1.1 Practical issues

The solicitor in the private client department tends not to be involved with the many practical issues when a client intends to leave or come to the UK. These matters include visa applications, work permits and accommodation. Clearly, in these areas there are legal issues involved about which the solicitor may be asked to advise, but generally the client will be able to handle practical matters personally.

15.1.1.2 Legal issues

The solicitor should be asked to advise and become involved as early as possible where legal issues arise. Two particular aspects may call for early consideration, and appropriate advice must be given quickly before the client changes his residential or domiciliary status.

Ownership and devolution of property

The UK client may need advice in relation to a property he is proposing to buy in a foreign country. If, for example, he is purchasing a property in Turkey, he will need advice as to Turkish succession law and the extent to which he can leave that property by a will made in England or in Turkey.

As a minimum this advice should be given by a lawyer from, or specialising in the law of, the jurisdiction in which the property is situated, although ideally the lawyer should also be qualified in the law of England and Wales. Not only may the laws of the foreign country differ from those of the UK, but the law may vary from state to state within that country.

As indicated at **11.1**, where a UK client is making a will and has property located in any of the EU States which are bound by Brussels IV, it will be important to consider stating the choice of law to govern succession to the estate. This choice of law only affects succession law and has no effect on taxation.

Where more than one will is made to deal with property in different jurisdictions, it is important to ensure that the later will does not revoke the earlier will. The revocation clause must be limited to earlier wills dealing with the relevant assets.

A will can either be stated as 'dealing with all my assets other than those situate in [X]' or as 'dealing only with my assets in [Y]'. The choice will depend on the client's circumstances. For example, if the client's assets are all in the UK apart from a holiday home abroad, the first formulation will be appropriate; whereas if the bulk of the client's assets are elsewhere, the second will be more appropriate.

If limiting the will to assets in a certain jurisdiction, it is important to describe the jurisdiction correctly. In *The Royal Society v Robinson* [2015] EWHC 3442 (Ch), the will was declared to apply only to the testator's assets situate in the United Kingdom. He had substantial assets in Switzerland and had made a will dealing with those assets. His major non-Swiss assets were a bank account in Jersey and another in the Isle of Man. Unfortunately, the technical meaning of 'United Kingdom' does not include the Channel Islands or the Isle of Man. Stroud's *Judicial Dictionary* says under the entry of 'United Kingdom':

> The United Kingdom is a union of England and Wales with Scotland forming Great Britain (Union with Scotland Act 1706) and Northern Ireland (Union with Ireland Act 1800, Government of Ireland Act 1920). So apart from interpretation clauses the use of 'United Kingdom' in statutes shows that only Great Britain and Northern Ireland, but not the Channel Islands or Isle of Man are included therein.

That is confirmed by the Interpretation Act 1978, Sch 1 of which provides:

> The 'United Kingdom' means Great Britain and Northern Ireland whereas 'British Islands' means the United Kingdom, the Channel Islands and the Isle of Man.

The result was that his will failed to dispose of the bank accounts which would then pass on intestacy. Fortunately, the court admitted extrinsic evidence of the testator's intention and interpreted the words 'United Kingdom' in an extended way to include the offshore bank accounts.

Taxation, and in particular the concepts of residence and domicile

These concepts affect such matters as the basis of assessment, territorial scope and reliefs in relation to UK taxes. The private client will need to know the extent to which he becomes or remains liable to income tax, CGT and IHT following immigration to or emigration from the UK.

15.2 RESIDENCE AND DOMICILE

Whether a client is an immigrant or an emigrant, or whether he intends to invest in the UK or overseas, the rules of income tax, CGT and IHT can apply to him, but frequently in a modified form depending on his particular circumstances. The keys to an understanding of a client's tax position are the concepts of residence and domicile.

A statutory residence test has been introduced by the FA 2013, the details of which are contained within Sch 45. There is also extensive guidance published by HMRC: 'Guidance Note: Statutory Residence Test' (RDR3), updated in January 2020, and 'Guidance note for residence, domicile and the remittance basis' (RDR1), updated in July 2018. This test is used to determine whether an individual is resident in the UK for tax purposes in any tax year from 6 April 2013 onwards. The new test is not retrospective, however, and for various reasons it is necessary to know whether an individual was UK resident in the period prior to 6 April 2013. This requires applying the rules that operated before the new test was introduced, which are largely based on HMRC guidance and case law, unless the individual elects to use the new rules for this earlier period. For the time being, therefore, solicitors will need to understand both the old and the new rules.

15.2.1 Residence – position before 6 April 2013

There was no statutory definition of residence. Instead, the concept developed in a series of cases over many years. In order to give practical guidance, the Revenue produced some guidance in its booklet HMRC6 (2009) *Residence, Domicile and the Remittance Basis*. This replaced the previous guidance issued in booklet IR20 *Residents and non-residents – liability to tax in the UK*, which is relevant for the period before 6 April 2009. Although without statutory authority, and therefore capable of challenge, these booklets are generally accepted by practitioners as a basis from which to provide advice to immigrant and emigrant clients in relation to their status for tax years prior to 6 April 2013.

For the tax years before 6 April 2013, residence as a concept is concerned with physical presence in the UK. If an individual is physically present in the UK at some time in a tax year, it is a question of fact whether he is resident for tax purposes for that year. The fact that an individual is in the UK involuntarily is not generally relevant to this question. Basically, an individual will be considered resident in the UK if, for the time he is in the UK, it can be said to be his 'home'. It is not necessary that he owns a property in the UK; he may be resident even if he is living in hotel accommodation.

Any of the following tests may determine whether an individual is treated as resident in the UK in relation to the period before 6 April 2013.

15.2.1.1 183 days in the UK: temporary residence

An individual is treated as resident in a tax year pre-6 April 2013 if he is present for, in aggregate, 183 days or more in the year of assessment. For periods prior to 6 April 2008, the usual rule was to ignore days of arrival and departure when counting days, although in *Gaines-Cooper v Revenue and Customs Commissioners* [2007] STC (SCD) 23, the Revenue Special Commissioners indicated that in some circumstances these days could be counted.

However, from 6 April 2008 onwards the HMRC guidance indicates that if a person is in the UK at the end of a day (taken as midnight), that day will count as a day of presence. This will not be so if a person arrives in the UK on one day, in transit to a destination outside the UK, and continues the journey the next day without taking part in any activity unrelated to the journey, such as attending a business meeting.

Visits to the UK for some temporary purpose only (eg a holiday), and which are for less than six months, will not usually give rise to tax. In determining whether the visit is for a 'temporary purpose', any available accommodation in the UK is disregarded.

In addition to being resident whenever a person is in the UK for at least 183 days in a tax year, there are a number of other circumstances described in HMRC6 in which a person may be regarded as resident. Two examples of this are mentioned below.

15.2.1.2   Short-term visitors

Where a person makes visits to the UK over several years, but without any intention to remain for an extended period, he will be regarded as resident if his visits average 91 days per tax year over four years. In such a case, the visitor is usually treated as resident from the fifth year. Days spent in the UK because of exceptional circumstances beyond the individual's control may be ignored, for example an extended stay in the UK because of ill-health.

15.2.1.3   Longer-term visitors

Where a person comes to the UK with a purpose, such as employment, that will mean remaining for at least two years, he will be regarded as resident from the day of arrival.

15.2.2   Residence post 6 April 2013 – the statutory residence test

For the tax year 2013/14 and later, there is a statutory test to define residence for the purposes of income tax, CGT and IHT. There are, in fact, three tests set out in Sch 45 to the FA 2013: the 'automatic overseas' test, the 'automatic residence' test and the 'sufficient ties' test.

The statutory residence test is dealt with extensively in HMRC's Residence, Domicile and Remittance Basis Manual at RDRM11000 onwards. There are also guidance notes available: 'Guidance Note: Statutory Residence Test' (RDR3), updated in January 2020, and 'Guidance note for residence, domicile and the remittance basis' (RDR1), updated in July 2018.

Broadly, a person is UK resident in a particular tax year if, in that year, he satisfies either the automatic residence test or the sufficient ties test and does not satisfy any element of the automatic overseas test.

A person is not resident in the UK in a particular tax year if he satisfies the automatic overseas test or simply does not satisfy either of the other two tests.

The number of 'days' spent in the UK is extremely important when determining residence. A person is considered to have spent a day in the UK if here at the end of the day (midnight). This is subject to certain special rules which may count days even though the person was not here at midnight (to stop people flying in to an airport, conducting business and flying out again before midnight) or which may discount days if the person is in the UK due to exceptional circumstances.

Automatic overseas test

The details of this test are complex, but, broadly, a person is not UK resident in a tax year if, in that year, he satisfies any one of the following:

- He was UK resident in at least one of the previous three tax years and spends fewer than 16 days in the UK.
- He was not UK resident in any of the three previous tax years and spends fewer than 46 days in the UK.

- He works for sufficient hours outside the UK to qualify as working full time overseas, as calculated by the formula set out in Sch 45 to the FA 2013, and:
  - he spends fewer than 91 days in the UK in the tax year, and
  - he works in the UK for more than 3 hours a day on fewer than 31 days.
- He dies in the tax year and meets certain other conditions.

Automatic residence test

Again, the details of this test are complex, but, broadly, a person is UK resident in a particular tax year if he does not meet any of the automatic overseas tests and, during the relevant tax year, meets any one of the following:

- He spends at least 183 days in the UK.
- He has a home in the UK during all or part of the relevant tax year and meets the following further conditions. There must be at least one period of 91 consecutive days, at least 30 days of which fall in the tax year, when he has a home in the UK in which he is present on at least 30 days, and either:
  - he has no overseas home, or
  - he has an overseas home or homes in each of which he is present on fewer than 30 days in the tax year.

  Annex A, set out at RDRM13020 onwards, gives HMRC's view of what is a 'home'. At A4 it gives the basic test, which is that 'a person's home is a place that a reasonable onlooker with knowledge of the material facts would regard as that person's home'. An individual does not have to own the accommodation. Ownership, form of tenancy, or legal right to occupy the accommodation makes no difference. RDRM13050 and RDRM13060 give a number of examples of what is and what is not a home for this purpose.
- He works for sufficient hours in the UK to qualify as working full time in the UK, as calculated by the formula set out in Sch 45 to the FA 2013.
- He dies and meets various conditions, including that he had his main home in the UK and was resident in the UK for the three previous tax years.

Sufficient ties test

A person who does not satisfy either of the two tests above is UK resident in a particular tax year if he has sufficient ties to the UK.

This involves counting the days spent present in the UK in a tax year and combining this with other listed 'UK ties', which are the residence of the person's spouse and minor children (a 'family' tie), the location of the person's main home (an 'accommodation' tie), the extent to which the person does work in the UK (a 'work' tie) and whether the person spent more than 90 days in the UK in either or both of the previous two tax years immediately before the year under consideration (a '90 day' tie). Broadly, the longer a person has spent present in the UK in a tax year, then the fewer UK ties that need to be satisfied for that person to be resident. A distinction is made between persons who have been resident in any of the previous three tax years and those who have not. The latter need to spend longer in the UK (plus have sufficient UK ties) to be regarded as resident.

Obviously the number of permutations is enormous. There is very good Revenue guidance available at RDRM11520 and in 'Guidance Note: Statutory Residence Test' (RDR3). By way of example, a person who was not UK resident for any of the three tax years before the tax year under consideration, but who has spent more than 90 days in the UK, will be deemed to be UK resident if they have two of the following ties:

- a family tie;
- an accommodation tie;

- a work tie;
- a 90 day tie.

If the same person had spent only 16–45 days in the UK, they would have to have all four ties before becoming resident.

(In **Chapter 4** we discussed the fact that the main residence exemption was not available for periods arising on or after 6 April 2015 unless a person had spent at least 90 midnights in the residence, with the result that it is difficult to maintain non-resident status and qualify for the main residence exemption.)

Schedule 45 to the FA 2013 contains detailed rules to identify when those leaving or coming to the UK part way through a tax year may be able to split the year and be treated as resident for only part of the year.

As before (see **15.2.1.1**), a person will be present in the UK on any day in which he is present in the UK at midnight (unless in transit).

There are also anti-avoidance measures to prevent people creating short periods of non-residence, during which large amounts of income are received.

Days spent in the UK can be disregarded if they are due to exceptional circumstances. Annex B, set out at RDRM13200 onwards, gives HMRC's view of what amounts to exceptional circumstances. It will always depend on the facts and circumstances of each individual case but can include inability to travel as a result of coronavirus restrictions.

15.2.2.1 Ordinary residence

The concept of ordinary residence was largely abolished by the FA 2013 from 6 April 2013. The concept remains relevant, however, for ascertaining an individual's tax position for the tax years before this date.

The phrase 'ordinary residence' has been used in legislation, particularly in relation to CGT, primarily to prevent an individual from avoiding liability to tax simply by ceasing to be resident in the UK.

The phrase is undefined, but the Revenue's view as to the meaning of ordinary residence, contained in HMRC6, is that if a person is resident in the UK year after year, this indicates that he normally lives there and is therefore ordinarily resident. HMRC6 contains guidance as to the circumstances in which, in the period prior to 6 April 2013, it regards a person as ordinarily resident for a tax year.

15.2.3 Domicile

Unlike residence and ordinary residence, an individual's domicile is not confined to determining liability to taxation. It is relevant to many other matters, for example, when determining in private international law which system of law governs succession to property owned in a foreign jurisdiction. The domicile of a deceased determines whether or not a claim can be brought under the Inheritance (Provision for Family and Dependants) Act 1975.

Like residence and ordinary residence, domicile is not defined in statute but its meaning has been established by the courts in a number of decisions. An individual can only be domiciled in a country which has its own system of law, for example, England and Wales.

An individual is usually domiciled in the country which he considers as 'home'. Thus, an individual who emigrates to the USA where he lives for 20 or 30 years will not necessarily cease to be domiciled in some part of the UK. Domicile is distinct from nationality or residence, although according to the guidance in HMRC6 both may have an impact on assessing domicile. It is not possible to be without a domicile, and a person can only have one domicile at a time. There are no current proposals to provide a statutory test for domicile. However, in relation to establishing domicile for tax purposes only, there are important deeming provisions (see **15.3.3** and **15.3.5**).

15.2.3.1 Domicile of origin

Every individual must have a domicile. Normally, a domicile of origin will be determined at birth, ie, children acquire as domicile of origin their father's domicile at the date of their birth (or the mother's if the parents are unmarried). This may not be the country in which the child is actually born; nor need it be a country which the child has visited.

15.2.3.2 Domicile of dependency

Children under 16 who derive their domicile of origin from their father will acquire a new domicile, ie, a domicile of dependency in place of their domicile of origin if their father acquires a new domicile (see below).

15.2.3.3 Domicile of choice

Domicile can change where an individual voluntarily acquires a new domicile, ie, a domicile of choice. There is a heavy burden of proof before an individual can show that a domicile of choice has been acquired. Domicile is a matter of intent but a mere intention to change domicile is insufficient. Many factors are relevant including abandoning an existing domicile. There must be residence in the new country; intention alone is not enough: see *Kelly v Pyres* [2018] EWCA Civ 1368. Moreover, unless all connections with the previous domicile are broken, it may be difficult (if not impossible) to show the acquisition of a domicile of choice.

Clients who, at the time of emigrating from the UK, are considering acquiring a new domicile of choice should compile all available evidence of intention. Inter alia, the following should be considered:

(a) they should take up residence in the country involved, preferably acquiring property in that country and selling all property in the UK; and

(b) they must have a permanent intention to remain indefinitely in the new country in order to show a change in domicile. This requirement as to intention is often the most difficult obstacle for a client to overcome when endeavouring to change domicile. Ideally, they should make a written statement, or statutory declaration, before leaving the UK, setting out all personal circumstances giving rise to the decision to change domicile. Such a statement is not conclusive but will always be of assistance when attempting to convince third parties, particularly the Revenue, of the change of domicile; and

(c) in addition to purchasing a residence in the new country, they should forge as many associations with that country as possible while at the same time ending associations with the old country. They should consider a new business or employment, make a will valid under local law, open a new bank account, sell investments and reinvest in the new country, etc. Purchasing a burial plot in the new country is often regarded as helpful.

15.2.4 United Kingdom

The UK consists of England and Wales, Scotland and Northern Ireland. As explained at **15.1.1.2**, it does not include the Channel Islands or the Isle of Man, which, because of their relatively lower tax rates, are often termed 'tax havens'.

It is technically incorrect to refer to a person as domiciled in the UK. An individual has a domicile in a territory or a state which has its own legal system. Thus, an individual may be domiciled in Scotland or in England and Wales or in Northern Ireland. For brevity, however, this chapter refers to a person domiciled in any part of the UK as 'UK domiciled'.

15.3 TAXATION OF THE INDIVIDUAL AND THE FOREIGN ELEMENT

The effect of the rules as to residence and domicile on an individual's liability to tax depends upon the tax involved. Spouses are independent persons for tax purposes. Their residence status and their domicile are determined by reference to their individual circumstances and so may not coincide with the status of their spouse.

Transfers of property between spouses both of whom are domiciled in the UK are free of IHT by virtue of the spouse exemption. However, transfers by a UK domiciled spouse to a non-UK domiciled spouse are only exempt up to a cumulative limit of £325,000 (for the tax year 2013/14 and beyond; for transfers prior to this, the limit was £55,000) (IHTA 1984, s 18(2)). Since 6 April 2013 it is possible, in certain circumstances, for a non-domiciled spouse to elect to be treated as domiciled in the UK, thus becoming eligible for the full spouse exemption for IHT. The conditions to be met for the election to be made are set out in s 177 of the FA 2013.

The Finance (No 2) Act 2017 introduces new deemed domicile provisions for income tax, CGT and IHT. The new provisions apply as from 6 April 2017.

15.3.1 Income tax and CGT

15.3.1.1 Income tax

Very broadly, an individual who is UK resident in a tax year is liable to income tax in that year on his worldwide income, ie, he must pay income tax on all income whether its source is within the UK or elsewhere. Special rules apply in some situations to individuals who are resident but not domiciled in the UK; see **15.3.2.4**.

A non-UK resident is only liable to income tax on income arising from a source within the UK. The rules to determine whether a person is resident in the UK are considered at **15.2**.

Whether a source of income is within the UK depends on the type of income. For example, income from employment within the UK, rent from land within the UK and dividends from companies whose membership register is kept within the UK are all sources of income within the UK. If the duties of the employment, the situation of the land or the membership register are outside the UK, the income will have a non-UK source.

15.3.1.2 Capital gains tax

An individual who is UK resident (or, in tax years prior to 2013/14, resident or ordinarily resident) is generally liable to pay CGT on gains made on disposals of assets wherever they are situated.

Before 6 April 2019, an individual who was not resident in the UK was not normally liable to CGT whether the gains arose on disposals of assets in the UK or elsewhere. On 6 April 2015, the disposal of residential property in the UK by a non-UK resident became chargeable to CGT. (See TCGA 1992, s 1 and ss 14B–14H.)

Finance Act 2019, s 13, Sch 1, Pt 1, paras 1, 2 made significant changes to the taxation of gains made by non-residents.

A person who is UK resident for a tax year is chargeable to capital gains tax on chargeable gains accruing to the person in the tax year on the disposal of assets wherever situated (TCGA 1992 s 1A(1)). For these purposes, a person is 'UK resident' for a tax year if the person is resident in the UK during any part of the tax year. The position of personal representatives and trustees continues unchanged.

Under s 1A(3), a person who is not UK resident for a tax year is chargeable to capital gains tax on chargeable gains accruing to the person in the tax year on the disposal of:

(a)   assets situated in the UK that have a relevant connection to the person's UK branch or agency and are disposed of at a time when the person has that branch or agency (see s 1B);

(b)   assets not within para (a) that are interests in UK land; and

(c)   assets (wherever situated) not within para (a) or (b) that derive at least 75% of their value from UK land where the person has a substantial indirect interest in that land (as defined in s 1D and Sch 1A).

For this purpose, a person is 'UK resident' for a tax year if resident in the UK during any part of the tax year.

Schedule 1A broadly provides that an asset derives at least 75% of its value from UK land if it consists of a right or an interest in a company, and, at the time of the disposal, at least 75% of the total market value of the company's qualifying assets derives (directly or indirectly) from interests in UK land. A person has a substantial indirect interest in UK land if, at any time in the period of two years ending with the time of the disposal, the person has a 25% investment in the company.

Thus, from 6 April 2019, the scope of UK tax is broadened for non-UK tax residents to include disposals of all real estate located in the UK, not just residential property, and disposals of entities such as companies deriving at least 75% of their value from UK land.

There is an exclusion for UK property-rich entities where all (or almost all) of the property has been used for trading purposes (TCGA 1992, Sch 1A, para 5). In addition, HMRC will only be able to apply UK capital gains tax to the disposal of UK property-rich entities if the tax treaty with the vendor's country of residence gives taxing rights to the UK for this type of disposal—currently not all UK tax treaties include this clause, so there will have to be a gradual replacement of all those treaties which do not give such taxing rights to the country where real estate is located.

In addition, it is possible to rebase property values to April 2019 (TCGA 1992, Sch 4AA). There are options to calculate the gain or loss on a disposal using the original acquisition cost of the asset or using the value of the asset at commencement of the rules in April 2019. Both options are available for direct and indirect disposals. For indirect disposals, where historical cost is used and it gives rise to a loss rather than a gain, the loss is not allowable for offset against any other gains.

Where the seller is an individual, he has the same annual exemption and is subject to the same tax rates as a UK resident. The seller may also make use of the main residence relief (see **4.7.3**) but only if the requirements are satisfied. An owner disposing of a property cannot count certain years of ownership as years when the property was his principal residence. Broadly, these are any years where (i) neither the owner nor his spouse was resident in the same jurisdiction as the property, and (ii) the owner spent less than 90 days at the property.

All sales of land (residential and non-residential) made by non-residents must be reported within 60 days of completion using a non-resident Capital Gains Tax Return, irrespective of whether or not there is tax to pay. Any tax due must be paid within the same period. See Finance Act 2019, s 14 and Sch 2.

Gains arising to companies will be charged to corporation tax. See **15.3.6**.

15.3.2   Effect of ceasing to be resident for income tax and CGT

If an individual is resident in the UK for part of a tax year and absent for the remainder of it, the general rule is that income tax and CGT is charged for the whole tax year. In certain circumstances it is possible to split the tax year so that an individual is treated as resident in the UK for only part of the year. For example, where an individual leaves to live permanently outside the UK, the Revenue treats him as non-resident from the day after the day of departure.

For the period prior to 6 April 2013, this occurred on a concession basis, but the detailed rules are now contained in the FA 2013, Sch 45.

Tax planning by emigrating from the UK is perhaps the ultimate form of tax avoidance. To be successful, the individual will need to convince the Revenue that he is no longer resident in the UK on the date on which the liability to tax arose.

The operative date will depend on the tax in question. For CGT purposes, liability arises on the date of disposal of the asset in question. This is generally the date on which a binding contract is made (and not the date of later completion). If an individual is still a UK resident when the terms of the contract were substantially agreed, the Revenue may argue that this should be taken as the date of disposal, even though a formal contract had not yet been made. For effective tax planning, therefore, a client may be best advised to become non-resident well before negotiations are concluded.

15.3.2.1 Temporary non-residence – CGT

To prevent abuse by UK resident individuals leaving the UK on or after 17 March 1998, FA 1998, s 127 introduced a new anti-avoidance measure into TCGA 1992, s 10A. This provision, which applied to the period before 6 April 2013, prevented a person avoiding CGT by simply becoming non-UK resident for a short period and making the disposal during this time. This was done by charging the gain in the tax year of that person's return to the UK, unless the person was non-resident for more than five full tax years.

For the tax year 2013/14 and afterwards, the position is largely the same, though now a person must be away for at least five years, rather than five tax years, to avoid being a temporary non-resident (FA 2013, Sch 45, Pt 4).

15.3.2.2 Employment overseas

Although an employee going overseas to work full time on a contract of employment may not consider he is emigrating, he is effectively doing so for income tax and CGT purposes. The position in relation to the tax year 2013/14 and after is governed by the statutory residence test, and in particular the elements of the automatic residence and overseas tests that deal with full-time working.

Once in the overseas employment, the employee can dispose of assets within the UK without liability to CGT on gains realised. To achieve this, he should be advised to enter into contracts disposing of assets likely to realise substantial gains only after he has gone overseas and achieved non-resident status (see above).

Any income which the employee may have from sources within the UK remains subject to income tax.

15.3.2.3 Emigration within six years of a gift

Hold-over relief on the disposal of assets by way of gift has been discussed at **4.4.5.2**. The relief is available only if an election is made by the donor and donee, and if the donee was resident in the UK at the time. If the donee emigrates within six years of the gift, an emigration charge arises whereby the heldover gain becomes immediately chargeable. Tax is payable by the donee but the Revenue can recover it from the donor if it remains unpaid 12 months after the due date. The charge does not apply if the donee is an employee who leaves to work abroad under a full-time contract of employment.

EXAMPLE

In 2016, Dana gave her son her shareholding in ABC Ltd. The gain of £10,000 was held over. In 2019, her son emigrated from the UK and took up residence in France. The £10,000 is immediately chargeable, ie, at the rates of tax relevant in 2019. The actual value of the shareholding in 2019 is irrelevant.

15.3.2.4 Long-term immigrants – remittance basis

Prior to 6 April 2008, persons who retained their non-UK domicile enjoyed more relaxed rules. Broadly, persons who were resident but not domiciled in the UK were only taxed on their foreign income and gains to the extent that these were remitted to the UK.

The FA 2008 introduced changes to the remittance basis, which came into effect on 6 April 2008.

A person who is resident but not domiciled in the UK will be taxed on all foreign income and gains wherever arising each year unless, for the tax year in question, the person has *claimed* the remittance basis of taxation. If this is claimed, the person will only pay tax on income and gains arising in the UK and on income and gains remitted to the UK. By claiming the remittance basis, the person will not be able to use the income tax personal allowance or CGT annual exemption. A person can only claim the remittance basis for the year if he pays the 'Remittance Basis Charge'. From 6 April 2017, there are two levels of charge: £30,000 where the person has been resident in seven out of the nine tax years prior to the tax year in question; and £60,000 for those resident in 12 out of 14 tax years. Any period of residence prior to 6 April 2008 will be counted when assessing if a non-domiciled person has been resident for seven or 12 years. The person may choose each year whether to claim the remittance basis.

If a person who is resident but not domiciled in the UK has, in any tax year, less than £2,000 worth of income and gains which are not remitted to the UK then this person will automatically be taxed on the remittance basis, without having to pay the Remittance Basis Charge, and he will have the income tax personal allowance and CGT annual exemption available. See ITA 2007, s 809D.

From 6 April 2017 there are new deemed domicile rules. Persons who are deemed domiciled in the UK are unable to claim the remittance basis.

15.3.3 Deemed domicile for income tax and capital gains tax

The Finance (No 2) Act 2017 inserts a new s 835BA into ITA 2007 introducing for the first time the concept of deemed domicile in relation to these two taxes. Previously, deemed domicile existed only in relation to IHT. The provisions will take effect from 2017/18.

An individual not domiciled in the UK is to be regarded as domiciled in the UK for the purposes of the two taxes if either of the following conditions are met:

Condition A (the formerly domiciled individual)

Condition A is met if:

(a)   the individual was born in the UK;

(b)   the individual's domicile of origin was in the UK; and

(c)   the individual is UK resident for the relevant tax year.

This is designed to deal with the situation (regarded as abusive) of a UK national who works abroad and acquires a domicile of choice in the new jurisdiction and then returns to the UK claiming to still be domiciled in the new jurisdiction. Mr Gulliver of HSBC was a high-profile example who attracted much adverse publicity. His domicile of origin was in the UK but, while working for HSBC, he acquired a domicile of choice in Hong Kong. When he returned to live in the UK, he claimed that he was still domiciled in Hong Kong and was, therefore, entitled to the remittance basis.

From 6 April 2017 such a person would be subject to income tax and CGT on their worldwide income and gains as soon as they became resident in a particular tax year.

Condition B (15 out of 20 rule)

Condition B is met if the individual has been UK resident for at least 15 of the 20 tax years immediately preceding the relevant tax year.

But, to provide transitional relief, Condition B is not met if:

(a)   the individual is not UK resident for the relevant tax year; and

(b)   there is no tax year beginning after 5 April 2017 and preceding the relevant tax year in which the individual was UK resident.

For example, Margot, a Swiss national, was resident in the UK from February 2002 to March 2017. She is not deemed domiciled in 2017/18. If she was resident from February 2003 to March 2018, she would be deemed domiciled in 2018/19.

Once a person is deemed domiciled, they are unable to claim the remittance basis (as to which see **15.3.2.4** above).

15.3.4 Inheritance tax

Residence is not relevant as a concept to determine liability to IHT. Instead, an individual's domicile governs liability to IHT.

An individual who is domiciled in (some part of) the UK is liable to IHT on a transfer of value of assets whether the assets are in the UK or elsewhere. If an individual is not domiciled in (some part of) the UK, liability arises only on the transfer of value of property situated in the UK, although there are some exceptions to this rule, for example, exempt gilts (government stock).

There have always been deemed domicile rules for IHT. For 2017/18 onwards, the rules are changed.

15.3.4.1 Deemed domicile up to 2016/17

Section 267 of IHTA 1984 contains provisions extending the meaning of domicile. An individual not domiciled (some part of) in the UK under the principles discussed at **15.2.3** may nevertheless be deemed to be domiciled there for IHT. This can happen in one of two circumstances.

The domicile test

An individual actually domiciled in (some part of) the UK within the three years immediately preceding a transfer of value will be deemed domiciled there at the time of the transfer. The aim of this provision is to stop an individual moving their property out of the UK and then emigrating in the hope of avoiding IHT on future transfers of their property.

EXAMPLE

Alexis acquired a domicile of choice in California in January 2011 when she emigrated there from England. She died two years later. As Alexis had given up her English domicile within three years of her death (the transfer of value), her entire estate is chargeable to IHT.

The residence test

An individual who was resident in the UK for income tax purposes in not less than 17 of the 20 years of assessment ending with the year in which the transfer of value occurs is deemed to be domiciled in the UK. In determining whether an individual is resident in any year, the income tax tests discussed at **15.2** are used.

This provision is intended to bring long-term residents who have not become UK domiciliaries into the charge to IHT.

> **EXAMPLE**
>
> Alexandra's employment in the UK since July 1990 has just ended following the failure of her employer's business. As a result, she plans to return home to Greece as soon as possible. Last year, she gave some land she owned outside Athens to her daughter. In view of Alexandra's residence in the UK for over 20 years, she will be deemed domiciled in the UK, so that her death within seven years of the gift of the land would cause the gift to become subject to IHT.

If a person who had acquired deemed domicile under the 17 out of 20 rule ceased UK residence for at least four complete tax years, they lost their deemed domicile status from the start of the fourth year of non-residence. This was because if they remained non-resident in the fourth year, they would no longer have been UK resident for 17 of the previous 20 years.

15.3.4.2 Deemed domicile from 2017/18

For 2017/18 onwards a person is deemed domiciled in the United Kingdom if either of the following conditions are met:

Condition A (formerly domiciled individual)

Condition A is met if a person is a formerly domiciled resident for the tax year in which the relevant time falls. As for income tax and CGT, the term 'formerly domiciled resident' means an individual who was born in the UK, with a UK domicile of origin. However, the IHT test has an extra element. The individual must have been resident in the UK for at least one of the two tax years immediately preceding the relevant tax year. The relaxation for IHT reflects the fact that acquiring domicile for IHT purposes has such serious tax consequences: worldwide assets become subject to IHT.

> **EXAMPLE**
>
> Rufus was born in the UK in 1977 with a UK domicile of origin. He acquires a domicile of choice in Monaco in 2002 but becomes resident in the UK on 1 January 2020 (he retains his domicile of choice in Monaco). For income tax and CGT purposes he is deemed domiciled in the UK for 2019/20.
>
> However, if Rufus dies on 5 April 2020, he would not be deemed domiciled for IHT because he was not resident here in either of the two preceding tax years. If he dies on or after 6 April 2020 (still UK resident) then he will be deemed UK domiciled so that his worldwide estate is subject to IHT, including property in trusts set up when he was not UK domiciled.

Linked to this amendment is an amendment to IHTA 1984, s 48 (which deals with excluded property in relation to settlements). Property comprised in a settlement situated outside the United Kingdom is normally excluded property if the settlor was not domiciled in the United Kingdom at the time the settlement was made (IHTA 1984, s 48(3)). However, a new s 48(3E) provides that such property is not excluded property at any time in a tax year if the settlor was a formerly domiciled resident for that tax year.

The effect of this amendment is that when an individual who was born in the UK and who had a UK domicile of origin has created a trust whilst they were non-domiciled, that trust will be subject to IHT, whilst they are UK resident, in the same way as a trust which had been created by somebody who was domiciled in the UK.

Condition B (15 out of 20 rule)

Condition B is met if a person has been resident in the UK for at least 15 out of the previous 20 tax years ending with the tax year in question.

However, a person who would otherwise satisfy the test will not be deemed domiciled if they are non-UK resident in that tax year and have been non-resident for the previous three consecutive tax years. The effect of this limitation (which is only found in the IHT version of the 15-year rule, not in the income tax and CGT version) is to replicate the previous position on losing domicile under the 17 out of 20 rule. A deemed UK domicile will cease for IHT purposes after four tax years of non-residence.

Note, however, that if the individual returns to the UK within six tax years, they will immediately become deemed domiciled for IHT because they will fulfil the 15 out of 20 years test.

The 20-year window is not limited to tax years from 6 April 2017 onwards, and so tax years of UK residence before 6 April 2017 will be counted towards an individual's total. As a result, a non-UK domiciled individual who had been continuously UK resident since the tax year 2002–03 acquired a deemed UK domicile on 6 April 2017.

The effect is that a person must cease being UK resident for four complete tax years in order to escape the deemed domicile rules.

15.3.4.3 IHT on residential property held by an overseas structure

A person who is domiciled (or deemed domiciled) in the UK is subject to IHT on their worldwide assets. A person who is not domiciled here is subject to IHT only on their UK assets. Their non-UK assets are excluded property for IHT purposes.

Shares in a company registered outside the UK are non-UK assets. It, was, therefore a common tax planning ploy for non-domiciliaries to own their residences through an offshore company plus, since 2017/18, any enveloped dwellings.

The Revenue has made strenuous efforts to bring the value of such residences in the UK within the UK tax net. (See, for example, the annual tax on enveloped dwellings at **5.3.6**.)

The Finance (No 2) Act 2017 extended IHT to residential properties situated in the UK held or financially supported by or through overseas structures situated outside the UK. It does so by amending the definition of excluded property.

Paragraph 1 of a new Sch A1 inserted into IHTA 1984 provides that property is not excluded property where:

- the beneficial owner of the property is an individual domiciled outside the UK; and
- the property is held in a settlement where the settlor was domiciled outside the UK when the settlement was made.

Paragraph 2 applies similarly where the UK residential property interest is held through a close company or partnership.

15.3.4.4 Death of a UK domiciliary with foreign property

Succession

If the testator left two wills, one dealing with his foreign property, and an English will dealing with his other assets, a foreign lawyer should be instructed to prove the foreign will and to administer the foreign property in accordance with its terms.

If the testator left only an English will, this should be proved in the usual way and then a foreign lawyer instructed either to reseal the English grant in the foreign jurisdiction or to extract the appropriate grant in that jurisdiction using sealed and certified copies of the English grant and will. As a grant obtained in the UK contains a 'notation of domicile', ie the deceased's domicile at death is stated on the grant, the grant will be recognised in other parts of the UK without further formality (Administration of Estates Act 1971 (AEA 1971)). Thus, the English executors of a deceased client can prove title to property in Scotland or Northern Ireland without resealing their grant in either jurisdiction (and vice versa).

Devolution of foreign property, particularly land, is often subject to local succession taxes (or equivalent) and to local laws of entitlement which may override (to a given extent) the terms of an English will. For example, in Scotland, Spain and France a stated proportion of the testator's estate passes automatically (and not by will) to certain relatives; in the USA and Scandinavian countries there is 'community of property' provision for spouses. In view of these local succession laws, it is usually appropriate for the clients to be advised to make a will in the particular jurisdiction taking local law into account; any English will should in terms exclude the property in the foreign jurisdiction. The impact of an election for the law of the deceased's nationality under the EU Succession Regulation (Brussels IV) in relation to succession to property on death has been considered at **11.1**.

Inheritance tax

Worldwide assets are part of the estate of a client domiciled in the UK for IHT purposes (under either of the tests discussed above) and should be disclosed in Form IHT400. Subject to any relief under a double taxation agreement or convention, the English PRs are liable to pay any IHT which is due although their liability is limited to the extent of assets received or which might have been received but for their neglect or default (IHTA 1984, s 204). Unless the testator's will provides otherwise, the beneficiaries of the foreign property bear the burden of the IHT which that property attracts (IHTA 1984, s 211). Thus, the UK PRs, having paid the IHT to the Revenue, will need to recover an equivalent amount from the beneficiary of the property.

15.3.4.5 Death of a non-UK domiciliary with UK property

Succession

Foreign PRs may obtain title to the property in the UK by resealing their foreign grant in the appropriate court in the UK. Except in Scotland (where local laws apply), succession to the property is generally in accordance with the terms of the deceased's will. The impact of Brussels IV in relation to succession to property on death has been considered at **11.1**.

Inheritance tax

Certain government stock and other property is exempt from IHT, even though situated in the UK, if owned by an individual who is neither domiciled nor ordinarily resident in the UK. Otherwise, property physically situated in the UK is subject to IHT. All such property should be disclosed in Form IHT401.

Since 6 April 2017, any UK residential property owned indirectly (eg via a company or trust) by a non-UK domiciled person is subject to IHT.

15.3.5 Double taxation treaties

An individual may be liable to tax in the UK and in a foreign country at the same time. The client may be 'dual resident' because the residence criteria in the two countries where he has lived treat him as resident in each country. If there is a double taxation agreement between the countries, this will provide relief from double taxation of income and gains. If no double taxation agreement exists, unilateral relief may be granted by one of the countries. There are no special EU tax rules and the rules of individual Member States have not yet been harmonised, but there are various double taxation provisions and reliefs between EU countries.

15.3.6 The annual tax on enveloped dwellings (ATED)

ATED was introduced by the Finance Act 2013, Part 3 from 1 April 2013 as part of a package of measures aimed at making it less attractive to hold high-value UK residential property indirectly, eg through a company, in order to avoid or minimise taxes such as stamp duty land tax (SDLT) and CGT on a subsequent disposal of the property.

ATED is an annual charge on UK dwellings held by a non-natural person, for example a company. The ATED year runs from 1 April to 31 March. Tax is due for that period if, on any day, the non-natural person is entitled to an interest in a dwelling that exceeds £500,000.

ATED is payable annually in advance by 30 April and a return must also be filed by that date. ATED is based on the taxable value of the property. Properties are revalued for the purposes of ATED every five years.

15.4 TRUSTEES AND THE FOREIGN ELEMENT

The residence and ordinary residence of trustees is generally determined separately from the status of the settlor or the beneficiaries and without regard to the location of the trust assets.

Before 6 April 2007, the test for whether trustees were UK resident was different for income tax (FA 1989, s 110) and for CGT (TCGA 1992, s 69) purposes. Since 6 April 2007 the test is the same (ITA 2007, s 475 and TCGA 1992, s 69, as amended by FA 2006). Under these sections, for both income tax and CGT, trustees of a settlement are together treated as if they were a single person, and this deemed person is treated as resident in the UK whenever either:

(a)   all the trustees are resident in the UK; or

(b)   at least one trustee is resident in the UK and the settlor was resident or domiciled in the UK when the settlement was created. (If the settlement was created before 6 April 2013, the condition also applied if the settlor was ordinarily resident.)

The sections also provide that a trustee not resident in the UK is treated as if resident at any time when he acts as trustee in the course of a business which he carries on in the UK through a branch, agency or permanent establishment there.

15.4.1 Income tax

Non-resident trustees are not liable to UK income tax other than on income arising in the UK (see above). In such cases, basic rate tax (20%) is generally deducted at source so that the trustees receive income net of tax. Trustees of no interest in possession settlements are liable to tax at the 'trust rate' or 'dividend trust rate' (see **14.5.2**); in practice, the Revenue often cannot collect this extra tax from the non-resident trustees because there is no means of withholding it at source, nor can it enforce the liability in the overseas jurisdiction.

15.4.2 Capital gains tax

Non-resident settlements have been popular with clients and estate planners as providing a ready method of sheltering the trust's gains from CGT. Non-resident trustees are in the same position as individuals who are not resident in the UK. Thus they are not liable to pay CGT on their chargeable gains on disposal of trust assets, provided the settlement is a non-resident settlement for the entire tax year in question. If the trustees become non-resident part way through the year, the Revenue will not split the year for assessment purposes so allowing avoidance of CGT for the period when the trust is non-resident. Ideally a client should be advised to set up his non-resident trust, or export his existing trust (see **15.4.4.1** below), well before 6 April in the relevant year.

Note, however, that the provisions discussed at **15.3.1.2** above, which introduced a CGT charge for non-UK residents who dispose of residential property in the UK, also cover non-UK resident trusts making such disposals.

15.4.3 Anti-avoidance legislation

Ever since the introduction of CGT in 1965, estate planners have advised clients to use non-resident settlements (normally discretionary settlements) to shelter the trustees' gains from

CGT. Over the same period, various legislative attempts have been made to counter loss of revenue through use of these settlements, but only recently has the large-scale use of non-resident settlements been substantially halted. Even now some opportunities remain for use of such settlements.

On the whole, clients were less concerned with avoidance of inheritance tax (or its predecessor capital transfer tax) or income tax in relation to their non-resident settlement, although sometimes this was the result even if not the overriding intention. Often clients wished for some continuing enjoyment from the settled property or its income. The real objective, therefore, was sheltering the non-resident gains from CGT while, so far as the legislation permitted, continuing to enjoy the property.

Anti-avoidance legislation is always complex even if the objective is reasonably certain. Whether the objective is achieved, is, of course, another matter. Apart from 1965 (with the introduction of CGT), there have been two principal occasions when anti-avoidance legislation has been introduced: the first by FA 1981, s 80; and the second 10 years later by FA 1991, Sch 16. Neither of these was entirely successful, in that estate planners continued to find ways round the provisions and so defeat the intention of the legislation. Each of these provisions has been retained, and strengthened, and appear now as ss 86 and 87 of TCGA 1992, with a supplementary charge under TCGA 1992, s 91.

TCGA 1992, s 86 provides that gains realised by non-UK resident trustees are attributed to its settlor where the settlor has an interest in a settlement and is both UK resident and domiciled in the UK. The settlor is entitled to recover the tax so paid from the trustees. The section does not apply in relation to a protected settlement (that is one that satisfies Conditions A–D in TCGA 1992, Sch 5, para 5A). Instead, capital gains will only be chargeable under TCGA 1992, s 87 to the extent that they are matched to benefits received from the trust.

TCGA 1992, s 87 imposes a charge on a beneficiary on payments received, or other benefits enjoyed, to the extent that it is matched with gains realised by the trustees. An amount equal to the gains realised in a year (on actual and deemed disposals) by the non-resident trustees which, had the trustees been UK resident, would have been chargeable to capital gains tax (the s 1(3) amount for the year), will be apportioned to a beneficiary to the extent that it is matched with a capital payment received. This charge applies to any settlement irrespective of the domicile of the settlor.

TCGA 1992, s 91 imposes a supplementary charge designed to discourage the long-term retention of gains within an offshore trust. In essence, the longer trust gains remain undistributed (within the first six-year period), the greater the potential tax charge when an individual receives a capital payment. The supplementary charge applies regardless of when the trust was established.

It is calculated by applying a notional rate of interest (currently 10% a year for a maximum of six years) to the amount of tax payable under the capital payments charge where an individual receives a capital payment. The amount of the capital payment is allocated to past gains previously made by the trustees and operates to increase the amount of tax due on the capital payments received by the individual. Hence, if an individual receives a capital payment of, say, £100,000 on which he has to pay capital gains tax of £20,000, he could be faced with an additional tax liability of as much as £12,000 (ie £20,000 × 60%) if the maximum supplementary charge were to apply.

A further provision, TCGA 1992 s 80, has introduced an export charge. Section 80 is discussed at **15.4.4** below. The other sections are beyond the scope of this book and will not be considered further. However, for anyone involved in advising settlor clients seeking to avoid CGT, they must be fully understood.

15.4.4   Anti-avoidance legislation – the position now

The current position in relation to anti-avoidance legislation is set out below.

15.4.4.1   Migrant settlements – export charge (TCGA 1992, s 80(2))

Consider the following example.

EXAMPLE

Derek Godfrey formed his electrical engineering company. He settled the shares on UK resident trustees to hold on family discretionary trusts. He continued to draw director's fees. Expecting imminent growth in value of the shares due to the success of the company, the UK trustees retired in favour of non-resident trustees. The company prospered. The non-resident trustees sold the shares realising a substantial capital profit.

Derek Godfrey's tax position:

(a)   deemed disposal on transfer of shares to the UK trustees: no significant capital gains realised and so covered by the indexation allowance and the annual exemption;

(b)   appointment of non-resident trustees: no disposal, the trustees are a single continuing body of persons (TCGA 1992, s 69, see **15.4**).

The consequence of these transactions (before 1981) was that any increase in value of the shares by the time the appointment of the new trustees was not charged to CGT. The gain (often large) was free of CGT. To counter this, an 'export charge' was introduced to tax gains which had accrued but which had not been realised to the date of the appointment of the non-resident trustees by FA 1981, s 83 (now TCGA 1992, s 80).

Advice to clients contemplating the 'export' of their settlement covers two main aspects; legal and taxation issues.

Legal issues

What is at issue is the export of a UK trust to avoid CGT. Export of the trust is simply achieved by appointing persons who are resident abroad as trustees and ensuring that the administration of the trust is carried on outside the UK. But what considerations should the present trustees have in mind when faced with a proposal that the trust be exported? First, there is no absolute bar in English law preventing the appointment of non-resident trustees of a UK trust and, secondly, such an appointment should be made only in 'appropriate circumstances' because the result is to remove the trust from control by the English courts. The following extract is from the judgment of Pennycuick V-C in *Re Whitehead's Will Trusts; Burke v Burke and Others* [1971] 1 WLR 833:

> The law has been quite well established for upwards of a century that there is no absolute bar to the appointment of persons resident abroad as trustees of an English trust. I say 'no absolute bar', in the sense that such an appointment would be prohibited by law and would consequently be invalid. On the other hand, apart from exceptional circumstances, it is not proper to make such an appointment, that is to say, the court would not apart from exceptional circumstances, make such an appointment; nor would it be right for the donees of the power to make such an appointment out of court. If they did, presumably the court would be likely to interfere at the instance of the beneficiaries. There do, however, exist exceptional circumstances in which such an appointment can properly be made. The most obvious exceptional circumstances are those in which the beneficiaries have settled permanently in some country outside the United Kingdom and what is proposed to be done is to appoint new trustees in that country.

Clearly, if the court would appoint non-resident trustees, it will be proper for the trustees themselves to do so, for example where all the beneficiaries are resident in the country where the trust is to become resident following the appointment. If the trustees made an appointment where the court might not, there is unlikely to be any real concern if all the beneficiaries have approved the non-resident appointment. This will require all beneficiaries to be ascertained and to be *sui juris*. If the trustees are in doubt about a proposed appointment, it would be sensible to apply to the court first (as in *Re Whitehead*).

In many cases, there will be appropriate express provision in the trust instrument for the trustees to retire in favour of non-resident trustees. Such a power can be exercised without further consideration by the trustees, provided its exercise is in the best interests of the beneficiaries.

The choice of overseas jurisdiction requires some thought by the trustees. It is prudent to appoint the non-resident trustees in a jurisdiction which will, if necessary, enforce the trustees' duties; the concept of a trust and the division of legal and beneficial ownership is not known in many civil law jurisdictions. Care should also be taken to choose a country where tax laws are less stringent than the UK since, otherwise, the trustees may be taxed as heavily, if not more so, than in the UK. It is also sensible to choose a jurisdiction which is likely to be stable – the Channel Islands or the Isle of Man – and to select reputable trustees, for example a well-known trust company or a firm of lawyers practising within the jurisdiction.

Taxation issues

The export charge is levied under TCGA 1992, s 80 in a manner familiar to the CGT legislation. When the trustees become non-resident in the UK, they are deemed to have disposed of the trust assets at market value and to have re-acquired them at the same value. The retiring trustees are primarily responsible for the tax due on the chargeable gain; if it is not paid by them within six months of the due date, the Revenue can recover the tax from any person who was a trustee in the 12 months before the export of the trust (unless, broadly, when he ceased to be a trustee there was then no proposal to export the trust). Because of their personal liability for the tax, the retiring trustees should retain sufficient assets under their control so that they can pay the tax due.

This export charge may not necessarily deter the use of a non-resident settlement by a settlor, particularly where the growth in the settled assets is expected to occur after the export rather than before it.

The charge is suspended in cases where an 'inadvertent' change in the residence status of the settlement occurs provided the UK resident status is resumed within six months. For example, the death of the only UK resident trustee leaving two non-resident trustees, would cause the settlement to become non-resident. If the trustee is replaced by another UK trustee within six months no charge is made under s 80.

Instalment option for the s 80 charge

The European Court of Justice in 2017 ruled that the immediate CGT charge on trustees, with no option to defer, was discriminatory according to EU principles (*Trustees of the P Panayi Accumulation and Maintenance Settlements v Revenue and Customs Commissioners* (Case C-646/15) EU:C:2017:682).

As a result, Finance Act 2019 introduced CGT exit charge payment plans, providing an option to pay the tax over six years in equal instalments with interest accruing on any outstanding tax. The details of the deferral arrangements are contained in a new Sch 3ZAA to the Taxes Management Act 1970. The change takes effect from 6 April 2019.

The deferral option is only available to trustees relocating within the EU or EEA and only where the trust carries out an economically significant activity. Security may be required if HMRC considers that there would be a serious risk to the collection of tax. The deferral ends if the taxpayer becomes bankrupt or resident outside the EEA. The measure includes an anti-avoidance provision to render any deferral plan void if the exit charge is deliberately triggered to benefit from the tax deferral.

The term 'economically significant activity' has the same meaning as in TCGA 1992, s 13A(4), but substituting references to companies with references to trustees. It appears to derive from the requirement for a trust to be 'profit-making' in order to benefit from the freedom of establishment in EU law, a condition that was found to be met in *Panayi* because the trust was carrying on an economic activity given that the trust assets were intended to generate profits for the beneficiaries to enjoy.

SUMMARY

(1)   Private client work can have an overseas dimension in various ways. UK clients may:

   (a)   own property overseas;

   (b)   spend time outside the UK.

(2)   Non-UK clients may spend time within the UK.

(3)   The tax position of these clients depends on whether they are regarded as resident and/or domiciled within the UK in any tax year.

(4)   The test for residence for tax years prior to 2013/14 is based on HMRC guidance and is largely based on the amount of time spent in the UK. From 6 April 2013 the test will be a statutory one, based on a number of factors.

(5)   The test for domicile is derived from case law and largely depends upon assessing the legal state with which a person has the closest links. HMRC also deems a person to be domiciled for tax purposes if he has been resident in the UK for sufficient time.

(6)   Broadly, a person who is not UK resident in a tax year pays income tax only on income from UK sources, and no CGT on disposals.

(7)   A person who is not domiciled within the UK is only liable to IHT on a transfer of value of UK property.

(8)   Dealing with overseas matters in relation to individuals and trusts requires a detailed understanding of a very large body of complex law.

REVIEW ACTIVITY

Which ONE of the following is CORRECT?

A   Domicile is mainly relevant to income tax.

B   Residence is relevant to CGT and income tax.

C   There is a statutory test for domicile.

D   Residence is mainly relevant to IHT.

Answer: B

Residence does have some relevance to IHT but it is domicile that is most relevant to this tax, and residence is mostly relevant to income tax and CGT. There is no statutory test for establishing a person's domicile, and no plans to create one. There is a statutory test for residence since 6 April 2013.

APPENDICES

INCOME TAX RATES AND ALLOWANCES

Rates	2022/23	2021/22
Basic rate	20% £0–£37,500	20% £0–£37,700
Higher rate	40% £37,500–£150,000	40% £37,700–£150,000
Additional rate	45% Over £150,000	45% Over £150,000
Savings income		
Starting rate for savings limit (applies only to the extent that non-savings/dividend income falls below personal allowance +£5,000)	£5,000	£5,000
At or under starting rate for savings limit	0%	0%
At or under basic rate limit	20%	20%
Above basic rate limit	40%	40%
Above additional rate limit	45%	45%
Dividend income		
At or under basic rate limit	8.75%	7.5%
Above the basic rate limit	33.75%	32.5%
Above additional rate limit	39.35%	38.1%

Allowance	2022/23	2021/22	Reduction in tax 2022/23 10%	2021/22 10%
	£	£	£	£
Personal				
For people born after 5/4/38	12,570	12,570		
Married couple				
born before 6/4/35	9,415	9,125	941.50	912.50
Blind person	2,600	2,520		
Transferable tax allowance between spouses where neither is a higher rate taxpayer	1,260	1,260		

Note:

(a) The 'Reduction in tax' columns show the amount of tax credit available where relief is restricted to 10%. It is given by reducing the individual's total liability by the amount of the credit.

(b) The personal allowance for individuals of any age is reduced if they have net income above £100,000. The allowance is reduced by £1 for every £2 of income over £100,000, so for example a person with £110,000 net income would lose £5,000 of personal allowance.

(c)   From 6 April 2016:

(i)   there is a personal savings allowance of £1,000 for basic rate taxpayers and £500 for higher rate taxpayers. Banks and building societies ceased deducting 20% basic rate tax from savings income;

(ii)   there is a dividend tax allowance for all individuals. This was £5,000 in 2016/17 and 2017/18 but was reduced to £2,000 from 2018/19. Above this the tax rates for dividends will be 8.75%, 33.75% and 39.35% for basic, higher and additional rate taxpayers. The dividend tax credit is abolished.

(d)   From 6 April 2018 there are also allowances for the first £1,000 of income from self-employment, a 'trading allowance' and the first £1,000 of income from rental income (unless such income is covered by the Rent a Room Scheme).

INVESTMENT AND FINANCIAL PRODUCTS

The purpose of this Appendix is to provide a brief introduction to some of the more popular types of investment and financial products currently available to individuals and trustees. It is not intended to be a definitive list. Where appropriate there is a brief summary indicating risk and showing income and capital growth potential for the investment, and suggestions as to the type of client for whom the investment might be suitable, though many factors will determine the actual choice of investment for a particular client. The tax rules are those for the client and not for the product.

The investments listed are:

(1) BANK ACCOUNTS

The two most common accounts are the current account and the deposit account.

Current account

The current account is one where the saver's money is immediately available to him, and he may have a cheque book and a cash card to enable him to spend the money in or withdraw the money from the account at any time. Because the money is always available, the bank is unlikely to pay interest to the saver on the amount in the account.

Deposit account

A deposit account is an account which pays interest to the saver. The saver can withdraw money from the account on demand but, depending on the terms of the account, may lose interest equivalent to that which would have been earned during the notice period. The bank will require notice (generally of seven days, but again depending on the terms of the account) of an intended withdrawal to release funds from the account. Amounts in accounts and transactions are shown by the bank on regular statements which are sent to the saver.

Tax

All interest paid by a bank on these accounts will be paid gross for tax years 2016/17 onwards.

Suitability

The majority of a solicitor's clients – both individuals and trustees – will have at least a current account in which a sufficient balance is maintained to enable regular expenditure (such as utility bills) to be met.

However, because of the lack of interest or comparatively poor interest rates, it is inadvisable for the majority of a client's savings to remain in such an account.

Banks and building societies encourage people to place their savings with them by offering interest on the money deposited. The bank or building society then uses this money to fund loans and mortgages to borrowers. The borrowers pay back not only the amount borrowed but also interest on the loan. This rate of interest is higher than that paid to the people saving with the bank or society. The difference covers the institution's running costs and provides a profit for the bank or society.

EXAMPLE

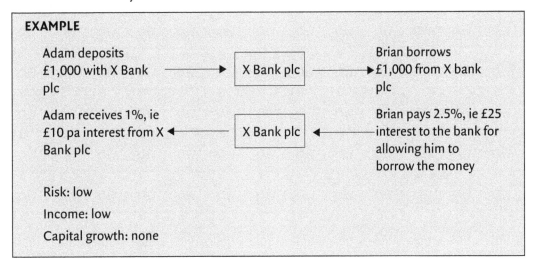

Adam deposits £1,000 with X Bank plc → X Bank plc → Brian borrows £1,000 from X bank plc

Adam receives 1%, ie £10 pa interest from X Bank plc ← X Bank plc ← Brian pays 2.5%, ie £25 interest to the bank for allowing him to borrow the money

Risk: low

Income: low

Capital growth: none

(2) BUILDING SOCIETY ACCOUNTS

Building societies offer deposit accounts and an array of share accounts. Ownership of an account is evidenced by a passbook held by the account holder in which the building society records all payments to and withdrawals from the account. Interest rates vary from time to time.

Deposit accounts

Money is repayable on demand and interest calculated on a daily basis is paid on the amount in the account. In the event of the building society ceasing to exist, deposit account holders will receive back their money in priority to all other savers. Hence, this is the safest type of building society account and, therefore, pays a lower rate of interest than a share account.

Share accounts

There are a wide variety of accounts offered by the various societies. For small sums or as an alternative to a current bank account, an ordinary share account offers a higher rate of interest than a deposit account and access to all money in the account on demand. Where immediate access is not required, higher rates of interest are paid on 'notice' accounts, for example, 28-day access account. The saver has to give the society a specified length of notice of his intention to withdraw his money. The longer the notice period, the higher the rate of interest paid on the account.

These accounts often also have a tiered interest system so that interest is paid at different rates on the amount in the account.

EXAMPLE

Charlene has £60,000 in a 60-day notice account. She is paid interest on:

(a)   the first £25,000 @ X% pa;

(b)   the next £25,000 @ X + 0.25% pa;

(c)   the balance @ X + 0.5% pa.

The best rates for both bank and building society accounts are often paid on accounts which have internet-only access.

Tax

The tax treatment of building society accounts is exactly the same as for bank accounts.

Suitability

Building societies offer a relatively safe investment with a reasonably good rate of return. Most clients concerned with financial planning should consider holding at least one share account as they offer liquidity and interest. However, if the interest is required to supplement income, the underlying value of the capital will be eroded by inflation.

Trustees with wide express investment powers can invest in all types of building society account.

Risk: low.

Income: low.

Capital growth: none.

(3) TESSAS

Tax Exempt Special Savings Accounts (TESSAs) were introduced by the Government in January 1991, and were offered by most banks and building societies. They allowed a person to invest up to £9,000 gradually over five years, and to receive tax-free income. When a TESSA matured after five years, it was possible to reinvest all of the capital (but not the interest) in a 'follow up TESSA'.

It became impossible to start a new TESSA after 5 April 1999, when Individual Savings Accounts (ISAs) became available (see (**21**) below). When a TESSA matured after this date, it could be transferred into an ISA – a ' TESSA-only ISA', which can be held in addition to other ISAs.

From 6 April 2008, such accounts are treated as ISA cash accounts.

(4) NATIONAL SAVINGS

National Savings are schemes offered by the Government which guarantee the security of the money invested with it. There are a number of National Savings products and some of the most common are identified below.

National Savings Bank accounts

This bank offers an investment account (operated by post only) and a direct saver account (operated online or by phone). They are both open to persons aged 16 and above.

Risk, income and capital growth: low.

Investment account

The minimum investment at any time is £20 and the maximum that can be held in the account is £1 million.

The rate is variable (currently 0.01%) and is added once a year on 1 January. Money can be withdrawn at any time without notice or penalty. The National Savings website says: 'We are not promoting this account on our website, but if you do want to find out more about it, please contact us.'

Tax

All the interest is taxable and is paid gross.

Suitability

Being able to deal with the account by post may appeal to the elderly. The annual interest payment can be a deterrent for those needing regular income. The rate of interest is the lowest currently offered.

Direct Saver account

The minimum investment is £1 and the maximum that can be held in the account is £2 million.

The rate is variable (currently 1.20%) and is added once a year on 1 April. Money can be withdrawn at any time without notice or penalty.

Tax

All the interest is taxable and is paid gross.

Suitability

The operation of the account only by phone or online may make it unsuitable for some. Again, the annual interest payment can be a deterrent for those needing regular income.

Income bonds

Income bonds provide a regular monthly income. Ownership is evidenced by a bond or certificate. Anyone aged 16 or above may purchase these. The minimum purchase is £500 and the maximum holding £1 million. Income is paid monthly to the investor. The interest rate may vary from time to time. At the time of writing it was 1.20%.

Tax

All the interest is taxable and paid gross.

Suitability

The bond provides an attractive rate of interest for non-taxpayers and a regular income. It is, therefore, particularly suitable for elderly clients with limited savings. The main disadvantage is the lack of protection of the capital against inflation.

Risk, income and capital growth: low.

Guaranteed Income Bonds

At the time of writing, these bonds are only available to customers renewing a maturing bond. They are not on general sale. The minimum investment is £500 and the maximum is £10,000 in any one issue. Each bond must be for a minimum of £500. Once renewed, they must be held for the full term which can be one, two, three or five years. Current rates depend on the length of the term, ranging from 1.8% for a one-year term to 2.5% for a five-year term.

If a bond is renewed for another term of the same length, the interest rate quoted at the time of renewal will be paid at maturity, even if rates go down before the maturity date. If renewal is for a different term, the rate paid will be the rate on offer on the date of maturity.

There is no maximum limit when renewing a maturing bond, but no extra money can be added to the investment. Interest is paid once a month.

Tax

Interest is taxable and is paid gross.

Suitability

The rate of interest is slightly more attractive than the rate available on income bonds. Additional disadvantages are that only a limited amount can be invested and the fact that funds cannot be withdrawn before the end of the fixed term.

Guaranteed Growth Bonds

As with guaranteed income bonds, these are only available to customers renewing a maturing bond. They are not on general sale. The minimum investment is £500 and the maximum is £10,000 in any one issue. The minimum investment is £500 and the maximum is £10,000.

Interest is added on each anniversary of investment and is fixed at the rate on offer at the time of the renewal. Rates are as follows at the time of writing:

1-year term, Issue 68:	1.85% gross/AER
2-year term, Issue 60:	2.25% gross/AER
3-year term, Issue 63:	2.55% gross/AER
5-year term, Issue 56:	2.55% gross/AER

Tax

Interest is taxable and is paid gross.

Suitability

As with income bonds, the rate of interest is reasonable, as compared to other interest-bearing accounts, but interest is only added yearly. There is no protection against inflation. Bonds must be held for the full term so they are not suitable for anyone who needs liquid funds.

Risk, income and capital growth: low.

National Savings Certificates

These are currently only available to customers with maturing certificates.

When on offer, National Savings Certificates can be purchased from the Post Office, by phone or online, and offer tax-free interest. There are different types of Certificate:

- A Fixed Interest Savings Certificate is a lump sum investment that earns fixed rates of interest over a set period of time (called an 'investment term'). Fixed Interest Savings Certificates are designed to be held for their full term. An investor can access the investment before the end of the term, but there will be a penalty (equal to 90 days' interest on the amount cashed in), so to achieve maximum return the Certificates must be held for the full term.

  Fixed Interest Savings Certificates are not always on general sale. They are sold in 'issues', each with a specific interest rate that is guaranteed for the period of the investment term. Issues can be withdrawn at any time. Current rates for those reinvesting are as follows:

2-year term	2.15% tax-free/AER
5-year term	2.45% tax-free/AER

  Certificates can be renewed by post, online or by phone if registered for the service. The minimum amount that can be renewed is £100.

  The minimum for each issue is £100 and the maximum is £15,000 per person per issue. For trust investments the limit is £15,000 per trust per issue.

  The interest for each issue of each investment is guaranteed. It is earned daily and added to the Certificate on each anniversary. It can only be withdrawn when the Certificate is cashed in.

- An Index-linked Savings Certificate is also a lump sum investment, but instead of paying a fixed rate of interest each year, the investment's value moves in line with the Consumer Prices Index. The investment also earns interest daily which is added to the Certificate on each anniversary. Current rates for those re-investing are as follows:

2-year term	Index-linking to CPI + 0.01% tax-free/AER
3-year term	Index-linking to CPI + 0.01% tax-free/AER
5-year term	Index-linking to CPI + 0.01% tax-free/AER

    Index-linked Savings Certificates are designed to be held for their full term. An investor can access the investment before the end of the term, but there will be a penalty (equal to 90 days' interest on the amount cashed in).

    The age limit and maximum/minimum investment limits are the same as for Fixed Interest Savings Certificates.

Tax

There is no income tax or CGT to pay.

Suitability

Because of their favourable tax treatment, National Savings Certificates have historically offered an attractive investment to higher-rate taxpayers. However, current rates are unattractive, although comparable with interest rates available elsewhere.

Because the interest is compounded and paid out only when the Certificates are redeemed, this is not a suitable investment for anybody requiring a regular income.

Risk and income: low.

Capital growth: medium (interest is added to the capital).

Children's Bonds

These are similar to National Savings Certificates but can be bought for children under 16. Bonds are not always on general sale. At the time of writing none are available. Junior ISAs are available (see below).

They sold in 'issues', each with a specific interest rate that is guaranteed for the period of the investment term, which is five years. They are designed to be held for the full term and can then be reinvested for another term. They can be cashed in early but with a penalty.

Parents and legal guardians can apply on behalf of their child under 16 online, by phone or by post.

Grandparents and great-grandparents can apply on behalf of their grandchild or great-grandchild under 16 but can only apply by post. No one else can buy Children's Bonds.

For each issue and for each child, the minimum that can be invested is £25 and the maximum is £3,000. The interest earned is added to the value of the Bond on the anniversary of investment.

Children's Bonds are owned by the child, but until the child's 16th birthday the parent or guardian nominated on the application looks after the Bond, regardless of who bought it. Grandparents who buy Children's Bonds must nominate one of the child's parents or guardians to look after the Bond until the child is 16.

Each Bond will finally mature once it reaches the first five-year anniversary on or after the child's 16th birthday. When this happens, the child will not be able to hold the Bond for another term. They can choose to reinvest the money in other National Savings products or cash in the Bond.

Tax

The interest earned is completely free of UK income tax and capital gains tax for both the child and the parents. Even if the child starts work and becomes a taxpayer before cashing in their Bonds, they still will not have to pay tax on the interest.

Children's Bonds can be held in addition to Junior ISAs and they are not linked to tax years.

Suitability

The Bonds are obviously attractive for parents and grandparents who want a safe, tax-free investment.

Premium bonds

Premium bonds can be purchased from the Post Office and online. Bond holders are automatically entered for regular prize draws. Bonds are divided into £1 units and each unit has a separate chance in the draws, ie a £100-bond has 100 chances of winning a prize in every draw. Prizes range from £25 to £1 million. Bond holders can reclaim their money from the bonds at any time. Anyone aged 16 and above may purchase these. The minimum purchase is £25 and the maximum holding is £50,000.

Tax

All prizes are totally tax free.

Suitability

Statistics suggest that holders of bonds to the maximum limit are likely to receive sufficient prizes to represent an acceptable return on the amount of prizes each year, making it a worthwhile purchase for wealthy higher-rate taxpayers. For lower holdings, there is no income and no capital growth, merely the gamble that a bond will win one of the larger prizes. The annual prize fund interest rate is 1.4% (dropping to 1% from December 2020), but of course this does not mean that a particular bond holder will receive that rate. It could be more or less.

Trustees whose investment powers come from TA 2000 cannot purchase premium bonds as they involve no income or capital growth, and they are unlikely to be suitable for most trusts.

Risk, income and capital growth: low.

Green Savings Bonds

Money raised on these bonds will be used for green projects chosen by the Government. HM Treasury plans to allocate an amount equivalent to the funds raised from Green Savings Bonds to its chosen green projects within two years.

The bonds are issued for a fixed term. The current issue is for three years at a rate of 3%. Between £100 and £100,000 can be invested. Money cannot be withdrawn before maturity. The bond can only be bought and managed online.

Tax

The interest payable is liable to income tax in the year of maturity. There is no CGT liability.

Suitability

They are suitable for those who want a guaranteed interest rate, fixed for three years and who wish to invest in green projects

(5) LOCAL AUTHORITY BONDS

These bonds are a way of investing in local authorities. When a local authority needs to raise money, it may encourage investors to deposit money with the authority in return for a competitive rate of interest. The minimum investment is usually £1,000 with no maximum. The bond will last for between one and four years, and must be held to maturity. The local authority guarantees the rate of interest to be paid throughout the period.

Tax

There is no CGT on these bonds. The interest is paid net of basic rate tax.

Suitability

The guaranteed interest rate may be attractive at a time of falling interest rates and is usually competitive when compared to other forms of interest-only savings. The safety of the money invested depends upon the standing of the local authority. Because it is a fixed-term investment, these bonds are not suitable for people needing immediate access to their capital. The bonds may be suitable investments for some trustees.

Most local authorities are too small to raise money through the bond market on their own, and councils have historically borrowed money from the Public Works Loan Board, a branch of the Treasury, to finance capital spending projects.

The Municipal Bonds Agency was set up with the backing of the Local Government Association with the idea that multiple councils banded together would have enough clout to raise hundreds of millions of pounds. The theory was that investors would be reassured by lending across a diverse 'pooled' spread of councils.

However, the Agency has not been a success, and more than three years after its launch, it is still struggling to issue its first bond as investors question the creditworthiness of the sector. The fiscal crisis at Northamptonshire County Council did not help. In March 2018, the UK Government sent commissioners into the Council to take direct control of its finances.

On 1 May 2020, the *Financial Times* reported that cash-strapped UK local authorities were grouping together for the first time to raise hundreds of million of pounds of debt to shore up their finances during the coronavirus pandemic. A group of up to 30 councils, including Westminster City in London and Barnsley borough in Yorkshire, plans to issue three bonds this year through the UK Municipal Bonds Agency with the aim of raising at least £250 million with each. The driver for the new set of bonds was the government's decision late in 2019 to raise the interest rate sharply on its own local-authority loans, granted by the Public Works Loan Board, inspiring councils to look elsewhere for new and cheaper sources of funding.

Risk, income and capital growth: low.

(6) GILTS

'Gilts' is the popular name for government stocks otherwise known as 'gilt-edged' securities. They are issued by the UK Government as a way of raising money, and are a secure form of investment as interest and repayment are guaranteed by the Government.

The majority of gilts pay a fixed rate of interest ('the coupon') over the life of the stock and guarantee repayment of the nominal value of the stock (known as par value) on a given date (known as the redemption date). Interest is usually paid half yearly in two equal amounts.

> **EXAMPLE**
>
> John purchases £100 nominal of 10% Treasury Stock 2021. He will receive an annual guaranteed income of £10 (10%) gross until 2021 when he will be paid £100.

Normally, when the Government issues the gilt, it does so at a discount to its par (nominal) value.

> **EXAMPLE**
>
> Assume that in 2009 the Government issued 10% Treasury Stock 2021 at 94p. This means that for every 94p invested with it in 2009, the Government guarantees to pay £1 on redemption in 2021.
>
> So when John purchased £100 nominal in 2009, it actually cost him £94. If he holds the stock until the Government redeems it at par, he will receive £100, ie, a profit of £6.

Once a person has purchased a gilt, he does not have to continue holding it until its redemption date. He can sell his holding to another investor via the stock market. The stock market determines how much a stock is worth on any given day prior to its redemption date. The seller pays commission to the stockbroker for arranging the sale.

> **EXAMPLE**
>
> Having bought £100 nominal 10% Treasury Stock 2021 in 2009, John needed some money in 2018. He therefore decided to sell his stock. The market price on the day of sale is 96p. John will receive £96 less commission.

Tax

The profit made from selling or redeeming a gilt is exempt from CGT. All interest payments are liable to income tax.

Gilts can be bought and sold through a stockbroker. Interest on all gilts is paid net of lower rate tax, meaning that non-taxpayers have to reclaim the tax deducted.

Suitability

Higher-rate taxpayers appreciate the CGT exemption but capital gains tend to be moderate and sales (as opposed to redemption) are subject to commission charges. A fixed rate of interest can be advantageous at times of falling interest rates but, conversely, unattractive if interest rates rise during the period of ownership for people on a limited income. A guaranteed rate of return can help budgeting. Gilts are often suitable investments for trustees where a beneficiary requires income.

Risk: low.

Income: medium/high.

Capital growth: if held to redemption, depends on whether bought for a premium or at a discount; otherwise prices vary according to the coupon and prevailing interest rates.

(7) QUOTED SHARES

An investor may wish to invest money in a company listed (quoted) on the Stock Exchange. The aim is to receive an income and also real (net of inflation) capital growth from the investment. Income is received in the form of dividends paid by the company. The size of a dividend is decided by the company and is normally paid in two, not necessarily equal, instalments. The dividend can vary from year to year.

The capital value of the shares is determined by the market and is based on a number of factors including past and projected profits and takeover rumours.

Shares are, therefore, a speculative investment which may increase or decrease (sometimes spectacularly) in value, and the value of which can change daily. Spectacular slumps in the stock market occurred as a result of the banking crisis in 2008 and the Covid-19 pandemic in 2020.

> **EXAMPLE 1**
>
> In 2015, Taj bought 1,000 shares in A plc at £1 each (cost £1,000). In 2016 he received a dividend of £70 and in 2018 a dividend of £83 as the company made good profits, had good industrial relations and a secure market for its products.
>
> Early in 2022, shares in A plc were listed as being worth £1.20 each. Taj sold his 1,000 shares for £1,200 less commission.

> **EXAMPLE 2**
>
> In 2015, Victor bought 1,000 shares in B plc for £1 each (cost £1,000 plus commission and stamp duty). Soon afterwards the company suffered a strike by its workforce and introduced a new product, which incorporated a faulty design and had to be withdrawn and compensation paid to people who had already bought the product. In 2019 the company borrowed money to enable it to pay shareholders a dividend. Victor received £50. Shortly afterwards the company went into liquidation. Victor's 1,000 shares are now worth £20.

Tax

All profits on the disposal of shares are liable to CGT. Any losses made on disposal can be set against gains in the same tax year and any excess carried forward to set against gains in future years.

Since 6 April 2016 dividends are paid gross. They are taxed at lower rates than other investments. The rates are 8.75% for basic rate taxpayers, 33.75% for higher rate taxpayers and 39.35% for additional rate taxpayers.

Suitability

Because of the financial risks, shares should be purchased only by those who can afford to lose the money invested. In return for that risk, shares offer both income and capital gains opportunities but fairly substantial sums need to be invested in a 'portfolio of shares' (ie, several shareholdings in different companies) to produce significant gains.

Shares are often purchased by trustees and may form the bulk of trust investments.

Risk: medium/high.

Income: low/medium.

Capital growth: medium/high.

(8) INVESTMENT TRUSTS

Investment trusts are quoted companies whose assets consist solely of shares in other companies. The investment trust company may specialise in acquiring shares in companies in one particular sector of the market, or it may own shares in a wide variety of companies. The advantage for the investor holding shares in the investment trust is that he can have an indirect interest in a number of companies with the investment management handled by professional managers: the investment trust.

The investment trust pays dividends and the value of investment trust is determined by the stock market.

Tax

Dividends paid on shares in investment trusts are taxed in the same way as dividends on other quoted shares.

When an investor disposes of his shares in an investment trust, a liability to CGT can arise.

Suitability

Investment trusts are suitable for anybody, including trustees, who might reasonably consider investing in quoted shares, and also smaller investors who lack the expertise to manage their own portfolio or for whom transaction costs on shares are high compared to their amount of investment. The risk of loss as compared with investment in individual companies may be reduced due to the spread of investment by the trust, but an investment trust may have to be held for several years to realise much capital growth.

Risk: medium.

Income: medium.

Capital growth: medium/high.

(9) UNIT TRUSTS

Unit trusts provide a method of investing on the stock market for anybody who wishes to invest in a range of companies but lacks the time or expertise to manage his own share portfolio.

Unit trusts are offered by a number of banks and other institutions who employ investment managers. The managers charge an annual management fee for their expertise and there is also an initial 'setting-up' charge. The investor hands his investment money to the investment manager in return for a number of units. The value of the units is determined by the value of the shares in the companies in which the managers invest. The investment manager then uses the investor's money to buy shares in other companies. Different unit trusts invest in different types of company, for example, one may invest only in UK government securities; another may invest only in companies quoted on stock exchanges of countries in the Far East (eg, Japan and Hong Kong).

An investor can sell his units back to the unit trust managers at any time. If the unit trust has performed well, the sale price should be greater than the price at which the investor purchased his units. Unit trusts have two prices: the bid price which is what an investor will receive if he sells his units, and the offer price which is the price at which the units can be purchased.

> **EXAMPLE**
>
> Daisy decides to invest £1,100 in the Magic Unit Trust which invests in UK companies. On the day of her investment the bid price is £1 and the offer price £1.10. She receives 1,000 units.
>
> Daisy must wait until the bid price of units in Magic Unit Trust increases to at least £1.10 before she sells in order to get back her full investment. The bid price must increase further for her to make a capital gain on her investment.
>
> Unit trusts also pay dividends or interest to investors.

Tax

Dividends paid to unit holders are taxed in the same way as dividends on quoted shares. Interest is taxed in the same way as bank or building society interest. Since 6 April 2007, UK resident non-taxpayers have been able to receive the interest gross.

Any profit made by an investor on the sale of his units is liable to CGT.

Suitability

Anybody, including trustees, wishing to invest in UK or overseas companies but without the time or expertise to manage their own portfolio, should consider unit trusts. However, the initial costs mean that unit trusts are not suitable for short-term investment.

Risk: medium.

Income: low/medium.

Capital growth: medium/high.

Note: Open-ended investment companies (OEICs) are a more modern version of the unit trust. An OEIC has all the characteristics of a unit trust but uses the structure of a corporation, as is commonly done in the rest of Europe and in the USA.

Like a unit trust, an OEIC is a collective investment pooling the resources of many investors. Both are open-ended and have to dispose of assets if there is a run on the fund.

Structurally OEICs are different from unit trusts. They are formed as limited liability companies. People invest in them through the purchase of shares, but these are traded in the same way as unit trusts. The shares have a single price for buying and selling. The tax treatment of OEIC funds and their investors' proceeds is identical to that for unit trusts.

(10) PERSONAL EQUITY PLANS (PEPS)

A personal equity plan (PEP) provided a way of making a tax-free investment in shares. The scheme was introduced by the Government in 1987 as a way of encouraging investment in UK companies. A maximum of £6,000 per annum per taxpayer could be invested in a general PEP plus another £3,000 in a single company PEP (in the shares of a single company), making an overall limit of £9,000 per annum.

The income and capital gains generated by the investments held were not subject to income tax or CGT.

New PEPs could not be started after 5 April 1999 when ISAs (see (**21**)) became available. Existing PEPs continued after this date, but from 6 April 2008 all PEPs are treated as ISAs (stocks and shares accounts).

(11) INSURANCE BONDS

Usually known as 'investment bonds' or 'single premium bonds', insurance bonds are single premium (one off capital payment, not the more usual regular insurance premiums) non-qualifying policies (ie, not satisfying ICTA 1988, s 267 and so attracting tax at maturity). The bonds are normally 'unit linked' with-profit policies, so that bonuses are added to the value of the units by the life company.

Income and capital are retained within the bond. Withdrawals up to 5% of the premiums paid can be taken tax free for the first 20 years of the bond.

Tax

No tax is payable by the investor during the life of the bond provided withdrawals do not exceed 5%. Gains arising on maturity of the bond are subject to higher-rate tax (as non-qualifying policies) but not to basic rate tax.

Suitability

These bonds are suitable for higher-rate taxpayers with a lump sum to invest as there is no tax to pay during the life of the bond. The 5% tax free withdrawal represents the income entitlement from the investment. Ideally the bond should be planned to mature when the investor's tax rate has fallen below higher rates (so as to avoid income tax), for example, the bond could mature following retirement when income is lower.

Risk: medium.

Income: low (max 5%). Capital growth: medium/high.

(12) GUARANTEED BONDS

These are single premium non-qualifying life policies which last for a fixed period. Guaranteed income bonds guarantee income at fixed rates, and guaranteed growth bonds guarantee a fixed return when the bond ends.

Tax

As non-qualifying life policies, there is no basic rate liability but higher rate tax may be payable.

Suitability

Both bonds may be suitable for basic rate taxpayers (as only higher rate tax may be payable) with capital to invest.

Risk: low/medium.

Income: low/medium (none on guaranteed growth bonds). Capital growth: medium (income on guaranteed income bonds).

(13) ENTERPRISE INVESTMENT SCHEME (EIS RELIEF)

This scheme, introduced by the FA 1994, encourages investment in smaller, higher-risk companies. Because of the generous nature of the relief, and in an attempt to restrict its abuse, there are many detailed conditions in the ITA 2007.

Individuals who invest capital in qualifying companies and meet certain requirements for the following three years obtain income tax relief at 30% of the amount invested. Since April 2012 the maximum amount that may be invested in a tax year is £1 million. For investments made or after 6 April 2018, the limit is increased to £2 million provided at least £1 million is invested in Knowledge Intensive Companies.

Capital gains made on disposal are free of CGT provided the shares are held for at least three years. If shares are disposed of at a loss, the investor can elect that the amount of the loss, less income tax relief given, can be set against income of the year in which they were disposed of or on income of the previous year instead of being set off against any capital gains.

Payment of CGT on the disposal of any kind of asset can be deferred when the gain is invested in shares of an EIS qualifying company, but the investment must be made one year before or three years after the gain arose. In this case a connection to a company does not matter.

Qualifying investments are shares in unquoted trading companies carrying on trading activity in the UK. UK resident taxpayers may obtain the relief but they are not eligible if they are 'connected with' the company, for example, as an employee or paid director. Further, combined shareholdings of the investor and his 'associates' must not exceed 30% of the share capital.

> **EXAMPLE**
>
> £50,000 is invested in EIS shares in May 2012 (2012/13).
>
> (a) The initial investment – attracts 30% relief, so that the effective cost of the shares is £35,000.
>
> (b) If shares are sold more than three years later – any gain is free of CGT.

Since 2017/18, a variant of the scheme called the Seed Enterprise Investment Scheme has been available. It is designed to help companies which are starting to trade raise money. Individuals can invest up to £100,000 in a tax year and obtain income tax relief at 50% of the amount invested.

A further variant called Social Investment Tax Relief is designed to encourage private individuals to invest in social enterprises including charities. These enterprises cannot access the conventional Enterprise Schemes. The relief was introduced in 2014 and expanded in 2017. Social Investment Tax Relief allows individuals to help social enterprises grow by offering a tax relief on investments. Individuals can invest up to £1 million and are entitled to income tax relief at 30% of the amount invested. Gains are not subject to CGT.

Suitability

Investors with substantial capital to invest in unquoted trading companies with which they are not connected. Although income tax relief at 30% is available on the investment, dividends received will attract income tax. Generally, it should be remembered the company's articles of association and questions of marketability of the shares may make it difficult to find a buyer for the shares. The danger is getting 'locked into' the investment – or perhaps only being able to sell at a reduced price. EIS eligible companies normally also attract IHT business property relief which represents an additional attraction for taxpayers trying to minimise their IHT bill.

Risk: medium/high.

Income: possibly none, depending on whether the company pays dividends.

Capital growth: medium/high (but marketability may make sale difficult).

(14) OFFSHORE FUNDS

These funds are managed by companies registered outside the UK tax and regulatory system under the Financial Services Act 1986 in places such as the Channel Islands and the Isle of Man.

Funds actively marketed in the UK (being approved by the Securities and Investments Board (now the Financial Services Authority)) are either Distributor Funds (ie, a fund which pays dividends equivalent to 85% of its income) or Accumulator Funds (where gross income is retained within the fund to increase its value).

Tax

Dividends from Distributor Funds are paid gross but are taxable on receipt into the UK. Income and capital gains of Accumulator Funds are subject to tax on sale of the investment and rates then prevailing.

Suitability

These funds are similar to UK unit and investment trusts and so are suitable for anyone with capital to invest. Distributor Funds (paid gross) may be particularly suited to non-taxpayers. Accumulator Funds are more likely to be attractive to higher-rate taxpayers who can afford to retain their investment offshore until after retirement when their tax rates are lower.

Risk: medium/high.

Income: medium/high.

Capital growth: medium/high.

(15) PENSIONS

Pension schemes are a way of saving for old age, so providing an income after retirement.

The main categories of scheme include State pensions, occupational pensions for employees, and personal pension schemes.

The State scheme

The State scheme is funded by the self-employed, employees and employers paying National Insurance (NI) contributions. Originally, the scheme had two parts – a compulsory contribution and an additional voluntary State pension – but this changed from 6 April 2016. Up to April 2002, the additional State pension was called the State Earnings-Related Pension Scheme (SERPS). This was based on the employee's record of NI contributions and level of earnings as an employee. It was possible for employers and employees to 'contract-out' and was not available to the self-employed.

On 6 April 2002, the Government reformed SERPS and replaced it with the State Second Pension. Any SERPS entitlement already built up is protected. The State Second Pension provided a more generous additional State pension for employees and certain carers and people with long-term illness or disability whose working lives were interrupted or shortened.

All employers, employees and the self-employed had to contribute to the compulsory part of the scheme. Provided a person had made sufficient contributions during his or her working life, he or she will receive the old age pension at State pension age. The Pensions Act 2007 provides for the State pension age for both men and women to rise from 65 to 68 in stages by 2046. The timetable for this has changed several times in recent years. Currently, the legislation (the Pensions Act 2011 and the Pensions Act 2014) provides for the retirement age for men and women to increase to 66 between December 2018 and October 2020, and then to 67 between 2026 and 2028. Under the Pensions Act 2014 there will be review of the State pension age at least once every five years. This will be with a view to achieving the position that people will spend a certain proportion of their adult life able to retire. According to the Chancellor's comments in the 2013 Autumn Statement, this proportion should be one-third. The review will therefore take into account various factors, such as life expectancy, to assess whether the State pension age should be raised more quickly.

The additional pension is paid by the State if employer and employee have paid extra NI contributions. Contributions are based on the employee's annual earnings and there is no income tax relief for the employee's contributions. The pension is currently paid at State pension age. It is possible to 'contract out' of the additional State pension. In this case, a lower level of NI contributions is payable but only the old age pension will be received after retirement. The Government has previously actively encouraged 'contracting out'; however, the Pensions Act 2007 introduced some restrictions on the ability to contract out, which apply from April 2012.

The State scheme changed again in 2016, and the changes apply to men born on or after 6 April 1951 and women born on or after 6 April 1953. Anyone in this category who reaches State pension age after 5 April 2016 is eligible for some new State pension (which replaces the State pension and Second State Pension) if they have at least 10 qualifying years of NI contributions. To obtain the full State pension a person must have at least 35 years of contributions. Those who have made contributions in the period before 6 April 2016 will have these factored into the calculation, and it may mean that they receive an extra amount.

Occupational pension schemes

These are often called company pension schemes, but they apply equally to those employed by partnerships and other non-corporate entities. Schemes may be contributory or non-contributory.

A non-contributory scheme is one where only the employer pays into the scheme to provide his employees with appropriate pension benefits on retirement. Such payments by the employer are not treated as an emolument of the employee for his income tax purposes and are based on a percentage of the employee's earnings.

In a contributory scheme, both the employer and employee contribute. Again, the employer's contributions are based on a percentage of the employee's annual earnings and do not count as emoluments. The employee's contributions are an agreed minimum percentage of earnings. He may also pay additional voluntary contributions (AVCs) into the scheme, or free-standing AVCs (FSAVCs) into a separately run scheme.

All contributions and AVCs are paid into a fund which is invested by the trustees of the pension scheme with the aim of increasing the value of the fund.

There are two main types of scheme:

(a)   Salary related schemes (also known as 'defined benefit' schemes). The pension the employee gets is based on the number of years employed by the scheme provider and the level of earnings (usually at the date of retirement or the date when the employee leaves).

(b)   Money purchase schemes (also known as 'defined contribution' schemes). The employee's contributions (together with any provided by the employer) are invested. The final pension is based on the amount invested and how well the investments have performed. The money is used to purchase an annuity.

Businesses are increasingly closing their salary schemes and turning to money purchase schemes which are cheaper to provide.

On retirement, an employee will receive either an annual pension based on the amount of his final salary, or a cash lump sum and a smaller annual pension.

Legislation controls the maximum amount of pension and lump sum which can be received without incurring a tax penalty.

In relation to defined contribution pensions, since 6 April 2015 there has been greater flexibility as to how the pension holder may access his pension. Previous restrictions on how the fund must be invested and how much may be taken as a lump sum have been relaxed, although this may still be constrained by the specific terms and conditions agreed between the pension provider and the pension holder.

Where an employee dies before retirement age, a lump sum based on contributions made to the scheme may be payable to the employee's dependants. Having started to receive a pension, all rights to it cease on the employee's death. However, an employee can elect to receive a smaller pension than he would normally be entitled to with the guarantee that, on his death, the pension will continue to be paid to his widow for the remainder of her life.

Workplace pensions

The Pensions Act 2008 contains measures to encourage more people to save in private pension schemes. Most of these measures came into effect in October 2012. They include the automatic enrolment of employees aged 22 and above who are not already in a qualifying pension scheme and who satisfy certain other criteria within either their employer's workplace scheme or a new savings vehicle (a 'personal account scheme'). Employers are under a duty to contribute a minimum amount either into the workplace scheme or the personal account scheme. The process started with larger employers from October 2012. From January 2016 employers with fewer than 30 staff have to provide a pension scheme and enrol employees. Employees have the right to opt out.

Self-employed pension schemes

These schemes are available to the self-employed and to employees who either do not wish to join their employer's occupational pension scheme, or whose employers do not provide an occupational pension scheme.

An individual taking out a scheme for the first time is now limited to a personal pension, but until 1988 pension provision was made through retirement annuity contracts. Although it is no longer possible to buy new retirement annuity contracts, it is still possible for contributions to be made to contracts taken out before 1988, and most people who have existing retirement annuity contracts continue to pay into them in preference to acquiring a new personal pension because the various maximum limits are often more favourable.

Personal pensions

Contributions are paid to the pension fund company – usually one of the life assurance companies – which invests them to provide a cash lump sum and/or an annual income and annuity, for the individual when he reaches retirement age. The pension can start at any time between the ages of 55 and 75 years.

On retirement, the individual can choose how to take benefits from the fund. As indicated in relation to occupational pension schemes above, the Government has relaxed restrictions on how a person may take his pension entitlement. The individual can buy an annuity or withdraw some or all of the funds as a capital sum. The first 25% is tax free; the balance is taxed as if it was income, so very high rates will be paid if the whole amount is withdrawn in one tax year.

Undrawn funds remaining invested at death (the 'pension pot') can be passed on to whomever the individual chooses. The tax treatment depends on whether the individual dies before reaching 75.

Death under 75

The pension pot can be paid to any individual free of tax either as a lump sum or as income drawdown.

Death at 75+

If the pot is paid to an individual as a lump sum, it is taxed at the beneficiary's marginal rate. Because the whole sum is received in one tax year, this is likely to be 45%. If the recipients leave the pot invested and withdraw funds gradually, although tax is again charged at their marginal rate, it is likely that they can escape paying tax at the 45% rate.

If the individual dies before retirement, the pension company will pay out a lump sum calculated in accordance with the scheme. To avoid this sum forming part of the individual's estate on death, and so chargeable to IHT, death benefits should be settled during the individual's life on, usually, discretionary trusts for the family and dependants. Pension pots are very valuable assets, particularly from an IHT point of view. A terminally ill person who is under 75 at the date of death can pass on their entire pot tax free.

Stakeholder pensions

In essence these are personal pension schemes which meet the following Government-imposed minimum standards:

(a)   annual management charges must not exceed 1.5% for the first 10 years, and thereafter must not exceed 1% (where a person joined a stakeholder pension scheme before 6 April 2005, the charges must not exceed 1% at any time);

(b)   there must be no initial charges or exit penalties;

(c)   the scheme must accept contributions of as little as £20 gross;

(d)   the rules must allow for contributions to be stopped, started and changed without penalties;

(e)   scheme managers must be authorised by the FSA or have trustees;

(f)   members must be provided with a default fund for investment if they do not want to make investment choices themselves;

(g)   other investment choices offered must meet diversification and suitability criteria;

(h)   a 'lifestyling' investment option must be available. Lifestyling involves the gradual transfer from higher risk investments to lower risk investments as a member approaches their selected retirement date. Lifestyling must commence at least five years before the member's selected retirement date. It is designed to shield the member's accumulated fund from investment volatility in the period leading up to the member's selected retirement date;

(i)   transfers in from other UK schemes must be accepted without additional charges (including contracted-out benefits);

(j)   members must be provided with a detailed statement each year;

(k)   membership must be available to all employees with a particular employer. It cannot be restricted to certain classes or employees.

Many providers are offering charges which are substantially lower than 1% (sometimes as little as 0.4%).

As from October 2001, employers with five or more staff had to offer a stakeholder scheme. However, since 1 October 2012 and the introduction of workplace pensions, employers need not offer access to a stakeholder scheme to new employees.

Tax relief

Before 6 April 2006 there were a number of rules regulating the types of pension a person could have, how much a person could contribute to each type of pension and the tax relief available.

Since 6 April 2006 most of these rules have been replaced with a single regime. It is possible to save in more than one type of pension scheme at the same time, and there is no limit on the amount that may be saved, though there are limits on the tax relief available.

Tax relief is given each year on contributions made by a saver on the lesser of the value of that person's earnings or £40,000. This means that for every £1 paid in, the Government will pay an extra 25p (or more if the person is a higher rate taxpayer). From 6 April 2016 the £40,000 maximum is subject to a tapering reduction where, broadly, a person has income of at least £200,000.

Non-taxpayers may also benefit from this but up to a limit of £3,600 gross, ie the non-taxpayer pays in £2,880 in a tax year and the Government will add in a further £720.

When a person comes to take his or her pension, there may be a charge to tax if the total pension 'pot' at this point exceeds the 'Lifetime Allowance', which was set at £1 million from 6 April 2016. From the 2018/19 tax year the Lifetime Allowance increased annually by reference to the Consumer Prices Index and in 2021/22 was £1,073,100.

(16) LIFE ASSURANCE (INSURANCE)

There are a number of life assurance products, only the most common types of which are dealt with below.

Whole life assurance (whole of life assurance)

In return for a regular monthly or annual premium an assurance company will contract to pay out an agreed fixed sum on the death of the life assured.

Most assurance companies refuse to insure the life of anybody over the age of 80 years and the older a person when they enter into a contract, the more expensive the premium. For example, a person aged 30 years might insure his life for a given sum for £50 per annum, while a person aged 60 years might pay £100 per annum for the same level of life cover.

Whole life policies can be written on single lives and also on joint lives. In the latter case, two lives are insured and the assurance company will either pay out on the first death or on the death of the survivor of the joint lives depending on the policy purchased. It is also possible for a person to insure a second person's life provided that he has an insurable interest in the second life. The fixed sum is paid out to the proposer on the death of the life assured.

If the policy is non-profit only a specified sum is payable on death. If it is with profit or unit linked there is an investment element. The sum assured will be paid with bonuses (with profit) or accumulated units (unit linked).

Tax

Premiums may be paid out of capital or income. No income tax relief is available for premiums paid.

On the death of the life assured, the assured sum forms part of his estate and will be liable to IHT unless the policy has been written in trust or assigned.

Suitability

Whole life assurance is suitable for anyone who wishes to provide a lump sum for his family or dependants on his death.

This may be to provide another asset, or to provide cash with which to meet debts such as an IHT bill or a mortgage or to provide funds to buy a deceased partner's share or the shares of a deceased shareholder/director whose shares might have to be sold to an outsider if the other members cannot afford to buy them.

It is not suitable for anybody wishing to save to provide a benefit for themselves.

Term assurance

In return for the payment of a regular premium the assurance company will pay out an agreed sum if the life assured dies within a fixed period of time from the purchase of the assurance policy. The term assurance provides protection only. There is no investment element.

If the proposer ceases to pay the premiums during the agreed term or the life assured survives the term, the policy comes to an end. It has no surrender value.

Tax

The tax treatment is the same as for whole life assurance.

Suitability

Term assurance is suitable for anyone, including trustees who needs to provide a lump sum with which to pay IHT which would become chargeable on a lifetime transfer if the transferor died within seven years of the transfer.

It may also be used by an individual to cover a fixed-term commitment such as a mortgage or school fees.

It is not suitable for anyone aiming to provide a benefit for himself.

Endowment assurance

In return for regular premiums, the assurance company contracts to pay the sum assured on the earlier of a given date or the death of the life assured. In these cases, there is clearly the possibility of personal enjoyment of the policy proceeds by the life assured.

The policy may be with profits or unit linked. It can be written on single or joint lives. There is an investment element.

Endowment policies provide protection as well as a sum payable on the maturity date for the policy or the earlier death of the life assured. These policies are frequently used in planning for the repayment of mortgages (where they are linked to the date for repayment of the mortgage) or school fees (where they are planned to mature at a time appropriate to payment of the fees). The risk is that the amount eventually paid out may not be sufficient to meet the amount due.

Tax

Policies are normally for a minimum period of 10 years so that as 'qualifying policies' under ICTA 1988, s 267 the sum payable on maturity is tax free. If the life assured survives to the given date, he will receive the assured lump sum free of all taxes. If the payment is made on death, the sum forms part of the estate of the assured.

Suitability

Endowment assurance is suitable for any taxpayer looking to build up a tax-free lump sum over a long period either for his own benefit or to meet commitments such as the repayment of a mortgage or the payment of school fees.

Keyman assurance

Where a person is a 'key' man or woman within an organisation, his or her premature death will affect the profitability of the company or partnership. The company or partnership may, therefore, insure that person's life so that the company or partnership receives a lump sum on the death of the 'key' man. The life assurance may be a whole life, term or endowment policy.

(17) PERMANENT HEALTH INSURANCE (PHI)

A person who is in employment anticipates receiving a regular wage or salary or share of partnership profits in return for working. If that person becomes disabled and, therefore, unable to continue working, he will lose this source of income. He can, therefore, insure himself by paying an annual premium so that if he is no longer able to work, the insurance policy will provide him with regular sums of money for a stated period or up to a stated age. There is a limit on the annual amount which can be received from PHI.

Payment may not commence immediately after the disability arises as the policyholder can defer claiming benefit, for example, for three months. The longer the agreed period of deferral, the lower the annual premium.

An employer often provides PHI through group arrangements. Contributions paid are generally deductible as trading expenses.

Tax

An individual does not receive tax relief on the premiums paid.

Once benefits are claimed they are taxable as income.

Suitability

Permanent health insurance is suitable for anyone in work who has dependants, but cover may not be available for a person who is already in poor health when he applies to purchase the insurance cover. It is particularly suitable for the self-employed for whom replacement of income when permanently disabled will be essential. The effect on the business through absence of the 'owner' may cause it to fold.

(18) ANNUITIES

In return for the investment of a capital lump sum, a life company will guarantee a regular amount of income (annuity) to the investor – purchased life annuity. The annuity can be paid annually, quarterly or monthly as the investor wishes. A good rate of return can be obtained if the annuity is purchased when interest rates are high. But the cost of the annuity depends partly on the age of the annuitant and may not be worthwhile until he reaches 70 years of age. On the death of the annuitant or expiry of the agreed term, usually no capital is returnable.

Tax

The Revenue regards purchased life annuity payments as being partly income and partly a return of the original capital invested (ICTA 1988, s 656). Only the income element is subject to income tax at the annuitant's income tax rates and is received net of lower rate tax. Some or all of this tax can be recovered by non and lower rate taxpayers.

No tax is payable on the capital element.

Suitability

Annuities are suitable for anyone who needs a guaranteed income or income for life and who can afford to spend capital. The main disadvantages are that the real value of the income may be eroded by inflation and that once purchased there is no ability to surrender the annuity or recover the initial capital investment. Annuities may be suitable for elderly clients, or younger clients with children wishing to make provision for school fees.

Risk: low.

Income: medium/high (depending on age at purchase).

Capital growth: nil.

(19) SCHOOL FEE PLANS

There are a number of commercial plans available or parents can create their own provision. Those listed below are intended to give an indication of how some of these plans work. The deciding factor as to the type of plan is often whether the parent can afford a 'one off' lump sum payment out of capital, or whether the cost of the plan has to be met from income.

Funding from income

Life assurance schemes

Certain qualifying with profits or endowment life assurance policies enable the proceeds to be received completely tax free provided that premiums are payable for at least 10 years. The idea is that a series of such policies are purchased each maturing in consecutive years to provide annual funds for annual school fees.

Deferred annuities

Monthly premiums are paid to purchase an annuity equivalent to the level of fees whose payment is deferred until the fees are needed. The premium payments need not commence until shortly before school fees start to become due and continue until the last term for which fees are required.

The income element of the annuity will be subject to income tax at the parent's highest marginal rate.

Funding from capital

Compounding

Many schools offer their own fee plan. In return for a guaranteed level of fees parents pay a lump sum to the school in advance of the child starting at that school.

This can result in a substantial saving to the parents but care should be taken to check what happens to the lump sum if the child does not subsequently start at that school or leaves before the anticipated year.

There should be no tax consequences.

Educational trusts

There are a number of charitable educational trusts which, in return for an administration fee, invest the parents' lump sum in the purchase of an annuity payable termly to meet the fees. The annuity can start immediately or be deferred. The longer the deferral (eg, the plan is established on the birth of a child, to commence when he is 7 years old) the greater the value of the annuity. Any over-provision against the school fees can be paid to the parent.

Any annuity paid to the school is unlikely to be subject to income tax, but any surplus paid to the parent will suffer income tax at his rate(s) on the income element.

Gilt-edged securities

A lump sum can be invested in gilts with a range of redemption dates to mature over the school life of the child. If suitable redemption dates are not available, long-dated gifts can be purchased and holdings sold as and when school fees become due.

There is no CGT to pay on any gains made on the redemption or sale of gilts.

(20) MORTGAGES

Mortgages cannot be described as investments from the point of view of the borrower. They can, however, be linked to insurance policies which are investments. The insurance policy is designed to repay the mortgage debt at the end of the term or on the earlier death of the borrower so that the property on which it is secured can pass free of mortgage to the beneficiary under the borrower's will or intestacy.

There are many types of mortgage. The borrower must be advised to 'shop around' to find the type which best suits his particular circumstances. This is particularly true for the first-time buyer needing a large mortgage (or large as a proportion of the purchase price for the house).

In principle, there are two types of mortgage: the repayment mortgage and the interest only mortgage.

Repayment mortgages

Here, the monthly repayment is partly interest and partly a repayment of the capital sum outstanding. In the early years, the payments are largely of interest but include some capital repayment. As the capital is repaid, the proportion of interest in the monthly repayment reduces and the capital proportion increases.

To cover the possibility of the borrower dying before the capital is repaid at the end of the mortgage term, the lender will require a mortgage protection policy. A decreasing term assurance (with no investment element) is usual. It is decreasing in that the cover provided equates to the reducing capital sum due to the lender.

Interest only mortgages

In these cases, the lender does not expect monthly repayment of capital but he will require interest on the amount borrowed. The capital remains due at the end of the mortgage term. Arrangements should be made by the borrower to fund this liability (sometimes the lender will lend only if adequate arrangements have been put in place). There are two main types of interest only mortgages.

The 'endowment mortgage'

This is a misleading phrase for a commonly met arrangement. There are two transactions – the mortgage and the endowment policy. The premiums on the policy attract no tax relief and represent a further outlay by the borrower but he is, at least, acquiring a valuable asset.

The policy is assigned to the lender. At the end of the mortgage the policy will mature. After the mortgage debt is discharged, any balance will be paid to the borrower. If the policy was a 'with profits' policy, there may be a sum due to the borrower.

Some 'with profit' policies assume that when bonuses are added at the end of the term, the sum assured will then be the equivalent of the sum borrowed. In such cases, the premium payable on the policy may be reduced because the sum assured is reduced. This will be attractive to many borrowers but increases the risk that the policy may not be sufficient to pay off the sum borrowed when it matures.

A 'pension mortgage'

This phrase is also misleading. Again there are two transactions – the mortgage and the pension. The assumption is that the repayment of the mortgage at the end of the term is funded from the 'tax free' lump sum payable from a personal pension (see (**15**)).

While superficially very attractive (bearing in mind the favourable tax position of a personal pension), it must be remembered that the real purpose of the pension is to provide an income for retirement (and not a lump sum to repay a mortgage debt).

(21) INDIVIDUAL SAVINGS ACCOUNTS (ISAS)

Individual Savings Accounts (ISAs) become available from April 1999 to replace TESSAs (see (**3**) and PEPs (**10**)) from that date.

These accounts allow savers to invest a limited amount each tax year as a cash deposit or by acquisition of shares, and enjoy tax-free income and capital gains. Since ISAs were introduced in April 1999, there have been several changes to their rules.

The position before 1 July 2014

Before 1 July 2014, the principles governing ISAs were similar to those now in place, but the rules were less flexible as they restricted the amount of the annual allowance that could be invested in a cash ISA.

The position since 1 July 2014

All ISAs existing at this date and those created on or after 1 July 2014 are called New Isas (NISAs).

There are three different types of basic NISA: cash NISAs, stocks and shares NISAs and innovative finance NISAs. Innovative finance NISAs include peer-to-peer loans and 'crowdfunding debentures'.

Each tax year, UK resident adult savers may invest up to a maximum amount in these accounts. In the 2021/22 tax year the maximum total amount that may be invested is £20,000. This amount may be invested wholly in a cash NISA or wholly in a stocks and shares NISA, or may be split in any proportion between one of each type of NISA. So, for example, in the 2021/22 tax year an adult may choose to invest £20,000 in a cash NISA, or instead invest £12,000 in a cash NISA and £8,000 in a stocks and shares NISA.

There are also Junior ISAs, Help to Buy ISAs (see below) and Lifetime ISAs (see (**22**)).

A UK resident person who is aged between 16 and 18 may invest up to the maximum amount each tax year, but only in a cash NISA.

It is possible for savers to transfer existing NISAs to NISAs with other providers, including transferring what is held in a cash NISA to a stocks and shares NISA and vice versa.

Income and capital gains arising from NISAs are exempt from income tax and CGT.

Spouses can each have their own investments in NISAs. There is no minimum investment, neither is there any overall lifetime limit. Since 6 April 2015 a surviving spouse of a person who died on or after 3 December 2014 may receive a further NISA allowance based on the value of NISAs held at death by his or her spouse. The rules as to how this operates are complex.

The tax-free status of investments held in an ISA used to end on death. However, from 6 April 2018, the tax-free status continues throughout the administration period (or for three years whichever is the shorter). This will simplify things for personal representatives as, subject to the three-year time limit, there will be no income tax or capital gains tax on investments retained in an ISA during the administration period.

Junior ISAs were introduced in November 2011. Any child born before 1 September 2002 or during 2011 or later may invest up to a maximum amount (£9,000 in 2022/23) each year in any combination of cash or stocks and shares NISAs. When the child reaches 18, the Junior ISA becomes a standard adult ISA. (Children born between 1 September 2002 and 31 December 2010 are excluded, as these children were eligible to invest in Child Trust Funds, which are outside the scope of this book.) Parents or a guardian with parental responsibility can open a Junior ISA for under-16s. No one else can, although, once opened, others can contribute up to the annual limit.

The child can take control of the account at 16, but cannot withdraw the money until 18.

'Help to Buy' ISAs, aimed at helping those who are saving to buy their first home, were introduced from 1 December 2015. The amount that could be saved was limited: up to £1,200 could be contributed in the first month and up to £200 per month thereafter. They are now closed to new applicants, but those who have already taken one out can continue to save up to £200 per month until November 2029. Alternatively, funds can be transferred into a Lifetime ISA but only up to the annual maximum figure that can be invested (£4,000, see (**22**) below).

In addition to the savings being tax free, the government will contribute 25% of the amount saved (up to a maximum of £3,000 additional funds). Only cash sums can be saved. There is no stocks and shares option. The maximum price of property which can be bought using the scheme is £250,000 (£450,000 in London).

Taxpayers with both a Help to Buy ISA and a Lifetime ISA can only use the bonus from one towards a property purchase.

(22) THE LIFETIME INDIVIDUAL SAVINGS ACCOUNT (LISA)

This allows savers to invest up to £4,000 every year by depositing cash or investing in stocks and shares. The £4,000 counts towards the annual ISA limit of £20,000.

It is designed for two specific purposes. The first is for first-time buyers to use towards a deposit for a residential property. The second is for retirement. If funds are taken out to buy a first home, the LISA can be kept open to continue saving for retirement.

Anyone aged 18 to 39 can open a LISA. A saver with a LISA can continue to save into the LISA until they reach 50.

The state adds a 25% bonus every year of saving until age 50. The bonus is payable only on contributions, not on interest earned or stocks and shares growth/loss. If funds are withdrawn for any reason other than the specified one, there is a 25% charge. On 1 May 2020, the penalty was reduced to 20% between 6 March 2020 and 5 April 2021 to help savers who need to access their savings early as a result of the Covid-19 pandemic.

The overall ISA limit is £20,000 in the 2022/23 tax year. Taxpayers are allowed to split this between a LISA (up to the maximum £4,000) and putting the remainder in a cash ISA, stocks and shares ISA.

LISAs are intended for persons who have never owned a property. This includes owning a property (or a share of one) that was inherited, even if it was sold straightaway. The property purchased must cost less than £450,000. Investors can transfer money from a Help to Buy ISA to a Lifetime ISA.

Savers can have a Help to Buy ISA and a LISA, though it is not possible to get the first-time buyers' bonus on both.

If an investor dies with funds invested, the LISA comes to an end on the date of death.

DISCRETIONARY SETTLEMENT

Table of contents

SETTLEMENT

DATE: [   ]

PARTIES:

(1)   [   ] (the 'Settlor'); and

(2)   [   ] (the 'Trustees').

RECITALS

(A)   The Settlor wishes to make this Settlement and has transferred or delivered to the Trustees or otherwise placed under their control the property specified in the Schedule. Further money, investments or other property may be paid or transferred to the Trustees by way of addition.

(B)   It is intended that this Settlement shall be irrevocable.

PART 1 – OPERATIVE PROVISIONS

1. Definitions and construction

In this Deed, where the context admits, the following definitions and rules of construction shall apply.

1.1   The 'Trust Fund' shall mean:

    (a)   the property specified in the Schedule;

    (b)   all money, investments or other property paid or transferred by

            any person to, or so as to be under the control of, and, in either case, accepted by the Trustees as additions;

    (c)   all accumulations (if any) of income added to the Trust Fund; and

(d)   the money, investments and property from time to time representing the above.

1.2   The 'Trust Period' shall mean the period ending on the earlier of:

(a)   the last day of the period of 125 years from the date of this Deed, which period, and no other, shall be the applicable perpetuity period; and

(b)   such date as the Trustees shall at any time specify by deed, not being a date earlier than the date of execution of such deed or later than a date previously specified.

1.3   The 'Beneficiaries' shall mean:

(a)   the Settlor's children and remoter issue;

(b)   the spouses, widows and widowers (whether or not such widows or widowers have remarried) of the Settlor's children and remoter issue;

(c)   [   ];

[(d)   Charities;] and

[(e)]   such other objects or persons as are added under clause 3.

1.4   'Charity' shall mean any trust, foundation, company or other organisation whatever established only for purposes regarded as charitable under the law of England and Wales.

1.5   The expression 'the Trustees' shall, where the context admits, include the trustees for the time being of this Trust.

1.6   References to the children, grandchildren and issue of any person shall include his children, grandchildren and remoter issue, whether legitimate, legitimated[, illegitimate] or adopted [but shall exclude any illegitimate person and his descendants].

1.7   Words denoting the singular shall include the plural and vice versa.

1.8   Words denoting any gender shall include both the other genders.

1.9   References to any statutory provision shall include any statutory modification to or re-enactment of such provision.

1.10   The table of contents and clause headings are included for reference only and shall not affect the interpretation of this Deed.

2. Power to receive additional property

The Trustees may, at any time during the Trust Period, accept additional money, investments or other property, of whatever nature and wherever situate, paid or transferred to them by the Settlor or any other person. Such additional money, investments or other property shall, subject to any contrary direction, be held upon the trusts and with and subject to the powers and provisions of this Deed.

3. Power to add Beneficiaries

3.1   The Settlor, or such person as the Settlor shall have nominated in writing, may, at any time during the Trust Period, add to the Beneficiaries such objects or persons or classes of objects or persons as the Settlor or such other person shall, subject to the application (if any) of the rule against perpetuities, determine.

3.2   Any such addition shall be made by deed:

(a)   naming or describing the objects or persons or classes of objects or persons to be added; and

(b)   specifying the date or event, not being earlier than the date of execution of the deed but before the end of the Trust Period, on the happening of which the addition shall take effect.

[3.3   This power shall not be exercised so as to add to the Beneficiaries either the Settlor or any person who shall previously have added property to the Trust Fund or the spouse for the time being of the Settlor or any such person.]

4. Discretionary trust of capital and income

4.1   The Trustees shall hold the capital and income of the Trust Fund upon trust for or for the benefit of such of the Beneficiaries, at such ages or times, in such shares, upon such trusts (which may include discretionary or protective powers or trusts) and in such manner generally as the Trustees shall in their discretion appoint. Any such appointment may include such powers and provisions for the maintenance, education or other benefit of the Beneficiaries or for the accumulation of income and such administrative powers and provisions as the Trustees think fit.

4.2   No exercise of the power conferred by sub-clause 4.1 shall invalidate any prior payment or application of all or any part of the capital or income of the Trust Fund under the trusts of this Deed or made under any other power conferred by this Deed or by law.

4.3   Any trusts and powers created by an appointment under sub-clause 4.1 may be delegated to any extent to any person, whether or not including the Trustees or any of them.

[4.4   Notwithstanding clause [   ], the Trustees may not release or restrict this power during the Settlor's lifetime without his written consent.]

4.5   The exercise of the power of appointment conferred by sub-clause 4.1 shall:

(a)   be subject to the application, if any, of the rule against perpetuities; [and]

(b)   be by deed, revocable during the Trust Period or irrevocable, executed during the Trust Period [; and

(c)   be subject to the written consent of the Settlor during his lifetime].

5. Income trusts in default of appointment

The provisions of this clause shall apply during the Trust Period until, subject to and in default of any appointment under sub-clause 4.1.

5.1   The Trustees shall pay or apply the income of the Trust Fund to or for the benefit of such of the Beneficiaries as shall for the time being be in existence, in such shares and in such manner generally as the Trustees shall in their discretion from time to time think fit.

5.2   Notwithstanding the provisions of sub-clause 5.1, the Trustees may at any time in their discretion accumulate the income by investing it in any investments authorised by this Deed or by law and, subject to sub-clause 5.3, shall hold such accumulations as an accretion to capital.

5.3   The Trustees may apply the whole or any part of the income accumulated under sub-clause 5.2 as if it were income arising in the then current year.

6. Power to apply capital for Beneficiaries

The provisions of this clause shall apply during the Trust Period notwithstanding the provisions of clause 5 but subject to any appointment made under sub-clause 4.1.

6.1   The Trustees may pay or apply the whole or any part of the capital of the Trust Fund to or for the benefit of all or such of the Beneficiaries, in such shares, and in such manner generally as the Trustees shall in their discretion think fit.

6.2   The Trustees may, subject to the application (if any) of the rule against perpetuities, pay or transfer any income or capital of the Trust Fund to the trustees of any other trust, wherever established or existing, under which any Beneficiary is interested (whether or not such Beneficiary is the only object or person interested or capable of benefiting under such other trust) if the Trustees in their discretion consider such payment or transfer to be for the benefit of such Beneficiary.

7. Trusts in default of appointment

From and after the expiration of the Trust Period, and subject to any appointment made under sub-clause 4.1, the Trustees shall hold the capital and income of the Trust Fund upon trust absolutely for such of [ ] as shall then be living and, if more than one, in equal shares per stirpes, provided that no issue shall take whose parent is alive and so capable of taking.

8. Ultimate default trusts

Subject as above and if and so far as not wholly disposed of for any reason whatever by the above provisions, the capital and income of the Trust Fund shall be held upon trust for [ ] absolutely.

9. Administrative powers

The Trustees shall, in addition and without prejudice to all statutory powers, have the powers and immunities set out in Part 2 of this Deed. No power conferred on the Trustees shall be exercised so as to conflict with the beneficial provisions of this Deed.

10. Extended power of maintenance[1]

The statutory provisions for maintenance and education shall apply but so that the power of maintenance shall be exercisable in the discretion of the Trustees and free from the obligation to apply part only of the income for maintenance where other income is available.

11. Extended power of advancement[1]

The statutory provisions for advancement shall apply but so that the power of advancement shall extend to the whole, rather than one half, of the share or interest of the person for whose benefit the advancement is made.

12. Appointment of new trustees

12.1 During the lifetime of the Settlor the power of appointing new trustees shall be vested in the Settlor.

12.2 A person may be appointed to be a trustee notwithstanding that such person is not resident in the United Kingdom. Remaining out of the United Kingdom for more than 12 months shall not be a ground for the removal of a trustee.

13. Proper law, forum and place of administration

13.1 The proper law of this Trust shall be that of England and Wales. All rights under this Deed and its construction and effect shall be subject to the jurisdiction of, and construed according to, the laws of England and Wales.

13.2 The courts of England and Wales shall be the forum for the administration of these trusts.

13.3 Notwithstanding the provisions of sub-clauses 13.1 and 13.2:

    (a)   The Trustees shall have power, subject to the application (if any) of the rule against perpetuities, to carry on the general administration of these trusts in any jurisdiction in the world. This power shall be exercisable whether or not the law of such jurisdiction is for the time being the proper law of this Trust or the courts of such jurisdiction are for the time being the forum for the administration of these trusts, and whether or not the Trustees or any of them are for the time being resident or domiciled in, or otherwise connected with, such jurisdiction.

    (b)   The Trustees may at any time declare in writing that, from the date of such declaration, the proper law of this Trust shall be that of any specified jurisdiction. No exercise of this power shall be effective unless the law of the jurisdiction specified is one under which this Trust remains irrevocable and all, or substantially all, of the trusts, powers and provisions contained in this Deed remain enforceable and capable of being exercised and so taking effect.

    (c)   Following any exercise of the power contained in sub-clause 13.3(b), the Trustees shall, by deed, make such consequential alterations or additions to this Deed as they consider necessary or desirable to ensure that, so far as may be possible, the trusts, powers and provisions of this Deed shall be as valid and effective as they were immediately prior to such change.

    (d)   The Trustees may, at any time, declare in writing that, from the date of such declaration, the forum for the administration of these trusts shall be the courts of any specified jurisdiction.]

14. Exclusion of Settlor and spouse

14.1 No discretion or power conferred on the Trustees or any other person by this Deed or by law shall be exercised, and no provision of this Deed shall operate directly or indirectly, so as to cause or permit any part of the capital or income of the Trust Fund to become in any way payable to or applicable for the benefit of the Settlor or any person who shall previously have added property to the Trust Fund or the spouse for the time being of the Settlor or any such person.

14.2 The provisions of sub-clause 14.1 shall not preclude the Settlor or any such person from exercising any statutory right to claim reimbursement from the Trustees for any income tax or capital gains tax paid by him in respect of income arising to the Trustees or capital gains realised or deemed or treated as realised by them.

14.3 Subject to sub-clause 14.2, the prohibition in this clause shall apply notwithstanding anything else contained or implied in this Deed.

15. Exclusion of Trusts of Land and Appointment of Trustees Act 1996, s 11(1)

Section 11 (trustees' duty to consult beneficiaries) of the Trusts of Land and Appointment of Trustees Act 1996 shall not apply to the trusts contained in this Deed.

PART 2 – ADMINISTRATIVE PROVISIONS

SCHEDULE
[The initial Trust Fund]

Signed as a deed and delivered   )
by [   ]   )
in the presence of:)

[1]It is no longer necessary to make these amendments to the Trustee Act 1925, s 31 and s 32, as the Inheritance and Trustees' Powers Act 2014 amended the sections for trusts created or arising on or after 1 October 2014.

SETTLEMENT FOR BEREAVED YOUNG PERSONS

EXTRACT FROM WILL CREATING A SETTLEMENT FOR BEREAVED YOUNG PERSONS

[Note that such a settlement can only be created by a parent in favour of their children.]

1.   Definitions and construction

In this Will, where the context admits, the following definitions and rules of construction shall apply.

1.1   The 'Trust Fund' shall mean:

(a)   the sum of [   ];

(b)   all accumulations (if any) of income added to the Trust Fund; and

(c)   the money, investments and property from time to time representing the above.

1.2   The 'Trust Period' shall mean the period ending on the earlier of:

(a)   the last day of the period of 125 years from the date of my death, which period, and no other, shall be the applicable perpetuity period; and

(b)   such date as the Trustees shall at any time specify by deed, not being a date earlier than the date of execution of such deed or later than a date previously specified.

1.3   'Primary Beneficiary' shall mean:

my children, namely

[   ] who was born on [   ];

[   ] who was born on [   ];

[   ] who was born on [   ]; and

[   ] who was born on [   ].

1.4   'Beneficiary' shall mean any person actually or prospectively entitled to any share or interest in the capital or income of the Trust Fund.

1.5   The 'Closing Date' shall mean whichever shall be the earlier of:

(a)   the date on which the first Primary Beneficiary to do so attains the age of 25; and

(b)   the date on which the Trust Period shall determine.

1.6   The expression 'the Trustees' shall, where the context admits, include the trustees for the time being of this Trust.

1.7   References to the children, grandchildren and issue of any person shall include his children, grandchildren and remoter issue, whether legitimate, legitimated[, illegitimate] or adopted [, but shall exclude any illegitimate person and his descendants].

1.8   Words denoting the singular shall include the plural and vice versa.

1.9   Words denoting any gender shall include both the other genders.

1.10   References to any statutory provision shall include any statutory modification to or re-enactment of such provision.

1.11   The table of contents and clause headings are included for reference only and shall not affect the interpretation of this Will.

2. Gift to Trustees

I give the Trust Fund to the Trustees to hold on the trusts set out in clause 3.

3. Principal trusts

3.1   The Trust Fund shall be held upon trust for such of the Primary Beneficiaries as:

(a)   attain the age of 25 before the end of the Trust Period; or

(b)   are living and under that age at the end of the Trust Period

and, if more than one, in equal shares absolutely.

3.2   The provisions of sub-clauses 3.3, 3.4 and clause 4 shall apply to the share of the Trust Fund to which any of the Primary Beneficiaries is or may become entitled under sub-clause 3.1. In those provisions, such share is called the 'Share' and that one of the Primary Beneficiaries who is primarily interested in the Share is called the 'Primary Beneficiary'.

3.3   If any Primary Beneficiary shall die during the Trust Period, under the age of 25 and leaving children who survive him, the Share of such Primary Beneficiary shall be held upon trust for such of the children of the Primary Beneficiary as attain the age of 25 before the end of the Trust Period, or are living and under that age at the end of the Trust Period, and, if more than one, in equal shares absolutely.[1]

3.4   No Primary Beneficiary shall be entitled to any share of the Trust Fund without bringing any assets or interest advanced to him or paid or applied for his benefit (in exercise of any of the powers conferred by sub-clause 4.2 or clause 9) into account in such manner as the Trustees shall in their discretion determine with a view to achieving an equitable division of the unadvanced part of the Trust Fund.

[1] If a child dies under the age of 25 and with children who survive, the portion of the settlement funds held for the substituted grandchildren will be held on relevant property trusts, not s 71D trusts. The substitution does not affect the status of the rest of the settlement. The settlement will, therefore, contain both relevant property and s 71D trusts.

Most settlors will want to provide for bereaved grandchildren and so will include a substitution provision, even though there will be anniversary and exit charges on the portion held for the grandchildren.

4. Trusts for Primary Beneficiaries under 25

This clause shall apply, during the Trust Period, in respect of the Share of any Primary Beneficiary who is living and under the age of 25.

4.1   The Trustees may pay or apply any income of the Share to or for the maintenance or education or otherwise for the benefit of the Primary Beneficiary, or any other Primary Beneficiaries who are for the time being living and under the age of 25.

4.2   Subject as above, the income of the Share shall be accumulated as an accretion to the capital of the Share. Any such accumulations may, at any time, be paid or applied in the manner set out in sub-clause 4.1 as if they were income of the Share arising in the then current year.

4.3   The Trustees may also pay or apply any capital of the Share to or for the maintenance, education, advancement or otherwise for the benefit of the Primary Beneficiary. No capital may be applied in such a way that the income of it might meanwhile be dealt with except by being applied for the maintenance, education or otherwise for the benefit of one or more of the Primary Beneficiaries for the time being living and under the age of 25 or by being accumulated.[2]

[2] The trustees can use this power to advance capital to beneficiaries early. If they do it before the beneficiary reaches 18 there will be no exit charge; if the beneficiary has already reached 18 at the time of the advance, there will be a charge based on the period that has elapsed since the beneficiary's 18th birthday.

The power is wide enough to allow the trustees to settle funds on further trusts if they think that a beneficiary is insufficiently mature to deal with an absolute advance. Settling the funds will be an exit from the original s 71D settlement, and the new settlement produced will be a relevant property settlement subject to both anniversary and exit charges.

The powers conferred by this clause are limited to the share of each primary beneficiary who is under 25.

5. Trust to accumulate

Subject as above, so long as no Primary Beneficiary has attained the age of 25 and further Primary Beneficiaries may come into existence, the income of the Trust Fund shall be accumulated.

6. Ultimate default trusts

In the event of the failure or determination of the above trusts, the capital and income of the Trust Fund shall be held upon trust for [such of the Primary Beneficiaries as are living at the date of this Will, and if more than one, in equal shares] absolutely.

7. Administrative powers

The Trustees shall, in addition and without prejudice to all statutory powers, have the powers and impunities set out in Part 2 of this Will. No power conferred on the Trustees shall be exercised so as to conflict with the beneficial provisions of this Will.

8. Extended power of maintenance[3]

The statutory provisions for maintenance and education shall apply, but so that the power of maintenance shall be exercisable in the discretion of the Trustees and free from the obligation to apply part only of the income for maintenance where other income is available.

9. Extended power of advancement[3]

The statutory provisions for advancement shall apply, but so that the power of advancement shall extend to the whole, rather than one half, of the share or interest of the person for whose benefit that advancement is made.

[3] It is no longer necessary to make these amendments to the Trustee Act 1925, s 31 and s 32, as the Inheritance and Trustees' Powers Act 2014 amended the sections for trusts created or arising on or after 1 October 2014.

WILL – OUTLINE STRUCTURE

Opening	Name, address, occupation and date (unless at end of will)
Revocation	Previous wills and codicils
Executors and trustees	Individuals (lay, professional); trust corporation
Specific bequests/devises	Particular items owned
Pecuniary legacies	Money
Residuary gift	Absolute or contingent gifts to individuals or class of individuals
	Substitution provision in case prior gift fails
Powers of executors and/or trustees	Implied by statute Express provision
Attestation	Signed by the testator in the presence of two independent witnesses
	Witnesses sign in the presence of the testator

TRUST DISTRIBUTION ACCOUNT

JOHN BALE TRUST

(a) Tom Bale set up an accumulation and maintenance trust for his nephew John under which John became entitled to the trust capital on his 18th birthday on 10 February 20–.

(b) The trustees being satisfied that no capital tax liability arises (no IHT since the trust is an accumulation and maintenance trust; no CGT because their annual exemption covers the gain on their deemed disposal caused by John's absolute entitlement) have transferred the investment in ABC plc to John.

(c) The dividend shown in the income account was received on 25 March 20– and it, together with the remaining cash has been transferred to John.

Capital account

Assets held on 10 February 20–	£
ABC plc ordinary shares	10,000.00
Cash	50.00
	10,050.00
Less: Lowe, Snow & Co's costs, disbursements and VAT on distribution of the funds	30.00
Balance held for John Bale	10,020.00

Income account

Income tax year 20–/20–

Dividend

ABC plc ordinary shares	10.00
Balance held for John Bale	10.00

Beneficiary's account

Capital, per capital account	10,020.00
Income, per income account	10.00
Total due	10,030.00
Represented by	
ABC plc ordinary shares	10,000.00
Balance of cash, now due	30.00
	10,030.00

Index